The Making of International Law in Korea

AF715064

The Making of International Law in Korea

From Colony to Asian Power

By

Seokwoo Lee and Hee Eun Lee

BRILL
NIJHOFF

LEIDEN | BOSTON

Library of Congress Cataloging-in-Publication Data

Names: Yi, Sog-u, 1967–, author. | Lee, Hee Eun, author.
Title: The making of international law in Korea : from colony to Asian power / by Seokwoo Lee and Hee Eun Lee.
Description: Leiden ; Boston : Brill, 2016. | Includes bibliographical references and index.
Identifiers: LCCN 2016006899 (print) | LCCN 2016007338 (ebook) | ISBN 9789004315747 (hardback : alk. paper) | ISBN 9789004315785 (pbk. : alk. paper) | ISBN 9789004315754 (E-book)
Subjects: LCSH: Korea (South)—International status.
Classification: LCC KZ4483 .L5 2016 (print) | LCC KZ4483 (ebook) | DDC 341.26095195—dc23
LC record available at http://lccn.loc.gov/2016006899

Typeface for the Latin, Greek, and Cyrillic scripts: "Brill". See and download: brill.com/brill-typeface.

ISBN 978-90-04-31578-5 (paperback)
ISBN 978-90-04-31575-4 (e-book)

This paperback is also published in hardback under 978-90-04-31574-7.

Copyright 2016 by Koninklijke Brill NV, Leiden, The Netherlands.
Koninklijke Brill NV incorporates the imprints Brill, Brill Hes & De Graaf, Brill Nijhoff, Brill Rodopi and Hotei Publishing.
All rights reserved. No part of this publication may be reproduced, translated, stored in a retrieval system, or transmitted in any form or by any means, electronic, mechanical, photocopying, recording or otherwise, without prior written permission from the publisher.
Authorization to photocopy items for internal or personal use is granted by Koninklijke Brill NV provided that the appropriate fees are paid directly to The Copyright Clearance Center, 222 Rosewood Drive, Suite 910, Danvers, MA 01923, USA. Fees are subject to change.

This book is printed on acid-free paper and produced in a sustainable manner.

From 2003, I have been struggling to produce an English language international law textbook in Korea. Since that time, I have crossed paths with many teachers, colleagues, and friends who were able to help me overcome my mistakes and failures. Though this book continues to be a work in progress, I would like to express my special thanks to the following people who were integral to achieving my goal.

Dakas CJ DAKAS (Director, Institute of Advanced Legal Studies, Supreme Court of Nigeria, NIGERIA);
Seoung-Yong HONG (President, Joongbu University; President (ret.), Inha University, KOREA);
Hee Eun LEE (Professor, Handong International Law School, KOREA);
Pae-Keun PARK (Professor, Law School, Pusan National University, KOREA);
Young Kil PARK (Director of Maritime Territory Research Center, Korea Maritime Institute (KMI), KOREA);
Catherine REDGWELL (Chichele Professor of Public International Law and Fellow of All Souls College, Oxford, UK);
Harry N. SCHEIBER (Stefan A. Riesenfeld Professor of Law and History (Emeritus); Director, Law of the Sea Institute (LOSI), Boalt Hall School of Law, University of California, Berkeley, USA);
Clive SCHOFIELD (Professor and Director of Research, Australian National Centre for Ocean Resources and Security (ANCORS), University of Wollongong, AUSTRALIA);
Marie SHELDON (Publishing Director, International Law, Brill/Nijhoff);
Kevin YL TAN (Director, Equilibrium Consulting Pte Ltd; Professor (Adjunct), Faculty of Law, National University of Singapore, SINGAPORE; Editor-in-Chief, *The Asian Yearbook of International Law*);
Jon M. VAN DYKE (late Professor of Law and Carlsmith Ball Faculty Scholar at the William S. Richardson School of Law, University of Hawaii at Manoa, USA); and
Keyuan ZOU (Harris Professor of International Law, Lancashire Law School, University of Central Lancashire, UK).

Lastly, I would also like to dedicate this book with love to Yoon, my most perceptive reviewer in life both academic and personal.

Seokwoo Lee

I have been blessed to have spent my entire professional academic career thus far at one institution, Handong International Law School ("HILS"). My time here has allowed me to grow and mature as a teacher, writer, and most importantly, as a person. In particular, I am thankful to the Dean of HILS, Eric G. Enlow, my dear friend and co-worker, whose deep love of learning the law and intellectual curiosity has fueled my own academic pursuits and questions. I am also indebted to the faculty of HILS who have given me much towards my edification and have graced with me with greater insights into the "weightier matters of the law". I would be remiss if I did not also thank my friend and colleague, Seokwoo Lee, the co-author of this book, who has and continues to encourage me to produce international law scholarship. Finally, I would like to dedicate this book to my grandmother, Park, Jum Soon, whose faith and perseverance I am grateful for.

Hee Eun Lee

Contents

Preface

The Republic of Korea[1] was colonialized in the early 20th century, achieved its independence, and rose from the ashes of the Korean War to become an Asian power. Korea remarkably emerged from Japanese colonialism, and subsequently became a divided nation occupied by communist forces in the North and the United States in the South. This division culminated in the Korean War from 1950 to 1953 which ravaged the peninsula and left Korea as one of the poorest countries in the world. By 2014, Korea was ranked the 11th largest economy in terms of GNP.

Korea's modern history parallels the tumultuous events of Northeast Asia when the longstanding Sinocentric order was upended through Western colonialism and Japanese aggression, leading to World War II. For Korea, the post-World War II era was marked largely by the Cold War, and after the fall of the Soviet Union, it has been in the midst of a reconfiguration. The balance of power in the region can be ascribed to the economic prowess of both China and Japan, the nuclear ambitions of North Korea, and US national interests. As the post-Cold War era in Northeast Asia continues to be influenced by power politics, it has also seen an increased need for international law due to the forces of globalization, regional concerns over ocean resources, trade and other non-security matters. Particularly for Korea, international law has gained greater prominence as Korea has entered into free trade agreements with the European Union (into force in 2011), the United States (into force in 2012) and is currently negotiating a potential trade treaty with China and Japan. Moreover, a number of Koreans are serving as judges on the International Criminal Court (Song, Sang-Hyun served as its President) and the International Tribunal for the Law of the Sea, and former Minister of Foreign Affairs Ban, Ki-Moon serving as the United Nations Secretary-General.

Korea's ascent coincides neatly with the advent of globalization and growing importance of international law in managing the increasing interactions between states and other non-state entities such as multinational corporations, non-governmental organizations, and international organizations like the United Nations. Korea's rise has occurred in one of the most dynamic and dangerous parts of the world: Northeast Asia. Encompassing the People's

1 The Republic of Korea (ROK) is commonly known as "South Korea" and the Democratic Peoples' Republic of Korea (DPRK) is known as "North Korea". In this text, the term "Korea" will refer the Republic of Korea. Any indication of the DPRK will be referenced as "North Korea".

Republic of China, North and South Korea, and Japan, the region has undoubtedly taken on greater global geopolitical and economic significance. It is under these conditions that international law has taken on an increased role in Korea and beyond.

This textbook addresses the developments of international law in Korea from human rights concerns to law of the sea issues; from maritime delimitation and access to ocean resources to other non-security matters. It attempts to demonstrate to students the increasingly important role of international law in Northeast Asia. Korea, in particular, can no longer ignore the age-old global question: should states obey international law, and if so, why? For the Republic of Korea, the answer to this question is of utmost importance given its precarious position between two world powers, China and Japan, and its volatile neighbor to the north, the Democratic People's Republic of Korea. The purpose of this textbook is to help students of international law, particularly those in Korea, to understand and appreciate the significance of international law to the international relations of Korea.

Acknowledgments

We gratefully acknowledge the permissions extended by the following publishers and authors to reprint excerpts from the indicated publications.

American Society of International Law. Permission to reprint excerpts from Seokwoo Lee and Young Kil Park, "Republic of Korea v. Araye", 106 American Journal of International Law 630 (2012).

Asian Yearbook of International Law. Permission to reprint excerpts from Seokwoo Lee and Hee Eun Lee, "Positivism in International Law: State Sovereignty, Self-Determination, and Alternative Perspectives", 2010 Asian Yearbook of International Law 1 (2013).

Elsevier B.V. Permission to reprint excerpts from Seokwoo Lee, "Korea and the Safety of Navigation: Uncertainty Derived from Undefined Fences" in Securing the Safety of Navigation in East Asia: Legal and Political Dimensions, Shicun Wu and Keyuan Zou, eds. (Chandos Publishing, 2013)

Konrad Adenauer Foundation. Permission to reprint excerpts from Hee Eun Lee and Seokwoo Lee, "Lethal Maritime Conflicts between North and South Korea: Any Role for International Law?", 1 KAS Journal on Contemporary Korean Affairs 87 (2013).

Korea Legislation Research Institute. Permission to reprint excerpts from Seokwoo Lee, Yoonkyeong Nah, and Youngkwan Cho, "Korean-Chinese, Migrant Workers, Marriage Immigrant Women, and the Refugee Act", 3(2) KLRI Journal of Law and Legislation 345 (2013).

Lynne Rienner Publishers. Permission to reprint excerpts from Seokwoo Lee, "Dokdo: The San Francisco Peace Treaty, International Law on Territorial Disputes, and Historical Criticism", 35(3) Asian Perspective 361 (2011).

Martinus Nihjoff Publishers. Permission to reprint excerpts from Boo Chan Kim and Seokwoo Lee, "Protection of the Sea Lanes in the Jeju Waters and Maritime Cooperation in Northeast Asia" in Navigating Straits: Challenges for International Law, David D. Caron and Nilufer Oral, eds. (Martinus Nihjoff Publishers, 2014); Seokwoo Lee and Hee Eun Lee, "The Cheonan Incident: A Perspective from International Law and Politics" in Northeast Asian Perspectives on International Law: Contemporary Issues and Challenges, Seokwoo Lee and Hee Eun Lee, eds. (Martinus Nijhoff Publishers, 2013); Suk-Kyoon Kim and Seokwoo Lee, "The Legal Framework of Maritime Security in East Asia: A Comparative View" in Regions, Institutions, and Law of the Sea, Harry N. Scheiber and Jin-Hyun Paik, eds. (Martinus Nijhoff Publishers, 2013); Seokwoo Lee, "Intertemporal Law, Recent Judgments and Territorial Disputes in Asia" in Maritime Boundary Disputes, Settlement Processes, and the Law of the Sea, Seoung-Yong Hong and Jon M. Van Dyke, eds. (Martinus Nijhoff Publishers, 2009); and Seokwoo Lee and Young Kil Park, "The Legal Assessment of the Illegal Fishing Activities of Chinese Fishing Vessels: A Focus on Detention of Foreign Vessels", 1 Korean Journal of International & Comparative Law 31 (2013).

Oxford University Press. Permission to reprint excerpts from Seokwoo Lee & Jon Van Dyke, "The 1951 San Francisco Peace Treaty and Its Relevance to the Sovereignty over Dokdo", 9 Chinese Journal of International Law 741 (2010).

Pacific Rim Law and Policy Association. Permission to reprint excerpts from Seokwoo Lee, "The 1951 San Francisco Peace Treaty with Japan and the Territorial Disputes in East Asia", 11 Pacific Rim Law & Policy Journal 63 (2002).

Pae-Keun Park. Permission to reprint excerpts from Pae-Keun Park, "The 1965 'Korea-Japan Claims Settlement Agreement' and Individuals' Claims Rights," 68 Hosei Kenyu 648–674 (2001).

Pae-Keun Park and Brill. Permission to reprint excerpts from Pae-Keun Park, "Korean Response to Changes of the International Legal Framework for Fisheries in the Northeast Asian Seas" in Recent Developments in the Law of the Sea and China, Myron Nordquist, John Norton Moore and Kuen-Chen Fu, eds. (Brill, 2005).

Routledge Publishing Company. Permission to reprint excerpts from Seokwoo Lee, "Korea's Maritime Challenges and Priorities" in Maritime Challenges and Priorities in Asia: Implications for Regional Security, Joshua Ho & Sam Bateman, eds. (Routledge, 2012); Seokwoo Lee and Chang Hoon Shin, "Implications of the Border Regime between North Korea and China" in Asian Approaches to International Law and the Legacy of Colonialism: The Law of the Sea, Territorial Disputes and International Dispute Settlement, Jin-Hyun Paik, Seokwoo Lee, and Kevin Y.L. Tan, eds. (Routledge, 2013); and Seokwoo Lee, "Analysis of Korea's Claim of Sovereignty over Gando/Jiandao Area in China under International Law," in Asian Approaches to International Law and the Legacy of Colonialism: The Law of the Sea, Territorial Disputes and International Dispute Settlement, Jin-Hyun Paik, Seokwoo Lee, and Kevin Y.L. Tan, eds. (Routledge, 2013).

University of Hawaii Law Review. Permission to reprint excerpts from Seokwoo Lee, Yoonkyeong Nah and Youngkwan Cho, "Historical Issues between Korea and Japan and Judicial Activism: Focusing on the Recent Decisions of the Korean Constitutional Court Concerning Comfort Women", 35 Hawaii Law Review 857 (2013).

Walter De Gruyter GmbH. Permission to reprint excerpts from Chang-Hoon Shin and Seokwoo Lee, “North Korea and the Law of the Sea”, 8(1) Issues in Legal Scholarship 1 (2009).

The authors express their great appreciation for the contributions made to the research for this book by Professor Pae-Keun Park of Pusan National University Law School.

CHAPTER 1

Korea's Encounter with the Modern International Legal System

1 Introduction

1.1 *The International Order of East Asia in the Era of International Law: Acceptance and the Status of Korea in International Law*

Before the introduction of *Jus Publicum Europaeum* into East Asia, there existed an "international" regional normative system that regulated the relations between and among China and the many political entities around her such as Korea, Japan, and Vietnam among others. This regional normative system was referred to as the "Sinocentric order".

The Sinocentric order was based on the concept of Sinocentrism. Sinocentrism was a belief that understood the world to be composed of a center and a periphery. The center was civilized China ruled by an emperor who received his mandate from heaven. The emperor was referred to as the "Son of Heaven" and the Chinese dynasties were called Celestial Empires. Uncivilized people or barbarians supposedly inhabited the outer regions. Naturally, relations between civilized central China and the uncivilized peripheral political entities around her were understood as a relationship between superior and inferior.

The inferior paid tribute to superior China regularly as a function of the tributary system. It may be said that this was the most important component of the Sinocentric order. Sometimes the Sinocentric order and the tributary system were treated as one in the same. As a matter of fact, under the Sinocentric order, the trade of goods between China and other dynasties was conducted only in the form of the peripheral entities' payment of tribute and the reception of return bestowals from China. The trade under the tributary system was sometimes more beneficial to the tribute-payer than the tribute-receiver.

The second feature of the Sinocentric order was the Chinese emperor's installation of kings in the peripheral dynasties. This meant that in formal terms, a king of a peripheral dynasty such as the king of Korea or king of Vietnam was a subject of the Chinese emperor.

The last feature of the Sinocentric order was the use of the Chinese calendar. Under the Chinese calendar system, years were counted by using the Chinese era reign name. Consequently, this third feature of the Sinocentric order

© KONINKLIJKE BRILL NV, LEIDEN, 2016 | DOI 10.1163/9789004315754_002

meant the official use of the Chinese era reign name by tributary dynasties. As the use of the Chinese calendar was an important element of the Sinocentric order, if a tributary dynasty began to use its own inherent era reign name, that meant and symbolized an exit from the Sinocentric order and becoming an equal with China in its normative or legal status.

Under the Sinocentric order, Chinese dynasties had taken the policy of "rein and bridle". This policy meant keeping peripheral dynasties and tribes under the Chinese bridle through the use of appeasement by their rulers rather than the use of force. On the basis of this policy, China did not intervene in the domestic affairs of the barbarians and the use of force was not the means by which China accomplished its foreign policy goals. Barbarians were allowed autonomy and their inherited customs were respected by China.

Korea had been a tributary dynasty like Ryukyu (Okinawa), Vietnam, Thailand, Laos, and Burma. It had willingly accepted the Sinocentric order and was a dynastic kingdom which paid tribute most frequently. This frequency of tribute payment was understood as a privilege rather than a burden. Korea herself had pride in her own level of civilization and referred to itself as a "little Chinese civilization". Japan also paid tribute to China. However, it was not a typical tributary dynasty because its payment of tribute was sporadic. The relation between Japan and China was marked by a lack of contact in comparison to Korea.

The fact that Korea had paid tribute regularly to China and accepted her own inferior status to China without any serious resistance under the Sinocentric order may give the impression that Korea had been thoroughly under the control of China. However, the Chinese policy of "rein and bridle" respected the inherited customs of the tributary polities and allowed their domestic self-government. Korea was no exception in this respect. Under the Sinocentric order, the political and legal matters of Korea were totally left in the hands of Koreans. This is the reason why the relationship between Korea and China under the Sinocentric order is called a formal or ceremonial one.

When Korea opened its doors to the West for the first time, Western countries had difficulty understanding the status of Korea since it was under the Sinocentric order. A question was raised among Western countries as to whether Korea was a vassal state or an independent sovereign state. It was rather advantageous for Korea to be regarded as a vassal state in terms of avoiding international responsibility, whereas it also hoped to be recognized as an independent sovereign state in all other respects. On the contrary, China put an emphasis on the status of Korea as an independent state so that it would not carry the burden of the international responsibility for Korea as a suzerain state which it was supposed to assume. However, it continued to assert Korea's dependency on China with the intention of putting Korea under its political influence. Despite this initial confusion, Western countries treated Korea as a sovereign state. Japan made continuous efforts to receive confirmation from China that Korea was indeed an independent sovereign state so that it could prepare its first step to invade Korea by ending the dominant-subordinate relationship between China and Korea.

1.2 *The Status of International Law in the Domestic Legal System of Korea*

Article 6, paragraph 1 of the Korean Constitution stipulates that "treaties duly concluded and promulgated under the Constitution and the generally recognized rules of international law shall have the same effect as the domestic laws of the Republic of Korea." In accordance with this, international law has been generally accepted as domestic law and incorporated into the Korean legal system. This provision stipulates that treaties have the same effect as the domestic law of Korea. There is no specific reference to customary international law, but "generally recognized rules of international law" is generally understood to mean customary international law. Therefore, customary international law has also been incorporated into the domestic legal system under the provision of the Korean Constitution. In this sense, Korea is a monist state insofar as the incorporation of international law into domestic law is not required for international law to apply. Both treaties and customary international law, however, need to be self-executing or directly applicable in order for it to be applied in litigation.

The constitutional provision stipulates that treaties and customary international law have the same effect as the domestic laws of Korea, but it does not explicitly identify the level of effect international law has within the domestic legal system. Due to this constitutional vagueness, the level of effect of international law within the domestic legal system has been left to theoretical interpretation. Article 5 of the Addenda of the Constitution stipulates that "... treaties in force at the time this Constitution enters into force, shall remain valid unless they are contrary to this Constitution." Thus, theories suggesting that a treaty is above or on the same level of the Constitution are very rare. The majority opinion is that both treaty and customary international law generally have the same effect as statutes as indicated by judicial decisions. Accordingly, treaties or customary international law that are contrary to the Constitution are invalid within the domestic legal system. In the event treaties or customary international law are in conflict with statutes, their validity is decided based on the principles of *lex posterior derogat legi priori* and *lex specialis derogat legi generali*.

Article 60, paragraph 1 of the Korean Constitution stipulates that consent to ratification by the National Assembly is required for "treaties pertaining to mutual assistance or mutual security; treaties concerning important international organizations; treaties of friendship, trade and navigation; treaties pertaining to any restriction in sovereignty; peace treaties; treaties which will burden the State or people with an important financial obligation; or treaties related to legislative matters." Based on this provision, some theories, which are supported by judicial decisions, suggest that treaties concluded with the consent to the ratification by the National Assembly have the same effect as statutes. However, treaties that are merely concluded by the executive branch only have the same effect as decrees which are lower than statutes.

1.3 *Treaty Making in Korea*

Under Article 73 of the Korean Constitution, treaty making is within the authority of the President. All working-level work for treaty making is carried out by the International Legal Affairs Bureau of the Ministry of Foreign Affairs and a procedure of consultations with various domestic institutions should be followed before the President is able to conclude and ratify treaties. From a procedural standpoint, there are three types of treaties that can be concluded in Korea: treaties requiring the consent to the ratification of the treaty by the National Assembly, treaties not requiring the consent to the ratification by the National Assembly, and the so-called "treaties by notification" made with a simple procedure through the Minister of Foreign Affairs.

The first step in the domestic procedure for treaty making is an examination made by the International Legal Affairs Bureau of the Ministry of Foreign Affairs. The International Legal Affairs Bureau reviews the wording of the treaty texts, classifies the type of treaty, determines whether there are legal conflicts with other treaties or domestic laws, and whether a treaty would require the consent to the ratification by the National Assembly. With this step completed, the proposed treaty is then sent to the Ministry of Government Legislation for review. It is required under the Law of Government Organizations that the Ministry of Government Legislation reviews all proposed legislation before being sent to the State Council for deliberation. Treaties are treated as such. A review is made the Ministry of Government Legislation is to find out whether the proposed treaty is in conflict with existing domestic law. In addition, the Ministry of Government Legislation examines whether the proposed treaty requires the consent to ratification by the National Assembly as stipulated in Article 60, Paragraph 1 of the Constitution, and provides opinions on it.

When the review of the proposed treaty by the Ministry of Government Legislation is completed, the treaty is then submitted to the State Council.

Article 89, paragraph 3 of the Constitution stipulates that the proposed treaty shall be referred to the State Council for deliberation. Before being sent to the State Council, the proposed treaty is reviewed by the Council of Vice-Ministers where practical discussions regarding the treaty text take place.

When the proposed treaty is reviewed and approved by the State Council, it is then sent for approval by the Prime Minister and finally by the President. With the completion of this procedure, the person appointed by the President with full powers signs the treaty that contains the treaty text that has already been approved. However, there are exceptional cases when the treaties are signed first and, then sent to the State Council for deliberation.

If a signed treaty requires ratification by the President, it must go through the ratification procedure again. However practically, a treaty concluded through the resolution by the State Council, approval of the Prime Minister and the President, they are ratified without the additional ratification procedure involving the President.

Article 60, paragraph 1 of the Constitution stipulates that the National Assembly shall have the right to consent to the conclusion and ratification of treaties. In other words, the consent by the National Assembly is certainly required for "treaties pertaining to mutual assistance or mutual security; treaties concerning important international organizations; treaties of friendship, trade and navigation; treaties pertaining to any restriction in sovereignty; peace treaties; treaties which will burden the State or people with an important financial obligation; or treaties related to legislative matters". The Administration submits to the National Assembly a motion for the consent to the ratification as a general item, not as a legislative bill. The National Assembly decides only on whether it consents to the ratification of the treaty which is ultimately decided in the Assembly plenary session after going through an internal procedure of the National Assembly. The resolution is passed if more than half of all votes cast by more than one half of voters eligible vote in favor. Regardless of whether treaties are formal or informal or whether the consent to the ratification by the National Assembly is required or not, all treaties that become binding within Korea are promulgated domestically by being noticed in the Official Gazette.

In Korea, there are treaties that are signed and concluded with the full power of the Minister of the Foreign Affair, without needing to go through the whole procedure of deliberation by the State Council; President's approval; or consent to the ratification by the National Assembly. These are referred to as *goshiryu joyak*, which can be put into "treaties by notification". These treaties refer to supplementary agreements concluded within the scope authorized by the treaty provisions in order for the implementation or execution of the original treaty, or a minor modification by an organizational resolution of a multilateral treaty provision adopted by an international organization.

The treaties that fall into this category are concluded by the Minister of Foreign Affairs in consultation with related ministries. Generally, treaties that are noticed in the Official Gazette (*Gwanbo*) as "treaty" and promulgated whereas treaties by notification are posted in *Gwanbo* as *Goshi* (notification) by the Ministry of Foreign Affairs. Pursuant to the Vienna Convention on the Law of Treaties Article 2(1)(a), there is no doubt that treaties by notification are considered treaties that are legally binding in Korea.

2 Conceptions of International Law

2.1 *Positivism in International Law*

Contemporary international law and its jurisprudence appear to be taking on a more self-reflective attitude in coming to terms with some of the core assumptions that have dominated international law since the age of European imperialism. One such assumption is that international law is concerned primarily with the actions of states and that those state acts have been and continue to be the basis for the content of international law. Part of the historical narrative of international law is that this positivistic approach departed from an earlier notion that international law emanated from natural law that found its source not necessarily from the purposeful action of states, but from obligations that existed beyond the states themselves. Accordingly, what can be found in Article 38 of the Statute of the International Court of Justice (ICJ) in what law the Court will apply to disputes between states, namely treaties and international custom, supports the sense that international law has had a strong positivist strand. State action in the form of treaty making and the state practice element of international custom confirm the sense that international law is made by the states themselves, a product of sovereign will. However, it is from that very point of positivism in international law that has been under attack not only from other legal philosophical schools in terms of methodological approaches in deducing the content of international law and explaining why states observe international rules, but it has also come under suspicion from others who question the very content of international law and its checkered history.

Third World Approaches to International Law (TWAIL) have pointed to the period of colonial expansion when colonialism was viewed as a legitimate exercise of state power as to when the contemporary rules of international law took shape. Given the impact of this period on international law, TWAIL scholars look upon the colonial era with a great deal of skepticism on an international system that saw powerful states exploit weaker entities through colonialism utilizing existing concepts of international law to justify their activities. TWAIL views the colonial period as the critical moment in understanding the proliferation of international law as a transnational phenomenon because of the expansive nature of the colonial project. By focusing on European colonialism, TWAIL desires to permit the expansion of the forum in which the history of repression can be reflected and criticized upon international law.

One of TWAIL's major contributions to the study of international law is that it has brought to light how the practice of powerful states shaped the content of contemporary international law. It posits that through an examination of European colonialism, international law today can be better understood if seen in light of the European states and their historical encounter with what was then the uncivilized world. This can be seen in how the present rules that govern the disposition of international disputes that deal with fundamental concepts of state sovereignty such as territorial integrity along with the conspicuous failure during the colonial period to recognize self-determination as a legitimate legal principle. By relying on legal positivism as its philosophical base, international lawyers of that time helped to lay the groundwork for an approach to international law that reflected the European experience of statecraft and international relations. As one TWAIL scholar put it, the "sovereignty doctrine is understood as a stable and comprehensive set of ideas that was formulated in Europe and that extended inexorably and imperiously with empire into darkest Africa, the inscrutable Orient, and the far reaches of the Pacific, acquiring control over these territories and peoples and transforming them into European possessions." As such, it is in that sense that there is a felt unfairness because of the absence of any meaningful contribution from other non-European states in the development of international law and skewed international law in the favor of hegemonic states.

The positivism that marked this earlier generation of international law that conveniently justified the colonial activities of European states, continued to make its marks on the very principle that was supposed to remedy the injustice caused by international law's non-recognition of nations as states—self-determination. With the end of World War II and the advent of the United Nations (U.N.), the former colonial holdings of the imperial powers had their opportunity to participate in the international system as legally equal players. The principle of self-determination enshrined in the U.N. Charter, International Covenant on Civil and Political Rights, and International Covenant on Economic, Social, and Cultural Rights gave former colonies the right to statehood. However, there were clear restrictions in the application of the self-determination principle. States that were both colonizers and former colonies which had become newly independent sought to place definite limits on the application of self-determination so as to be not too destabilizing. The European colonial states naturally desired to see the principle only applicable to the areas outside of Europe it formerly governed, while the newly independent states in Africa desired to maintain the principle of *uti possidetis* and keep the pre-existing colonial borders with the hope of securing post-colonial stability. Since states, especially those that were newly conceived, were concerned for survival, international rules that promoted their interests in establishing stability regarding their territorial boundaries made sense despite the emergence of the principle of self-determination which seemed to defy traditional norms. Thus, positivism in international law helped to create the conditions for an instrumentalism in its use so as to maintain the status quo ante. It has continued to do so because it has colored basic principles of international law such as state sovereignty.

2.1.1 State Sovereignty and the Impact of Colonialism in International Law

State sovereignty is one of the most fundamental principles of international law. It is the basis upon which states claim the legal right to manage its own affairs to the exclusion of others. As expressed under classical international law, the sovereignty of the state allows it to enjoy exclusive jurisdiction over subjects and matters that exist within its territorial boundaries. The notion that the nation-state exercises authority over a territorial jurisdiction marked a significant shift in understanding the nature of authority and accountability that had previously been hierarchical with various political authorities subject to the Holy Roman Emperor or the Pope. The end of the Thirty Years War in Europe saw the centralization and recognition of power in the princes who were treated as sovereigns. These rulers and the state powers they began to represent became the principal actors in the international system. The new world order that was established at the conclusion of the Peace of Westphalia in 1648 was founded on the sovereignty of these states, which has endured as the bedrock of classical international law and formed the foundation for understanding international relations for the next four centuries.

The state continues to be considered the primary actor in international relations and from the perspective of international law, continues to possess the right to be free from the interference of outsiders and refuse any form of unwarranted intrusions within its territories. It has found articulation in international society through Article 2(7) of the U.N. Charter which states that "[n]othing contained in the present charter shall authorize the United Nations to intervene in matters which are essentially within the domestic jurisdiction of any State or shall require the members to submit such matters to settlement under the present Charter...." The General Assembly, on multiple occasions during the Cold War, pronounced the importance of the non-intervention principle in relation to sovereign rights of member states. Adopted by an overwhelming majority in 1962, the Resolution on Permanent Sovereignty over Natural Resources declared that "[i]t is the duty of all States to refrain in their international relations from military, political, economic or any other form of coercion aimed against the territorial integrity of any State and the exercise of its national jurisdiction." In 1965, the General Assembly unanimously adopted the Declaration on the Inadmissibility of Intervention in the Domestic Affairs of State and the Protection of Their Independence and Sovereignty. It condemned the use of armed intervention and "all other forms of interference" against sovereign states as well as attempts at coercion through political, economic and any other means to gain advantages at the expense of the target state.

From this basic notion of state sovereignty, the corollary of rules and principles such as sovereign equality, non-intervention, and self-determination were eventually derived and utilized in the conduct of international relations. While the essential conceptual framework for state sovereignty and the derivative legal principle of non-intervention has held together for centuries, the interpretation given to important definitional elements of these principles has not necessarily remained constant. Territorial sovereignty which European states enjoyed was not extended by the leading international law publicists during the period of European colonial expansion. A utilitarian, pragmatic, and positivist approach in understanding the principle of state sovereignty that offered a legal justification for the colonial enterprises of the various European empires created legal space for empires to grow territorially. These objective positive actions of treaty making with local "states" that ceded territory or the outright taking of territory deemed *terra nullius* by European states were taken to be legitimate.

The recent decisions of the ICJ in relation to territorial claims involving former colonial territories make this point clear. Territorial disputes between *Qatar and Bahrain* in 2001, between *Nigeria and Cameroon* in October 2002, and the *Ligitan and Sipadan* dispute of December 2002 share a similarity in that significant weight was given to the decisions of the colonial powers ruling at the time in the final judgment. In a pending case before the ICJ, *Case of Territorial and Maritime Dispute between Nicaragua v. Colombia*, one of the determinative issues involves the validity of the Barcenas-Esguerra Treaty of 1928, a treaty that was claimed to have been illegally concluded under U.S.

occupation recognizing the sovereignty of Colombia over the islands in dispute. In this case, the key to its resolution would be the assessment of Nicaragua's legal arguments in emphasizing the historical circumstances after 1909, namely the assertion of illegal conclusion of the Barcenas-Esguerra Treaty under U.S. occupation and the want of effectiveness of other treaties such as the Chamorro-Bryan Treaty of 1914 that were concluded under duress. The ICJ has generally given preference to relying on the positive acts of dominant states, including treaty making and other state acts, in navigating through the historical evidence of territories in dispute. The Court's tendency to rely on positive state action has not come without criticism by a minority of the Court.

In a separate opinion in the *Maritime Delimitation and Territorial Questions between Qatar and Bahrain*, Judge Kooijmans took exception to this approach and stated, "[O]nly by taking into account the full spectrum of the Parties' history, can their present rights be properly evaluated. By not giving the full historical context its due, however, the Court has ... unnecessarily curtailed its scope for settling the dispute in a persuasive and legally convincing way." In his separate opinion in the *Land and Maritime Boundary between Cameroon and Nigeria* case, Judge Ranjeva expressed his concern saying, "The inequality and denial of rights inherent in colonial practice in relation to ... colonies is currently recognized as an elementary truth; there is a resultant duty to memorialize these injustices and at the same time to acknowledge an historical fact."

The "historical-critical method," first referenced by Judge Ranjeva in the *Case Concerning the Sovereignty over Pedra Branca/Pulau Batu Puteh, Middle Rocks and South Ledge*, provided a new direction for the development of future decisions with regard to colonial issues. In his declaration appended to the Court's judgment, Judge Ranjeva stated that in interpreting the facts of the case, the decision was reached without having taken into consideration the political and legal order prevalent at the time. He observed that while the relations between the colonial powers were governed by international law, the relationship between the United Kingdom and Johor could not be seen as having been established as between sovereigns, equal subjects of international law. Thus, "the sovereignty granted to indigenous authorities did not have the same significance as that in relations between colonial Powers," and their only role was "to submit to the will of the colonial Power ..." He questioned how Johor's title over the islands in question could have been extinguished without its consent and emphasized that in the absence of proof, the conclusion of the transfer of title relied upon presumptive consent as evidenced by Johor's silence in the face of decisions made by the British government regarding the islands. It was under these circumstances that the Sultan of Johor could not express any form of opposition to the decision of the British government. Judge Ranjeva reached the conclusion that it was difficult to infer an international transfer of title by acquiescence since Johor was merely exercising its colonial territorial title according to the rules and practice of the colonial powers and that the silence of Johor could not be interpreted against such circumstances.

Judge Ranjeva's approach to these issues is emblematic of a desire for alternative approaches in settling these issues rather than relying primarily on legal positivism. Given the impact of positivism on the shaping of international law, there is a need for viable alternative philosophical perspectives that can provide the basis for fairer international rules that depart from "a Eurocentric conception of international law based on notions of otherness."

The recent decisions of the ICJ in dealing with the disposition of territorial disputes originating from the period of European colonial expansion reveal the lingering impact of positivism in international law. These positivist presuppositions impacted the way states resolved important issues such as what political groups were entitled to be treated as states and ultimately who had state sovereignty, and related issues such as when intervention is possible or called for. Therefore, when it came to determine how to deal with indigenous peoples and their rulers, the European states, using existing principles of international law, had to find a way to deal with these native peoples. Ultimately, the classification between civilized and uncivilized mattered because it was the basis upon which whether the already recognized principles and rules of international law would apply to these indigenous societies such as whether to treat their political unity as states or give them lesser designations such as protectorate or colony. This distinction was critical in offering a legal justification for permitting colonial expansion.

3 International Relations in Northeast Asia

3.1 *Brief Historical Context of International Relations in Northeast Asia*

The Korean peninsula is the point of contact shared by the three great powers of East Asia. China, to the west, viewed it as a protective buffer for its exposed eastern flank. Japan, to the east, used the peninsula as a staging ground for military access to the Asian heartland. Russia, to the north, saw the peninsula as a natural extension of its own territory, providing warm weather ports that would otherwise be beyond reach. Nevertheless, for most of its history until the beginning of the twentieth century, Korea has been able to maintain a distinct and autonomous identity. It did so largely by using China's enormous cultural and political influence as a shield behind which it was able to flourish in relative isolation.

The relationship between China and Korea developed in three fundamental phases. The first phase, beginning in the early third century or late second century before the Common Era, is characterized by China's intermittent and occasionally successful attempts to conquer and incorporate the politically divided Korean peninsula. By 676 CE, these efforts had resulted in a unified peninsula, but one that was under Korean rather than Chinese control. The second phase was characterized by Korea's slow pull into a Chinese cultural orbit, culminating in its participation in the Chinese tributary system as China's most favored tributary state. Finally, Korea entered into the modern system of treaty-based international relations. That phase began in 1875, when Korea signed the Treaty of Ganghwa with Japan. Article I of that document stated that Korea was an autonomous state, thereby beginning a break with Chinese suzerainty and establishing Korea as a sovereign nation in accord with the Western concept of that word. The phase ended, however, with the complete elimination of Korean sovereignty as Japan made Korea its protectorate in 1904–1905 and fully annexed the country on August 29, 1910.

3.1.1 The Unification of the Korean Peninsula

The peoples living on the Asian mainland and the Korean peninsula have always engaged in some level of trade or contact, but the first political engagement by China came when the Han emperor Wudi systematically attempted to unify the frontier territories that bordered China. In 109 BCE, Wudi successfully launched a land and sea invasion of Chosun (Chinese: Chaoxian), a kingdom in the northwest of the Korean peninsula. China maintained direct control over that area by way of four administrative commanderies for the next four centuries. Control ended when the Chinese government was forced to move its capital further south because of civil war and external invasions. After that relocation in 317 CE, China was never able to exert direct control over any portion of the Korean peninsula again.

In the fifth and sixth centuries, China reunified under the Sui dynasty and attempted to reassert its control over the Korean peninsula. At that time, Korea consisted of three independent kingdoms: Kogoryŏ in the north; Paekche in the southwest; and, Silla in the southeast. In 612 CE, the Sui invaded Kogoryŏ with a force of up to 300,000 men, laying siege to its capital, Pyeongyang. The siege proved unsuccessful, and as winter was setting in, the Chinese forces began a retreat. The Kogoryŏ general, Ulchi Mudŏk, ambushed the retreating army, reducing it to only 2,700 men, if later reports are to be believed. Regardless of the exact number, this devastating loss and the enormous expense proved deadly to the Sui dynasty, eventually leading to its overthrow by the Tang.

While Kogoryŏ was occupied with the invading Chinese forces, Paekche took advantage of the power vacuum by attacking the neighboring kingdom of Silla. A particularly devastating attack took place in 642, when Paekche seized forty of Silla's border forts. By 650 CE, the Sui dynasty had collapsed, but the Paekche attacks continued. Silla appealed to the Tang court for assistance. Sensing a different strategy for the conquest of the Korean peninsula, in 650 CE, the Tang emperor agreed to assist Silla sending Chinese forces to attack Paekche. The combined forces of Tang and Silla pushed through Paekche and continued on to attack Kogoryŏ from its exposed southern flank. Silla forces captured Pyeongyang in 668 CE, leading to the collapse of Kogoryŏ.

China's military presence on the peninsula was short lived, however. Once the Tang forces had served their purpose, Silla refused to provide further logistical assistance to the Chinese. Without Silla's help in providing provisions for the Tang army, the army's continued presence on the Korean peninsula was untenable. By 676 CE, the foreign forces had withdrawn and a Korea that was geographically unified and politically independent came into existence for the first time.

3.1.2 Korea and the Chinese Tributary System

After 676 CE, Korea was politically unified under Silla, but the dominant cultural influence remained Chinese. In its efforts to court China's favor, Silla had become increasingly sympathetic to the Chinese worldview. Although military and political differences forced the two apart, the cultural influence remained. Over the following centuries, Korea increased its cultural connection to China, a connection that culminated in Korea's formal inclusion in China's tributary system. The depth of their relationship allowed Korea to participate in the richness of Chinese culture and to take a privileged position under China's protective umbrella.

Confucianism and the Confucian understanding of authority lay at the heart of China's tributary system. For Confucius, political stability was grounded on a strong and morally upright center that provided a point of orientation for those in its political orbit. "He who exercises government by means of his virtue may be compared to the north polar star, which keeps its place and all stars turn towards it." For China and its tributaries, China was the middle kingdom, the stable center around which others turned. Political authority was also metaphorically modeled on China's paternalistic familial relations. "The duties are those between sovereign and minister, between father and son, between husband and wife, between elder brother and younger, and those belonging to the intercourse of friends." Korea, as a tributary state, was viewed as son or younger brother to China.

The success of the tributary system rested on the regular missions between China and its tributary states. The missions would take place at regular intervals, up to three times a year, and also for any special events such as the emperor's birthday, the winter solstice, the death of an emperor, or when a new Korean king was enthroned. "During the two and one-half centuries from 1637 to 1894, no less than 507 Korean missions came to Peking, while 169 Chinese missions went to Korea." During those missions Korea presented local goods as a tribute to the Chinese emperor, and received goods from China in return. The missions also provided an important source of information, allowing Korean access to Chinese literary, artistic, and scientific advancements.

The mutual obligations that arose out of this tributary "imposed on both parties moral rather than legal obligations." Although trade ties were an important element to the missions, it was not their primary goal. Rather, Korea's acknowledgment of Chinese suzerainty provided China with an important affirmation of its self-understanding as the center of the world. At the same time, Chinese acknowledgment and reception of Korean leaders provided them with important certification of their legitimate claim to the thrown.

Much like a father's obligation to a child or an older brother's obligation to a younger brother, China also had a moral obligation to look after the welfare of its tributary states. That obligation was tested in 1592 when Japanese forces led by Toyotomi Hideyoshi invaded Busan on the Korean peninsula with an initial force of 52,000 troops. The Korean army was unable to resist, and the Korean court retreated to safety to the Chinese border. Ming dynasty China, recognizing a threat to both its tributary and its own sovereignty, responded by sending troops into Korea in January of 1593. The Chinese forces were assisted in this campaign by a Korean naval commander, Yi Sun-sin, who successfully designed and deployed "turtle boats," the world's first ironclad ships. The combined forces drove the Japanese back but could not evict them from the country. The result was a stalemate until late 1598, when Hideyoshi died and Japanese forces withdrew.

The effort to protect its tributary state and its own border took its toll on the Ming. Less than twenty years later, a rising Manchu state on the northern border sensed Chinese weakness. In 1616, China was attacked by the Manchurian state and requested Korean assistance. The Korean king, Kwanghaegun, sent troops, but ordered them to remain neutral until it was clear which side was more likely to win. Enraged upon learning of the King's disloyalty, a coup was mounted by Korean forces loyal to the Ming and Kwanghaegun was overthrown.

In retrospect, Kwanghaegun's hesitation might have been the strategically better choice. The Manchurians were successful in their attempt to overthrow the Ming dynasty and declared themselves the new rulers of China. As punishment for Ming loyalty, the new Qing rulers invaded Korea in 1627, looting Pyeongyang. Korea, remained a tributary state to the Qing until the end of the nineteenth century. The Koreans were never fully comfortable with their professed loyalty to a Manchurian dynasty, however. They remained in the minds of many Koreans pretenders to a culture that they did not fully understand, little brothers, themselves, that had breached propriety and usurped the thrown. "As a result the idea came about among Koreans that since China was ruled by a dynasty of questionable legitimacy, and since its rulers were not fully civilized, Korea remained the last true bastion of civilization (that is, Confucian civilization.)"

3.1.3 The Fall of the Tributary System and the Rise of Treaty-Based Relations

The tributary system served Korea well for most of its history. It allowed the small kingdom to exist in relative peace and obscurity without great interference from its much larger neighbors. Although Korea paid tribute to China, it remained fully autonomous in relation to its internal and external affairs, choosing its own leaders and conducting its own trade. That autonomy began to collapse as Western powers weakened China's influence over the region, substituting nominal "sovereignty" for the practical autonomy that it had once enjoyed.

Western European nations forged the concept of national sovereignty at the Peace of Westphalia, in 1648, in order to end the religiously motivated Thirty Years War. At its foundation, the peace agreement established that there was no higher political authority than the nation-state, each nation-state was regarded as the political equal of any other, and each had absolute sovereignty within its own borders.

The mirage of political equality between greater and lesser powers held for a time in Europe but could not be maintained when Western industrialized powers contacted the non-industrialized nations of East Asia. When the Asian nation states refused to recognize the Westerners as equals, equality was forced upon them. The Treaty of Nanking, signed in 1842, is indicative of the treaties that opened Japan and China to the West. Ostensibly proclaiming equality between the powers, they in fact were treaties "imposed by the victor upon the vanquished at gunpoint, without the careful deliberation usually accompanying international agreements in Europe and America."

The new world order exposed Korea to forces that were well beyond its control. Compounding the problem, Korea's internal politics were in great flux. In 1864, the 25th king of Chosun died without having named an heir. The

Queen dowager unexpectedly named an 11 year old son of Prince Hŭngsŏn, who was to control the reins of power until his son came of age. In honor of his new authority, Prince Hŭngsŏn was given the title of Taewŏn'gun, or Grand Prince.

Taewŏn'gun was determined not to negotiate with the foreign powers, proclaiming that "To not fight against the invading Western barbarians and instead negotiate for peace is to sell the country." The most immediate push for trade came from the East rather than the West, however. In 1875, two years after Taewŏn'gun stepped down from power and his son became King, the Japanese employed the same tactics against Korea that had been applied against the Japanese by Western powers. Having rapidly accepted Western technology, the Japanese were able to send a modern warship to the Korean-controlled Ganghwa Island, in order to provoke a fight and intimidate the new government. Fighting did, in fact, break out, as the warship *Unyokan* approached Korean defensive batteries. Japan retaliated by attacking Ganghwa Island as well as the harbor at Pusan, further demanding that Korea provide access to its ports as reparations for the injustice that Japan claimed it had suffered.

The new king, posthumously named King Kojong, was more amenable to Korea's participation in the new world order than his father, Taewŏn'gun, had been. Certainly intimidated by the Japanese show of force, he was also compelled by the new technology and the opportunities that it presented. On February 26, 1876, Korea signed the Ganghwa Treaty, opening three ports to unrestricted trade with Japan and, perhaps more significantly, declaring that Korea was "an autonomous state enjoying the same rights as Japan." For the first time, Korea had engaged in direct negotiations with a foreign power which resulted in a treaty based, at least in part, on the principles of Western sovereignty rather than on the more traditional relations between suzerain and tributary.

China was neither blind nor indifferent to Japan's expanding influence on the Korean peninsula. It felt threatened by a modernized Japan on its eastern border, but it no longer had the power to contain Japan on its own. In order to work around this strategic weakness, Li Hongzhang, a Viceroy of China and architect of nineteenth century Chinese foreign policy, devised the strategy of "using the barbarian to control the barbarian." Li Hongzhang hoped that by bringing Korea into treaty relationships with as many other foreign powers as possible, the Western nations would each have an interest in preventing any one of them from gaining exclusive control.

King Kojong was amenable to the strategy and interested in expanding Korea's Western contacts. On May 22, 1882, representatives of the United States and Korea signed and sealed the Treaty of Peace, Amity, and Commerce between the two nations. Similar treaties followed with Britain and Germany in 1883, Italy and Russia in 1884, and France in 1886. Each of these treaties contained an attachment that indicated Korea's ambivalent feelings to the new world order. For instance, the treaty with the United States had an attachment that stipulated that, "the king of Korea, as an independent monarch, distinctly undertakes to carry out the Articles contained in the Treaty, irrespective of any matters affecting the tributary relations subsisting between Korea and China, with which the United States has no concern." On the one hand, the treaty establishes Korean sovereignty in relation to Western powers, but on the other hand, it maintains its place in the Confucian world order, with which the West "has no concern."

The conflicting impulses found in the treaties' language were found in Korean society, as well. On the one hand, elements of Korean society wanted to push for a faster embrace of Western influence and modern technology. On the other hand, other more traditional Korean groups called for the complete rejection of these newly established foreign contacts. Parties on both sides of the rift led unsuccessful coups against Kojong in the tumultuous 1880s.

In 1879, Japan agreed to help Kojong train and equip a modern fighting force, which would generally be known by its Japanese title of *kunrentai*. This highly trained squadron quickly enlisted more than 1,000 men. The additional funds that the new soldiers received were taken from the support that had previously been provided to Korea's traditional army. The old guard resented their decreased support and resented the apparent pro-Japanese stance that the newly trained soldiers took. In 1882, the Korean army led a coup, adopting as their spiritual leader Taewŏn'gun, the isolationist, anti-Japanese father of Kojong that had been forced to retire in 1873.

In an expression of nationalism, the soldiers stormed the capital and burnt the Japanese legation, forcing the Japanese minister to flee Korea. The Japanese, in turn, wanted to invade Korea and abduct the Taewŏn'gun, who had become the symbol of the movement. The Chinese intervened, sending 4,500 troops to protect the Korean capital. The Chinese were also able to entice the Taewŏn'gun to their legation for protection, and eventually took him back to China. The soldiers' coup attempt resulted in the return of an enormous Chinese military presence to the Korean peninsula.

Following the soldier's attempted anti-Japanese coup, a group of young Korean reformers attempted a pro-Japanese coup two years later. The Kapsin coup, as it is known, was organized by a group of radical Korean officials who attempted to take advantage of a draw down in Chinese forces brought about by a French threat to Indochina. On December 4, 1884, the officials staged an intricate coup that expected Japanese military assistance which, in the end, did not materialize. The Chinese military that had remained in the capital were able to crush the resistance, and the coup leaders were exiled to Japan.

Both China and Japan recognized that Korea's internal struggles had come dangerously close to drawing the two powers into direct conflict with each other. Neither country was prepared for that, however. On April 18, 1885, China and Japan agreed to the Convention of Tianjin. The Convention stipulated a mutual withdrawal of Japanese and Chinese forces from the Korean peninsula, along with a promise that neither side would again send in troops without first notifying the other. It was a short-lived effort to cool the overheated tensions on the peninsula.

Within ten years, another, larger movement arose which threatened the stability of the Korean government more than either of the previous coup attempts had. The Tonghak religious movement was founded in the 1860s as a reaction to the increasing pervasiveness of foreign influence. "Tonghak" meant "Eastern learning," and the movement embraced a blend of Taoism, Buddhism, egalitarian reforms, and anti-foreign sentiment. Its founder, Ch'oe Cheu, was executed in 1864 for heresy against Neo-Confucianism. The religion grew after his execution, leading to a demand for the founder's posthumous exoneration. By 1893, the pressure had grown so great that King Kojong agreed to the exoneration. He later had a change of heart and refused to exonerate Ch'oe Cheu, after all. The indignation felt by the Tonghak followers led to a successful rebellion in the southwestern province. In 1894, the Tonghak army defeated the government forces and occupied all of the major cities in the southwest including the provincial capital.

The Korean government requested assistance from China, once again. China agreed by sending 3,000 men to suppress the Tonghak rebellion. Before doing so, however, China notified Japan of its impending invasion, in accord with the terms of the Convention of Tianjin. Not willing to have an unchallenged Chinese military presence in Korea, Japan sent its own force of 7,000 troops. The Japanese army successfully suppressed the Tonghak rebellion, but it did not stop military operations until it had destroyed the Chinese army as well. The Sino-Japanese war was over almost as quickly as it started. In November 1895, China signed the Treaty of Shimonoseki, relinquishing all claims to Korea.

After 1895, Japan worked to secure its hold over the Korean peninsula against other foreign influence. In 1904, Japan crossed the Yalu River, Korea's northern border, moving against Russian forces that were stationed there. Simultaneously, Japan moved against ships in the Russian fleet that were moored at Port Arthur (today's Lüshun). In August 1905, the United States brokered a peace agreement between the two, the Portsmouth Agreement, in which Russia conceded Japanese dominion over the Korean peninsula.

Japan also worked to consolidate its control over Korean domestic policies through a series of agreements beginning in 1904, while the Russo-Japanese War was still underway. On August 22, 1904, Japan forced Korea to sign the First Japanese-Korean Agreement. That agreement required, among other things, that "The Korean Government shall first consult the Japanese Government before concluding treaties with foreign powers . . ." In effect, the First Japanese-Korean Agreement made Korea a protectorate of Japan. That relationship was formalized with the 1905 Protectorate Treaty. Finally, the Kingdom of Korea was eliminated entirely on August 29, 1910, when Prime Minister Yi Wan-Yong signed the Treaty of Annexation, making Korea a part of Japan. With that treaty, Korea began a new phase of its existence and forever lost China as its older brother.

4 Western International Law

4.1 *Introduction of Western International Law into East Asia*

When international law of Western origin appeared in East Asia and it was asserted as the new international order in the region through the superior military power of Western states, it became inevitable that many matters of an international character should be rethought according to the newly introduced concepts of international law. One of the most important matters of review was the legal status of Korea. From the viewpoint of international law, Korea could be considered a vassal state whose suzerain state was China. This *prima facie* impression is totally understandable as Korea paid tribute to China and in many respects Korea was not equal to China. The difference in the title of the respective rulers of each country could show that the two states were not sovereign equals. Therefore, it would have been natural for Westerners to inquire as to whether Korea was a sovereign independent state or a vassal state of China under the system of international law with which they were familiar with and which they wanted to adopt as regulating norms of the relations between East Asian states and Western states.

This was not a question of a solely theoretical nature but had practical significance. Depending on the answer to the question, Korea might or might not, for example, conclude treaties with Western states, send and receive diplomatic missions to and from the Western states and owe responsibility for the legal problems that occurred between her and Western states. Whether Korea could declare war was another question the answer to which might be varied according to the status of Korea under international law.

The following incidents are a few of the historical instances in which the international legal status of Korea became problematic. In March 1866, many Roman Catholics suffered persecution and the Korean government executed many Koreans and nine French priests. This incident was reported by the French Bishop Ridel to Admiral Roze, commander of the French fleet in China. France decided to dispatch troops to Korea and demand the conclusion of a trade treaty. One legal problem that emerged from this incident was determining which state, Korea or China, was responsible for the lives of the French priests. Faced with this problem, the Office of Foreign Affairs, *Zongli Yamen* (統理衙門), which was established as the initial organ in charge of diplomacy during the Qing dynasty, denied any Chinese responsibility. It said that Chosun was "entirely independent" in her relations with other states. France, for her part, was said to have sent an official letter to the Chinese government on July 13, 1866, in which France manifested her intent not to recognize any authority of China over Korea.

A similar problem was raised when the American warship, General Sherman, was burnt by the people of Pyeongyang and all the crew members were killed. At this time, China showed the same attitude that such matters were not under its jurisdiction, because all the domestic affairs of Chosun were put under the jurisdiction of Chosun since it enjoyed its own autonomy under the Sinocentric order. Prince Kung's reply to the inquiry of W. Williams, the acting U.S. Minister to China at that time, shows the Chinese attitude with regard to Korean status under the Sinocentric order and the bearer of legal responsibility when this kind of incident occurs.

...

Another noticeable scene where the international legal status of Korea was questioned appeared when Korea was to conclude the Treaty of Amity and Commerce with the United States. Needless to say, this treaty was a treaty between Korea and the United States. However, on behalf of Korea all the negotiations were led by China and Korea only signed the treaty without having had any direct negotiation with the United States. In mediating the conclusion of the treaty, China pursued two mutually paradoxical objectives. One was to let Korea conclude a treaty with the United States. The capacity to do so was only recognized to a sovereign independent state. The other was to keep her as a dependency of China and to maintain Chinese political influence upon it. When Li Hongzhang (李鴻章), the Chinese Viceroy of Zhili and Minister of Beiyang, had a talk with Admiral Shufeldt, the U.S. representative for the negotiations, he proposed a draft of the treaty composed of 10 articles.

The first draft article provided that Korea was a 屬邦 (*sokbang* in Korean and *shubang* in Chinese) of China. This is the so-called "dependent country clause" (屬邦條項).

The meaning of shu (屬) is "to be of", "belonging to", "connected with", "pertaining to", "depending on", or "subordinate to". Bang (邦) means "a state", "a country" or "a nation". Therefore, "the position of a country such as Korea" as a shubang of China "can best be described as a 'belonging or dependent country'". Translating it into terms like "vassal kingdom" or "fief" is "misleading, for the character *shu* carries with it the idea of kinship, not that of a merely legal relation". In that sense, *sokbang* or *shubang* (屬邦) can be best translated into "belonging or dependent country". As a result, article 1 of the proposed draft is to be read as follows: "Korea is a 'dependent country' of China. However, the affairs of domestic politics and diplomacy may be constantly managed autonomously for the future." (朝鮮爲中國屬邦 而內政外交事宜 向來均得自主)

China strongly argued the acceptance of this article by the U.S., a demand refused by Shufeldt. Compromise was reached at the third conference between Li and Shufeldt. Instead of inserting an article concerning Korean dependency upon China in the text of the treaty, they decided to make Korea send the Document of Reference (照會文) which confirmed the traditional tributary relation between Korea and China. Two days after the conclusion of the treaty, on May 24, 1882, the Korean king handed the document to Shufeldt and it was translated into English by him and forwarded to the U.S. government in Washington D.C. On June 26, 1882, United States minister to China, Holcombe, also translated the document and sent it to U.S. Secretary of State Frelinghuysen. Holcombe's translation seemed to be more refined and was said to be accepted by China as the official translation:

> Cho-sen has been from ancient times a state tributary to China. Yet hitherto full sovereignty has been exercised by the Kings of Cho-sen in all matters of internal administration and foreign relations. Cho-sen and the United States, in establishing now by mutual consent a treaty, are dealing with each other upon a basis of equality. The King of Cho-sen distinctly pledges his own sovereign powers for the complete enforcement in good faith of all the stipulations of the treaty in accordance with international law.
>
> As regards the various duties which devolve upon Cho-sen as a tributary state to China, with these the United States has no concern whatever.
>
> Having appointed envoys to negotiate a treaty it appears to be my duty, in addition thereto, to make this preliminary declaration.

In the translation, Chosun is described as "a state tributary to China" and "a tributary state to China". However, at the same time, phrases such as "full sovereignty", "dealing with each other upon a basis of equality", and "the King of Chosen distinctly pledges his own sovereign powers" are used, which express Chosun as a sovereign state. A Chinese reading of the document would have focused on the words of "a state tributary to China" and interpreted them as expressing Chosun's traditional dependency to China. The U.S. would have focused on other phrases which describe Chosun as a sovereign independent state. In this sense, the Document of Reference may be said to show the difficulty in attempting harmonize a normative fact which has different meanings in two different international systems of order.

Judicial Decisions

A. Treaties and International Agreements

(1) *Direct Application of Treaties*

Constitutional Court [97 Heon-ba 65] Decision issued November 26, 1998.

[Facts: Pursuant to the signing of the WTO Agreement, Korea's tariff rates changed, thereby increasing the criminal sentence of the Accused. The Defense asserted that the penalty increase based on a treaty and not a domestic legislation violated the principle of legality [*nullum crimen, nulla poena sine lege*] of the Constitution. The Constitutional Court held that even if a criminal sentence were to be increased by a treaty, this still had the same effect as an increase caused by domestic legislation. It was an example of recognition of direct application of treaties.]

The Claimant alleges that in order to increase the punishment of tariff violation, there must be an amendment of the tariff laws or the Act on Aggravated Punishment of Specific Crimes. Thus he argues that increasing the punishment for tariff violation solely based on a treaty is a grave violation of fundamental rights and also runs counter to the principle of legality.

The Constitution states, in the latter sentence of article 12(1), "No person may be punished, placed under preventive restrictions, or subject to involuntary labor except as provided by law and through lawful procedures," thereby regulating criminal punishment through law and due process; while article 13(1) provides, "No citizen may be prosecuted for an act which does not constitute a crime under the law in force at the time it was committed," thereby prohibiting criminal punishment of an act not constituting a crime at the time of commission. Article 6(1) states, "Treaties duly concluded and promulgated under the Constitution and the generally recognized rule of international law have the same effect as the domestic laws of the Republic of Korea," providing that treaties duly concluded and promulgated have the same effect as domestic laws. The Marrakesh Agreement was duly concluded and promulgated thereby having the same effect as domestic laws; thus, even if crimes were to be created or punishments increased by this Agreement, it would be as if done so by domestic laws. In other words, even if the punishment for tariff violation were to be increased by the Marrakesh Agreement, it cannot be said that it was an unlawful criminal punishment or a punishment for an act that did not constitute a crime at the time of commission. Therefore, we cannot conclude that the old Act on Aggravated Punishment of Specific Crimes article 6(2)(1) or the Act on the Marketing and Price Stabilization of

© KONINKLIJKE BRILL NV, LEIDEN, 2016 | DOI 10.1163/9789004315754_003

Agricultural and Fishery Products article 10(3) either violates the principle of legality or the fundamental human rights and personal liberty of the Claimant.

(2) *Self-Executing Treaties*

Supreme Court [96 Da 55877] Judgment issued March 26, 1999.

[Facts: The Plaintiff, while heading the Kumho Company Trade Union, was pronounced guilty for violating the article 13(2) of the Labor Dispute Adjustment Act prohibiting third-party intervention. After the conviction was affirmed by the Supreme Court (92 Do 70 Judgment), he became the first Korean to report this case to the Human Rights Committee (HRC) established under the Optional Protocol to the International Covenant on Civil and Political Rights (ICCPR) on July 7, 1992. On August 5, 1995, the HRC found that the punishment of Jong-Kyu Sohn violated the right to freedom of expression as provided in the Covenant; and the HRC, while stating that Jong-Kyu Sohn was entitled to an effective remedy, including appropriate compensation, further invited the Korean government to review article 13(2) of the Labor Dispute Adjustment Act (CCPR/C/54/D/518/1992). When the government did not carry out the decision of the HRC, Jong-Kyu Sohn brought a suit against the government for damages, pointing to article 2(3) of the ICCPR.]

Article 2(3) of the above international covenant provides for the obligation of states under international law to secure legal systems that would ensure effective remedy for persons whose rights or freedoms as recognized in the covenant are violated. Remedies such as compensation suits against the state can be claimed based on domestic law, e.g., State Compensation Act; therefore, the above provision does not individually create a special right for a person to claim remedies, e.g., compensation against a member state of the convention.

(3) *Effect of Treaties as Domestic Law*

a. Constitutional Court [99 Heon-ma 139, 143, 156, 160 Consolidated] Decision issued March 21, 2001. (Affirming the unconstitutionality of the ratification of the Fisheries Agreement between Korea and Japan, etc.)

Article 6(1) of the Constitution states, "Treaties duly concluded and promulgated under the Constitution and the generally recognized rule of international law have the same effect as the domestic laws of the Republic of Korea." The Agreement at bar is a treaty "duly concluded and promulgated under the Constitution" regarding the fisheries between our country and Japan and therefore has the same effect as domestic "laws". Thus, as observed above, a Constitutional Appeal can be made regarding a law in the exceptional circumstance of when a fundamental right is infringed by an ordinance that is not separately executed.

b. Constitutional Court [2002 Heon-ma 611] Decision issued April 24, 2003. (Affirming the unconstitutionality of Medical Treatment Law article 5, etc.)

The Claimants allege that the provision regarding preliminary examination breaches the "Regional Convention on the Recognition of Studies, Diplomas and Degrees in Higher Education in Asia and the Pacific," thereby failing to recognize the education obtained abroad and thus additionally limiting the achievement of domestic licenses. Our country is a signatory of this Convention (Treaty no. 990, entered into effect Sept. 29, 1989); and though it has a legal effect, its status is not constitutional and therefore cannot be a criterion for the evaluation of the validity of the preliminary examination provision.

c. Constitutional Court [2000 Heon-ba 20] Decision issued September 27, 2001. (Constitutional Appeal regarding the Articles of Agreement of the International Monetary Fund article 9(3))

Article 68(2) of the Constitutional Court Law provides that the object of trial shall be "law," which should be read as including "treaties." This court has earlier made a judgment on the text of a treaty on the grounds that a treaty having the same effect as domestic law can be subject to evaluation of its constitutional validity (Constitutional Court, 97 Heon-ga 14, Apr. 29, 1999, Casebook 11–1, p. 273). The article in this case was concluded and ratified by the National Assembly and therefore has the effect of domestic law pursuant to Article 6(1) of the Constitution, which would be equivalent to the effect of legislation. Because this particular article regards the immunity from jurisdiction, its nature of direct application would make it subject to evaluation of constitutional validity.

(4) *Precedence in the Application of Treaties as* Lex Specialis

Supreme Court [82 Da-ka 1372] Judgment issued July 22, 1986.

As there has yet to be any domestic legislation concerning carriage by air, the legal relationship would be that it would be subject to the application of civil law, or *lex generalis*. Regarding international air transport, however, the government has declared the "Protocol to Amend the Convention for the Unification of Certain Rules Relating to International Carriage by Air Signed at Warsaw on October 12, 1929" (hereinafter "Hague Protocol") as Treaty no. 259, after having passed the resolution in the Cabinet

Council and subsequently ratified by the National Assembly on October 11, 1967. Article 23(2) of the Hague Protocol provides, "Adherence to this Protocol by any State which is not a Party to the Convention shall have the effect of adherence to the Convention as amended by this Protocol[,]" while Article 19 states, "As between the Parties to this Protocol, the Convention and the Protocol shall be read and interpreted together as one single instrument and shall be known as the *Warsaw Convention as amended at The Hague, 1955*." Thus Korea's signing of the Hague Protocol gave it an effect equivalent to signing the "Convention for the Unification of Certain Rules Relating to International Carriage by Air" (hereinafter "Warsaw Convention") concluded on October 12, 1929 in Warsaw; and the Warsaw Convention, as amended by the Hague Protocol, now has the same effect as that of domestic laws of Korea. Therefore, regarding the laws of international carriage by air, the Warsaw Convention amended in the Hague in 1955 (Amended Warsaw Convention) shall have precedence in its application as *lex specialis* in the general body of civil law.

(5) *Harmonious Interpretation of Domestic and International Law*

Constitutional Court [2004 Heon-ba 47] Decision issued April 24, 2008.

Opinion of Judge Song, Doo-hwan Regarding Unconstitutionality

Further, Article 6(1) of the Constitution states, "Treaties duly concluded and promulgated under the Constitution and the generally recognized rule of international law have the same effect as the domestic laws of the Republic of Korea[,]" which makes clear the accommodation and respect for international law. Currently, our country is a party to most international human rights covenants, having been ratified by the National Assembly, and is a member of the International Labour Organization (ILO). Therefore, the interpretation of individual articles of the Constitution must be done in harmony with international norms set out by the U.N., e.g., Universal Declaration of Human Rights, International Human Rights Covenants, ILO Agreement and recommendations, etc. If domestic laws do not comply with these norms, though they may not immediately be declared unconstitutional, the above norms must be utilized as important standards in determining the constitutionality of such laws.

(6) Whether Agreed Minutes is a Treaty

Constitutional Court [99 Heon-ma 139, 142, 156, 160 Consolidated] Decision issued Mar. 21, 2001.

[Facts: The 1998 Fisheries Agreement between Korea and Japan was obtained through the consent of the National Assembly and was subsequently ratified, but the government did not forward the annexed Agreed Minutes to the National Assembly for ratification. The following case is the decision of the Constitutional Court regarding the issue of whether the Agreed Minutes are subject to ratification of the National Assembly as a treaty.]

There seems to be no definite principle determining the legal effect of Agreed Minutes under international law. In order for Agreed Minutes to be considered a "treaty," its satisfaction of the legal characteristics of a treaty would provide important evidence. Treaties are not limited to those actually termed "treaties" but rather are "international agreement concluded between states in written form and governed by international law, whether embodied in a single instrument or in two or more related instruments and whatever its particular designation (Vienna Convention on the Law of Treaties art. 2(1)(a)."

The preamble of the Agreed Minutes states, "The government officials of the Republic of Korea and Japan have agreed to record the following regarding the relevant articles of the Fisheries Agreement between the Republic of Korea and Japan signed today." According to this, two legal actors, the Republic of Korea and the state of Japan, reached an "agreement" regarding certain matters. Whether such agreement amounts to an "international legal relationship" will be the dispositive factor determining whether the Agreed Minutes can be categorized as a "treaty."

Turning to the actual contents of the Agreed Minutes, paragraph 1 states that the governments of both countries shall closely cooperate to maintain good fisheries order in the East China Sea; paragraph 2 states that our government has intentions to cooperate with the governments of Japan and third countries not to damage fisheries relations; paragraph 3 states that the government of Japan has intentions to cooperate with governments of third countries with fisheries relations to make possible certain fishing activities by nationals and fishing vessels of the Republic of Korea in certain areas of the East China Sea; and paragraph 4 states that both countries have intentions to negotiate to maintain good fisheries order in the East China Sea on the basis of fisheries agreements concluded or to be concluded through the Korea-Japan Joint Fisheries Committee or other committees. These provisions show a declaration of intentions to cooperate towards a fisheries order, and it would be difficult to say that there is a purpose of reaching an immediately binding legal relationship. Article 14 of the Agreement further states that Annexes I and II form an indivisible part of the agreement, indicating that the annexes are integral elements of the agreement itself. However, considering that it does not provide for the Agreed Minutes, it would be difficult to say that the Minutes also form an integral part of the Agreement at hand that forms a treaty. Therefore, the assertions of the Claimants are without merit.

(7) *Legal Nature of the Joint Statement of ROK-US Ministers of Foreign Affairs*

Constitutional Court [2006 Heon-ra 4] Decision issued March 27, 2008.

[Issue: On January 19, 2006, Korea and the United States issued a joint statement on the Launch of the Strategic Consultation for Allied Partnership which contained the following:

Joint Statement on the Launch of the Strategic Consultation for Allied Partnership:

> The ROK, as an ally, fully understands the rationale for the transformation of the U.S. global military strategy, and respects the necessity for strategic flexibility of the U.S. forces in the ROK. In the implementation of strategic flexibility, the U.S. respects the ROK position that it shall not be involved in a regional conflict in Northeast Asia against the will of the Korean people.

The Claimant in this case (member of the National Assembly) asserts that while the U.S. armed forces stationed in Korea under the ROK-US Mutual Defense Treaty is necessary for the defense of the Korean Peninsula, consent to strategic flexibility in the Joint Statement violates the defense treaty and ultimately alters its effect, which would naturally violate Claimant's rights by not obtaining National Assembly ratification pursuant to Article 60(1) of the Constitution. The following is the judgment of the Constitutional Court regarding the legal nature of this joint statement.]

Treaties are "international agreement concluded between States in written form and governed by international law, whether embodied in a single instrument or in two or more related instruments and whatever its particular designation." [...] While the consent of the National Assembly to the conclusion and ratification of treaties pertaining to important matters is required by law (Constitution art. 60(1)), the National Assembly is granted this right regarding particular treaties provided by law in Article 60(1) of the Constitution.

As the Joint Statement at bar only contains statements of respect, by Korea and the United States toward each others' position and contains nothing establishing legal rights or obligations, it cannot be regarded as a treaty. Even without having to consider whether it falls under the category of Article 60(1) treaties, we cannot hold that the National Assembly has the right to ratify this Joint Statement or that the Claimant, a congressman, holds the right of deliberation.

As this case is grounded on the belief that the Joint Statement is a treaty subject to the consent of the National Assembly on its conclusion and ratification, upon which the Claimant's right to deliberation is based, the case is improper for lack of subject matter.

B. International Customary Law

(1) *Application of International Customary Law*

Supreme Court [97 Da 39216] Judgment issued December 17, 1998.

[Facts: In this case regarding the scope of sovereign immunity, the Court issued a holding based on a theory of limited sovereign immunity. As Korea is not a party to any treaties nor has enacted domestic legislation regarding sovereign immunity, this decision can be seen as having been issued on the basis of international customary law.]

1. According to the trial court, the Plaintiff was hired by the United States Army and Air Force Exchange Service, a non-appropriated fund organization affiliated with the United States of America and was stationed at Camp Casey, 2nd Infantry Division until unreasonably dismissed on November 8, 1992. With the United States as Defendant, he sought to nullify the dismissal and to be compensated for the lost wages from the day of dismissal to his reinstatement. A state, under international law and custom, does not submit to the jurisdiction of another state. Unless an exception has been made through treaties or diplomatic privileges have been renounced, our courts cannot exercise jurisdiction over a foreign state as defendant. Because there is no evidence that the United States neither submitted to the jurisdiction of our courts through any treaty provisions nor renounced its diplomatic privileges, this case is illegitimate for lack of jurisdiction.
2. According to international customary law, while a sovereign act of a state is not subject to the jurisdiction of another state in principle, one cannot say that it is customary that even the judicial acts of a state are immune to the jurisdiction of another state. It thus follows that unless there are special circumstances, e.g., a foreign judicial act done within the territory of the Republic of Korea could fall within our jurisdiction or is sufficiently related that the exercise of jurisdiction can unjustifiably interfere with the sovereign activities of the other state, our courts cannot exercise jurisdiction over judicial acts with this state as defendant. The decision of the Supreme Court that previously differed in this regard [74 Ma 281, Decision of May 23, 1975] shall be amended accordingly.
3. Thus the trial court ought to have determined whether our courts could exercise jurisdiction over the employment contract and dismissal based on the consideration of the overall circumstances, e.g., duties and activities of by the United States Army and Air Force Exchange Service, the plaintiff's position and his assigned tasks, and sovereign activities of the United States and their relation to the Plaintiff's tasks, after which it should have considered the legal nature of the employment contract and dismissal at hand, as well as their relation to

the sovereign activities. However, the trial court decision, in holding that this case was illegitimate for lack of jurisdiction without having fully considered the nature of this employment contract and dismissal, shows a misunderstanding of the principles of law regarding the exercise of jurisdiction over foreign states and thus violated the law by not fully trying the case. There are reasons for pointing this out in particular among other issues of appeal.

CHAPTER 2

The Legacy and Impact of Japanese Colonialism

1 Introduction

Following Commodore Matthew Perry's entry into Japanese ports and the subsequent signing of the Treaty of Kanagawa, Japan actively pursued Westernization and quickly engaged in treaty making, concluding one of friendly relations with Korea in 1876, also known as the Treaty of Ganghwa. In this newly introduced treaty regime, Japan became a signatory of the Geneva Conventions in 1886, followed by the signing of the Declaration of Paris the following year. This was the beginning of its entry into the "Family of Nations," as it was the one and only Asian country to do so at that period of time. The ultimate breakthrough occurred in 1894 with the signing of the Anglo-Japanese Treaty of Commerce and Navigation, only 16 days prior to Japan's declaration of war on China, which recognized the equal freedoms of residence, travel, property, trade, and navigation. Throughout the war with China, Japan appealed to the West through letters and writings of Japanese scholars, testifying to its "scrupulous observance of international law." In regards to Japan's civilized and law-abiding character, Sakayue Takahashi wrote that "the Japanese nation laid stress upon the law of war, even before they were confronted ... [and] refrained from revenge." In a letter addressed to the *Japan Mail*, he also wrote:

> I have seen to-day in a copy of the *Japan Mail* that reached me, that Mr[.] Creelman, the war-correspondent of the *New York World*, wrote to that paper to the following effect: "Torpedo-boats were going through the waves, sinking junks loaded with men, women and children endeavouring to escape." ... While regretting for the sake of Mr[.] Creelman, whose honour as a gentleman may be impaired by such absurd fabrications, I fear that the public might be led astray by what he has written, and therefore I feel constrained to refute the false statements made by him.

The Sino-Japanese War came to an end on April 17, 1895 with the conclusion of the Shimonoseki Treaty providing for, among others, the complete independence of Korea and the cession of certain territories. The same year, Japan established a pro-Japanese cabinet in Korea, which was soon ousted by Queen Min. Japan immediately responded by brutally murdering the Queen, thereby angering not only the Korean people but also Russia, who went on to deploy

© KONINKLIJKE BRILL NV, LEIDEN, 2016 | DOI 10.1163/9789004315754_004

units to assist Korea. Under a strong Russian influence, a new Korean Empire was established.

Having lost control of the Korean Peninsula, Japan began to ally itself more with the West, signing its first mutual defense treaty with England on January 30, 1902 and another on August 12, 1905. The latter recognized Japan's "guidance, management and protection" over Korea. Beginning in 1904, Japan forced Korea to sign a series of agreements including the 1905 Protectorate Treaty to consolidate its control. This culminating with Korea's signing of the Treaty of Annexation on August 29, 1910 which made Korea a part of Japan.

Around the same time in 1904, Japan moved against Russian forces by crossing the Yalu River, Korea's northern border, as well as the Russian fleet moored at Port Arthur. An important international legal issue in this case was whether a formal declaration of war had taken place—more specifically, if two diplomatic notes that were exchanged could be regarded as such a declaration. It is regarded that the Russo-Japanese War was significant in that "it was the first war in which both belligerents pledged to adhere to the international laws of war" signed at the 1899 Hague Convention. The following year in August 1905, the United States mediated the Portsmouth Agreement between the two, in which Russia conceded Japanese dominion over the Korean peninsula. Further, as all states involved equally claimed civilized statehood—with the exception of Korea and China, Japan was able to annex Korea with the diplomatic support of the United States and Britain and the indifference of other states. Also notable was Japan's interaction with the international community in proving itself impeccable in its adherence to international law. As one scholar notes:

> Many aspects of Japan's prosecution of the war were, so to speak, done by the book, and facilitated by the attachment of international legal advisors to each army in the field: Japanese treatment of prisoners of war was impeccable, and Japan received much praise for its creation of a bureau to manage prisoners—in the exact manner prescribed by the 1899 Hague Conference. Also praised by the international press was Japanese treatment of the sick, the wounded, and the dead, as well as Japanese Red Cross facilities, operations, and first aid. Japan's conduct of the siege and capitulation of Port Arthur was noteworthy for the care with which Japan protected Russian life and property there. The manner of the Japanese prosecution of the war was said to be a model of gentlemanly behavior—and this praise for Japan was of a piece with the otherwise distracting incidents examined in this article. With the Russo-Japanese War, Japan demonstrated a command of international law and a commitment to

> its principles. This mastery not only certified Japan's status as an equal among the civilized states but also invited Japan to participate in world affairs in the same manner as its fellows-by resorting to state will in situations defined by legal ambiguity or military necessity.

As mentioned above, by 1905, Japan had tacit recognition of Britain and the United States regarding its control over Korea despite the fact that both had signed treaties with Korea affirming its independence. Korea's fate was already evident, as stated by T.J. Lawrence: "I have no doubt that in the long run Korea will be annexed by one or the other of her powerful neighbors. It is the fate of small, weak, and corrupt states to fade out of the political map." Soon enough, Japan confirmed this in a treaty with Korea, which gave Japan control over "foreign relations and affairs of Korea." Such action went largely unchallenged, and vigorous protests of American missionaries and educators in Korea went unheeded by the United States and subsequently silenced by Japanese authorities. Finally, Korea was completely annexed on August 22, 1910 pursuant to the Japan-Korean Annexation Treaty.

2 Annexation by Japan

2.1 *The Legality of the 1910 Annexation of Korea by Japan*

From 1910 to 1945, Korea was annexed by Japan and thus fell under Japanese rule. The issue of how to comprehend and evaluate this historical fact forms the starting point and foundation of the bilateral relations of these two states. This is because the answers to the questions of whether Korea was a victim of Japanese rule, and, if it was a victim, depend upon an understanding and evaluation of the nature of that victimization and how Japan should take responsibility for its actions.

As this issue lies at the root of Korea-Japan relations, it was inevitably raised during the negotiations for the normalization of diplomatic relations between the two countries in the early 1960s. As the so-called "Kubota remark" demonstrated, the Japanese government once seemed to take the position that Japanese rule of Korea was not only legal under the international law of the time but also morally and politically justifiable. Currently, Japan admits that its rule over Korea was a morally unjustifiable act. However, from the days of the Korea-Japan normalization talks to the present, Japan's position that the annexation was legal under the international law of the time remains unchanged. In contrast, the Korean government has consistently maintained its position that

Japanese domination was not only morally unjustifiable one but also illegal and devoid of any ground in international law. The two sides failed to bridge the differences in their positions during the diplomatic normalization process. It is a well-known that Article 2 of the Treaty on Basic Relations between the Republic of Korea and Japan (1965) adopted an intentionally vague expression to evade a resolution of these differences, stating that the agreements signed by Korea and Japan on August 22, 1910 and prior to that "were already null and void."

2.1.1 Treaties under Examination

The issue of the legality of Japan's annexation of Korea can be traced to the validity of the 1910 Annexation Treaty. However, discussions about the legality of Japan's colonial domination of Korea are not confined merely to the 1910 Annexation Treaty alone but also include discussions about a number of other agreements that led up to Japan's formal annexation of Korea. This is because the 1910 Annexation Treaty is viewed as the result of a series of political steps developed with annexation in mind and the validity of the agreements that were concluded in this process is problematic. There are five agreements that are often questioned in discussions about the legality of the annexation. The following table summarizes the important contents of these five agreements and the reasons argued for their invalidity:

Date/Description	Reasons for Invalidity	Procedural Defects
February 23, 1904		
Japan's interests in emergency situations were to be maintained and permission was given to the expropriation of property necessary for military use. (Article 4)	Conclusion of the treaty was forced by the stationing of five Japanese battalions on the Korean peninsula creating a state of military occupation.	The treaty was concluded unilaterally by Japan without negotiations with any Korean representatives. The original text of the treaty was drafted after the signing date.
August 22, 1904		
Korea was required to utilize a Japanese financial advisor and a diplomatic advisor of foreign nationality was		An official Korean version of the agreement does not exist. The treaty was concluded unilaterally

Date/Description	Reasons for Invalidity	Procedural Defects
recommended by the Japanese government who had the obligation to consult with the government.		by Japan without negotiations with any Korean representatives. Texts of the treaty were added and promulgated after the date of signing pursuant to the directives of the Japanese government. A draft was signed as a memorandum and later added to the agreement. The memorandum lacked the proper delegation of authority.
November 17, 1905		
Japanese Ministry of Foreign Affairs was authorized to supervise and direct Korea's external relations. (Article 1)	The agreement was signed when Japanese troops surrounded the residence of the Korean Emperor. Japanese officials also entered the meeting room and intimidated Korean officials while heavily armed Japanese troops were present in major locations throughout Seoul.	The treaty lacks a name. Matters of great importance such as the power to handle foreign relations were transferred in a manner and form that lacked the regular formality of a treaty. The document that evidenced the delegation of signing authority to the representative of the government does not exist. The instrument of ratification does not exist. The Korean Foreign Minister was forced to sign and seal. The treaty was not ratified.

(cont.)

Date/Description	Reasons for Invalidity	Procedural Defects
July 24, 1907		
Korea was required to adhere to the directives of the Japanese Resident-General. (Article 1)		
The Japanese Resident-General had the power to approve Korean legislation and important administrative matters. (Article 2)	A mixed brigade was dispatched to assist Japanese troops stationed in Korea.	Full powers granted by the Korean Emperor and the instrument of ratification do not exist. The Korean Emperor's signature and seal are lacking.
Korea could not employ foreign advisors without the consent of the Japanese Resident-General. (Article 6)		
August 22, 1910		
There is a concession to Japan of all rights of sovereignty over the entirety of Korea permanently and completely. (Article 1)		A royal edict proclaiming the annexation possessing the royal seal was not signed by Emperor Sunjong. The treaty was signed by the Japanese Resident-General acting as a representative of the Japanese government even though this post was created by the 1905 Treaty and put under the auspices of the Korean Emperor.

3 San Francisco Peace Treaty

The San Francisco Peace Treaty, which came into force in 1952, provided for the legal resolution of Japan's involvement in World War II against the Allied Powers and "settle questions still outstanding as a result of the existence of a state of war between them." The Peace Treaty deliberately left unresolved the territorial disposition of strategic islands and islets in East Asia in response to the commencement of the Cold War between the United States and the Soviet Union. As a result, the Peace Treaty served to protect Japan from a potential communist threat in East Asia which has affected the present-day conflict between Japan and her immediate neighbors, China, Korea and Russia, in their disputes over sovereignty and maritime delimitation.

3.1 *The 1951 San Francisco Peace Treaty and Its Relevance to the Sovereignty over Dokdo*

3.1.1 San Francisco Peace Treaty (1951)

The San Francisco Peace Treaty, signed on 8 September 1951, provided the terms for terminating the state of war between Japan and the Allied Powers, to "settle questions still outstanding as a result of the existence of a state of war between them," such as the status of the minor islands that were under Japanese sovereignty at the end of the war. In Article 2(a), "Japan, recognizing the independence of Korea, renounces all right, title and claim to Korea, including the islands of Quelpart, Port Hamilton and Dagelet [Ullungdo]." Dokdo was not mentioned in the Treaty, but Korean commentators are quick to point out that "while the Peace Treaty only specified three among the total of 3,215 islands [belonging to Korea], they were listed merely to illustrate the status of the remaining outlying islands." Many other Korean islands are also not explicitly mentioned.

...

3.1.2 A Geopolitical Analysis of the Post-World War II Documents

By the time the San Francisco Peace Treaty was finalized in 1951, the United States was more preoccupied with the Cold War and its competition with the Soviet Union than with regional disputes over territory between Japan and Korea. The decision to refrain from resolving Dokdo's sovereignty had more to do with the goal of furthering U.S. Cold War strategy than with the merits of this matter.

In a memorandum by the UK Delegation to the U.S. Department of State on the drafting of the territorial clause of the San Francisco Peace Treaty, a British diplomat wrote that "[i]n determining which of the minor islands shall remain under Japanese sovereignty the decisive considerations must be strategic." The United States came to agree with this conclusion. The strategic considerations that loomed large during this period included future U.S. use of Dokdo, the utility of a short treaty in negotiating with other Allies and the need for a buffer zone around Japan to assist in limiting Communist influences.

3.1.2.1 *William Sebald's Plan and the First Nine Drafts of the Treaty*

William J. Sebald, who had a major political and strategic influence on the first nine drafts of the Treaty, graduated from the U.S. Naval Academy in 1922. He served in the U.S. Navy during World War I, received his LL.B. from the University of Maryland in 1933, practiced law at his father-in-law's firm in Japan during 1933–1939, again served in the U.S. Navy during World War II and in 1945 became Political Advisor to the Supreme Allied Commander, General Douglas MacArthur.

The first five drafts of the peace treaty were completed on 19 March 1947, 5 August 1947, 8 January 1948, 13 October 1949 and 2 November 1949. The 19 March 1947 draft provided that "Japan hereby renounces all rights and titles to Korea and all minor offshore Korean islands, including Quelpart Island, Port Hamilton, Dagelet Island and Liancourt Rocks (Takeshima)...," and this language remained essentially unchanged during the next four drafts. These early drafts provide proof of an original intention on the part of the Allied Powers to recognize Korea's sovereignty over Dokdo.

In late 1949, however, the United States re-evaluated this position, based at least partially on strategic considerations. Sebald focused on these considerations in his "Comment on Draft Treaty of Peace with Japan," written 19 November 1949:

> It is suggested that Liancourt Rocks [Dokdo]... be specified in our proposed Article 3 as belonging to Japan. Japan's [claim] to these islands is old and appears valid, and it is difficult to regard them as islands off the shore of Korea. Security considerations might also conceivably render the provision of weather and radio stations on these islands a matter of interest to the United States.

As explained above, in SCAPIN No. 1778, issued 16 September 1947, the Allied Powers had asserted jurisdiction over Dokdo for use as a bombing range, and had engaged in merciless shelling of these islets shortly thereafter. SCAPIN No. 1778 and Sebald's 1949 memorandum reveal that the United States was motivated primarily by its own security needs. The sixth draft of the San

Francisco Peace Treaty, completed on 8 December 1949—19 days after Sebald's memo—introduced new language in the territorial clause, stating that:

> The territory of Japan shall comprise the four principal Japanese home islands of Honshu, Kyushu, Shikoku, and Hokkaido and all adjacent minor islands, including the islands of the Inland Sea (Seto Naikai); Tsushima, Takeshima (Liancourt Rocks), Oki Retto, Sado, Okujiri, Rebun, Riishiri and all other islands in the Japan Sea (Nippon Kai) within a line connecting the farther shores of Tsushima, Takeshima and Rebun..." This draft used the Japanese name for Dokdo—"Takeshima"—and would have recognized Japan's sovereignty over the islets.

The seventh draft of the San Francisco Peace Treaty, dated 11 days later, on 19 December 1949, switched positions once again and recognized Korea's sovereignty over Dokdo, but this version was short-lived and was quickly replaced by the eighth and ninth versions, on 29 December 1949 and 3 January 1950, which again recognized Japanese sovereignty. Sebald's thinking is revealed in documents relating to these drafts such as the "Commentary on Draft Treaty of Peace with Japan" released on 29 December 1949, which argued that the Japanese historical claim was strong, incorrectly asserting that "Takeshima has no Korean name and does not appear ever to have been claimed by Korea" and noting that the islands "have been used by U.S. forces during the occupation as a bombing range and have possible value as a weather or radio station site."

3.1.2.2 *John Foster Dulles and U.S. "Strategic Ambiguity"*

The tenth draft of the Peace Treaty was completed on 7 August 1950. Two important events occurred between the ninth and tenth drafts, which affected the approach taken by the United States regarding Dokdo. The first was the appointment in April 1950 of John Foster Dulles to oversee the peace treaty process, and the second was the outbreak of the Korean War on 25 June 1950. The War complicated the geo-political situation and led to the U.S. position of "strategic ambiguity".

...

As a result of Dulles's influence, these new treaty drafts were significantly shorter and more vague than previous versions. The logic behind this approach was that by not addressing every detail in the Treaty, U.S. negotiations with its Allies could proceed more quickly, thus allowing for an earlier signing of the Treaty. As the Cold War intensified and the fighting in the Korean peninsula expanded, the rebuilding of Japan and restoration of Japan's role in Northeast Asia came to be seen by the United States as matters of vital importance.

The Allied Powers feared that heavy-handed, punitive measures against Japan would devastate Japan's already fragile economy, promote Japanese resentment towards the United States and increase the risk of communism taking root in Japan. The signing of the San Francisco Peace Treaty was a necessary step towards repairing U.S.–Japan relations as well as the Japanese economy and advancing U.S. efforts to insulate Japan from the spread of communism in East Asia. Dulles thus favoured a speedy end to negotiations, even if issues such as Dokdo's sovereignty were left unanswered.

Dulles's motives for leaving the sovereignty of Dokdo ambiguous were also related to the strategic positioning of U.S. military force in East Asia, especially after the Korean War broke out. Soon after 25 June 1950, when North Korea's army invaded Korea, the 24th U.S. Infantry Division, which had been occupying Japan, was quickly dispatched into Korea, leaving Japan vulnerable to a Soviet invasion. To combat this potential danger, General MacArthur created in 1950 a force of 75,000 Japanese men known as the "National Police Reserve", which would later become the Japanese Self-Defense Force.

Before the U.S. occupation forces could be diverted from Japan and utilized in Korea, however, the Peace Treaty with Japan had to be completed, so that administrative responsibilities could be transferred from SCAP to Japanese leadership. This transition became urgent during these months, because Korea needed additional U.S. military resources to avoid being overwhelmed by the Communist North Koreans. Dulles thus decided to expedite the completion of the San Francisco Peace Treaty by drafting a short version of the document, which avoided some of the issues that might have required prolonged negotiations.

The decision to eliminate a reference to Dokdo in the Treaty was probably also influenced by the perceived need to create a geopolitical buffer zone around Japan to halt the spread of communism. The ability of the United States to maintain its presence in Korea was far from certain, and the situation grew bleaker in November 1950 when China entered the war as an ally of North Korea. The fear of losing Korea to Communism may explain why Dulles never wrote a draft treaty specifically granting Dokdo to Korea. If Korea had sovereignty over Dokdo, but was then taken over by the North, the Communist forces would have a spot in the East Sea dangerously close to Japan from which to launch attacks. Dulles's concern regarding such a scenario was demonstrated during a U.S. House of Representative Subcommittee meeting on 11 January 1951, when he explained: "With Communist domination of China and Manchuria, Sakhalin, the Kuriles, and possibly all of Korea, Japan would be placed in an invidious position and would be vulnerable to Communist domination unless the United States and the other friendly powers were able to assure Japan of a reasonable political, economic and military stability over the future." The Korean Ambassador to the United States sent a letter to the U.S. Secretary of State on 19 July 1951, asking that Liancourt Rocks be added to the list of islands that Japan would renounce in Article 2(a) of the Peace Treaty, but Assistant Secretary of State Dean Rusk replied on 10 August 1951 (one month before the signing of the Peace Treaty) that the United States could not agree to this change because Dokdo "was according to our information never treated as part of Korea," noting that Japan had claimed it since 1905.

The intensity of the Korean War fighting helps explain why recognizing Korea's sovereignty over Dokdo might have seemed to be inconsistent with the strategic interests of the United States, but it is less clear why the United States declined to recognize the sovereignty of Japan over the islets. Why did the drafters of the San Francisco Peace Treaty choose to omit any reference to Dokdo when the inevitable result would be decades of international dispute between Korea and Japan?

...

3.1.2.3 *U.S.–Japan Collusion against Korea*

Despite numerous attempts made during the drafting process to convince the United States to define Dokdo as Korean territory, U.S. diplomats ultimately declined Korea's request. U.S. leaders also excluded Korean delegates from the Peace Treaty signing ceremony in San Francisco in 1951, thus depriving Korea of its final chance to argue its position.

The United States had originally intended to invite Korea to the signing ceremony as a means of extending international legitimacy to the newly created Republic of Korea, but on 19 July 1951, Dulles met the Korean ambassador to the United States and reversed his position. Dulles claimed that Korea could not be a signatory to the treaty because "only those nations in a state of war with Japan and which were signatories of the United Nations Declaration of 1942 would sign the treaty."

Dulles probably had some other motive for excluding Korea, because Vietnam, Laos and other nations that were not signatories of the 1942 U.N. Declaration were included in the ceremony. John Price has suggested that the United States wanted to exclude Koreans living in Japan from the property benefits that allied civilians would receive under the treaty, explaining that "Dulles suggested that many of these Koreans were undesirables, being in many cases from North Korea and constituting a center for Communist agitation in Japan." Because of their desire to expel these Koreans from Japan, the United States and Japan agreed to prevent Korean delegates from signing the treaty.

3.1.3 Impact of the Cold War on the Drafting of the San Francisco Peace Treaty

A review of this early Cold War history reveals that the U.S. approach towards Dokdo's sovereignty was based on geopolitical considerations rather than on an examination of Dokdo's history. U.S. diplomats did not want to shut the door on the possibility of using Dokdo for U.S. military needs and had a substantial interest in having the San Francisco Peace Treaty signed quickly, to limit the possibility that Japan or Korea might fall under the Communist sphere of influence. These diplomats may also have realized the value of creating a buffer zone as well as a wedge issue between Japan and Korea, for insurance in the event of the collapse of the Korean government.

The decision to exclude any reference to Dokdo in the territorial clause of the San Francisco Peace Treaty was not based on an assessment of historical claims to Dokdo, but rather on the dynamics and tension of the emerging Cold War. Because these geopolitical considerations dominated the drafting of the ultimate text of the Treaty, and because the final Treaty text makes no reference to Dokdo, the Treaty cannot be viewed as a factor in determining sovereignty over Dokdo.

Also significant is the recognition that the final text of the Treaty was not designed to be comprehensive, and was not intended to resolve all disputes, but was written in a short form in order to enable Japan to consolidate itself against Communist threats, and to allow the United States to focus on the defense of the Korean peninsula from the Communist military activity. The omission of any reference to Dokdo cannot, therefore, be viewed as creating an ambiguity, because the Treaty did not purport to address all controversies.

3.1.4 Events Subsequent to the 1951 Peace Treaty

Because the textual clause of the Peace Treaty makes no mention of Dokdo, the events that followed in the years after its signing are not "interpretive" evidence under Articles 32 and 33 of the Vienna Convention on the Law of Treaties. But these subsequent events are still of interest with regard to Dokdo's sovereignty, and the decisive and consistent actions taken by Korea to consolidate its possession of Dokdo certainly support Korea's claim of sovereignty over these islets.

The status of Dokdo remained controversial after the Peace Treaty was signed in September 1951. Five months later, on 18 January 1952, Korean President Syngman Rhee issued a presidential proclamation that created the "Peace Line," a territorial boundary averaging 60 miles off the coast of Korea, which explicitly identified Dokdo as a Korean territory. Japan protested this Peace Line and declared that it did not recognize Korea's claim to Dokdo.

Several months later, Japan issued a tacit protest through the U.S.–Japan Security Treaty, which had designated Dokdo as an area for U.S. military training. After receiving a similar protest from the Korean government, the U.S. military announced on 27 February 1953 that Dokdo would be excluded from its training area. The United States sought to avoid any direct involvement in this issue, but did publicize Dean Rusk's 10 August 1951 Note to the Korean Ambassador in Washington, DC, when the question was raised in 1953, and stated then that "[w]e have publicly declared our view that this Island belongs to Japan, but no one in Japan or elsewhere seriously expects U.S. to take military action under the [U.S.–Japan] Security Treaty to reclaim this Island for Japan." In May 1954, citizens of both Japan and Korea, under the protection of patrol boats from their respective governments, landed on Dokdo and proceeded to erect signs claiming sovereignty while dismantling the signs erected by the other nation.

3.1.4.1 *1954–1965: Korea Physically Possesses Dokdo; Rejects Japan's International Court of Justice Proposal; and Normalizes Relations with Japan in the 1965 Treaty*

After Korea erected a lighthouse on Dokdo in August 1954, the nature of the situation changed. With Korea physically possessing the island, Japan increased its mode of protest and in September 1954 proposed that the matter be submitted to the "authoritative" International Court of Justice (ICJ), but Korea rejected this proposal.

Between 1952 and 1960, Japan sent 24 notes to Korea on the Dokdo matter and Korea responded with 18 notes back to Japan. The matter was also raised again through diplomatic channels during the protracted negotiations that led to the signing of the 1965 Korea–Japan Treaty, but because of Korean resistance on this issue, from 1957 when the talks were resumed until the signing in 1965, the Dokdo problem was never adopted as an official agenda item, to be recorded in the minutes. There is absolutely no direct reference to Dokdo in the various documents of the Korea–Japan Treaty signed in 1965. Originally, Japan thought of writing down the problem in the Treaty or failing that, as planned in advance, in the instruments to be exchanged agreeing to take the case to the ICJ. However, the Korean side rejected both plans by arguing that Dokdo could not become an agenda item as it was Korea's inherent territory.

Korean Ambassador Jae-hee Oh, who was involved in these negotiations, explained that on the day scheduled for the signing of the 1965 Normalization Treaty, Japan offered language to be inserted in the dispute-resolution protocol that would say "Disputes such as Dokdo/Takeshima shall be resolved through a conciliation procedure." The Korean negotiators refused to consider this insertion. After an awkward hour had passed, the Japanese Prime Minister agreed to take out the reference to Dokdo, and the treaty was then signed.

According to the Japanese view of the negotiations, the general language that remained in the agreement covering all disputes, which says that they are to be resolved "through arbitration in accordance with the procedure agreeable to both countries", preserves their position on Dokdo. But Korea has rejected the idea that Dokdo is covered by this side agreement, referring to this notion as "a far-fetched construction of the instruments," with Korean Foreign Minister Lee Dong-won stating that "since Takeshima/Tokdo was not an object of dispute, it could not be covered by the exchange document." Korea's position has always been that Dokdo is inherent Korean territory, and thus that the island cannot be viewed as an issue either in the treaty or before the ICJ.

3.1.4.2 *Since 1965*

In the decades that followed the 1965 Normalization Treaty, "Korea and Japan sought to avoid the controversial issue of Dokdo, with each side maintaining its own position on the matter." Japan stepped up its rhetoric in the mid-1990s, claiming an exclusive economic zone in 1996 and asserting its claim to Dokdo repeatedly. In 1999, Korea and Japan established a provisional fishing zone in the East Sea, which includes Dokdo, but this agreement was unpopular in Korea, and the Korean government "has unilaterally refused to promote the joint regulatory measures that had been agreed upon." On 26 February 2005, Japan's Shimane Prefecture promulgated "Takeshima Day," further exacerbating relations between the two countries. But Korea's possession of Dokdo has continued and has been unchallenged except through verbal protests. This long period of effective occupation, especially when coupled with Korea's strong historical claim to Dokdo, provides substantial support for Korea's claim of sovereignty over these islets.

Article 32 of the Vienna Convention on the Law of Treaties discourages the use of the negotiating history (*travaux preparatoires*) of a treaty to provide meaning to the Treaty unless the treaty's language "(a) leaves the meaning ambiguous or obscure; or (b) leads to a result which is manifestly absurd or unreasonable," but Article 31(3) allows evidence of the subsequent actions and agreements of the parties to be examined to provide guidance regarding the understanding of the treaty's terms. Relevant subsequent activities would seem to include the actions of Korea in gaining possession of Dokdo by 1954, the protests of Japan since then and the events surrounding the 1965 Normalization Treaty. The consistent approach of the ICJ and other international tribunals examining sovereignty disputes has been to focus on actual demonstrations of effective control, particularly in the past century. Korea's possession since the early 1950s would provide substantial support for Korea's claim to sovereignty to Dokdo. Japan's protests provide some support for Japan's claim, but a tribunal adjudicating this matter would have to determine whether they are adequate. Japan's willingness to enter into the 1965 Normalization Treaty with Korea without any reference to Dokdo would serve to undercut Japan's claim and could be viewed as having acquiesced to Korea's sovereignty, particularly if a tribunal were to contrast this action by Japan with its refusal to normalize relations with Russia until the Northern Territories dispute is resolved.

The formal rules of interpretation found in Articles 31 and 32 of the Vienna Convention on the Law of Treaties thus appear to support Korea's position on Dokdo. The 1951 San Francisco Peace Treaty makes no mention of Dokdo, and so an international tribunal would likely take that on face value, and conclude that the Peace Treaty has no relevance to Dokdo. If, on the other hand, the tribunal were to conclude that the Peace Treaty's failure to mention Dokdo creates an "ambiguity," then the tribunal could examine the *travaux preparatoires*, in which case it would find further ambiguity in the conflicting drafts and notes pointing in different directions. Perhaps the most important pre-1951 document is SCAPIN No. 677, which separated Dokdo from Japan, as well as SCAPIN No. 1778, authorizing bombing operations in and around the island. As one Korean scholar has explained, "because SCAPIN No. 677 specified that Dokdo was Korean territory, the Treaty of Peace with Japan would have had to explicitly overturn this stipulation in order to supersede the original designation."

If a tribunal were then to look at the subsequent events, as it is authorized to do under Article 31(3), it would probably focus on the actual Korean occupation of Dokdo and the Japanese acceptance of the 1965 Normalization Treaty without any reference to Dokdo, both of which provide support for Korea's position. Japan's protests are not irrelevant, but they would probably not be viewed as sufficient to overcome the acquiescence evidenced by the 1965 Treaty and Korea's continued occupation of the island.

3.1.5 The Unique Status of Peace Treaties

The preceding sections have explained that the omission of any reference to Dokdo in the territorial clause of the 1951 San Francisco Peace Treaty should not be viewed as an ambiguity triggering sophisticated tools of interpretation, and that the Treaty should be viewed as irrelevant to Dokdo's sovereignty. Nonetheless, because the Treaty is frequently addressed by commentators discussing Dokdo, two other issues related to the Treaty are examined now—whether the 1951 Peace Treaty should be viewed as having a "constitutive" status and whether it should apply at all to Korea, which is not a party to it.

Peace treaties have always had a special status in international law. Because they define boundaries and relations among States, they are generally viewed as "constitutive" documents that provide the defining underpinnings for the sovereign State system and the fundamental principles of international law. Normally, treaties that are imposed by the threat or use of force are void, as enunciated in Article 52 of the Vienna Convention on the Law of Treaties. But a peace treaty is by definition the result of military activity. The victors will typically believe that the other side was the aggressor, and thus that the use of force resulted from the nefarious transgressions of the losing party, but in some military conflicts it is difficult to be sure which side "started" the war. Especially for those central peace treaties that have ended protracted wars, the (exhausted) international community has tended to accept the validity of the peace treaty without regard to which country was the initiator of the conflict, perhaps because the only real alternative is the unrealistic one of re-fighting the war to punish the victorious initial aggressor. In his separate opinion in the Advisory Opinion on the International Status of South West Africa, Lord A.D. McNair explained that:

> [F]rom time to time it happens that a group of great Powers, or a large number of States both great and small, assume a power to create by a multi-party treaty some new international regime or status, which soon acquires a degree of acceptance and durability extending beyond the limits of the actual contracting parties, and giving it an objective existence.

In other words, a "constitutive treaty" creates an "objective regime" that establishes a new framework applicable to all States, even those that are not contracting parties to the treaty. The States that are not contracting parties have not "consented" in the usual sense to the regime established by the constitutive peace treaty, but—unless they challenge the result militarily—they are deemed to have accepted the treaty and the new boundaries and relationships established by it, and thus the treaty becomes part of the general customary international law applicable to all countries. By accepting the treaty and acting in accordance with it, the non-contracting parties engage in State practice with the requisite *opinio juris* (the belief that the practice is required by law) to enable the treaty to be viewed as a reflection of binding customary law.

Peace treaties thus have an effect *erga omnes* and are applicable to all the world, without regard to who has signed the treaty. *Obligatio erga omnes* are obligations owed not merely to certain States and their nationals, but "towards the international community as a whole."

Should the 1951 San Francisco Peace Treaty be viewed as a constitutive treaty capable of defining Korea's boundaries? The answer is clearly "no" because Korea's existence and boundaries pre-existed the Treaty, and because the Treaty did not purport to provide definitive boundaries for Korea. The final draft of the Treaty, as explained above, was shortened in length so that an early agreement could be reached, and the parties recognized that a number of territorial disputes were not addressed or resolved in the Treaty. The territorial clause of the Treaty, Article 2(a), does not purport to define boundaries of Korea, but rather assumes that Korea's borders have been established by something outside the Treaty. The Treaty thus must be viewed as irrelevant to the question of Dokdo's sovereignty.

3.1.6 The Application of the 1951 San Francisco Peace Treaty to Korea

The legal issue that commentators have grappled with is the application of the San Francisco Peace Treaty to countries that were not contracting parties, which are generally referred to as "third parties". Korea was not a contracting party to the Treaty, so should this Treaty have any effect at all with regard to a dispute between Korea and Japan? The applicable rules are found in Articles 34, 35 and 36 of the Vienna Convention on the Law of Treaties:

> *Article 34—General Rule Regarding Third States*
> A treaty does not create either obligations or rights for a third State without its consent.
>
> *Article 35—Treaties Providing for Obligations for Third States*
> An obligation arises for a third State from a provision of a treaty if the parties to the treaty intend the provision to be the means of establishing the obligation and the third State expressly accepts that obligation in writing.
>
> *Article 36—Treaties Providing for Rights for Third States*
> 1. A right arises for a third State from a provision of a treaty if the parties to the treaty intend the provision to accord that right either to the third State, or to a group of States to which it belongs, or to all States, and the third State assents thereto. Its assent shall be presumed so long as the contrary is not indicated, unless the treaty otherwise provides.
> 2. A State exercising a right in accordance with paragraph 1 shall comply with the conditions for its exercise provided for in the treaty or established in conformity with the treaty.

The 1951 San Francisco Peace Treaty addresses its applicability to countries that are not contracting parties in Article 25, which states that the Treaty "shall not confer any rights, titles, or benefits on any state which is not an Allied Power." The complete language of Article 25 is as follows:

> For the purpose of the present Treaty the Allied Powers shall be the States at war with Japan, or any State which previously formed a part of the territory of a State named in Article 23, provided that in each case the State concerned has signed and ratified the treaty. Subject to the provisions of Article 21, the present Treaty shall not confer any rights titles or benefits on any State which is not an Allied Power as herein defined; nor shall any right, title or interest of Japan be deemed to be diminished or prejudiced by any provision of the Treaty in favor of a State which is not an Allied Power as so defined.

Article 21 provides the exception to Article 25, and states that "[n]otwithstanding the provisions of Article 25 of the present Treaty, China shall be entitled to the benefits of Articles 10 and 14(a)(2) and Korea to the benefits of Articles 2, 4, 9 and 12 of the present Treaty." Article 2 is the territorial article wherein Japan recognizes "the independence of Korea" and "renounces all right, title and claim to Korea, including the islands of Quelpart, Port Hamilton and Dagelet [Ullungo]." Article 4 concerned debts and submarine cables, Article 9 required Japan to enter into negotiations regarding fisheries and Article 12 required Japan "to enter into negotiations for the conclusion with each of the Allied Powers of treaties or agreements to place their trading, maritime and other commercial relations on a stable and friendly basis."

Korea thus gained certain definite benefits from the San Francisco Peace Treaty, including a confirmation of its independent existence. John Foster Dulles explained to the Koreans a month before the signing of the treaty that they "would benefit from all of the general provisions of the treaty equally with other nations." By the terms of Article 25, however, Korea cannot utilize the dispute resolution procedures in Article 22, which allows any party to refer "a dispute concerning the interpretation or execution of the Treaty" to the ICJ for binding determination (and, similarly, Japan cannot invoke this provision to bring a claim in the ICJ against Korea).

Articles 34–36 of the Vienna Convention on the Law of Treaties constitute a codification of the longstanding maxim *pacta tertiis nec nocent nec prosunt*, stating that agreements neither give rights nor impose obligations on third parties. The 1951 Peace Treaty by explicit design does convey specific benefits on Korea, but excludes Korea and Koreans from other aspects of the Treaty's provision. With regard to the territorial provision in Article 2, because it was by design not comprehensive in its language, and because it says nothing about Dokdo's sovereignty, it cannot be viewed as having any effect on the Dokdo matter.

3.1.7 Conclusion

This section has provided an overview of the ways in which the 1951 San Francisco Peace Treaty might be viewed as relevant to the Dokdo matter. This "constitutive" treaty brought the Pacific and Asian aspects of World War II and defined the boundaries of Japan, thus establishing an objective regime that has had an effect *erga omnes* and which has thus been accepted by countries that were not contracting parties to the treaty. Korea's independence was recognized in this treaty, and it gained other benefits from it.

The Peace Treaty did not purport to be comprehensive and it does not resolve a number of territorial issues, including that of Dokdo, and so it is largely irrelevant to claims of sovereignty over Dokdo. The United States was clearly concerned with its own security interests, including the emerging Cold War and the Korean War, during this period, and apparently sought to maintain some flexibility on this issue, in case Korea was lost to the Communists, and perhaps also to maintain some tension between Korea and Japan if Korea remained independent.

Within five months of the signing of the Peace Treaty, Korea made it clear that it continued to claim sovereignty over Dokdo, and by 1954, Korea had built a lighthouse on the island. Japan registered regular protests, but entered into the 1965 Normalization Treaty with Korea even though this treaty made no mention of Dokdo. This action could be viewed as acquiescence to Korea's sovereignty, especially if one contrasts this acceptance with Japan's rigid refusal to normalize relations with Russia until the Northern Territory dispute is resolved.

The San Francisco Peace Treaty is constitutive and some of its provisions have an effect *erga omnes*, but its territorial clause does not purport to define Korea's boundaries in any detail and does not mention Dokdo, and thus this Treaty cannot be viewed as being relevant to the Dokdo matter. More important to claims of sovereignty would be the actions that have been taken subsequent to the Treaty, particularly Korea's immediate possession and exercise of control over Dokdo and Japan's acquiescence that can be found in its acceptance of the 1965 Normalization Treaty.

3.2 *The 1951 San Francisco Peace Treaty and Territorial Disputes in East Asia*

3.2.1 Japan's Territorial Disputes

...

Japan is a party to three ongoing territorial disputes that, arguably, could have been prevented by more diligent diplomacy fifty years ago: against Russia, Japan continues to claim sovereignty over the Southern Kurile Islands/Northern Territories (Kurile Islands); against the People's Republic of China (China) and the Republic of China (Taiwan) over the Pinnacle Islands/Senkaku Islands/Diao-yu-tai (or Tiao-yu-tai) (Senkaku Islands); and against Korea over the Liancourt Rocks/Dokdo/Takeshima (Liancourt Rocks).

... Unlike the disputes over the other islands, the Liancourt Rocks dilemma suffers from a paucity of scholarly research, particularly in the western world. Recently, the territorial dispute over the Liancourt Rocks re-surfaced largely as a consequence of new exclusive economic zone claims by the disputants, together with their respective ratifications of the Law of the Sea Convention. If considered to be "islands" under the Law of the Sea Convention, the Liancourt Rocks would include 16,600 square nautical miles of marine space. Thus, national pride (as much as contestation over territory, resources, and the associated maritime area) is a typical feature of the islands in dispute.

Since the Treaty of Peace with Japan (San Francisco Peace Treaty) effected the final disposition of territories in East Asia following the conclusion of World War II, its text should be the starting point for research into the territorial disputes over islands in East Asia. For that purpose, although there could be other versions, this section examines the following treaty drafts: March 19, 1947; August 5, 1947; January 8, 1948; October 13, 1949; November 2, 1949; December 8, 1949; December 19, 1949; December 29, 1949; January 3, 1950; August 7, 1950; September 11, 1950; March 12, 1951; March 17, 1951; April 7, 1951; May 3, 1951; June 14, 1951; July 3, 1951; July 20, 1951; and August 13, 1951.

...

3.2.2 The Liancourt Rocks

The Liancourt Rocks include two tiny rocky islets, the East Island (Tongdo/Onnajima) and the West Island (Sodo/Otokojima), as well as numerous small reefs. The Liancourt Rocks are located 93 kilometers east of Korea's Ullung Island and 157 kilometers northwest of Japan's Oki Islands. Korea and Japan have contested the ownership of Liancourt Rocks, which are currently occupied by Korea, since the end of World War II. Korea's status as a former colony of Japan has complicated the dispute because after 1910 there was no border between the two countries. Therefore, in contrast to the disputes over the Kuriles and the Senkakus, the two parties have relied on the priority of their historical claims, rather than invoking the favorable interpretation of treaties.

Under the terms of the Law of the Sea Convention, the outcome of maritime boundary disputes often depends on the ownership and classification of islands or rocks capable of sustaining human habitation or economic life. As a result, sovereignty over the Liancourt Rocks has become increasingly important, although the size of their territory is relatively small. If considered to be "islands" under the Law of the Sea Convention, ownership of the Liancourt Rocks could affect 16,600 square nautical miles of marine space. Thus, the issues at stake in the Liancourt Rocks dispute go beyond mere national pride.

3.2.2.1 *The Status of the Liancourt Rocks Prior to 1945*

Japan annexed Korea in the aftermath of the Russo-Japanese War in a series of agreements made between 1904 and 1910. During this period, Japan specifically laid its claim to the Liancourt Rocks by officially incorporating them into Shimane Prefecture. A Cabinet Decision on January 28, 1905 and the Shimane Prefecture Notice 40, issued on February 22, 1905, declared that the island 85 miles northwest of the Oki Islands should be designated as "Takeshima" and be placed under the jurisdiction of the head of Oki Islands. During World War II, the 1943 Cairo Declaration primarily decided the terms of territorial disposition with respect to Korea. The Potsdam Proclamation, in stating: "Japanese sovereignty shall be limited to the islands of Honshu, Hokkaido, Kyushu and Shikoku, and such minor islands as we determine," indicated that other minor Japanese islands might be detached from Japan, at the discretion of the Allied Powers.

3.2.2.2 *The Postwar Status of the Liancourt Rocks*

The status of the Liancourt Rocks was not addressed in Article 2(a) of the San Francisco Peace Treaty. Instead, the treaty provided that "Japan, recognizing the independence of Korea, renounces all right, title and claim to Korea, including the islands of Quelpart, Port Hamilton and Dagelet." Following Japan's surrender, the Supreme Commander for the Allied Powers removed the Liancourt Rocks from Japanese jurisdiction, and U.S. armed forces controlled and used the area as a bombing range.

On January 18, 1952, President Syngman Rhee of Korea issued the Korean Presidential Proclamation of Sovereignty over the Adjacent Sea, creating the so-called "Peace Line" or "Syngman Rhee Line," which claimed Korean jurisdiction over waters within a line running an average of 60 nautical miles from the Korean coast. Aimed principally at excluding the Japanese from the East Sea/Sea of Japan, the Rhee Line explicitly stated Korea's claim to the Liancourt Rocks. Japan responded by protesting Korea's unilateral proclamation of jurisdiction over the high seas, and by declaring its non-recognition of the Korean claim to the Liancourt Rocks.

Korea has taken numerous steps to develop the disputed area since 1952, including the recent construction of a wharf on the Liancourt Rocks. There has also been the continuous Korean presence on the Liancourt Rocks of at least one or two fishing families and a permanent coastguard.

Despite disagreement over the ownership of the Liancourt Rocks, the two claimants signed the Treaty on Basic Relations between Korea and Japan on June 22, 1965, which normalized their diplomatic relations. The treaty did not address the status of the Liancourt Rocks.

The territorial dispute over the Liancourt Rocks resurfaced in 1996 as a consequence of new, revised and modified exclusive economic zone (EEZ) claims by both sides in the wake of the ratification of the Law of the Sea Convention. In particular, Japan's declaration of an EEZ represented a marked departure from its previous policy of restraint regarding territorial issues. Japan's EEZ claims were construed by Korea as an attempt to usurp Korean sovereignty over the disputed territory, and provoked a harsh response.

More recently, Korea and Japan signed a fisheries agreement, which took effect on January 22, 1999. This agreement sets quotas for each state's fishermen in the other's EEZ and establishes a joint fishing zone around the Liancourt Rocks.

3.2.2.3 *Competing Claims to the Liancourt Rocks*

The official Korean position is that at one time the Liancourt Rocks were part of the Kingdom of Korea. Korea's claims are based on numerous Korean historical records, including some written in the eighth century, indicating that the Liancourt Rocks became part of Korea in 512 AD. Additionally, Korea asserts that various maps verify its title to both the Liancourt Rocks and Ullung Island, of which, Korea argues, the Liancourt Rocks are appendages.

On the other hand, Japan's historical claims are based on records documenting Japanese ownership of the Liancourt Rocks from 1650, which indicate the granting of the Liancourt Rocks to what is known today as Tottori Prefecture.

Japan also relies on other pre-nineteenth century documents providing evidence of Japanese fishermen's use of the Liancourt Rocks during the seventeenth and nineteenth centuries, and Japanese hunting of sea lions on the Liancourt Rocks during the early twentieth century.

3.2.3 The Wartime Declarations

There was general agreement that the San Francisco Peace Treaty could only endorse the territorial agreements made at Cairo, Yalta, and Potsdam. In fact, the territorial dispositions of the San Francisco Peace Treaty followed the terms of these agreements and U.S. studies and policy decisions relating to the implementation of these agreements.

The pertinent provisions of these agreements are: "Japan will... be expelled from all other territories which she has taken by violence and greed" in the Cairo Declaration on December 1, 1943; "The Kuril islands shall be handed over to the Soviet Union" in the Yalta Agreement of February 11, 1945; "Japanese sovereignty shall be limited to the islands of Honshu, Hokkaido, Kyushu, Shikoku, and such minor islands as we determine" in the Potsdam Proclamation of July 26, 1945; and "[Japan]... accepts the provisions set forth in the [Potsdam Proclamation]" in the Japanese government's statement accepting U.S. terms of surrender, dated August 14, 1945.

3.2.3.1 *The Cairo Declaration*

The Cairo Declaration referred specifically only to "the territories Japan has stolen from the Chinese, such as Manchuria, Formosa and the Pescadores," although it did add "Japan will also be expelled from all other territories which she has taken by violence and greed." As to the words of the Cairo Declaration, there were harsh responses from Japan, for example, "the expulsion of Japan from the territory which she took by violence and greed is difficult for the Japanese to understand, since all countries have acquired additional territory in such a way."

3.2.4 Interpretation of the Supreme Commander for the Allied Powers' Instructions

The General Headquarters of the Supreme Commander for the Allied Powers gave an instruction No. 677 entitled "Governmental and Administrative Separation of Certain Outlying Areas from Japan" on January 29, 1946, which stated, "The Imperial Japanese Government is directed to cease exercising, or attempting to exercise, governmental or administrative authority over any area outside of Japan, or over any government officials and employees or any other persons within such areas." It further stated, "For the purpose of this directive, Japan is defined to include the four main islands of Japan (Hokkaido, Honshu, Kyushu and Shikoku) and the approximately 1000 smaller adjacent islands... and excluding... (c) the Kurile (Chishima) Islands, the Habomai (Hapomaze) Island Group (including Suisho, Yuri, Aki-yuri, Shibotsu and Taraku Islands) and Shikotan Island."

This instruction has been considered one of the significant legal instruments deciding the destiny of the Kurile Islands especially favoring Russia. Russia continuously maintains that SCAPIN No. 677 decreed the cessation of Japanese administration over various non-adjacent territories, including the Kurile Islands, and this is a strong indication of what the Allied Powers desired. In response to this Russian claim, Japan argues that SCAPIN No. 677 suspended only Japanese administration of various island areas, including the Kurile Islands, and it did not preclude Japan from exercising sovereignty over this area permanently.

The United States recognized that the question of international sovereignty was outside SCAP's authority. As SCAPIN No. 677 itself stated, "Nothing in this directive shall be construed as an indication of Allied policy relating to the ultimate determination of the minor islands referred to in Article 8 of the Potsdam Declaration." The United States also pointed out that in all SCAPINs to the Japanese Government regarding authorization of areas for Japanese fishing and whaling which were established under SCAP, there appeared a statement providing essentially that "the present authorization is not an expression of Allied policy relative to ultimate determination of national jurisdiction, international boundaries or fishing rights in the area concerned or in any other area." Therefore, it was the U.S. position that SCAPIN No. 677 was an operational directive to the Japanese Government tentative in character and that specifically stated it was not an Allied policy determination of Japanese territory. In the same vein, the SCAP General Order No. 1 merely stated that Japanese troops in Sakhalin and the Kurile Archipelago should surrender to the Commander of the Soviet Forces Far East, and it did not and was not intended to touch upon the final disposition of these islands.

There is also, however, a report, titled "Summaries of FEC Policy Statements and Certain SCAP Directives to the Japanese Government, with Proposals for Disposition in the Peace Settlement with Japan," regarding the relationship between territorial questions and SCAPIN No. 677, which "defines present area of Japanese jurisdiction and provides a starting point for decisions on details of territorial adjustments."

SCAPIN No. 677 further stated, "For the purpose of this directive, Japan is defined to include the four main islands of Japan ... and the approximately 1,000 smaller adjacent islands ... and excluding ... Liancourt Rocks. ..." This instruction is also considered one of the significant legal instruments that could decide the destiny of the Liancourt Rocks in favor of Korea. Korea continuously maintains that SCAPIN No. 677 decreed the cessation of Japanese administration over various non-adjacent territories, including the Liancourt Rocks, and this is a strong indication of what the Allied Powers desired to remove from Japanese jurisdiction. In response to this Korean claim, Japan argues that SCAPIN No. 677 suspended only Japanese administration of the various island areas, including the Liancourt Rocks, and it did not preclude Japan from exercising sovereignty over this area permanently, as the United States also opined in the same vein.

A later instruction, SCAPIN No. 1778 of September 16, 1947, designated the islets as a bombing range for the Far East Air Force and further provided that use of the range would be made only after notification through Japanese civil authorities to the inhabitants of the Oki Islands and certain ports on Western Honshu. The action of the U.S.-Japan Joint Committee in designating these rocks as a facility of the Japanese Government is therefore justified according to Japanese interpretation. Again, SCAPIN No. 677 did not purport to express Allied policy as to the "ultimate determination of national jurisdiction, international boundaries or fishing rights in the area concerned or in any other area." SCAPIN No. 1033 of June 22, 1946, also provided that "Japanese vessels or personnel thereof will not approach closer than twelve (12) miles to Takeshima (37 [degrees] 15<prime> North Latitude, 131 [degrees] 53<prime> East Longitude) nor have any contact with said island.... The present authorization is not an expression of allied policy relative to ultimate determination of national jurisdiction, international boundaries or fishing rights in the area concerned or in any other area."

3.2.5 Draft Treaty Clauses Concerning the Disposition of the Liancourt Rocks

> In the course of private talks on other matters, [U.S. Secretary of State Dean Rusk] referred to the Korea-Japan negotiations, and said that [the United States] hoped for an early conclusion.... [President Chung-Hee Park of Korea] stated that one of the irritating problems, although it was a small one, in the negotiations was Tokto Island (Takeshima). These are uninhabited rocks in the Sea of Japan that are claimed by both Korea and Japan. Korean security forces actually guard them, and the Koreans believe that they historically belong to Korea. The Japanese believe they have a like claim. President Park said he would like to bomb the island out of existence to resolve the problem. Secretary Rusk... suggested that perhaps a joint Korean-Japanese commanded light house be set up and the problem of to whom it belonged left unanswered, letting it die a natural death. President Park commented that a joint lighthouse with Korea and Japan just would not work.

The terms of the territorial disposition regarding Korea followed the terms of the Cairo Declaration of December 1, 1943, confirmed at Potsdam on July 26, 1945, to the effect that "Japan will also be expelled from all other territories which she has taken by violence and greed. The aforesaid three great powers, mindful of the enslavement of the people of Korea, are determined that in due course Korea shall become free and independent." It also declared that Quelpart Island, Port Hamilton, Dagelet (Utsuryo) Island, and all the other off-shore Korean islands were naturally to be included in the new independent Korea, for they were historically and administratively part of Korea and were inhabited primarily by Koreans. The Potsdam Proclamation in stating, "the terms of the Cairo Declaration shall be carried out and Japanese sovereignty shall be limited to the islands of Honshu, Hokkaido, Kyushu, Shikoku, and such minor islands as we determine," indicated that other minor Japanese islands may be detached from Japan, at the discretion of the Allied Powers. As for the other areas, it was stipulated only that Japan shall renounce right, title and claim to them, and no reference was made as to their status following such renunciation. Further, Japan accepted the terms of the Potsdam Proclamation.

3.2.6 The Implications of Drafts on the Territorial Dispositions over the Liancourt Rocks in the San Francisco Peace Treaty

When Japan agreed in Article 2 of the San Francisco Peace Treaty to renounce "all right, title and claim to Korea, including the islands Quelpart, Port Hamilton, and Dagelet," the Liancourt Rocks were not included within the area to be renounced. Japan has, and with reason, assumed that its sovereignty still extends over the Liancourt Rocks, and the Koreans have disputed this assumption. Therefore, as Charney points out, "There is even a dispute over whether by implication or, by general terms, the victors in World War II intended to return the disputed [Liancourt Rocks] to Korea."

During the course of drafting the San Francisco Peace Treaty, Korea's views were solicited, in consequence of which the Korean Ambassador requested the U.S. Secretary of State in a letter of July 19, 1951 to amend Article 2(a) of the draft treaty so as to include the Liancourt Rocks as well as Quelpart, Port Hamilton and Dagelet among those islands over which Japan would renounce right, title and claim by virtue of recognizing Korea's independence. In his reply to the Korean Ambassador, Mr. Dean Rusk, the Assistant Secretary of State, stated in a letter dated August 10, 1951 that the United States could not concur in the proposed amendment as it applied to the Liancourt Rocks, since according to his information the Liancourt Rocks had never been treated as a part of Korea—they had been under the jurisdiction of the Oki Islands Branch Office of Japan's Shimane Prefecture since 1905 and it did not appear that they had ever before been claimed by Korea. As a result, Article 2(a) of the San Francisco Peace Treaty made no mention of the Liancourt Rocks.

Accordingly, it appears that the United States viewed the San Francisco Peace Treaty as constituting a determination that the "minor islands" would be left to Japan under the Potsdam Proclamation, and that the treaty left the

Liancourt Rocks to Japan. The United States' stated position was simply that of one of the several signatories of the treaty, and that Article 22 of the San Francisco Peace Treaty, providing for reference to the International Court of Justice, was drafted in order to settle disputes arising from the treaty.

In determining what course of action should be taken in light of this development, a question arose about whether the statement made in Mr. Rusk's letter entailed the legal conclusion that the San Francisco Peace Treaty left the Liancourt Rocks to Japan. On the one hand, it may be argued that the determination of the minor islands to be left under Japanese sovereignty required by the Potsdam Proclamation has been made by the treaty; i.e., Japan retained everything not renounced under Article 2; that Korea, prior to the signing of the treaty, specifically asked for a renunciation of the Liancourt Rocks by Japan and was turned down; that, therefore, it was the intent of the drafters of the treaty that Japan not renounce the Liancourt Rocks; and that these islands were accordingly included in the minor islands determined to remain under Japanese sovereignty.

On the other hand, it may be argued that Mr. Rusk's letter refusing to include the Liancourt Rocks in the islands renounced in connection with Korea was based on the U.S. understanding of the historical facts, providing that "Dokdo ... was according to our information never treated as part of Korea," and that his statement left the door open for Korea to show that it had in fact treated the Liancourt Rocks as part of Korea prior to 1905, when the Japanese placed the Liancourt Rocks under the jurisdiction of Shimane Prefecture. Under this theory, Korea would still be free to establish legally, if it could, that the "Korea" renounced in the San Francisco Peace Treaty included the Liancourt Rocks. This rationale is supported by the fact that the reports on the Liancourt Rocks were based for the most part on Japanese language sources available in the Department of State and the Library of Congress, studies prepared by the Department of State, and studies by the Japanese Foreign Office.

3.2.7 Conclusion

Although careful drafting of the San Francisco Peace Treaty could have put an end to territorial disputes over islands, today, almost half a century later, territorial disputes remain. This is not surprising given that historical facts were not a major factor in the post-World War II territorial dispositions in East Asia. Territorial provisions of the San Francisco Peace Treaty largely reflected the Allied Powers' policy in East Asia, which failed to give serious consideration to rival claims to title over specific territories. The fact that the Allied Powers were more concerned with their own geopolitical and strategic interests resulted in a failure to resolve territorial disputes in East Asia.

It is one thing to determine the abstract legal question of sovereignty over the disputed islands in East Asia, but it is quite another to effectuate it in practice. Given the institutional void in the East Asian region insofar as the resolution of territorial disputes is concerned, and given the current political atmosphere in the region, one is skeptical about the likelihood of a regional dispute resolution any time soon.

Nevertheless, it is imperative that the disputants approach the issues through dialogue and with a spirit of compromise. An all-or-nothing approach, which obviously does not accommodate the mutual interests of the disputants, will only aggravate an already precarious situation. Therefore, various confidence-building measures, including joint development of the disputed maritime zone for the mutual benefit of all the affected parties, should be attempted first, prior to any hasty attempt to resolve the question of sovereignty over the disputed territories. Finally, every effort should be made to determine the real worth of the disputed territories instead of placing undue reliance, as is presently the case, on exaggerated notions of what is at stake.

4 Colonial Claims against Japan

4A *1965 Korea-Japan Claims Settlement Agreement*

4.1 *The 1965 Korea-Japan Claims Settlement Agreement and Individuals' Claims Rights*

In 1965, Korea and Japan concluded "the Agreement on the Settlement of Problems Concerning Property and Claims and Concerning Economic Cooperation between the Republic of Korea and Japan" (1965 Claims Agreement) and settled the so-called "claims rights" problem between the two States. Namely, the Agreement provides in Article 2, paragraph 1, "The High Contracting Parties confirm that the problems concerning the property, rights, and interests of the two signatories and their nationals (including juridical persons) and the claims rights between the High Contracting Parties and between their nationals … have been settled completely and finally." The plain meaning of the clause appears to mean that Korean nationals, as individuals, ceased to have any right to bring lawsuit against either Japanese people (including Japanese juridical persons) or the Japanese government. However, regardless of this clause, many Korean nationals have raised various kinds of "claims" in Japanese courts both against Japanese government and against Japanese companies. And recently, these "claims" even came to be raised in a Korean court and United States courts.

How can Korean nationals bring suits against the Japanese government and people? Were the individual rights to property, rights, interests and the claims rights of each state's nationals not waived by Article 2, paragraph 1 of the 1965 Claims Agreement, and therefore is it not impossible for Korean nationals to bring suits against the Japanese Government and companies? Or is it only the right of diplomatic protection by the state that was waived by the clause, and therefore is it still possible for the Korean nationals to bring such suits? It may be said that this question has been one of the main legal issues in the several cases before Japanese courts. However they do not seem to have answered it clearly. Moreover, it would clearly be one of the most important legal points in the cases before the Korean court and United States courts.

4.1.1 International Law Concerning the Interpretation of Treaties

The question outlined above is a typical problem of treaty interpretation. Needless to say, the interpretation of treaties is regulated by international law. The current positive international law concerning this issue is "the Vienna Convention on the Law of Treaties" (hereinafter Vienna Convention on Treaties), concluded in 1969. Both Korea and Japan are signatories to this Convention, so it may appear to be applicable in interpreting the 1965 Claims Agreement. However, while the 1965 Claims Agreement was concluded and entered into force in 1965, the Vienna Convention on Treaties was concluded in 1969 and entered into force in 1980. Therefore, a problem of intertemporal law exists in applying the Vienna Convention to the 1965 Claims Agreement.

On this point, Article 4 of the Vienna Convention on Treaties states, "Without prejudice to the application of any rules set forth in the present Convention to which treaties would be subject under international law independently of the Convention, the Convention applies only to treaties which are concluded by States after the entry into force of the present Convention with regard to such States." This Article sets forth the principle of non-retroactivity for the Convention. Therefore, in interpreting the 1965 Claims Agreement, it is necessary to ascertain the international laws pertaining to treaty interpretation that existed at the time when the Korean-Japan Agreement was concluded.

Before the Vienna Convention on Treaties was concluded in 1969, no rules of international law regulating interpretation of treaties existed in the form of a "treaty." Therefore, to the extent that such rules of international law were in effect, they would have existed as norms of customary international law. It is unclear whether in 1965, such norms of customary international law existed as to the issue of treaty interpretation, and even among scholars, the opinions were divided as between those who acknowledge that customary norms of treaty interpretation existed at the time and those who do not.

In this context, the various approaches to treaty interpretation argued at that time can be summarized as follows: (1) the subjective (or intent of the parties) approach, which regards ascertainment of the intentions of the parties to the treaty as the aim and goal of treaty interpretation, (2) the objective (or textual) approach, which seeks to ascertain the meaning of the text of a treaty, and (3) the teleological (or object and purpose) approach, which argues that those who interpret a treaty must first ascertain the object and purpose of the treaty and then interpret it to give effect to that object and purpose.

In attempting to ascertain the norms of customary international law which were in effect around the year 1965—and if such norms were not in existence, to ascertain the appropriate principles of treaty interpretation from the point of view of jurisprudence—most representative works of international law scholars published around the year 1965 may be consulted. In Hans Kelsen's work, published in 1966, the primary purpose of the interpretation of treaties is deemed to be the determination of the intent of the parties. To effectuate this purpose, it is said that the historical circumstances behind the conclusion of a treaty—including the political or economic circumstances at the time—are to be considered. This methodology also incorporates interpretation according to its wording—the so-called logico-grammatical interpretation—as a method of interpreting treaties. At the same time, endorsing this method, Kelsen adds, "The wording of a legal instrument may not be in conformity with the ascertainable intentions of its authors. The wording may go beyond, or remain behind, their intentions." This point seems to be particularly relevant in interpreting the 1965 Claims Agreement.

Next, in his textbook of international law published in 1959, A. Verdross, on the basis of his review on prior case precedents and the works of international law scholars, presents 11 principles of treaty interpretation. Key portions of these principles are as follows: (1) The leading principle says that the true intention of the parties must be pursued because all international treaties are *negotia bonae fidei.* (2) However, the intention of the parties must be found first of all from the treaty itself. Therefore, if a clear and plain meaning comes out from the context of a treaty, then it is only when the meaning leads to an absurd result, or when the fact that the parties wanted some other meaning is proved, that interpretation may deviate from the wording. (3) Ambiguous treaty norms are to be interpreted in the light of general international law, as well as the principles which regulate the material matters to which the treaty belongs. When dubious, the formulation history of the treaties (*travaux préparatoires*) can also be invoked. Because the treaties of contracting character are applied only to the specific relations which are within the sights of the treaties, an application of a treaty norm, by analogy, to similar cases is in principle allowable only to the treaties which include the *general* norms.

If one is to assume that the intentions of the parties to a treaty are reflected in the text of the treaty, then the subjective and objective approaches are in essence different expressions of the same methodology. The representative works of international law scholars can be said to have endorsed the position that the subjective and objective approaches must be utilized in the way of supplementing each other. And, if a teleological approach is added to them, the principles of treaty interpretation as described above may be said to be fully applicable in interpreting the 1965 Claims Agreement. In other words, Article 2, paragraph 1 of the 1965 Claims Agreement should be interpreted according to its purposes, by way of ascertaining the intent of the parties through making the meaning of the text clear. In the interpretation, the historical circumstances of the time when the 1965 Claims Agreement was concluded must be considered. And, if the text of the treaty is ambiguous, the preparatory materials of the treaty (*travaux préparatoires*) must also be used to aid the task of interpretation.

4.1.2 The Purpose of the 1965 Claims Agreement and Related Circumstances

The fundamental purpose of the Agreement was to normalize relations between the states and in doing so, to resolve the complicated issues of property rights between them. In order to accurately understand the purpose of the 1965 Claims Agreement, as well as the meaning of the Agreement's text and the intentions of the parties, it is necessary to review the circumstances that led up to the conclusion of the Agreement.

One of the main problems that needed to be resolved in normalizing relations between Korea and Japan was the issue of property rights and claims, namely the issue of Japanese property existing in Korea and property claims that might be thought to be held by the Japanese government or Japanese nationals against the Korean government or Korean nationals, and conversely, the issue of Korean property existing in Japan and property claims that might be thought to be held by the Korean government or Korean nationals against the Japanese government or Japanese nationals. These issues existed because, in the process of ruling Korea as a colony, Japan often brought Japanese property into Korea or took Korean property to Japan. The nationals of each country also crossed into the other country to conduct economic activities there.

As to Japanese property existing in Korea, this property came to be vested in the Military Government in Korea through Ordinance No. 33, issued on December 6, 1945 by the Headquarters of the United States Army Forces in Korea. On September 11, 1948, it was then transferred to the Government of Korea pursuant to the "Initial Financial and Property Settlement between the Government of the Republic of Korea and the Government of the United States of America." At the time, Japan objected to such measures, claiming that they violated international law and were unlawful. However, the U.S. took the position that Japan's property rights were extinguished by Article 4, paragraph 2 of the 1951 Peace Treaty and that Japan could not make valid claims as to those rights. The U.S. notified both Korea and Japan of this position. Ultimately, Japan accepted the position of the U.S. on December 31, 1957, and consequently, the only issue that remained between Korea and Japan was the problem of Korean property existing in Japan and property claims that might be thought to be held by the Korean government or Korean nationals against the Japanese government or Japanese nationals.

During the negotiations regarding the normalization of relations, Japan took the position that it would recognize only the "claims" having an irrefutable legal foundation and proof of facts. However, in light of the fact that during the war there had been heavy bombing and destruction in Japan, and that the Korean War erupted in 1950 and had lasted to 1953, substantiating the proof of facts or legal foundations for these claims was obviously difficult. As a result of these difficulties, the two states decided to resolve the problem through a "political agreement." It was under this circumstance that Article 2, paragraph 1 of the 1965 Claims Agreement was concluded.

It has been asserted that the 1965 Claims Agreement was concluded pursuant to the 1951 Peace Treaty between Japan and the Allied Powers, and specifically pursuant to Article 2 and Article 4 of this Treaty. However, it is axiomatic that a treaty is not binding on those states that are not parties to it. As Korea was not a party to the 1951 Treaty, it was not bound by any provision of that Treaty when it concluded the 1965 Claims Agreement. As the work of Professor In-Sup Chung makes clear, while the 1951 Treaty may have played a political role in sparking the Korea-Japan talks, it did not create the legal framework for the 1965 Claims Agreement. It is crucial that a clear, legal distinction be made between peace treaties (like the 1951 Treaty) that seek to resolve postwar problems between belligerents, and agreements (like the 1965 Claims Agreement) that relate to the establishment of diplomatic relations between states together with the resolution of property disputes.

4.1.3 Intentions of the Governments

4.1.3.1 *Japanese Government*

When one examines accessible public records, it is easy to see that the Japanese government has clearly represented that Article 2, paragraph 1 of the 1965 Claims Agreement does not extinguish individual rights but only the state's right of diplomatic protection, leaving no room for question on this point. For example, when Mr. Ishibashi, a member of the House of Representatives of the Japanese Diet, inquired on November 5, 1965 at the "Special Committee on the Treaty between Japan and Korea" whether the treaty extinguished not only the right of diplomatic protection but also individual claims rights, Mr. Shiina, Minister of Foreign Affairs, responded, "In my view, the expression that the individual claims rights are extinguished is not proper ... It is not that the government first took the individual claims rights to its hand, and then relinquished them. It is only that the government waived its right of diplomatic protection as to claims against Korea, meaning that as a result, even if Japanese people were to make claims individually [against the Korean Government or Korean people], Korea would not acknowledge such claims ... If I have ever used the expression of 'waiver of them [individual claims rights],' I would like to take this opportunity to correct it." This statement by Foreign Minister Shiina was made in the consideration and ratification process of the 1965 Claims Agreement and as such, has a decisive importance on the interpretation of Article 2, paragraph 1 of the Agreement.

This position on the part of the Japanese government has been consistent, and was repeated on several occasions in response to the inquiries in the Diet. The most widely known example of this position came out from the Committee on Budget of the House of Councilors held on August 27, 1991. At the Committee, then government delegate Mr. Yanai stated, "By the so-called Japan-Korea Claims Agreement, the claims rights problem between the two states are settled finally and completely. The meaning of this is that all are settled including the claims rights of the nationals of both nations as existed before. However this means waiving of the rights of diplomatic protection which both Japan and Korea possessed as States. Accordingly, this does not mean the extinguishments of so-called individual claims rights in the sense of domestic law. It only means that the Korean and Japanese governments, as Governments, cannot raise problems regarding these claims by exercising their respective rights of diplomatic protection." This statement shows the Japanese Government's interpretation of the clause clearly.

Several records of Japanese Diet also support both Mr. Shiina's and Mr. Yanai's statements. On April 6, 1993, at the Committee on Foreign Affairs of the House of Councilors, Mr. Tanba, the Director-General of Treaties at Ministry of Foreign Affairs at the time, stated, "[Our] government has long been representing that the claims rights individuals may have are not waived directly by the effect of the Treaty." He also stated on May 26, 1993 at the Committee on Budget of the House of Representatives, "What is said in Article 2, paragraph 1 of the Treaty is only a relinquishment of the right of diplomatic protection, with regard to all the 'property, rights and interests' and 'claims rights'. In this point, things are just as you [Mr. Utsnomiya, a member of the House of Representatives] said."

On March 25, 1994, at the Committee on Cabinet of the House of Representatives, Mr. Takeuchi, Foreign Minister's Secretary, stated that "with regard to property claims issues between Japanese and Korean citizens, the right of diplomatic protection, which both states have as State, was waived... As we have stated before, the terms of the treaty itself does not extinguish individual property rights or their claims rights directly within the meaning of domestic law."

And as recently as March 14, 2000, Mr. Fukushima, a member of the House of Councilors, inquired, "What about Foreign Affairs Ministry's then Director-General of Treaties Yanai's statement of August 27, 1991 that only the right of diplomatic protection was waived and that individual claims rights were not extinguished?" Mr. Hosokawa, Director-General of Civil Affairs of the Ministry of Justice, responded, "We are well aware of Mr. Yanai's answer, and we also agree with his statement."

In addition, in relation to the interpretation of Article 14(a)(2)(I) and Article 19(a) of the 1951 Peace Treaty, the Japanese government has consistently taken the position that the waiver of "rights to claims" encompassed only the state's right of diplomatic protection and did not extend to individual rights. Japan has also taken this position in relation to the interpretation of Article 6 of the "Joint Declaration of Japan and Union of Soviet Socialist Republics." On March 25, 1994, at the Committee on Cabinet of the House of Representatives, Mr. Nishida, Director of the Russia Division of the Europe-Asia Bureau, stated as follows: "In Article 6 of the Japan-USSR Joint Declaration which is currently in effect between Japan and Russia, the governments waived their rights to claims. As only the governments' own rights to claims and the so-called right of diplomatic protection are waived, claims of our citizens against Russia or against its citizens were not waived by the clause." Also, on March 4, 1997, at the First Sub-Committee of the Committee on Budget of the House of Representatives, Foreign Minister's Secretary Togo stated, "Though all rights to claims were waived in Article 6, paragraph 2 of the Japan-USSR Joint Declaration, it does not mean that the Declaration prevents individuals from raising claims."

4.1.3.2 *Korean Government*

Immediately after the conclusion of the 1965 Claims Agreement, in regard of Article 2, paragraph 1 of the Agreement, the Korean government appears to have adopted a different interpretation from that of the Japanese government. The Korean government issued a publication on August 15, 1965, in which the government explains that all rights to property and claims rights on the part of both states and their nationals were extinguished by the 1965 Claims

Agreement. However, if it is true that Korea intended to waive all property rights and claims rights through the Agreement, then there exists an unequivocal difference of intent between the two contracting parties.

The significance of this difference of intent is as follows: A treaty signifies, by definition, a manifest *agreement* of intentions of the contracting parties. If such an agreement of intentions did not occur in the conclusion of the 1965 Claims Agreement, Article 2, paragraph 1, then this would mean that the provision of the Agreement could not have become a treaty and is therefore null and void for that reason. If this is what really happened, Article 2, Paragraph 1 of the 1965 Claims Agreement could not have regulated the property issues as a valid treaty provision, and again the result would be that an invalid provision has been misconstrued as a valid one by both governments. However, this conclusion does not seem to be a logically reasonable one, especially since this provision has had a certain concrete regulatory force in the past. If good faith is to be maintained in interpreting a treaty provision, it must be interpreted in the way of making it meaningful and valid rather than making it meaningless and invalid.

One important fact to be taken note of is that the Korean government's position in relation to Article 2, paragraph 1 has not been consistent. As can be seen above, in its publication issued directly after the conclusion of the 1965 Claims Agreement, the Korean government took the position that all property, right, and interests, and the claims rights of Korean nationals had been extinguished. However, the Korean government changed its attitude and has adopted the position that the Agreement did not extend to claims by individuals, and this position has been expressed repeatedly. In July 10, 1991, Minister of Foreign Affairs Sang Ok Lee stated in a response to a question in the Korean National Assembly, "At the governmental level, this issue [problems of the property, rights, and interest and claims rights] has been resolved by the Treaty Regarding Claims and Economic Cooperation, concluded in 1965 during the normalization of relations between Korea and Japan". On September 20, 1995, Minister of Foreign Affairs No Myoung Kong stated in the Reunification and Foreign Affairs Committee of the Korean National Assembly, "From a governmental standpoint, I believe that our government has resolved the issue of monetary compensation from Japan". At the same meeting, he also stated, "The government acknowledges the claims rights of individuals." These statements clearly show that the Korean government is not of the opinion that individual rights were extinguished by the Agreement.

As recently as October 24, 2000, the Korean Ministry of Foreign Affairs and Trade responded to an inquiry by a member of National Assembly, Mr. Won Woong Kim, who inquired, "Is it the Korean government's position, as Japan asserts, that all claims for compensation have been extinguished by the 1965

Claims Agreement? If this is the government's position, what is the basis for this opinion? Are these claims extinguished only as to governmental claims, or as to individual claims as well? I request that the Korean government present its official position on this matter." Mr. Chung Bin Lee, Minister of Foreign Affairs and Trade, responded, "The Korean and Japanese governments, in order to resolve issues regarding claims such as forced laborers and forced military draftees, concluded 'The Agreement on the Settlement of Problems Concerning Property and Claims and Concerning Economic Cooperation between the Republic of Korea and Japan' in 1965. The claims problem was thereby settled as between the two governments ... However, the Korean government's position is that the Agreement does not affect individuals' claims rights or their rights to bring lawsuits or other legal actions."

How can these contradictory pronouncements by the Korean government be analyzed and understood? The first possibility is to conclude that the government's position, as described in "The Explanation of the Treaty and Agreements between the Republic of Korea and Japan," did not express the true intentions of the Korean government. Alternatively, one could conclude that the intentions expressed after 1965, namely that the 1965 Claims Agreement did not extinguish individuals' claims rights, did not reflect the true intentions of the Korean government. The final possibility is to conclude that the intentions of the Korean government changed over time.

Among these three possible conclusions, the second seems to be the most unreasonable interpretation as Korean government's intentions expressed after 1965 have been repeated several times and also are recent ones. Therefore, the remaining possibilities of understanding these *prima facie* contradictory attitudes of the Korean government are either to regard the Korean government as having the opinion that individual claims were not extinguished though there were discrepancy between its real intention and its expression, or to regard it as having changed its own opinion over time.

If the Korean government is seen to have changed its opinion, then the problems of the conclusion and validity of the treaty arise again. Taking this point into account, and considering the fact that Japan's position has remained remarkably consistent, the most reasonable interpretation that upholds the validity of the treaty seems to conclude that the parties agreed not to extinguish the rights of individuals.

4.1.4 Interpretation of the 1965 Claims Agreement

4.1.4.1 *Text of the Agreement and Its Interpretation*

Article 2, paragraph 1 of the 1965 Claims Agreement states, "[t]he problems concerning the property, rights and interests of the two signatories and their nationals (including juridical persons) and the claims rights between the High Contracting Parties and between their nationals... have been settled completely and finally." As is shown above, the Japanese government has consistently taken the position that this provision of the Agreement did not extinguish the claims rights of individuals; it only waived the rights of diplomatic protection as to those claims. The Korean government's position has been less consistent, but recent pronouncements, repeated over time, have expressed the position that individuals' claims rights were not extinguished. Japan's consistent position, repeated several times through communications to the Japanese Diet, has become a matter of public record. The Japanese government's interpretation also has the character of the "authoritative interpretation" of the text.

When all of these points are taken into consideration together, it is clear that the wording of the 1965 Claims Agreement cannot be interpreted simply as a complete waiver of all claims of the governments and their nationals. Here exists really a situation as pointed out by Kelsen, "The wording of a legal instrument may not be in conformity with the ascertainable intentions of its authors. The wording may go beyond, or remain behind their intentions." This is the reason why the 1965 Claims Agreement should be interpreted as having waived only the right of diplomatic protection.

4.1.4.2 *Meaning of "Property, Rights, Interests" and of "Claims Rights"*

If Article 2, paragraph 1 of the 1965 Claims Agreement only waived the right of diplomatic protection, then the next question is, "What kinds of rights were waived as a matter of diplomatic protection?" This is the problem of interpreting the words, "property, rights, and interests" and "claims rights."

Generally speaking, "property, rights, interests" seem to be the rights that can be realized under national law, and that "claims rights" seem to be the rights that are recognizable under international law. However, when we review the way that these terms were used during the negotiations that led up to the 1965 Claims Agreement, it is apparent that the terms should not be understood in their "general ordinary meaning". As a matter of fact, the parties to the treaty, Korea and Japan, attributed specific meanings to those words.

Professor In-Sup Chung has accurately pointed out that "during the negotiations for the conclusion of the Agreement, the Korean government had used the term 'claims rights' as substantial rights that could be claimed against Japan on a clear legal foundations." The so-called "Eight Items," or the Outline of Claims which were argued by the Korean government during the treaty negotiations, were a kind of consolidated contents of those "claims rights." However, in the process of the codification of the Agreement, Japan also took the position that "claims rights" must mean only the legal status of being able to make claims, not the substantial rights. Article 2 was drafted in such a way as accepting this argument of Japan. And accordingly, the provision of section 2(a) was included in the Agreed Minutes annexed to the 1965 Claims Agreement, which states: "It is understood that the words 'Property, rights, and interests' mean all kinds of substantial rights of which the property values are recognized on the basis of law."

It is natural that the Japanese government understands the meaning of the terms, "property, interests, rights" and "claims rights," in this manner. The Director-General of the Treaties Bureau, Mr. Tanba, stated in a response to the Japanese Diet, "'Property, rights, and interests' mean all kinds of substantial rights which are recognized under law to be of property value. The term 'claims rights,' referenced in the Claims Agreement, is not included in the concept of 'property, rights, and interests,' and refers to the legal status of being able to make claims for which the existence of legal rights itself is in question." The concrete examples of "property, rights, and interests" offered in the Japanese Diet included "creditor's rights, rights to collateral, and the right to demand payment of receivables," and the examples of "claims rights" included "claims for compensation for damages for which evidence is lacking, pain and suffering claims, wage claims, etc."

Therefore, the most significant difference between the terms "property, rights, and interests" and "claims rights" is that, while the former mean established rights with clear and solid legal foundations, the latter are unsettled rights for which the legal foundations can be disputed.

4.1.5 Government's Capacity to Waive Individual Rights

One of the main legal issues concerning the interpretation of Article 2, paragraph 1 of the 1965 Claims Agreement is "Whether a State can extinguish its nationals' individual rights through a treaty or not."

It is generally said that a state may compromise or release claims, leaving the individual or corporation concerned without any remedy. However, some international law scholars have different views on this problem. For example, Professor Dong-Hoon Kim argues in his article on the 1965 Claims Agreement that a government may not waive individuals' property and rights, and another scholar argued that this is the common view. Therefore, there seems to be no settled opinion on this issue among the scholars of international law.

What is decisive, however, regarding the interpretation of Article 2, paragraph 1 of the 1965 Claims Agreement is whether Japan has, in real fact, extinguished individual rights or not. It does not automatically follow that, in concluding a treaty, states always do, in fact, what they are able to do in theory.

It would have been possible for the Japanese government to obtain the consent of the Korean government to extinguish the rights of the Korean and Japanese people by the terms of the treaty rather than by separate domestic measures. However, Japan did not actually do so. Japan did not extinguish the rights of the Japanese and Korean nationals by the Agreement, but only diplomatic protection of those rights. Thus, the rights of the citizens of the respective countries could not be extinguished without internal measures extinguishing them.

Even though the Japanese government could have secured a waiver of individuals' rights through the terms of the 1965 Claims Agreement, Japan in fact did not and could not seek such a clause. This is likely a result of the democratic controls over the treaty ratification procedure. Article 73 of the Japanese Constitution requires that the treaties negotiated by the Cabinet be first approved by the Diet, thereby institutionalizing democratic control over the treaty ratification process. The Japanese government likely was fully aware of the fact that a treaty extinguishing the individual rights of Japanese citizens would not have been approved by the Diet, in which case there would be no ratification and the treaty would not have entered into force. As already discussed above, at the Special Committee on the Treaty between Japan and Korea, Mr. Ishibashi as a member of the House of Representatives strongly challenged the government by asking whether the Treaty extinguished the rights of the Japanese citizens, and in response, Foreign Minister Shiina stated that the Treaty "only waives rights to diplomatic protection but not individual rights."

4.1.6 Domestic Measures in Korea and Japan

If Article 2, paragraph 1 of the 1965 Claims Agreement is interpreted as set forth above, then it can be said that only the state's right of diplomatic protection, not individuals' rights, was waived. If the meaning of "property, rights and interests" and also of "claims rights" is understood in this manner, then we must ask, "What is the legal significance of the domestic legislation passed in Korea and Japan following the conclusion of the 1965 Claims Agreement?"

4.1.6.1 *Japan's Legislation No. 144*

In the same year that the 1965 Claims Agreement was concluded, Japan enacted on December 17 the "Law Regarding Measures to be Taken with Respect to the Property Rights of the Republic of Korea upon Enforcement of Article II of the Agreement on the Settlement of Problems Concerning Property and Claims and on Economic Co-operation between Japan and the Republic of Korea" (Law No. 144). Through this legislation, Japan attempted to extinguish the "property, rights and interests" of Korean nationals.

The specific rights of Korean nationals purportedly extinguished by Law No. 144 included the creditor's rights, rights to collateral, possessory rights, and rights related to securities. It is unquestionable that these rights correspond to the "property, rights and interests" provided in Article 2, paragraph 1 of the 1965 Claims Agreement. However, it is also beyond any question that Law No. 144 does not include rights which correspond to the "claims rights" under the 1965 Claims Agreement. The reason for this is that Law No. 144 contains no provisions relating to "claims rights." Moreover, the "claims rights" provided in the 1965 Claims Agreement refer to those claims that are not yet settled and therefore, cannot be extinguished by law. Therefore, the "claims rights" of Korean nationals have not been extinguished, even by Japanese domestic law, namely Law No. 144.

This point is again affirmed by the position of the Japanese government as expressed through its response to the Diet. Specifically, Director-General of Treaties, Mr. Tanba has stated, "In referring to the waiver of claims rights, the waiver does not also extinguish individuals' rights to bring suit in the other state's courts... How those courts decide cases brought by individuals, in this case Philippines or Korean nationals, is up to the Judiciary, and the Administration is paying close attention."

In addition, Secretary to the Minister of Foreign Affairs, Mr. Takeuchi also stated with regard to Article 2, paragraph 1 of the 1965 Claims Agreement, "Regarding our domestic legal treatment of matters, an individual's own government—in this case, Korea—cannot exercise, according to the built-in mechanism of the treaty, its right of diplomatic protection. With regard to an individual's claims right... an individual's right to bring a suit in court is not deprived by the treaty."

It may be argued that Law No. 144 is "the implementing legislation" of the 1965 Claims Agreement. However, if the Agreement is interpreted to be only a waiver of the right of diplomatic protection, then it is impossible to adopt this view. The Agreement waives the right of diplomatic protection and therefore it is secured that Korea, on the governmental level, cannot submit any objection to Japan's domestic measures. It was on this basis that Japan enacted domestic legislation and attempted to unilaterally extinguish the property, rights, and interests of Korean nationals. The domestic legislation was not meant to implement the 1965 Claims Agreement. Rather, having secured the guarantee that Korea could not make any objection, Japan enacted the legislation to unilaterally extinguish individual rights of Korean nationals. Also of decisive importance is the fact that Law No. 144 contains no provisions regarding "claims rights," and therefore did not extinguish individual rights as to those claims.

Additionally, it is highly likely that Japan's attempt to extinguish individual rights of Korean nationals through Law No. 144 violates the Japanese Constitution. Article 29, section 1 of Japan's Constitution protects "the right to property" and prohibits the violation of that right. The intended beneficiaries of this provision are not specified in the Constitution, but can be interpreted as including foreign nationals. Therefore, Law No. 144 may be said to be null as it violates Article 29 of the Japanese Constitution.

Moreover, Article 29, section 3 of the Japanese Constitution states, "Private property may be taken for public use upon just compensation therefor." The rights of Korean nationals were *prima facie* extinguished by Japanese domestic legislation, but "just compensation" was never provided. Because this also is in violation of the Constitution, it can be said that Korean nationals' rights were not extinguished either by treaty or by Japanese domestic law.

4.1.6.2 *Korea's Domestic Measures*

In 1966, Korea enacted the "Legislation Concerning the Distribution and Management of the Claims Treaty Fund." In January 1971, Korea enacted the "Legislation Concerning Report of Individual Claims Against Japan," and began processing property claims of Korean nationals against Japan and Japanese nationals. In December 1974, Korea enacted the "Legislation Concerning Compensation of Individual Claims Against Japan." Under this legislation, Korea distributed compensation funds pursuant to the reported claims by Korean nationals according to the 1971 law. All these laws were repealed in December 31, 1982 as their objectives were deemed to be fulfilled.

It has been argued that after having received Japan's lump sum payment of funds under the 1965 Claims Agreement, the duty to compensate Korean nationals was transferred from the Japanese government to the Korean government, and that the latter carried out this duty by enacting domestic legislation. However, this view seriously miscomprehends the fundamental objectives of Korea's domestic measures. The funds that were paid to Korea by Japan have no legal relationship to the "property, rights, interests" or the "claims rights," the diplomatic protection for which was waived pursuant to Article 2, paragraph 1 of the Agreement. The explanation of the Japanese government is clear on this point: "As Korea says, the $500,000,000 fund provided to Korea under Article 1 does not have the character of a debt or liability for the claims of Korea against Japan. This fund was provided solely for the purpose of economic cooperation."

As Professor Yoshio Hirose points out, the decision of whether or not to distribute the funds received pursuant to the Agreement was entirely assigned to Korea as a matter of domestic jurisdiction. The 1965 Claims Agreement did not create any obligations of international law, under which Korea was obligated to distribute the funds to its own nationals. On this point, the Agreement is fundamentally different from, for example, the Peace Treaty signed by Italy and the Allied Powers after the World War II. Articles 74(E), 76(2), and 79(3) of that Treaty impose obligations on Italy to provide compensation to its own nationals in relation to their claims against the Allied Powers. In contrast, Korea had no obligations under the 1965 Claims Agreement to provide compensation, on behalf of Japan, to Korean nationals.

The Korean government was of the intention to use the funds "to construct multi-purposed dams, to import vessels and equipment for fishing, to expand railroads and ports and other infra-structures, without using them for the specific individual, groups of individuals or region." The fact that Korea had no intention of distributing these funds to its nationals as compensation for the waiver of claims was unequivocally communicated to and understood by Japan during the negotiations for the conclusion of the Agreement. In consideration of the fact that the Korean government had given up the right of diplomatic protection, and that on this basis Japan had enacted legislation unilaterally extinguishing the individual rights possessed by Korean nationals, Korea provided through domestic legislation a remedy in the context that the exercise of rights or submission of claims by individuals had become, from a "practical" standpoint, quite difficult.

Even putting aside the legal analysis, if we assume that all "property, rights, interests" and "claims rights" of Korean nationals were waived by treaty and that the received funds represented compensation for those rights, then each of the approximately 1,700,000 victims would have received $176 each in compensation for their suffering. Some commentators view this to be a ridiculous result of such an interpretation.

4.1.7 Remaining Issue —Interpretations of Japanese Courts

As both Article 2, paragraph 1 of the 1965 Claims Agreement and Article 14(a)2(I) and Article 19(a) of the 1951 Peace Treaty waived Japanese nationals' property rights, these clauses seem to have some similarity. And the Japanese government interprets these clauses to waive only diplomatic protection and not individual rights. However, concerning the interpretation of Article 14(a)(2)(I) and Article 19(a) of the 1951 Peace Treaty, Japanese courts have rejected the government's view for the most part. In other words, contrary to the Japanese government's position, the majority of Japanese courts interpret the clauses to directly extinguish Japanese nationals' individual rights.

However, almost all of the judgments of Japanese domestic courts are about the 1951 Peace Treaty. The 1951 Peace Treaty and the 1965 Claims Agreement have two very different goals and objectives. Hence, the propriety of applying the same analysis used in the interpretation of the 1951 Peace Treaty to the 1965 Claims Agreement is highly questionable. The 1965 Claims Agreement is wholly different in its legal character from the Peace Treaty which settles war reparations by waiver of rights of a state and its citizens. In addition, not all Japanese courts have adopted this position. In interpreting Article 14(a)(2)(I) of the 1951 Peace Treaty, the Japanese Supreme Court found on July 4, 1969, that the clause "cannot be interpreted as disposing abroad properties belonging to Japanese nationals to fill up the amount of war reparations, on the basis of the exercise of autonomous exercise of governmental power to dispose properties of Japanese nationals. This is to be referred as only a promise not to exercise the right to make an objection or the right of diplomatic protection, which might be exercised in order to avoid disparate treatment of the property abroad by the foreign governments."

The Japanese Supreme Court's decision is consistent with its government's position that despite the fact that the 1951 Peace Treaty specifies a waiver of Japanese "*nationals*," only the diplomatic protection was waived by the Treaty. In addition, the various lower court decisions concluding otherwise, as numerous as they may be, remain lower court decisions, while this Supreme Court decision in agreement with the Japanese government is that of the highest court in Japan.

4.1.8 Conclusion

Based on the above examination it may be concluded as follows. First, Article 2, paragraph 1 of the 1965 Claims Agreement did not extinguish the "property, rights and interests" and "claims rights" of the nationals of one state against the government and nationals of the other. Rather, the Agreement only extinguished the states' rights to provide diplomatic protection as to the rights of their nationals. This interpretation is supported by the Japanese government's own consistent position and the corresponding Korean government's positions.

Second, the fact that the two governments were only able to extinguish diplomatic protection but not individual rights is a result of the democratic controls that were placed over the treaty ratification procedures.

Third, because the 1965 Claims Agreement did not extinguish Korean nationals' "property, rights and interests" against Japan or its nationals, Japan attempted to extinguish those rights by a domestic measure, legislation of Law No. 144. During treaty negotiations, the Korean government agreed not to object to such legislation, which is precisely the type of diplomatic protection waived by the treaty. However, Legislation No. 144 was in violation of the Japanese Constitution because it did not provide any compensation in exchange for its unilateral waiver of rights.

Fourth, even if Law No. 144 is valid, it only waived Korean nationals' "property, rights and interests" against Japan and not their rights to "claims." This is so because a "claims rights" in the context of the 1965 Claims Agreement refers to the "status where, if the legal existence of a right is in dispute, the alleged holder may make a claim or bring suit." The claims rights of individuals cannot be extinguished until they are consolidated as rights.

Fifth, the Korean government's distribution of the amount of the funds received from Japan was not to fulfill its obligations under the 1965 Claims Agreement. Korea had never owed such an obligation.

In conclusion, Korean nationals' "property, rights and interests" against Japan and its nationals are *prima facie* extinguished pursuant to Japanese domestic law, and all corresponding diplomatic protection by Korea as a state has been waived. On the other hand, Korean nationals' "claims rights" against the Japanese government and Japanese nationals are not extinguished by Japanese domestic law or by the 1965 Claims Agreement, though the diplomatic protection of them by Korea has been waived. Thus, even under Japanese domestic law, "claims" or the right to seek adjudication of the existence of a legal right survives. Therefore, even under Japanese domestic law, Korean nationals may make "claims" and can bring suit to settle the existence of legal rights against both the Japanese government and Japanese nationals. As appropriately expressed by lawyer and Diet member Utsunomiya, "[The Agreement] provides that the Korean government will not say anything, but does not extend to provide that Korean nationals will not say anything either."

Needless to say, the above conclusion also applies to Japanese nationals' property, rights, and interests and their claim rights against the Korean government and people. In other words, according to the above conclusion, their rights were not extinguished by the Japanese government in the 1965 Claims Agreement, and therefore they can institute lawsuits against the Korean government and people in spite of the Ordinance No. 33 of the Military Government in Korea, the "Initial Financial and Property Settlement between the Government of the Republic of Korea and the Government of the United States of America" and Japanese government's acceptance of these measures in 1957. If Japanese nationals begin to claim their own rights and bring lawsuits, the so-called problem will go back to the time before 1965. It goes without saying that this is the most undesirable situation for both States. Therefore, it is fully agreeable that the 1965 Claims Agreement should have settled completely and finally the problems concerning the property, rights, and interests and the claims rights of the nationals.

However, until now no lawsuit has been brought by Japanese nationals against the Korean government or nationals, and it does not seem likely to happen in the future. What does this fact mean? In this author's view, this means that the so-called "after-war compensation claims" raised by Korean nationals are the result of not having liquidated the negative historical legacy between the two Sates, and those who have suffered from that are "Korean" nationals. And again, many seem to admit the interpretation that Article 2, paragraph 1 did not extinguish the individuals' claims rights. This may be the result of the request that the so-called after-war claims raised by Korean nationals should not be thwarted by a specific treaty clause.

4B *Comfort Women and Forced Labor*

4.2 *Historical Issues between Korea and Japan and Judicial Activism: Focusing on the Recent Decisions of the Korean Constitutional Court Concerning Comfort Women*

4.2.1 "Comfort Women for the Japanese Military" Case

...

The Constitutional Court of Korea reached a decision (2006 Heonma 788 Decision [Gyeoljeong], issued August 30, 2011) concerning the issue of "Comfort Women for the Japanese Military," namely that a dispute of interpretation existed between Korea and Japan as to whether the compensation claim of the comfort women was extinguished pursuant to the Agreement between the Republic of Korea and Japan Concerning the Settlement of Problems in Regard to Property and Claims and Economic Cooperation (Claims Agreement) Article 2(1), and held that failure of the Government (Ministry of Foreign Affairs and Trade (MOFAT))[2] to resolve such dispute of interpretation pursuant to Article 3 of the above Agreement violated the Constitution.

The Supreme Court decision regarding "Compensation for Forced Labor" concerned the victims of forced labor who had been employed by Japanese munitions companies for the production of weapons during the colonial era. The victims filed a damage suit against these companies for unlawful acts and for the payment of unpaid wages, for which the Supreme Court upheld their right to compensation and payment of wages.

This section describes the progress leading up to such decisions, discusses their significance, and evaluates the implications of judicial activism in the issues concerning past history.

---

2 The Ministry of Foreign Affairs and Trade was renamed the "Ministry of Foreign Affairs" in 2013. Trade issues were given over to the Ministry of Knowledge Economy.

4.2.1.1 *Background*

From the early 1930's until the defeat of Japan in the Second World War in 1945, the issue of comfort women who were taken to the battlefield and forced into sexual slavery by the Japanese government and its military has remained a "psychological thorn" in the Korea-Japan relations, a representative issue of the past that still needs to be dealt with.

Comfort stations were first installed by the Japanese navy as a preventive measure for mass rape that could result in venereal diseases and opposition of local people during the 1932 Shanghai Uprising. With a mass dispatch of its soldiers to China in the Sino-Japanese War starting in July 1937, the Japanese army began installing comfort stations in conquered areas, the number increasing after the Nanking Massacre of December 1937. Besides providing "mental consolation" to the soldiers, comfort stations were installed in order to pacify discontent and to stir up morale to prevent desertion from a war that dragged on. Their purpose also entailed the prevention of leaking classified information, done by "hiring" women from colonies who could not speak Japanese. From 1941 and during the course of the Asia-Pacific War, Japan installed comfort stations in their conquered territories in Southeast Asia and the Pacific. Regions where comfort stations were installed, as identified in official documents were areas invaded by Japan, i.e., Chosun, China, Hong Kong, Macau, and the Philippines. The number of comfort women is estimated to be between 80,000 and 100,000 with some estimations reaching 200,000, 80% of whom were Chosun women, while others also came from the Philippines, China, Taiwan, and the Netherlands.

The issue of comfort women was not easily discussed in public due to the nature of the crimes, but with the launching of the Korean Council for Women Drafted for Military Sexual Slavery by Japan in November 1990, the issue of comfort women was finally raised in earnest. Various activities continued among civil groups, the Korean government, and international human rights organizations; and the weekly Wednesday protests urging for the resolution of the issue before the Japanese Embassy in Korea hit the 1000 mark (1992.1.8~2011.12.7).

The Japanese government, however, denied the very existence of comfort women at first, until documents showing direct involvement of the Japanese government were uncovered in addition to the testimonies of the victims. On August 4, 1993, together with the second Government Report, it acknowledged the involvement of the Japanese military and authorities, as well as the forced drafting and fatigue duty; and Chief Cabinet Secretary Yohei Kono released a statement recognizing the grave violation of their human rights and expressing his apologies. However, Japan maintained that legal responsibility regarding these comfort women had been settled by the 1965 Claims Agreement and refused compensation.

...

4.2.1.2 *Decision of the Constitutional Court*

With regard to the interpretation of Article 2(1) of the Agreement, the Japanese government and judiciary were of the position that the reparations claim of Korean nationals including the comfort women against the state of Japan was encompassed by the Agreement in this case and, with its conclusion and implementation, were waived or compensation terminated. On the other hand, the Korean government declared through the decision of the joint government-civic committee of August 26, 2005 that issues concerning crimes against humanity such as that of the comfort women where state authorities were involved were not settled by the Agreement in this case and therefore, the Japanese government still bears liability. Consequently, the Court found that there was a difference between the two states in the interpretation of the Claims Agreement.

The Constitutional Court thus held that there clearly was a difference between Korea and Japan in the interpretation of Article 2(1) of the Agreement as to whether the reparations claim of the Comfort Women is included in the claim against Japan, and this fell under the meaning of "dispute" in Article 3.

Concerning the Dispute Resolution Procedure provided for in Article 3 of the Claims Agreement, the Court also found that these provisions, at the time of its conclusion, anticipated disputes in the interpretation and established dispute resolution principles and procedures, while setting the subject of these acts as the contracting states themselves and ruled that since the above dispute exists, the Respondent ought to resolve the issue through diplomatic channels pursuant to the dispute resolution procedures of Article 3; and it ought to submit the case to an arbitration panel after having attempted to reach settlement.

The core issue in the decision of the Constitutional Court was, in the midst of such dispute in interpretation, whether the nonfeasance of the Minister of Foreign Affairs and Trade in not pursuing such dispute resolution procedures provided for in Article 3 of the Claims Agreement violated the fundamental rights of the Petitioners and was therefore unconstitutional. In other words, the issue was, where there is a dispute over the interpretation of a treaty, whether the government had a specific constitutional duty to pursue the dispute resolution procedures provided for in the treaty to resolve the issue. There was disagreement among the Constitutional Court justices concerning this issue.

4.2.1.3 *Majority Opinion*

Concerning the "Duty of the Korean government to pursue dispute resolution procedures," the majority opinion of the Constitutional Court stated that in light of the language of the Preamble, Article 2(2), and Article 10 of the Constitution and Article 3 of the Claims Agreement, the duty to take measures of dispute resolution pursuant to Article 3 is based on a constitutional demand to protect and to cooperate towards realizing the reparations claim of state nationals, whose human dignity and value were gravely violated by the systematic and continued criminal acts of the state of Japan. Without the performance of this duty, there is the possibility of Petitioners' fundamental rights being gravely violated; thus, the Respondent's duty to act is one deriving from the Constitution which is specifically provided for in the law.

The majority further held that the Korean government was also liable for the conclusion of the 1965 Claims Agreement, stating that though it had not done any acts to directly violate the fundamental rights of the comfort women, considering that the realization of the victims' reparations claim against the state of Japan and the restoration of their human worth and value has come to the current state of impairment because it has not clarified the substance of the claims but used a vague term of "all claims" in concluding the Claims Agreement in this case, it cannot be denied that the Korean government has the specific duty to act in order to remove the reason for malfunction.

Also holding that diplomatic measures neglecting the reparations claims of the victims do not fall within the scope of performance of its duties, the Court found that having Japan acknowledge its wrongdoing and bear legal liability is an issue altogether different from the Korean government providing funds for social security; and thus the provision of partial living support for the victims cannot be considered satisfying the duty to act.

Lastly, the Constitutional Court declared that the harm to comfort women, having been caused by the enforced mobilization and sexual slavery by the state of Japan and its military, is a unique harm, for which other precedents cannot be found. It thus held that the reparations claim that the comfort women have against Japan is not only a property right guaranteed by the Constitution, but its realization also signifies the *a posteriori* restoration of their dignity and value, as well as their personal freedom that were ruthlessly and continuously violated.

The Court also noted the urgency of the need to remedy the violations of the fundamental right, as well as its possibility of remedy, as the current living comfort women have all advanced in age so that any further delay in time may make it impossible to restore this historical injustice and the violated human worth and value of the comfort women. In pursuing dispute resolution measures, the Court further stated that the government's reasons of "possibility of developing into exhaustive legal arguments" or "diplomatic tension" are vague and abstract, and that it cannot be considered valid grounds for neglecting the remedy for the victims or a national interest that must be seriously considered.

4.2.1.4 *Concurring Opinion of Justice Cho, Dae Hyeon*

Justice Cho, Dae Hyeon added to the majority opinion, stating that in this situation where the victims' claim to reparations was being hindered by the Claims Agreement, there definitely lies the duty to pursue diplomatic negotiations or arbitration procedures. Thus, the Court should also declare the Republic of Korea liable for complete compensation of the damage incurred by the Petitioners in being unable to exercise their reparations claim against the state of Japan. He reasoned that because it is highly unlikely that the obstacle to victims' exercise of their reparations claim against Japan will be removed by diplomatic negotiations or arbitration procedures, and while there is sincere concern that it will give them false hope resulting in pains of frustration and despair, it must be even more emphasized that the Republic of Korea bears the duty to completely compensate them for their reparations claim against Japan. Furthermore, because the victims have all advanced in age, the state's compensation measures for the victims must be urgently implemented.

4.2.1.5 *Dissenting Opinion of Justices Lee, Kang-Kook; Min, Hyeong-Ki; and Lee, Dong-Heub*

These three justices of the Constitutional Court, unlike those in the majority, held that they could not conclude under the wording of the Constitution and the Claims Agreement that "the Respondent has the duty to pursue dispute resolution measures under Article 3 of the Agreement in this case for the Petitioners."

The dissenting opinion further stated that no matter how grave or urgent the state of violation of the fundamental rights of the Petitioners is in this case, the interpretation of the law, namely Articles 10 and 2(2) and the Preamble of the Constitution as well as Article 3 of the Claims Agreement, alone cannot generate the Korean government's specific duty to pursue dispute resolution procedures nor the people's right to petition for such a duty to act. Rather, the justices saw that the act of pursuing the dispute resolution procedure in Article 3 of the Agreement, in form and substance, a "discretionary act" of the two contracting parties. Thus, they held that the constitutional claim brought by the victims claiming that their fundamental rights were violated by the nonfeasance of the Korean government in failing to pursue the above dispute resolution procedures is illegitimate and must be rejected.

4.2.1.6 *Significance of the Decision of the Constitutional Court*

The majority's decision declaring the failure to act as unconstitutional is significant in that it is the first decision of the judiciary to order a positive act on the part of the government, especially in that the representative issue of comfort women requires urgent legal compensation.

The Constitutional Court held, in confirming that an interpretative dispute existed between Korea and Japan regarding the 1965 Claims Agreement, that actively protecting the right to claims of the victims whose human dignity and value were gravely violated by the systematic and continued criminal acts of the state of Japan was a positive duty of the government as required by the Constitution. This appears to be an aggressive attempt of the judiciary to pressure the government that has shown a passive stance in resolving the issue of comfort women.

In the decision, in particular, the Court saw the harm to comfort women, having been caused by the enforced mobilization and sexual slavery by the state of Japan and its military as "a unique harm, for which other precedents cannot be found" and ordered an active resolution of the issue in consideration of the fact that the current living comfort women have all advanced in age, so that any further delay in time may make it impossible to restore this historical injustice and the violation of human worth and value of the Comfort Women by realizing their reparations claim. Considering that nine more of the victims have passed away in the nine months following the decision of the Court, leaving behind approximately 60 survivors among the 234 victims registered with the government, the decision certainly has great implications.

Further, regarding the claim that the Korean government has taken necessary measures for the resolution of the comfort women issue in deciding to give financial support and compensation to the victims on its own rather than to demand monetary reparations from Japan, and to demand of the Japanese government instead a more important and fundamental issue of a thorough fact-finding, formal apology and display of regret, implementation of proper education of history, etc., in order to continually raise the comfort women issue in international society, the Court found that the diplomatic and domestic measures of the Korean government towards Japan that neglected the victims' right to claims of the victims could not be considered performance of its duties that are at issue in this case. The Court thus held that the specific role of the government in principle was to diplomatically demand reparations for the victims and, should the dispute be unresolved, to submit to arbitrations pursuant to Article 3 of the Claims Agreement.

This appears to be a forceful reminder from the judiciary regarding the extremely passive stance the government has shown in its attempts to diplomatically resolve the comfort women issue—a lukewarm attitude to avoid diplomatic friction with Japan, and ordering a more determined attitude towards the issue including submission to arbitration.

Thus, this decision of the Constitutional Court established an unprecedented principle of law, namely the "unconstitutionality of the Government's failure to take diplomatic actions." This decision is significant in that while criticizing the passive attitude of the government that failed to actively resolve the compensation issue for the comfort women, the Court also held for the first time that the government efforts to resolve the issue of right to claims for the war crime victims was a duty required by the Korean Constitution and thus provided a specific solution, thereby demonstrating an ambitious attitude of the judiciary towards historical issues.

4.2.1.7 *Response of the Korean Government*

Following the decision of the Constitutional Court, MOFAT established a Task Force for the Resolution of Comfort Women Issue pursuant to the Korea-Japan Claims Agreement (MOFAT-TF) and proposed a bilateral meeting for the resolution of the issue on September 15, 2011, all the while urging for sincere measures on the part of Japan by summoning Deputy Ambassador Kanehara. When the Japanese government did not respond, it proposed a bilateral meeting again in November. At the Korea-Japan summit meeting held in Tokyo on December 18, 2011, President Lee, Myung-Bak stated, "Korea and Japan must become sincere partners for mutual prosperity of the two countries and regional peace and security. To this end, the military comfort women issue which forms a stumbling block must first be addressed, and this takes true courage." He also stated that "the comfort women issue is one that can immediately be resolved if perceived differently" and that "it is an emotional issue before a legal one," urging Japan to consider the issue from a broader perspective that would help address other issues between the two countries. Prime Minister Yoshihiko Noda replied that the Japanese position concerning the comfort women issue was the same as before and that while "humanitarian efforts have been made, it would try to explore ideas from a humanitarian point of view."

Through this process, it can be observed that the Comfort Women issue is no longer buried under the theory of "future-oriented Korea-Japan relations" but has now become part of the Korea-Japan diplomatic agenda. More specifically, according to recent media reports, the MOFAT-TF is already discussing how to constitute the arbitration committee. Further progress has yet to be made, but the significance is clearly in line with the aggressive decision of the Constitutional Court, the long entrenched and neglected issue of comfort women is finally being discussed with specific purpose and direction.

4.3 *Historical Issues between Korea and Japan and Judicial Activism: Focus on the Recent Supreme Court Decision on Forced Labor*

4.3.1 Background

During the Japanese occupation of Korea, Japan began to run short of labor in the production of munitions as it fought the Sino-Japanese War and the Pacific War. On July 8, 1939, it legislated and promulgated the National Mobilization Law and in 1942 legislated and implemented the provision of mobilizing the Chosun people in order to procure a labor force from all regions of the Korean Peninsula through official arrangements. When the shortage of manpower and supplies continued, it implemented a *de facto* conscription of the Chosun civilian people under National Conscription Order beginning October 1944.

The victims of forced labor were either forcefully sent over to Japan with other conscripts pursuant to a conscription notice or were sent through their applications for employment in Japanese munitions company under deceitful job placements that guaranteed their return after their employment and training. These victims were then placed in companies such as Mitsubishi Heavy Industries and Nippon Steel Corporation, where they worked in three 8 hour shifts with one to two limited outings per month. Once their daily tasks were complete, they ate and slept at the quarters provided by the companies, where the quality and the amount of food provisions were severely insufficient and sleeping quarters cramped.

These quarters were also surrounded by barbed-wire fences that limited entry; and strict surveillance by military police during both working hours and holidays prevented the liberty of everyday life. The conscripts were subject to *de facto* forced labor, as any correspondence with family back in Korea was screened and censored and thus limited in content, and those caught escaping were severely beaten, and wages were not properly paid out.

When the Pacific War reached its peak and munitions facilities in Japan were destroyed by U.S. military airstrikes, some of the conscripts also perished at those facilities, and still others were exposed to radiation caused by the atomic bomb dropped on Hiroshima.

After liberation, compensation for forced laborers became an issue, and the governments of Korea and Japan discussed normalization of diplomatic relations and post-war compensation beginning in late 1952. Finally on June 22, 1965, Treaty on Basic Relations between the Republic of Korea and Japan for the Normalization of Diplomatic Relations was concluded together with its annexed agreement of Agreement between the Republic of Korea and Japan Concerning the Settlement of Problems in Regard to Property and Claims and Economic Cooperation (Claims Agreement). Through this Claims Agreement, Japan agreed to provide Korea with 300 million dollars in grants over a period of 10 years and 200 million dollars in loans while confirming that the problem of claims was completely and finally settled.

According to the Agreed Minutes drafted during this process, the scope of the "Outline of the Property and Claims Settlement Agreement between Korea and Japan (8 items)" included the restitution of claims of Korean organizations or natural persons against Japan and its people of their government bonds, public bonds, Japanese bank notes, outstanding receivables of drafted Koreans and other claims. In other words, the Korean government included the compensation for the conscripted workers in its negotiation of the Claims Agreement with Japan; and the Japanese government thus claimed that all rights to claims of the victims of forced labor was extinguished pursuant to the Agreement.

4.3.2 Suit against Mitsubishi Heavy Industries

On December 11, 1995, the victims of forced labor at Mitsubishi Heavy Industries filed a suit against the Japanese government and Mitsubishi Heavy Industries at the Hiroshima District Court for unlawful acts and for violations of international law, demanding payment of outstanding wages, damages, and compensation.

The Hiroshima District Court found, concerning the conscription circumstances of the victims, that "the conscription of the Plaintiffs under the law at the time cannot be an unlawful act in itself, nor can the process of conscription pursuant to the law be called a violation of the law" and thus rejected the claim of forced conscription and forced labor made by the victims. While the court did recognize some of the claims of the victims as being true such as the Japanese munitions companies unlawfully driving them to forced labor unlike their prior explanations, failure to pay out wages properly, failure to implement safety precautions, it still held that the right to request compensation for such damages had already lapsed since the statute of limitations had expired for the right to claim unpaid wages and, even if it had not, the rights were extinguished by the 1965 Claims Agreement between Korea and Japan.

The victims appealed to the Hiroshima High Court and while the case was still in progress, filed the same suit against Mitsubishi Heavy Industries before the Busan District Court of Korea on May 1, 2000. When the Hiroshima High Court also dismissed the case on January 19, 2005, the victims filed an appeal again, this time to the highest court of Japan.

On February 2, 2007, the Busan District Court ruled similarly, stating that the victims' right to compensation for damages and payment of wages was extinguished. The Supreme Court of Japan also dismissed the victims' case on November 1, 2007, thereby concluding the proceedings in Japan. Then, the victims appealed the decision of the district court to the Busan High Court, but the same dismissed the appeal on February 3, 2009 for reason of res judicata following the final decision in Japan.

4.3.3 Suit against (New) Nippon Steel Corporation

On December 24, 1997, the victims of forced labor at Nippon Steel Corporation filed a suit against the Japanese government and the New Nippon Steel Corporation at the Osaka District Court for unlawful acts and for violations of international law, demanding payment of outstanding wages, damages, and compensation.

The Osaka District Court dismissed the case on March 27, 2001 for the same reasons as the Hiroshima District Court. It further added that Nippon Steel Corporation for which the victims provided service at the time was dissolved pursuant to Japan's Emergency Corporate Accounting Measures Law and Corporation Reconstruction and Maintenance Law and ceased to exist. It held that the current New Nippon Steel Corporation is of independent legal personality from that of the previous Nippon Steel Corporation, on which legal responsibility does not transfer; and even if it did, the rights of the victims were extinguished pursuant to the 1965 Claims Agreement and thus declared the Plaintiffs' loss. The victims appealed to the Osaka High Court, but the appeal was dismissed on November 19, 2002, and the entire proceedings came to an end on October 9, 2003 when the Supreme Court rejected the case.

When the case closed in Japan, the victims filed the same claim before the Seoul Central District Court of Korea on February 28, 2005 against Nippon Steel Corporation. However, the Seoul Central District Court also dismissed the case on April 3, 2008 for the reason of *res judicata* pursuant to the final decision of Japanese courts. The victims appealed to Seoul High Court but were again denied for the same reason on July 16, 2009.

4.3.4 Decision of the Supreme Court

The Supreme Court stated, "In determining international jurisdiction, we must follow the basic principles of equity for both parties, fairness of trial, speed, and economy. More specifically, not only must individual interests be considered such as fairness, convenience and foreseeability for the parties to the litigation, but also state or judicial considerations of fairness, speed, efficiency, and effectiveness of trial. Among these various considerations, determining which interests need protection must be rationally determined by considering each individual case, practical relevance of the party to the forum, and the relevance between the forum and the issue at dispute as objective criteria." Based on this premise, the Court stated, "The damages claim resulting from unlawful acts in this case arises from the enforced mobilization of the previous Nippon

Steel Corporation, together with the state of Japan, for the purpose of forced labor, because the act of putting such mobilized persons to forced labor is an unlawful act for which the Plaintiff is claiming that the Defendant bears the liabilities of the previous Nippon Steel Corporation. In consideration of the fact that Korea, together with Japan, was the *locus delicti* where part of the acts in a series of unlawful acts that occurred, the Plaintiff victims reside in Korea, and that the issues are intimately related to historical and political changes," the Court held that it had jurisdiction over the case because Korea had *de facto* connection with the parties and issues of this case.

...

4.3.5 Decision Concerning the Extinction of Rights Pursuant to the 1965 Korea-Japan Claims Agreement

In its decision, the Supreme Court found that the "1965 Claims Agreement was aimed not towards compensating for Japanese colonization but towards resolving the financial and civil debt/credit relationship between Korea and Japan based on Article 4 of the San Francisco Peace Treaty. The funds for economic cooperation, granted to the Korean government by the Japanese government pursuant to Article 1 of the Claims Agreement, neither resolves the issue of rights based on Article 2 nor have the effect of legal consideration. In the process of negotiating the Claims Agreement, the Japanese government fundamentally denied legal compensation for forced labor by refusing to acknowledge the illegality of colonization; and the two governments were unable to reach an agreement concerning the nature of Japan's rule over the Korean Peninsula. In this situation, it is difficult to conclude that the right to compensation for crimes against humanity that state power was directly involved in or crimes directly connected to colonization was included in the scope of application of the Claims Agreement. Therefore, the individual rights to claim compensation for forced labor were not extinguished by the Claims Agreement, nor were Korea's rights to diplomatic protection of its nationals."

Further, the Supreme Court held, "For a state to be able to conclude a treaty which does not stop at abandoning diplomatic protection but goes on to directly extinguish the rights to claims of its nationals that have independent legal personality different from that of the state, without their consent, contradicts contemporary legal principles. Even if it were to be permissible under international law for a state to extinguish the rights of its nationals through treaties, considering that a state and its nationals are different legal persons, the people's rights cannot be deemed to have been extinguished unless specifically provided for in the treaty. Considering that there is not enough evidence to conclude that there was an agreement between the two governments regarding the extinguishing of individual rights to claims in the 1965 Claims

Agreement, and that Japan's Property Measures Law—extinguishing the rights of Korean people against Japan and its people—enacted immediately following the conclusion of the Claims Agreement can only be understood on the premise that the Claims Agreement alone could not have extinguished the individual rights of the Korean people, even if the rights of the victims were included in the scope of application of the Claims Agreement, the individual rights themselves cannot be deemed to have been automatically extinguished by the Agreement."

... The Supreme Court thus vacated the decision of the High Court and remanded the case for retrial.

4.3.6 Significance of the Supreme Court Decision

Korea has been greatly influenced by Japan since the Japanese occupation up to present in its legal system, judicial administration, interpretation of the law and application of legal reasoning. Thus, there have been many instances in which the decisions of the Japanese courts have been acted as precedents accepted without question. Likewise in this case, the district and high courts accepted the effect of the decision of the Japanese courts because they supposedly did not violate the good morals and social order of Korea and dismissed the petitions of the victims.

The Supreme Court decision, however, is significant in that it aggressively and independently recognized the compensation rights of the victims based on the Preamble of the Constitution and other related laws concerning the issues already judged and decided in Japanese courts. It declared that the Preamble of the founding Constitution and the current Constitution of the Republic of Korea "uphold[s] the cause of the Provisional Republic of Korea Government born of the Independence Movement of 1 March 1919" and that Japan's rule over the Korean Peninsula during Japanese Occupation Period was nothing more than an unlawful occupation by force from a normative perspective. The Supreme Court holding that the effect of the decisions of the Japanese courts premised on the legality of Japan's enforced annexation of Korea could not be recognized, as they squarely contravene with the Constitution of Korea, is significant as the aggressive and independent attitude of the judiciary concerning historical issues.

In judging the 1965 Claims Agreement in its decision, the Supreme Court restricted the Claims Agreement to one that resolved the financial and civil debt/credit relationship between Korea and Japan and found that the right to compensation for crimes against humanity that that the Japanese government was directly involved in or crimes directly connected to colonization was not included in the scope of application of the Claims Agreement. It thus held that neither the individual claims were extinguished nor diplomatic protection of Korea was abandoned. Such a holding squarely contradicts the official position of the Japanese government that claims that all legal compensation, including individual claims, was fulfilled by the 1965 Claims Agreement.

The Supreme Court decision, in particular, is a logical extension of the official position of the Korean government but takes a step further in its attitude towards the forced labor victims. While the Korean government had declared in 2005 through the decision of joint government-civic committee that compensation issues concerning comfort women, atomic bomb victims, and nations in Sakhalin were not settled by the Claims Agreement, it had failed to similarly recognize the rights of forced labor victims. Rather, because such were not clearly recognized as forced labor victims, their claims were assumed to have been settled by the Claims Agreement. This was because the outline of the eight items indicated in the Agreed Minutes to the Agreement included the restitution of the claims of Korean persons against Japan and its people of the outstanding receivables of the conscripted Koreans and other claims.

In spite of this, the Supreme Court stated "Even if the right to claims was indeed included in the scope of application of the Claims Agreement, individual rights themselves cannot be deemed to have been extinguished by the Claims Agreement alone. Rather, the state's diplomatic protection of that right is abandoned by the Claims Agreement, so that even if such a right were to be extinguished within Japan due to domestic measures taken by Japan, the Korean government would no longer have the means to protect this diplomatically. Therefore, the Agreement cannot restrict the victims' exercise of rights in the Republic of Korea."

War crimes committed by the Japanese government during the occupation are certainly not limited to that of this case. According to a survey conducted by the Committee for the Survey and Support of Forced Labor Victims and Casualties Abroad during Anti-Japan Resistance (Forced Labor Victim Survey Committee) under the Prime Minister, those recognized as victims of forced labor pursuant to the committee's analysis numbered 147,893 as of May 11, 2012. Their additional suits have already begun their countdown. Aside from forced labor, comfort women and victims of forced conscription into the Japanese military who they were victimized as soldiers or civilian employees, have yet to be properly compensated. Through the Supreme Court decision, compensation suits of war crime victims other than those engaged in forced labor can be actively reviewed.

Furthermore, similar issues can also be raised in other East Asian countries that were illegally occupied by Japan. If compensation for crimes committed during the Japanese occupation period would not be recognized up to present time pursuant to the logic of the government and courts of the state of Japan that caused harm, this Supreme Court decision expressly criticizes the decisions of the Japanese government and courts based on Japanese laws while also providing a reasoning that makes compensation possible for other victims. Therefore, this decision will also likely be viewed for its significance among other East Asian states.

...

4.3.7 Conclusion

Korea and Japan, having experienced a history of Japanese occupation in a relationship as an occupying power and its colony, cannot be free from the important historical issues of the past. From territorial disputes to historical understanding, cultural differences and economic cooperation, there are many challenges yet to be overcome. Some of these challenges can be peacefully overcome through diplomatic efforts from a future-oriented perspective on the part of both countries.

However, as for war crimes committed during the Japanese occupation period, avoiding legal responsibility will not settle the past as long as specific identifiable victims exist. As living witnesses and victims of history, sufficient compensation and a sincere apology would be the proper way to resolve the issue, and efforts toward this end would be the duty and reason for the existence of the state.

The Korean government cannot be free from criticism concerning their passive attitude towards the representative historical issues of comfort women and forced labor. More specifically, in negotiating post-war compensation following liberation, it hastily used an all-inclusive term "all claims" in concluding the 1965 Claims Agreement, thereby creating an obstacle to the realization of the victims' rights to claims. It also neglected the victims for a long time without having taken initiative to remove these obstacles. In the meantime, many of the victims have passed away without having received compensation or an apology. Therefore, the intervention of the judiciary in these historical issues through affirmative decisions holds great significance.

Of course, there are concerns for the possible adverse effects that such an aggressive intervention by the judiciary may have on diplomatic relations. In order to resolve the complex issues within Korea-Japan relations, there needs to be a broad range of negotiations through various means; but with the severely limiting aspect of judicial intervention may make resolution even more difficult. According to recent media reports, there has been some progress in the matter, with the Japanese government directly issuing apologies concerning the comfort women issue through its Prime Minister, as well as talk about considering the possibility of compensating the victims directly. However, the firm position taken by the Korean government concerning comfort women pursuant to the Constitutional Court decision has made it difficult to find a point of contact, thereby vitiating these plans.

A further issue can be raised as to whether a treaty concluded between states as parties pursuant to international law can be invalidated *ex post facto* through the decision of its judiciary. As raised by those opposing the unconstitutionality decision, although one can understand the desperation of the victims, forcing a diplomatic resolution by overstepping previous constitutional interpretations does not adhere to the limits of the judiciary within the framework of separation of powers.

However, separation of powers alone cannot be an autotelic value in itself. Also, considering that the fundamental purpose of the separation of powers is to affirmatively guarantee the basic rights of the people, the aggressive role of the judiciary in guaranteeing the people's rights coincides with the substance of the principle of separation of powers. Furthermore, ruminating on the fact that the resolution of historical issues has been left to the executive branch alone and that the promotion of such issues have progressed and regressed repeatedly based on the will of the head of that branch of government, the positive implications of an active role of the judiciary in its recent decisions are great.

4C *Dokdo*

4.4 *The San Francisco Peace Treaty, International Law on Territorial Disputes, and Historical Criticism*

As one of the most important territorial issues facing Korea, the issue concerning Dokdo at first blush seems to rest largely on an interpretation of the San Francisco Peace Treaty and its reference to Korean territory in relation to Japan's renouncement of territory it gained unlawfully. However, recent decisions by the International Court of Justice (ICJ) reveal that this territorial issue should not only include a close examination of the San Francisco Peace Treaty, but also the colonial context of Japanese acquisition of Korean territory such that the legal structure of Korea's claim of sovereignty over Dokdo can be restructured largely into the following stages: first, a "single unit" approach proving the historical title of Dokdo prior to the official incorporation into Japan's Shimane Prefecture in 1905 while emphasizing its subordinate relationship to Ullungdo; second, a legal and historical criticism of the process of Japanese colonization of Korea from 1905 until liberation in 1945; third, an emphasis on Korean independence following the Second World War and territorial disposition by the Allied Powers from 1945 to 1952, and the indeterminacy of title over Dokdo; and fourth, Korea's exercise of sovereignty over Dokdo following the declaration of the Peace Line in 1952 until today.

To determine the weight and validity of such a restructured approach to the Dokdo issue requires an evaluation of Korea's claim of sovereignty on the following points and issues: first, an evaluation of the Ullungdo Dispute of the 17th century, or an evaluation of the status of Dokdo in the Korean-Japanese diplomatic relations regarding Ullungdo; second, a determination of whether "Seokdo" mentioned in the Imperial Order no. 41 of Oct. 25, 1900 is actually Dokdo; third, whether the incorporation of Dokdo into Japan in 1905 should be understood as being part of the process of annexation of Korea that began in 1904; fourth, the attitude of the Allied Powers in their disposition of Japanese territory in order to conclude the San Francisco Peace Treaty; and fifth, Korea's exercise of sovereignty over Dokdo after 1952 and the role of that critical date. Upon this evaluation, one can discover a number of themes that are common to these issues such as the probative value of the evidence, positivism, colonization, history, otherness, etc. Thus, a study of the status and connotation of these words in modern international law must be rooted in the approach to the Korean territorial dispute in contrast to an approach to the issue based simply on a formalistic reading of the San Francisco Peace Treaty.

4.4.1 The San Francisco Peace Treaty and Its Relevance to the Sovereignty of Dokdo

When Japan agreed in Article 2 of the San Francisco Peace Treaty to renounce "all right, title and claim to Korea, including the islands Quelpart, Port Hamilton, and Dagelet", the drafters of the treaty did not include Dokdo within the areas to be renounced. Japan has, and with reason, assumed that its sovereignty still extends over Dokdo, and the Koreans have disputed this assumption. Therefore, as Charney pointed out, "There is even a dispute over whether by implication or, by general terms, the victors in World War II intended to return the disputed [Dokdo] to Korea".

During the course of drafting the San Francisco Peace Treaty, Korea's views were solicited, in consequence of which, the Korean Ambassador in his letter of July 19, 1951 requested the U.S. Secretary of State to amend Article 2(a) of the draft treaty so as to include Dokdo as well as Quelpart, Port Hamilton and Dagelet among those islands over which Japan would renounce right, title and claim by virtue of recognizing Korea's independence. In his reply to the Korean Ambassador dated August 10, 1951, Dean Rusk, the Assistant Secretary of State, stated that the United States could not concur in the proposed amendment as it applied to Dokdo since, according to his information, Dokdo had never been treated as a part of Korea, as it had been under the jurisdiction of the Oki Islands Branch Office of Japan's Shimane Prefecture since 1905 and it did not appear that they had ever before been claimed by Korea. As a result, Article 2(a) of the San Francisco Peace Treaty made no mention of Dokdo.

Accordingly, it appeared that the United States viewed that the San Francisco Peace Treaty constituted a determination of the "minor islands" to be left to Japan under the Potsdam Declaration, and that the treaty left Dokdo to Japan. The United States remarked, however, that its view was simply that of one of the several signatories of the treaty, and that Article 22 of the San Francisco Peace Treaty, providing reference to the ICJ, was drafted in order to settle the disputes deriving from the treaty.

In determining what course of action should be taken in light of this development, the question arose whether the statement made in Rusk's letter entailed the legal conclusion that the San Francisco Peace Treaty left Dokdo to Japan. On the one hand, it may be argued that the determination of the minor islands to be left under Japanese sovereignty required by the Potsdam Proclamation has been made by the treaty, i.e., Japan retained everything not renounced under Article 2, and that Korea, prior to the signing of the treaty, specifically asked for a renunciation of Dokdo by Japan and was turned down and that therefore it was the intent of the drafters of the treaty that Japan would not renounce Dokdo, and that these islands were accordingly included in the minor islands determined to remain under Japanese sovereignty.

On the other hand, it may be argued that Rusk's letter refusing to include Dokdo in the enumeration of islands renounced in connection with the renunciation of Korea was based on the U.S. understanding of the historical facts, providing that "Dokdo … was according to our information never treated as part of Korea", and that his statement left the door open to Korea to show that it had in fact treated Dokdo as part of Korea prior to 1905, when the Japanese placed Dokdo under the jurisdiction of Shimane Prefecture. Under this theory Korea would still be free to establish legally, if it could, that the "Korea" it renounced in the San Francisco Peace Treaty included Dokdo. This is all the more so given that the reports on Dokdo were based for the most part on Japanese language references available in the Department of State and the Library of Congress, and the studies prepared within the Department of State and by the Japanese Foreign Office on some of the islands.

4.4.2 Judicial and Arbitral Decisions Regarding Territorial Disputes that Have Required Interpretation of a Treaty

Some guidance regarding the relevance of the 1951 San Francisco Peace Treaty to Dokdo's sovereignty can be found by examining other cases adjudicating territorial disputes that have involved treaties. Examples of relevant cases include the *Temple of Preah Vihear Case, Case Concerning the Land, Island and Maritime Frontier Dispute* (*Gulf of Fonseca Case*), and the *Eritrea-Yemen Arbitration*.

In *Case Concerning the Temple of Preah Vihear* (*Thailand v. Cambodia*), the Temple of Preah Vihear is described in current tourist literature as occupying one of the most magnificent sites of any Khmer temple and as containing some of the most stunning sculptured stone carvings. The temple is nestled in the Dangrek Mountains, which provides the border between Thailand to the north and Cambodia to the south. The dispute regarding the exact location of the boundary dated back to 1904, when Cambodia was part of French Indo-China and Thailand was known as Siam, and the two countries entered into the Boundary Treaty of 1904. Ultimately this case revolved around Cambodia and Thailand's alternate interpretations of the Boundary Treaty of 1904 and the disputed validity of the French maps.

The ICJ's examination of the region's history revealed multiple instances during other treaty negotiations in which it would have been perfectly natural for Siam to bring up this issue, but the issue had never been raised in these subsequent events. "They did not do so, either then or for many years, and thereby must be held to have acquiesced." The Court also noted that, in contrast to the position Thailand presented to the Court, Siam had never advocated that the mixed commission strictly follow Article 1 of the 1904 Boundary Treaty. Given the court's finding that Siam had accepted the mapped boundary, the Temple of Preah Vihear was determined to be in Cambodia.

In the *Gulf of Fonseca Case* (*El Salvador v. Honduras*), in 1980, Honduras and El Salvador signed and ratified the General Treaty of Peace which defined the agreed portions of the boundary and provided for a Joint Frontier Commission to delimit the disputed six sectors of the boundary and resolve the legal status of disputed islands in the Gulf of Fonseca. The Court first determined that the specific islands under dispute were El Tigre, Meanguera, and Meanguerita. Next, the court examined the language of Article 26 of the Peace Treaty and compared both parties' differing interpretations of that provision.

The Court rejected the idea that sovereignty could be determined by occupation alone, because these islands were never *terra nullius*. Instead they were Spanish territories that were inherited by the new countries. Furthermore, the Court decided that the *uti possidetis juris* of 1821 was the primary evidence for finding title over the islands but, after concluding that the Spanish administrative boundary was ill defined and ambiguous, concluded that an exercise of authority by one party and acquiescence by the other could also be used as evidence of sovereignty. The Court justified its conclusion under the final sentence of Article 26 of the 1980 Treaty of Peace, which allowed other evidence besides Spanish administrative documents to be taken into account.

Turning to the specific islands themselves, the Court awarded the island of El Tigre to Honduras based on evidence that Honduras had occupied the island for more than 100 years, that El Salvador had previously recognized this exercise of authority by Honduras without objection, and that no colonial title refuting Honduras's sovereignty over El Tigre existed. El Salvador received the islands of Meanguera and Meanguerita because it had effectively possessed and controlled these territories since 1854 without any protest from Honduras until 1991. Because Honduras waited 137 years before objecting to El Salvador's effective control over the disputed islands, the Court found clear evidence of acquiescence.

In *Eritrea-Yemen Arbitration*, both parties claimed sovereignty over islands in the Red Sea, which serve as a natural boundary separating Eritrea and Yemen. Peace treaty interpretation was at the center of this conflict because both parties based their claims on different understandings of how the 1923 Treaty of Lausanne affected title over the islands. Article 16 of the Treaty of Lausanne addressed Turkey's surrender to the Allied Powers and the cession of some of the territories of the Ottoman Empire, but like the 1951 San Francisco Treaty of Peace, the 1923 Treaty of Lausanne did not specifically vest any nation with title to the disputed islands and left the procedure for making such a determination ambiguous.

The tribunal holds that the Treaty of Lausanne had an "effect *erga omnes*" and hence that its language and allocation of territory binds non-parties as well as those who signed the treaty. This conclusion, however, did not answer the question of whether the Treaty of Lausanne treated the Red Sea Islands as *terra nullius* or territories with undetermined ownership status. Because the Red Sea Islands did not revert back to Yemen nor become *terra nullius*, the arbitral tribunal determined their sovereignty based upon a showing by the parties of "an intentional display of power and authority over the territory, by the exercise of jurisdiction and state function, on a continuous and peaceful basis." The tribunal also looked at international law concepts such as contiguity and territorial seas when it made the final judgment, which divided sovereignty over the disputed islands between both parties.

The international judicial bodies' resolution of the disputed islands provides some guidance on the Dokdo matter, in particular the impact of a treaty on third parties discussed in the *Eritrea-Yemen Arbitration* because neither party was an original signatory of the Treaty of Lausanne. The tribunal was able to use the treaty to grant rights to Eritrea and Yemen by holding that it operated *erga omnes*. Therefore, even though Korea was a third party to the

San Francisco Peace Treaty, a tribunal may look to the Treaty for guidance regarding the Dokdo matter, if it sees this Treaty as having an *erga omnes* effect.

4.4.3 International Law on Territorial Disputes

Nevertheless, given the unsettled nature of the San Francisco Peace Treaty on the issue of sovereignty over Dokdo, the understanding and application of international law from the Korean perspective should be logically structured within the dimensions of mainstream positivist criticisms of international law along with alternative perspectives that reflect the Korean historical experience. Such an approach brings to light a difficulty and struggle seen in recent ICJ decisions on disputed territorial issues in the denial of the probative value of potentially controversial historical evidence. This problem is based on the decisions of the colonial powers that exercised authority over the territories at the time, as well as the interpretation and application of the applicable treaties that have been recognized to have absolute evidentiary value.

As a result, the jurisprudence of the ICJ and other international judicial organs were criticized as having resurrected the brutality of the colonization era by having unquestioningly accommodated the tyranny of indiscriminate territorial expansion of the colonial powers for the resolution of territorial issues related to the newly independent states. Third world international law scholars have continually questioned the Euro-centric perception of modern international law regarding territorial dispute and resolution. Such discourse among the international law scholars of the third world has led to criticism of the current international legal jurisprudence as mentioned above. However, this perception of the recent functionalist jurisprudence of international tribunals has not gained an all-around sympathy within the international legal academy.

Thus, by articulating not only the reasons for the application of international law to territorial disputes from a Korean perspective but also the limitations to be exposed in the process, there are expectations that overcoming such duplicity will ultimately function as an alternative solution to the Korean territorial issue of Dokdo.

4.4.3.1 *General Understanding of Territorial Disputes in International Law*

The general understanding of territorial disputes in international law has developed through decisions and awards by international judicial and arbitral bodies, and these cases generally involve either colonising countries or colonised/newly independent countries. Consequently, none of these cases parallels the situation that involves a former colonising country and a colonised/newly independent country. What this suggests is that since there have been no precedent cases directly involving a territorial dispute between former colonies and former imperial powers, any applicable legal principles did not count as major factors in formulating the relevant international law relating to territorial acquisition and loss in such situations. Thus, it is debatable whether the general rule of international law on territorial disputes can be applied, without modification, to the specific cases that cannot clearly fit into those general terminologies and categories.

In such circumstances, it is imperative to clarify the relevant norms of international law and develop new norms to address the very nature of the territories in dispute. This will be critical for formulating a broader framework for the appreciation of the nature of territorial disputes in Asia and in particular for the Dokdo issue, a move beyond a simple application of the San Francisco Peace Treaty.

4.4.3.2 *Recent Jurisprudence of International Law on Territorial Disputes*

If Korea, a state in dispute having undergone colonization, is unable to receive substantive evaluation of the historicity of its evidence to be utilized in its claim of sovereignty, it may result in feared outcomes as hypothesized in consideration of the current state of international legal jurisprudence. The problem is that, as mentioned above, despite the awareness of the need for an alternative to the mainstream positivist perspective, it is difficult to propose one fixed theory. This difficulty is aggravated because, in relation to the colonization issues, not only must one be aware of the general/universal understanding of the application of international law to regions, i.e., the Middle East or Africa, but one must also reflect on the implementation of Japanese imperialism in East Asia, as well as the unique application of international law to Korea at the time.

The debate about this third world perception and development of international law leading to criticism of the jurisprudence of current international judicial organs regarding territorial disputes is but a budding sprout when considering the foundations from which the legal principles were derived. For example, the jurisprudence regarding territorial disputes in cases, i.e., between *Qatar and Bahrain* in 2001, between *Nigeria and Cameroon* in October 2002, and the *Ligitan and Sipadan* dispute of December 2002, share a similarity in that significant weight was given to the decisions of the colonial powers ruling at the time in the final judgment.

In *Case concerning Maritime Delimitation and Territorial Questions between Qatar and Bahrain*, which concerned disputes between the two states over Zubarah, Hawar Islands, and Janan Island, the ICJ concluded that Bahrain had sovereignty over the Hawar Islands. Although Bahrain claimed, in support of its argument, that "its sovereignty over the Hawar Islands has been exercised continuously and uninterruptedly over the last two centuries and has been acknowledged by the inhabitants of the islands, and Qatar has never exercised any kind of competing authority over the islands" the ICJ considered only the British decision of 1939 throughout its reasoning, and this 1939 decision virtually served as the sole basis of the judgment.

Likewise, the ICJ found that Qatar had sovereignty over Janan Island including Hadd Janan, on the basis of the British Government's decision in 1939 on the question of sovereignty over Janan Island, as interpreted in 1947. Although the British Government concluded that Hawar Islands belonged to Bahrain and not to Qatar, no remarks were made regarding Janan Island, nor was it specified which islands were to be considered "Hawar Islands". Qatar, on its part, referred to the letters dated December 23, 1947, drafted in identical terms and sent by the British Political Agent in Bahrain to the Rulers of Qatar and Bahrain, in which the seabed between the two states was delimited by the British Government. In those letters, Janan Island was not regarded as being part of the islands of the Hawar group. The ICJ thus concluded that the British Government's 1947 letter provided an authoritative interpretation of the 1939 decision and its results.

In *Case concerning the Land and Maritime Boundary between Cameroon and Nigeria*, Nigeria contested Cameroon's claims and, *inter alia*, questioned the competence of the British to cede the Bakassi Peninsula to the Germans, arguing that since the territories that were the subject of the 1884 Treaty of Protection were protectorates and not colonies, Great Britain was incompetent to effect the purported cession to Germany.

In the *Case concerning the Sovereignty over Pedra Branca/Pulau Batu Puteh, Middle Rocks and South Ledge* between Malaysia and Singapore in 2008, the core issue of the case was the legal evaluation of a letter from the State Secretary of Johor in 1953 indicating Johor's official position towards the Singapore authorities in stating that the "Johore Government does not claim ownership of Pedra Branca" while Johor had sovereignty under international law. From this, we see the continuing trend of international tribunals in their jurisprudence—a complete reliance upon the most "objectively" certain evidence.

In this case, the ICJ decision, which appears to have partially accommodated the post-colonialist perspective critique, gave rise to a hope that a post-colonialist interpretation may possibly grow into a mainstream theory. In other words, as the separate opinion of Judge Kooijmans in the *Maritime Delimitation and Territorial Questions between Qatar and Bahrain* stated, "[Only] by taking into account the full spectrum of the Parties' history, can their present rights be properly evaluated. By not giving the full historical context its due, however, the Court has ... unnecessarily curtailed its scope for settling the dispute in a persuasive and legally convincing way"; and the separate opinion of Judge Ranjeva in *Land and Maritime Boundary between Cameroon and Nigeria* stating, "The inequality and denial of rights inherent in colonial practice in relation to ... colonies is currently recognized as an elementary truth; there is a resultant duty to memorialize these injustices and at the same time to acknowledge an historical fact"; provide an opportunity for theorization of the historical criticism approach, which would help subjugate the current international jurisprudence founded upon European imperialism and graft in the historical perception of East Asia.

4.4.4 Historical Criticism and Towards the Formation of a Fairer International Law

The historical criticism approach, first mentioned in the *Case concerning the Sovereignty over Pedra Branca/Pulau Batu Puteh, Middle Rocks and South Ledge,* provided a direction for development of future decisions with regard to colonial issues. Though not stated in the actual judgment, the reference to the historical criticism approach in separate opinions contributes greatly to the expansion of international legal perception regarding colonial settlement. The context in which Judge Ranjeva emphasized the historical criticism approach is in an opinion differing from that of the actual judgment regarding the transfer of sovereignty over Johore to Singapore. In this case, Judge Ranjeva questioned how Johor's title could have been extinguished without its consent. He further emphasized that in the absence of proof, the conclusion of the transfer of title relied upon presumptive consent, which is controversial in having downplayed the facts. Judge Ranjeva stated that in interpreting the facts the decision was reached without having taken into consideration the historical criticism approach toward their political and legal order prevalent at the time. He also stated that while the relations between the colonial powers were governed by international law, the relationship between the United Kingdom and Johor could not be seen as having been established as sovereign, equal subjects of international law. Thus, the sovereignty granted to indigenous authorities did not have the same significance as that in relations between colonial powers, and their only role was to submit to the will of the colonial powers. In this situation, the Sultan of Johor could not express any form of opposition to the decision of the British government. Judge Ranjeva reached the conclusion that it was difficult to infer an international transfer of title by acquiescence since Johor was merely exercising its colonial territorial title according to the rules and practice of the colonial powers and that the silence of Johor could not be interpreted against such circumstances.

In analyzing the recent jurisprudence of international tribunals, a psychological preference for "objectively" certain evidence, or "the least controversial" evidence can be deduced from the fact that they afforded great significance to the decisions of the colonial powers that were in control of the disputed regions at the time. Taking this into account in a hypothetical resolution of the territorial issue of Korea, i.e., Dokdo, before a third party mediator or international tribunal, there is also a need to predict the perspective from which such bodies will approach these issues.

In the case of Dokdo, it is difficult to ignore the possibility that great legal significance will be accorded to the process of territorial disposition by the Allied Powers according to the San Francisco Peace Treaty. This is because the intent of all interested parties including the U.S.—the central drafter of the treaty, the Allied Powers, i.e., United Kingdom and Australia, and the parties in dispute, Korea and Japan, were expressed in the negotiation process of the Peace Treaty. Further, the intent as documented in the materials will act as a useful mechanism in objectively evaluating and verifying Dokdo related evidence for each of the interested parties before future tribunals. In other words, the status of Dokdo under the San Francisco Peace Treaty is important in that while the territorial provision and its execution may not be the ultimate factor in determining the sovereignty issue, all relevant evidence may be re-evaluated within the framework of general principles of international law in relation to territorial acquisition.

The implications of the recent international legal jurisprudence in recognizing the absolute probative value of the decisions of the colonial powers exercising practical authority over territorial disposition for the Korean title dispute over Dokdo will also be applicable for other disputed titles where colonial context is a salient issue. Thus, subjugation of the recent jurisprudence regarding territorial disputes is an absolute requirement in strengthening Korea's claim of sovereignty over Dokdo.

The reason for insisting on terminology of colonization, history, third party, etc., is that it contributes greatly to approaching and understanding the East Asian territorial issues in relation to intertemporal law. In other words, it is closely related to understanding some fundamental questions such as: Did the legal concepts or systems of territorial acquisition exist at the material time? Assuming it did, what kind of role does it play in the resolution of relevant disputes today? If it did, what effect will the significant factual and legal change over the years have on the factual and legal development in the future?

Applying these questions to the current territorial issues, for example the Dokdo issue: Can Japan claim the international norms that were prevalent during the era of imperial colonization? Was it impossible for Korea to make any significant contribution to the formation or standardization of the relevant legal norms because of its status as a colonized state? Should one or more parties to a dispute be unable to carry out a meaningful role in the development of a normative system, must the intertemporal law be utilized for the resolution of the dispute? Must the intertemporal law be claimed even when it may result in an unfair and defective outcome? And must the intertemporal law be claimed when its results may result in impairment of *jus cogens*?

In the end, this is related to the understanding of this fundamental question: In situations where one cannot function as an actor but only as the object in the application of existing normative system, where the obvious logic or facts expressed as an actor are entirely misinterpreted and consequently act as restrictions, and where adequate channels of communication cannot be secured, how can one overcome the psychological discomfort of knowing that the status as an object will never change?

Ultimately, the function of the historical criticism approach against the Eurocentric positivist perspective of modern international law (based on third-party notions) seems to be the key challenge that is directly relevant to the search for solutions to the Dokdo issue between Korea and Japan. There is hope that in the above case, there will be an evaluation of their attempt at the formation of a fairer structure of international law in approaching territorial disputes, depending upon their accommodation of the historical criticism approach emphasized by Judge Ranjeva. In international dispute resolution, the historical criticism approach ought to be emphasized as a theoretical alternative to forming a fairer international legal structure.

4.4.5 Conclusion

The San Francisco Peace Treaty is constitutive and some of its provisions have an effect *erga omnes*, but its territorial clause does not purport to define Korea's boundaries in any detail and does not mention Dokdo.

The points made above reveal the two-sided nature of Korea's position in relation to the territorial issue of Dokdo where Korea is a disputant. It is prudent to approach the understanding of international law from the perspective of the current prevailing international law regime, which is based upon Eurocentric positivism; however, this approach lacks an appreciation of Korea's historical experience that includes the injustice of Japanese annexation and colonialism. The task for Korean international lawyers is to challenge the existing international law regime by promoting a perspective on international law that not only takes into account the historical experience of formerly oppressed countries like Korea, but seeks to bring the international system up to a standard of justice that is fair for all. Though there are scholarly approaches that raise this issue in Korea which have emphasized historical consciousness and decolonization, in order to formulate this as a comprehensive theoretical perspective, more needs to be done. The term, "historical criticism approach," which was a term that appeared in a recent judgment of the ICJ, is an encouraging indicator that should inspire international lawyers to employ this approach when dealing with territorial issues Korea is involved in. "It is a disciplinary project devoted to the academic task of revisiting, remembering and, crucially, interrogating the colonial past."

Judicial Decisions

A. Forced Labor Cases

(1) *Mitsubishi Heavy Industries* (2009 Da 22549 Verdict, issued May 24, 2012 [Supreme Ct.])

Case no. 2009 Da 22549
Issued May 24, 2012
Compensation for Damage (Others)

...

Verdict issued May 24, 2012.

Order
Vacate the lower court verdict and remand the case to Busan High Court.

Reasoning
We will now decide the issues on appeal.

1. Basic Facts
According to the reasoning of the lower court and the evidence lawfully accepted, the following facts can be found.

A. The deceased person who is not a party to this case (hereinafter "the Deceased") and Plaintiffs 2, 3, 4 & 5 (hereinafter together referred to as "Plaintiffs *et al.*") are Korean nationals who were domiciled in Korea between 1923 and 1926. Mitsubishi Heavy Industries Corporation (hereinafter "old Mitsubishi" to distinguish it from "the Defendant") is a company incorporated in Japan that operated factories and shipyards.

B. Having concluded the Annexation treaty with the Empire of Korea on August 22, 1910, Japan ruled over Korea through the Japanese Government-General. Japan entered into a war regime by starting the Manchurian Incident in 1931 and the Sino-Japanese War in 1937; and on December 8, 1941, it started the Pacific War. As Japan began to run short of labor and supplies due to the war, it enacted the National Conscription Order (no. 451) pursuant to the National Mobilization Law (no. 55, Apr. 1, 1938). (However, these were actually applied to foreign territories such as the Korean Peninsula from October 1 pursuant to Imperial Order no. 600 of the same year). It first actively pursued

© KONINKLIJKE BRILL NV, LEIDEN, 2016 | DOI 10.1163/9789004315754_005

the transfer of persons with special skills such as in manufacturing aircraft parts and steel mill furnace and in ship repair from Korea to Japan. (At first, its implementation was not forced due to concerns of resistance but rather took the form of recruitment pursuant to the labor mobilization plan.) When the shortage of labor and supplies continued and the Pacific War reached its peak around August 8, 1944, the Cabinet members passed the resolution 'on the bringing in of laborers from the peninsula, thereby applying the national conscription order to the general Korean population regardless of whether persons actually possessed special technical skills. National Conscription Order Article 18 provided for the payment of wages by the hiring company to the conscripts.

C. Plaintiffs *et al.* received their draft notices pursuant to the National Conscription Order in their places of residence in Gyeongseongbu (京城府) and Gyeonggi Province between August and October of 1944, after which they were assembled together with other conscripts near their areas of residence. They took the train to Busan, where they took the government ferry and arrived at Shimonoseki Port of Japan. There they took the train to Hiroshima where old Mitsubishi was located and were assigned to machine production and shipbuilding. Such process of transfer and assignment were conducted under the control of Japanese soldiers and police, as well as officials of Old Mitsubishi.

Plaintiffs *et al.* had to work in their respective workplaces everyday from 8 a.m. to 6 p.m.—except for two days of rest per month—where they cut iron plates, bent copper pipes, and worked in plumbing. Once their daily tasks were completed, they returned to *ryo*, the quarters provided by the companies, to eat and sleep. The quality and the amount of food provisions were severely insufficient; and in a room of about 12 *tatami* (Japanese floor mats), between 10 to 12 conscripts lived together. These quarters were also surrounded by barbed-wire fences; and strict surveillance by military police during both working hours and holidays prevented the freedom of everyday life. Any correspondence with family back in Korea was pre-screened and thus limited in content. They received their wages from Old Mitsubishi on the 28th of each month based on their days of work from the 21st of the previous month to the 20th of the following month. The Deceased received on average of 20 yen per month, while Plaintiff 2 received about 23–24 yen, Plaintiff 3 about 35 yen, and Plaintiff 4 about 30 yen.

D. With the dropping of the atomic bomb on Hiroshima on August 6, 1945, the factories and the shipyards of Old Mitsubishi were destroyed. With the declaration of Japan's surrender to the U.S. and the Allied Powers on the 15th, the Pacific War came to an end. When the atomic bomb was dropped, the Deceased tried to avoid the bombing but was hit by iron fragments and lost portions of flesh on his chin. On September 13, 1945, he put himself on a smuggling boat from Shimonoseki. Plaintiff 2, without any particular injury, put himself on a smuggling boat in Hakada in October; Plaintiff 3, with wounds on his arm and leg by glass fragments, took the returning ship prepared by the U.N. in Hakada; Plaintiff 4, without any particular injury, took a government ferry from Shimonoseki around August 30; and Plaintiff 5, without any particular injury, took a smuggling boat from Shimonoseki around October 20 to return to Korea.

Since their return, the Plaintiffs have been facing, up to the present day, not only various social and economic difficulties such as the loss of jobs they had prior to conscription and not being able to adjust back to life, but also numerous physical injuries resulting from exposure to radiation such as languor, shortness of breath, skin diseases, declining eyesight, etc.

E. After Japan was defeated, Old Mitsubishi was designated as a Special Accounting Corporation pursuant to Japan's Emergency Corporate Accounting Measures Law (1946 Law no. 7) and Corporation Reconstruction and Maintenance Law (1946 Law no. 40), enacted in an attempt to resolve the immense burden of reparations and liability of unpaid wages to be borne by Japanese companies, together with the zaibatsu dissolution policy of the Headquarters of the Supreme Commander for the Allied Powers in Japan. On July 4, 1949, it applied for the Reconstruction and Maintenance authorization pursuant to the Corporation Reconstruction and Maintenance Law and received a permit on November 3 of the same year.

Old Mitsubishi was set to be dissolved on January 11, 1950 pursuant to the Corporation Reconstruction and Maintenance Law; and on the same day, with the investment in kind taken from Old Mitsubishi, three new companies of Central Japan Heavy-Industries, Ltd. (later changed to New Mitsubishi Heavy-Industries, Ltd. on May 29, 1952, and Mitsubishi Heavy-Industries, Ltd. on June 1, 1964, hereinafter Central Japan Heavy-Industries), East Japan Heavy-Industries, Ltd. (later changed to Mitsubishi Heavy-Industries, Ltd. on June 1, 1964), and West Japan Heavy-Industries, Ltd. (later changed to Mitsubishi Shipbuilding, Ltd. on May 27, 1952) were established (hereinafter "the Second Companies"). On June 30, 1964, Central Japan Heavy-Industries, Ltd. (the name which had already been changed to Mitsubishi Heavy-Industries, Ltd.) merged with the other two companies to form the current Defendant. In being succeeded to the Second Companies, the employees of the Previous Company retained their positions and salaries, with their pension being calculated by adding the years worked at the Previous Company. All the presidents of the Second Companies had been executive directors at the Previous Company. Further, the Defendant considers Old Mitsubishi to be part of its own corporate history.

According to the Emergency Corporate Accounting Measures Law, companies designated as special accounting corporations had to set up an Old Account and a New Account (Article 7(1)) at the designated hour (referring to 00:00 hours on August 11, 1946, Article 1(1)). Regarding movable assets, real property, receivables and other properties, assets "necessary for the continuation of the current businesses that are part of the company objectives, and post-war restoration and improvement" were to be attached to the New Account at the designated hour, while others were to be attached to the Old Account in principle (Article 7(2)). Income and expenditures due to causes after the designated hour were to be kept in the New Account, while those occurring due to causes prior to the designated hour would be kept in the Old Account (Article 11(1)–(2)). Dissolution of old liabilities such as repayment were prohibited, while exceptional circumstances where repayment was acknowledged, had to be done through the Old Account; and where repayment was to be made through the New Account, it could only be done within set limits under certain conditions such as approval of a special manager (Article 14).

Pursuant to the Emergency Corporate Accounting Measures Law and Corporation Reconstruction and Maintenance Law, the Old Mitsubishi accounts were thus separated into Old and New Accounts as of August 11, 1946 midnight. After attaching the assets necessary for the continuation of the current businesses that were part of the company objectives, as well as post-war restoration and improvement to the New Account, these were taken to be invested in kind or businesses transferred to establish the three Second Companies. Old Mitsubishi was liquidated while bearing the liabilities of the Old Account occurring up to that point; and it was merged with Ryoju (菱重) Corporation established on May 25, 1957 and subsequently dissolved as of October 31, 1957.

F. After the Pacific War ended, the Allied Powers including the U.S. and the UK concluded the Peace Treaty with Japan in San Francisco on September 8, 1951 in order to resolve the issue of post-war reparations. Article 4(a) of this treaty provided for "the disposition of property of Japan and of its nationals in the areas referred to in Article 2, and their claims, including debts, against the authorities presently administering such areas and the residents (including juridical persons) thereof, and the disposition in Japan of property of such authorities and residents, and of claims, including debts, of such authorities and residents against Japan and its nationals, shall be the subject of special arrangements between Japan and such authorities."

Pursuant to the purpose of the provision in Article 4(a) of the Peace Treaty, discussion of normalization of diplomatic relations and post-war reparations began in late 1951 until the conclusion of the "Treaty on Basic Relations between the Republic of Korea and Japan for the Normalization of Diplomatic Relations" on June 22, 1965 and its annexed agreement of "Agreement between the Republic of Korea and Japan Concerning the Settlement of Problems in Regard to Property and Claims and Economic Cooperation" (hereafter "the Claims Agreement"). Article 1 of the Claims Agreement stated that Japan would provide Korea with $300 million in grants within a period of ten years and $200 million in loans. Article 2 further provided:

> The High Contracting Parties confirm that the problems concerning property, rights, and interests of the two High Contracting Parties and their peoples (including juridical persons) and the claims between the High Contracting Parties and between their peoples, including those stipulated in Article IV(a) of the Peace Treaty with Japan signed at the city of San Francisco on September 8, 1951, have been settled completely and finally.

The Agreed Minutes to the Claims Agreement (I) stated concerning Article 2 of the above as follows:

> (a) It is understood that "property, rights and interests" means all kinds of substantial rights which are recognized under law to be of property value;
> (e) It is agreed that measures to be taken in accordance with the provisions of paragraph 3 mean the internal measures of the respective countries which would be taken for the settlement of problem concerning property, rights and interests of the two countries and their nationals and problem concerning the claims between the two countries and their nationals, referred to in paragraph 1;
> (g) It is confirmed that problem concerning property, rights and interests of the two countries and their nationals and concerning the claims between the two countries and their nationals, which is settled completely and finally as mentioned in paragraph 1, Includes any claim falling within the scope of the "Outline of the Claims of the Republic of Korea against Japan" (the so-called "Eight Items"), which was submitted by the Korean side at the Japan-Republic of Korea negotiations and that, therefore, no contention can be made with respect to the above mentioned Outline of the Claims of the Republic of Korea against Japan.

The eight items outlined in the Agreed Minutes above were: "1) Return of gold and silver that were taken out of Korea by Japan between 1909 and 1945 through Cho** Bank; 2) Repayment of liabilities of the Japanese Government towards the Chosun Government General as of August 9, 1945; 3) Return of the money transferred from Korea after August 9, 1945; 4) Restoration of property in Japan, belonging to organizations whose headquarters or main offices are in Korea as of August 9, 1945; 5) Restitution of the claims of Korean organizations or natural persons against Japan and its people of their Government bonds, public bonds, Japanese bank notes, outstanding receivables of drafted Koreans, and other claims; 6) Legal recognition of claims possessed by Korean organizations or natural persons that are not included in items 1 to 5 to be independently exercisable after the Korea-Japan Summit; 7) Restitution of faults arising from the above property or rights claims; 8) Return and payment of the above must commence immediately after the establishment of the Agreement and be terminated within at least six months.

Pursuant to the conclusion of the above Claims Agreement, Japan enacted the Law on the Measures concerning the Property Rights of the Republic of Korea pursuant to the Execution of the Agreement between the Republic of Korea and Japan Concerning the Settlement of Problems in Regard to Property and Claims and Economic Cooperation (Law no. 144, hereinafter "Property Measures Law") on December 17, 1965. This law provided that "the claims of the Republic of Korea and its peoples are deemed extinguished as of June 22, 1965, except for those that fall within the scope of Article 2 property and benefits."

G. Plaintiffs *et al.* filed a suit against Defendant at the Hiroshima District Court of Japan for compensation (11,000,000 yen per person) for the torts committed by Old Mitsubishi such as forced labor and for the outstanding wages from the period of forced labor converted to present day amounts (99,014 yen for the Deceased; 96,056 yen for Plaintiff 2; 68,424 yen for Plaintiff 3; and 59,512 yen for Plaintiffs 4 & 5). When their cases were dismissed on March 25, 1999, they appealed to the Hiroshima High Court but were again rejected on January 19, 2005. Their appeal to the highest appellate court of the Supreme Court of Japan was also rejected on November 1, 2007, thereby concluding the litigation process (hereinafter "Japanese litigation" or "Japanese decisions").

Plaintiffs *et al.* instituted this suit against the Defendant, with identical claims, for the payment of compensation for torts and violation of international law in the courts of Korea immediately after the trial court decision of the previous case was issued by the Hiroshima District Court on May 1, 2000. The Deceased passed away on February 24, 2001 while this lawsuit was in progress at the trial court. His heirs agreed that Plaintiff 1 would be the sole beneficiary to the right to claims against the Defendant in this case; and thus Plaintiff 1 became the successor to the necessary legal procedures of the Deceased.

H. In their lawsuit to quash the refusal to disclose information (Seoul Administrative Court, 2002 Gu-Hap 33943) against the Minister of Foreign Affairs and Trade, Plaintiffs 2, 3, 4 & 5 received a decision in their favor on February 13, 2004 (Trial court decision confirmed by withdrawal of the appeal of the Minister of Foreign Affairs and Trade). Pursuant to this, the Korean government released certain documents related to the Claims Agreement, after which it launched the Joint Government-Civic Committee for the Follow-up Measures after the Release of Documents from the Korea-Japan Summit Meeting on August 26, 2005. The Korean government also formally announced regarding crimes against humanity where state authorities like the Japanese government had been involved (i.e. comfort women issue), that Japan's legal responsibility had not been resolved because the claims cannot be deemed to have been settled by the Agreement; and that the issues of Koreans in Sakhalin and atomic bomb victims were not included in the Claims Agreement.

C. Whether the claims of the Plaintiffs were extinguished by the Claims Agreement

The Claims Agreement was not a negotiation over compensation for Japanese colonization. It was rather a political agreement aimed at resolving the financial and civil debt/credit relationship between Korea and Japan based on Article 4 of the San Francisco Peace Treaty. The fact that the economic cooperative funds provided by the Japanese government to the Korean government pursuant to Article 1 of the Claims Agreement does not appear to resolve the issue of rights based on Article 2 nor have a legal compensatory relationship to the same; and the fact that in the process of negotiating the Claims Agreement, the Japanese government fundamentally denied legal reparations for forced labor without having even recognized the unlawfulness of its colonial rule, following which the two governments of Korea and Japan were unable to reach a consensus concerning the nature of Japanese control over the Korean Peninsula; and the fact that it is difficult to conclude that in such a situation, the claim to compensation for crimes against humanity involving the state powers of Japan or the crimes directly connected to its colonial rule were included in the scope of application of the Claims Agreement, show that not only were the individual rights to claim of compensation of the above Plaintiffs were not extinguished by the Claims Agreement, but it is also duly proper to conclude that the right to diplomatic protection of Korea was also not abandoned.

Further, it contravenes the principles of contemporary law to consider it possible for a state to conclude a treaty that does not stop at abandoning its right to diplomatic protection but proceeds to directly extinguish the individual rights of its nationals having a legal personality independent of the state without their consent. Even if it were to be permissible under international law for a state to extinguish individual rights to the claims of its nationals through a treaty, it would not be possible to conclude that a treaty can extinguish not only a state's right to diplomatic protection but also the people's individual rights without clear provisions in the treaty considering that a state and its peoples are independent legal subjects. The Claims Agreement does not have sufficient evidence to show that there was a consensus of the two governments concerning the extinction of individual rights to claims; and the fact that immediately following the conclusion of the Claims Agreement, Japan domestically enacted a Property Rights Measures Law regarding the rights of Korean peoples against Japan and its peoples, is premised on the fact that the Claims Agreement alone does not extinguish individual rights to the claims of the Korean people. Taking these points into consideration, even if the claims of the above Plaintiffs were to be included within the scope of application of the Claims Agreement, the individual rights themselves cannot be seen as automatically being extinguished by the Claims Agreement alone. Rather, the Claims Agreement would abandon Korea's rights to diplomatic protection concerning the rights to claims, so that even if such rights were to be extinguished in Japan through its domestic measures, Korea would be unable to exercise its rights (or be at loss of measures) to diplomatically protect them.

Therefore, because the compensation claims of the above Plaintiffs against the Defendant pursuant to its torts were not extinguished by the Claims Agreement, the above Plaintiffs can exercise such rights to claims against the Defendant.

...

5. Conclusion

Therefore, the original verdict is vacated, and the case is remanded and to be retried consistent with the opinion of the Supreme Court.

Presiding Justice Lee, In-bok
Chief Justice Kim, Nung-hwan
Justice Ahn, Dai-hee
Justice Park, Byoung-dae

(2) *New Nippon Steel Corporation* (2009 Da 68620 Verdict, issued May 24, 2012 [Supreme Ct.])

Case no. 2009 Da 68620
Compensation for Damage (Others)

...

Verdict issued May 24, 2012

Order
The lower court decision is vacated and the case is remanded to Seoul High Court.

Reasoning
We will now decide the issues of appeal.

1. Basic Facts

According to the reasoning of the lower court and the evidence lawfully accepted, the following facts can be found.

A. The Plaintiffs are natural persons domiciled in Korea between 1923 and 1929 and resided in Pyeongyang, Boryeong and Gunsan. The Nippon Steel Corporation (hereinafter "Old Nippon Steel") is a company established around January 1934 and operated steel mills in Kamaishi (釜石), Yawata (八幡), and Osaka (大阪) of Japan.

B. Japan faced a nationwide shortage in its labor force in the production of war supplies as it fought the Sino-Japanese War and the Pacific War. To resolve the issue, the Japanese government enacted the National Mobilization Law on April 1, 1938, implementing it in Korea starting May 5 of the same year. In October 1942, guidelines for importing Chosun people to Japan were issued in order to mobilize manpower through job placement by regional government offices. Aside from Old Nippon Steel, the Steel Control Association, an agency of the Japanese government responsible for the regulation and supervision of steel producers in Japan was established on April 26, 1941. The Association decided to aggressively expand the laborers from Korea and thus cooperated with its government to mobilize workers; and Old Nippon Steel played a dominant role in the Association with its holding the post of president.

C. Old Nippon Steel advertised for factory workers to work in Osaka Steel Mill in Pyeongyang around 1943. The advertisement stated that after working for two years at the Osaka Steel Mill, one would acquire technical skills and that afterwards they could find employment after training as a technician at a steel mill in Korea. Plaintiffs Yeo and Shin saw this advertisement around September of 1943. Attracted by the idea of finding employment back in Korea after acquiring technical skills, they applied, interviewed with the recruitment officer of Old Nippon Steel, was successful in securing employment, and under the guidance of an officer, went to the Osaka Steel Mill of Old Nippon Steel where they engaged in labor as trainees.

At the Osaka Steel Mill, Plaintiffs Yeo and Shin worked in three 8-hour shifts, were permitted outings once or twice a month, and received 2–3 yen as an allowance. Old Nippon Steel deposited into accounts under the names of the Plaintiffs without their consent because of a concern that they would waste their money if their entire wages were paid out to them. The account book and seal were kept by the headmaster of their dormitory. The Plaintiffs engaged in arduous work that did not pertain to their technical skills such as breaking and mixing coal in the furnace and were in danger of being burned as they removed coal residue in iron pipes. Food provisions were scarce. A policeman would come by often and tell the Plaintiffs, "Even if you run, we can catch you immediately." Because there were people keeping watch even inside the dormitory, the Plaintiffs did not think of running away. Plaintiff Shin once said that he wanted to run away, but this was discovered and he was beaten and punished by the headmaster.

Then around February 1944, Japan forcefully conscripted the trainees, but after their conscription, Plaintiffs Yeo and Shin were not given even their allowances. The factories at the Osaka Steel Mill were destroyed by an airstrike of Allied Forces in March 1945, and some of the trainees perished along with them. The rest of the trainees including Plaintiffs Yeo and Shin were assigned to the steel mills under construction in Cheongjin, Korea in June 1945 and were thus relocated. Plaintiffs Yeo and Shin demanded the return of their savings account where their wages had been deposited and the seal to the headmaster, but the headmaster did not return their account book or their seal even after their arrival in Cheongjin. Though Plaintiffs Yeo and Shin engaged in construction of factories for 12 hours each day, they did not receive any of their wages. When the Cheongjin factory was destroyed by a Soviet attack in August 1945, Plaintiffs Yeo and Shin escaped to Seoul while avoiding the Soviet military where they learned of Korea's liberation from Japan.

D. Plaintiff Lee was recommended by the mayor of Daejon in 1941 to be mobilized for national service. He crossed over to Japan where he engaged in labor at the Kamaishi Steel Mill of Old Nippon Steel. Though he had been told that they would put his wages into savings, he was not given any. Plaintiff Kim was recruited upon the orders of Gunsanbu (present day Gunsan City) in January 1943. Under the guidance of Old Nippon Steel, he crossed over to Japan where he engaged in labor at the Yahata Steel Mill of Old Nippon Steel but received no wages. He tried to run away but was discovered and was beaten for five days. When Japan was defeated in the war and each of the steel mills were destroyed by airstrikes between August and December of 1945 so that Old Nippon Steel could no longer utilize forced labor, Plaintiffs Lee and Kim returned to their respective homes.

E. Old Nippon Steel was designated as a "special accounting company or special accounting corporation" pursuant to Japan's Emergency Corporate Accounting Measures Law (Law no. 7, enacted August 15, 1946) and Corporation Reconstruction and Maintenance Law (Law no. 40, enacted October 19, 1946) and was dissolved as of April 1, 1950. With the investment of its assets, Yawata Iron & Steel (八幡製鐵), Fuji Iron & Steel (富士製鐵), Nippon Steel Steamship Co. (日鐵汽船) and Harima Refractories Co. (播磨耐火煉瓦) (hereinafter "the Second Companies") were established. Yawata Iron & Steel Corporation changed its name to Nippon Steel Corporation on March 31, 1970 and merged with Fuji Iron & Steel Corporation on May 29, 1970 to form the present-day Defendant.

According to the Emergency Corporate Accounting Measures Law, companies designated as special accounting corporations had to set up an Old Account and a New Account (Article 7(1)) at the designated hour (referring to 00:00 hours on August 11, 1946, Article 1(1)). Regarding movable assets, real properties, receivables and other properties, assets "necessary for the continuation of the current businesses that are part of the company objectives, and post-war restoration and improvement" were to be attached to the New Account at the designated hour, while others were to be attached to the Old Account in principle (Article 7(2)). Income and expenditures due to causes after the designated hour were to be kept in the New Account, while those occurring due to causes prior to the designated hour would be kept in the Old Account (Article 11(1)–(2)). Dissolution of old liabilities such as repayment were prohibited, while exceptional circumstances where repayment was acknowledged, had to be done through the Old Account; and where repayment was to be made through the New Account, it could only be done within set limits under certain conditions such as approval of a special manager (Article 14).

Pursuant to the Emergency Corporate Accounting Measures Law and Corporation Reconstruction and Maintenance Law, Old Nippon Steel accounts were thus separated into Old and New Accounts as of August 11, 1946 midnight, so that corporate activities after the designated hour were executed only from the New Account. After attaching the assets necessary for the continuation of the current businesses that were part of the company objectives, as well as post-war restoration and improvement to the New Account, these were taken to be invested in kind or businesses transferred to establish Second Companies on April 1, 1950. Liabilities in the Old Account mainly resulting from causes prior to the designated hour were left to the dissolution and liquidation process of Old Nippon Steel. As a result, among the assets of Yawata, Wanishi, Kamaishi, Fuji and Hirohata possessed by Old Nippon Steel, Yawata Iron & Steel Corporation succeeded the assets, businesses, board and employees of the Yawata Steel Works, while those of the other four steel works were succeeded by Fuji Iron & Steel Corporation.

F. The governments of the Republic of Korea and Japan began discussing normalization of diplomatic relations and post-war compensation at the end of 1951. Finally, on June 22, 1965, the "Treaty on Basic Relations between the Republic of Korea and Japan for the Normalization of Diplomatic Relations" and one of its annexed agreements, "Agreement between the Republic of Korea and Japan Concerning the Settlement of Problems in Regard to Property and Claims and Economic Cooperation ('Claims Agreement')" were concluded. Article 1 of the Claims Agreement stated that Japan would provide Korea with $300 million grant within a period of ten years and $200 million in loans. Article 2 further provided:

> 1. The High Contracting Parties confirm that the problems concerning property, rights, and interests of the two High Contracting Parties and their peoples (including juridical persons) and the claims between the High Contracting Parties and between their peoples, including those stipulated in Article IV(a) of the Peace Treaty with Japan signed at the city of San Francisco on September 8, 1951, have been settled completely and finally.
>
> 3. As a condition to comply with the provisions of paragraph 2 above, no claims shall be made with respect to the measures relating to the property, rights, and interests of either High Contracting Party and its people which were brought under the control of the other High Contracting Party on the date of the signing of the present Agreement, or to all the claims of either High Contracting Party and its people arising from the causes which occurred prior to that date.

The Agreed Minutes to the Claims Agreement (1) stated concerning Article 2 of the above as follows:

> (a) "Property, rights and interests" was understood to refer to all types of actual rights whose property values were recognized by law.
> (e) It was agreed that the measures to be taken pursuant to paragraph 3 referred to domestic measures in each state that would be taken in order to resolve the problems concerning property, rights, and interests of the two High Contracting Parties and their peoples stated in paragraph 1.
> (g) The problems concerning property, rights, and interests of the two states and their peoples and the claims between them that has been completely and finally settled, as referred to in (I) of this article includes all claims that are within the scope of the "Outline of the Property and Claims Settlement Agreement between Korea and Japan" (hereafter "the eight items") proposed by Korea at the Korea-Japan summit, thereby confirming that no claims could be made concerning the eight items.

Also included in the eight items identified in the Agreed Minutes above were outstanding receivables of the drafted Koreans, restitution of harm inflicted by war upon drafted Koreans, and the claims of Koreans against Japanese natural persons or organizations.

Pursuant to the conclusion of the above Claims Agreement, Japan enacted Law no. 144, "Law on the Measures concerning the Property Rights of the Republic of Korea pursuant to the Execution of the Agreement between the Republic of Korea and Japan Concerning the Settlement of Problems in Regard to Property and Claims and Economic Cooperation Article 2 (hereinafter "Property Rights Measures Law")" on December 17, 1965. The main point of this law was that the claims and security rights of the Republic of Korea and its peoples against Japan and its peoples, otherwise qualifying as property rights and concerns according to Claims Agreement Article 2, were deemed extinguished as of June 22, 1965.

G. Plaintiffs Yeo and Shin instituted a compensation suit against the Defendant for payment of wages and unlawful acts on December 24, 1997 in the Osaka District Court of Japan. On March 27, 2001, the court dismissed the suit. On November 19, 2002, the Osaka High Court dismissed the appeal, and the above suit was decided on October 9, 2003 (hereinafter "Japanese litigation" or "Japanese decisions"). Now, the Plaintiffs instituted this suit against the Defendant for the payment of compensation for its unlawful acts and violation of international law on February 28, 2005 in the Seoul Central District Court of Korea after the Japanese litigation was concluded. Their causes of the claim were identical to those asserted by Plaintiffs Yeo and Shin in the Japanese litigation.

H. Prior to the filing of this suit by the Plaintiffs, the Korean government released documents related to the Claims Agreement; and after the suit was filed, it launched the Joint Government-Civic Committee for the Follow-up Measures after the Release of Documents from the Korea-Japan Summit Meeting (joint government-civic committee) on August 26, 2005. It formally announced through the committee that "the Claims Agreement was aimed at resolving the financial and civil debt/credit relationship between Korea and Japan based on Article 4 of the San Francisco Peace Treaty. Regarding "crimes against humanity," where state authorities like the Japanese government may have been involved (i.e. comfort women issue), the Korean government also announced that Japan's legal responsibility had not been resolved because the claims cannot be deemed to have been settled by the Agreement; and that the issues of Koreans in Sakhalin and atomic bomb victims were not included in the Claims Agreement."

...

3. Judgment on the Appeals of Plaintiffs Yeo and Shin

Civil Procedure Act Article 217(3) provides, as one of the criteria for acknowledging the effect of foreign judgments, that such judgment does not violate "the good morals and other social order" of the Republic of Korea. Acknowledging the effect of foreign decisions, or determining whether the result of such recognition violates "the good morals and other social order" of Korea, must be determined by judging its effect on the fundamental moral convictions and social order that we seek to protect at that point in time in light of the issues dealt with in the foreign decision and their relevance to Korea. At the same time, not only the order, but also the reasoning of the foreign decision and the result of recognizing such a decision must be examined as a whole.

According to the evidence lawfully admitted by the lower court, the Japanese decision considered Plaintiffs Yeo and Shin as Japanese nationals at the time when their claims came into existence, by considering Korea, their place of residence, as part of Japanese territory. The law applicable to the claims of the above Plaintiffs was not decided from an international legal perspective in consideration of its foreign elements but Japanese law was applied from the outset. Concerning the circumstances surrounding the annexation of Korea by Japan, it premised, "Chosun was under the rule of Japan after the conclusion of the Annexation Treaty of 1910" and stated concerning the circumstances surrounding the conscription of the Plaintiffs, "Even if it were to be recognized that the Japanese government and the Japanese Government-General of Korea at the time promoted aggressive policies for mobilizing low-grade laborers during the war, the above Plaintiffs all responded to the labor recruitment and enlisted by their own volition until they came to work at the Osaka Iron Works. They were not forcefully taken against their will." The assertions of the Plaintiffs, that, "In September 1943, when the above Plaintiffs had applied, conscription pursuant to the guidelines for importing Chosun people to Japan was executed by recruiters (補導員) who secured the target number of laborers in a short period of time with the cooperation of regional administrative institutions, police and the Chosun Labor Association. The mobilized Chosun laborers were then guided by the recruiters of their respective businesses to Japan. This was implemented under the plans of the Department of Health and Human Services of the Japanese government and the Japanese Government-General of Korea to place a Chosun labor force into major enterprises to be incorporated into production organizations. These measures were a *de facto* forced taking or conscription," were not accepted. Further, the Japanese Decisions accepted the partial assertions of the Plaintiffs such as Old Nippon Steel unlawfully placing them in forced labor unlike their advertisements, and not paying the wages of the Plaintiffs nor performing the duty of occupational safety as *de facto* employers. Yet it also held that the liabilities of Old Nippon Steel were not succeeded by the Defendant because it had an independent legal personality; and even if this were not true, their claims were extinguished by the 1965 Claims Agreement between Korea and Japan, as well as Japan's Property Rights Measures Law, thereby dismissing the Plaintiffs' claims.

Thus, the reasoning of the Japanese Decision was premised on a normative understanding that Japan's colonial rule over Korea and its people was lawful, so that the application of National Mobilization Law and National Conscription Order to the above Plaintiffs was deemed valid.

However, the founding Constitution of the Republic of Korea provides in the Preamble, "We, the people of Korea, proud of a resplendent history and traditions dating from time immemorial, upholding the cause of the Independence Movement of 1 March 1919 establishing the Republic of Korea and declaring the great spirit of independence to the world, hereby establish an independent democratic nation"; while Supplementary Provision Article 100 states, "The current law is effective as long as it does not conflict with the provisions of this Constitution"; and Article 101 of the same provides, "The National Assembly enacting this Constitution may also legislate special laws punishing malicious crimes against the peoples committed prior to August 15 of the 4,278th year of Dangun." The current Constitution also states in the Preamble, "We, the people of Korea, proud of a resplendent history and traditions dating from time immemorial, upholding the cause of the Provisional Republic of Korea Government born of the Independence Movement of 1 March 1919 and the democratic ideals of the uprising on 19 April 1960 against injustice." In light of these constitutional provisions, Japan's control over the Korean Peninsula during the Japanese occupation period was an unlawful possession by force; and any legal interests resulting from such unlawful control, which is not compatible with the spirit of the Constitution of Korea, cannot be recognized as being effective. Then, because the reasoning of the Japanese decision directly contravenes the core value of the Korean Constitution which considers the conscription during Japanese occupation as unlawful, acknowledgement of such a decision of the Japanese court clearly violates "the good morals and other social order" of Korea. Therefore, we cannot acknowledge the effect of the Japanese decision in Korea.

On the contrary, however, the original court immediately dismissed the Plaintiffs' suit for *res judicata* based on the premise that acknowledging the effect of Japanese decisions would not violate "the good morals and other social order" of Korea and that they could not issue a judgment inconsistent with that of the Japanese courts. It thus did not try the case from an independent perspective of the Korean courts. Such a decision of the lower court is unlawful in that its misinterpretation of the law concerning acknowledgement of foreign decisions affected its decision. Therefore, the appeal of the Plaintiffs in pointing this out has merit.

4. Judgment on the Causes for Appeal of Plaintiffs Lee and Kim

...

B. Whether the Claims of the Plaintiffs were Extinguished by the Claims Agreement.

(1) In addition to the above judgment, the lower court held that the compensation claims of the Defendants based on unlawful acts under national law were extinguished by completion of prescription, to which the Plaintiffs raised their appeal claiming that the lower court misinterpreted the law concerning negative prescription. In judging this cause for appeal, a prerequisite requirement is whether the claims of the Plaintiffs were indeed extinguished by the Claims Agreement.

(2) The Claims Agreement was not a negotiation over the compensation for Japanese colonization. It was rather a political agreement aimed at resolving the financial and civil debt/credit relationship between Korea and Japan based on Article 4 of the San Francisco Peace Treaty. The fact that the economic cooperative funds provided by the Japanese government to the Korean government pursuant to Article 1 of the Claims Agreement does not appear to resolve the issue of rights based on Article 2 nor have a legal compensatory relationship to the same; and the fact that in the process of negotiating the Claims Agreement, the Japanese government fundamentally denied legal reparations for forced labor without having even recognized the unlawfulness of its colonial rule, following which the two governments of Korea and Japan were unable to reach a consensus concerning the nature of Japanese control over the Korean

Peninsula; and the fact that it is difficult to conclude that in such a situation, the claim to compensation for crimes against humanity involving the state powers of Japan or the crimes directly connected to its colonial rule were included in the scope of application of the Claims Agreement show that not only were the individual rights to claim of compensation of the above Plaintiffs not extinguished by the Claims Agreement, but it is also duly proper to conclude that the right to diplomatic protection of Korea was also not abandoned.

Further, it contravenes the principles of contemporary law to consider it possible for a state to conclude a treaty that does not stop at abandoning its right to diplomatic protection but proceeds to directly extinguish the individual rights of its nationals having a legal personality independent of its state without their consent. Even if it were to be permissible under international law for a state to extinguish individual rights to the claims of its nationals through treaty, it would not be possible to conclude that a treaty can extinguish not only a state's right to diplomatic protection but also the people's individual rights without clear provisions in the treaty considering that a state and its peoples are of independent legal subjects. The Claims Agreement does not have sufficient evidence to show that there was a consensus of the two governments concerning the extinction of individual rights to claims; and the fact that immediately following the conclusion of the Claims Agreement, Japan domestically enacted a Property Rights Measures Law regarding the rights of Korean peoples against Japan and its peoples, is premised on the fact that the Claims Agreement alone does not extinguish individual rights to the claims of the Korean people. Taking these points into consideration, even if the claims of the above Plaintiffs were to be included within the scope of application of the Claims Agreement, the individual rights themselves cannot be seen as automatically being extinguished by the Claims Agreement alone. Rather, the Claims Agreement would abandon Korea's rights to diplomatic protection concerning the rights to claims, so that even if such rights were to be extinguished in Japan through its domestic measures, Korea would be unable to exercise its rights (or be at loss of measures) to diplomatically protect them.

(3) Therefore, because the compensation claims of the above Plaintiffs against the Defendant pursuant to its unlawful acts were not extinguished by the Claims Agreement, the above Plaintiffs can exercise such rights to claims against the Defendant.

...

5. Conclusion

Therefore, the original verdict is vacated, (The Plaintiffs claimed a violation of international law and national law as causes for their compensation claim in this case. The lower court appears to have seen this as a separate subject matter, but as this ought to have been seen as a different method of raising issue in their claim of compensation rather than as an independent subject-matter. Thus, the entire decision of the lower court is vacated.) and the case is remanded and to be retried consistent with the opinion of the Supreme Court.

Presiding Justice Lee, In-bok
Chief Justice Kim, Nung-hwan
Justice Ahn, Dai-hee
Justice Park, Byoung-dae

B. Comfort Women Case

(1) *Constitutionality of Nonfeasance under Article 3 of the Agreement between the Republic of Korea and Japan Concerning the Settlement of Problems in Regard to Property and Claims and Economic Cooperation* (2006 Heonma 788 Decision, issued August 30, 2011 [Const. Ct.])

Case no. 2006 Heon-ma 788
August 30, 2011

Issue
Whether the Respondent's failure to resolve the conflict of interpretation between the Republic of Korea and Japan regarding the issue of Petitioners' reparations claim against the state of Japan by Japanese Comfort Women (military sex slaves) was extinguished pursuant to Article 2 paragraph 1 of the 'Agreement between the Republic of Korea and Japan Concerning the Settlement of Problems in Regard to Property and Claims and Economic Cooperation' (hereafter 'the Agreement') according to the procedure provided for in Article 3 of the above Agreement is unconstitutional?

Summary of Decision
In light of the language of the Preamble and Articles 2(2) and 10 of the Constitution and Article 3 of the Agreement, the Respondent's duty to pursue dispute resolution procedures pursuant to Article 3 of the Agreement is based upon a constitutional petition to protect and to endeavor to realize the reparations claim of its people, whose human dignity and worth have been gravely violated by the systematic and continued crimes committed by the state of Japan. If the duty is not performed, there is the possibility of the Petitioners' fundamental rights being gravely infringed upon; therefore, the Respondent's duty to act can be derived from the Constitution, an instance in which the duty is specifically provided for by law.

More specifically, the government did not commit acts that directly violated the fundamental rights of the Japanese Comfort Women. However, it cannot be denied that the Government had a specific obligation to act in order to remove any impediments to these reparations claims, in particular its failure to clarify the precise content of the Agreement in referring to "all claims." This failure of clarification caused an impediment to the realization of the reparations claims against Japan.

The question is whether the Respondent's nonfeasance—in not pursuing such a dispute resolution procedure—infringed upon the fundamental rights of the Petitioners. In determining whether this inaction can be seen as being properly within the scope of discretion attached to the rights of the state institution, several factors must be considered together: the urgency of the threat of the violation, the possibility of remedying the fundamental rights, and whether the decision to act would indeed be against national interest.

Regarding the crimes against humanity committed on a widespread scale by the state of Japan, the reparations claim of the Comfort Women against Japan is not limited to property rights guaranteed by the Constitution. Its realization also represents the *ex post facto* restoration of the human dignity and worth and personal freedom that was unmercifully and continuously violated. Therefore, the fundamental rights being infringed upon by the Respondent's failure to act are very important. Furthermore, the Comfort Women have all advanced in age; so any more delay in time may make it impossible to realize their reparations claim in order to remedy an historical injustice and to restore their violated human dignity and worth. Thus, the urgency of remedying the violation of their fundamental rights is clear; and when considering the circumstances and the domestic and international activities at the time the Agreement was concluded the possibility of remedy is certainly not trivial. Even taking into consideration the particular nature of diplomacy, which requires strategic decisions based on an understanding of international politics, we cannot agree that the vague and abstract reasons of the "possibility of developing into exhaustive arguments" or "uncomfortable foreign relations," as asserted by the Respondent as reasons for its nonperformance, are justifiable. We also disagree that any national interest exists that requires greater consideration than the remedy of Petitioners who are in danger of having their fundamental rights violated.

When taken into consideration altogether, pursuing dispute resolution procedures under Article 3 of the Agreement is the proper exercise of the discretionary powers within the limited rights of the state institution; and as Respondent's nonfeasance has resulted in a grave infringement of the Petitioners' fundamental rights, and is thus unconstitutional.

Separate Concurring Opinion of Justice Cho, Dae Hyeon

In addition to the majority opinion of the court, the court should also declare the Republic of Korea liable for the damages incurred by the Petitioners and be responsible for complete compensation as the Petitioners were unable to exercise their reparations claim against the state of Japan due to the Agreement in question.

Dissenting opinion of Justices Lee, Kang-Kook; Min, Hyeong-Ki; and Lee, Dong-Heub
For a Constitutional complaint regarding nonfeasance of administrative powers to be legitimate, a "duty to act deriving from the Constitution" must be specifically defined for the agent exercising governmental authority. The above duty to act can be derived from the following: the substance of the Constitution, its interpretation, and provisions of the law.

First, Article 10 of the Constitution establishes the duty to guarantee the human rights of its nationals, while Article 2(2) establishes the duty to protect Korean nationals residing overseas, and the Preamble declares a general yet abstract duty towards the people or state's basic order of values. A specific duty to act for its nationals cannot be derived from these provisions, which was already previously held to be so by this Court.

Next, the Republic of Korea and the state of Japan, as parties to the Agreement at issue, concluded a treaty premised on the liability against each other; therefore, Article 3 of the above Agreement cannot be seen as deriving "a duty for the government to act for the Petitioners." Furthermore, Article 3 does not detail any "obligatory" content; and while there is a precedent establishing that diplomatic settlement and request for arbitration, as provided in the above Article 3, falls under the "diplomatic discretion" of the government (Constitutional Court Decision of Mar. 30, 2000, 98 Heon-ma 206), the majority opinion ultimately counters the above precedent.

"Settlement through diplomatic channels," as provided for in Article 3 of the Agreement, is a highly political domain for which an objective legal standard is difficult to define such as the agent or method of implementation, and the degree and completion of such implementation. Thus, while it may be subject to judicial review of the Constitutional Court, it is an area requiring judicial restraint at the same time.

The fundamental rights of the Petitioners in this case, who were thoroughly deprived of human worth and value after being forcefully recruited by Japan as Comfort Women, desperately need to be remedied. To that end, we all earnestly hope for state endeavor in every possible way. However, the Respondent cannot be forced to seek diplomatic settlements by overstepping the boundaries of the Constitution, the regulations under the law, and the Constitutional interpretations of legal principles. This is the Constitutional limit placed on this Court by the principle of separation of powers.

...

Order
We find that the Respondent's nonfeasance in settling the interpretative dispute between the Republic of Korea and Japan pursuant to Article 3 of "Agreement between the Republic of Korea and Japan Concerning the Settlement of Problems in Regard to Property and Claims and Economic Cooperation," regarding the issue

of whether the reparations claims of the Petitioners against the state of Japan as Comfort Women was extinguished pursuant to Article 2(1) of the above Agreement, is unconstitutional.

Reasoning

1. Facts of the Case and Issue for Review

A. *Facts of the Case*

(1) The Petitioners are "Comfort Women" who were forcefully recruited by the Japanese to live lives of Comfort Women for soldiers and to suffer sexual abuse. Respondent is a state institution in charge of diplomacy, trade negotiations with other states and related responsibilities and adjustments, coordination of tasks relating to international relations, treaties and other international agreements, protection and support of overseas nationals, formation of policy regarding overseas nationals, and directing investigation and analysis services regarding international affairs.

(2) The Republic of Korea concluded the "Agreement between the Republic of Korea and Japan Concerning the Settlement of Problems in Regard to Property and Claims and Economic Cooperation" on June 22, 1965 (Treaty no. 172, hereafter "the Agreement").

(3) The Petitioners filed this case on July 5, 2006, to request a finding that the nonfeasance of the Respondent violated their fundamental rights and was therefore unconstitutional. More specifically, Japan denies compensation for the Petitioners by claiming that their reparations claim against the state of Japan as Comfort Women was been extinguished pursuant to Article 2(1) of the Agreement. On the other side, the Korean Government is of the position that the same right was not settled by the above Agreement, resulting in a conflict of interpretation between the two states. Thus, the Petitioners claim that the Respondent had the duty to take measures provided in Article 3 of the Agreement in order to settle the conflict of interpretation, but failed to do so.

B. *Issue under Review*

The issue under review in this case is whether the nonfeasance of the Respondent, in failing to settle the conflict of interpretation of Article 2(1) of the "Agreement between the Republic of Korea and Japan Concerning the Settlement of Problems in Regard to Property and Claims and Economic Cooperation," regarding the extinction of Petitioners' reparations claim against the state of Japan as Comfort Women pursuant to Article 3, violates the fundamental rights of the Petitioners.

The relevant provisions of the Agreement are as follows.

Relevant Provisions
Agreement between the Republic of Korea and Japan Concerning the Settlement of Problems in Regard to Property and Claims and Economic Cooperation (Treaty no. 172, signed June 22, 1965, entered into force Dec. 18, 1965)

The Republic of Korea and Japan,
Desiring to settle problems regarding the property of both countries and their peoples and the claims between both countries and between their peoples; and
Desiring to promote economic cooperation between the two countries,
Have agreed as follows:

Article 1
1. Japan shall supply the Republic of Korea with:
(a) Products of Japan and the services of Japanese people, free of charge, the total value of which will be so much in yen as shall be equivalent to three hundred million United States dollars ($300,000,000), at present computed at one hundred and eight billion yen (Y108,000,000,000), within a period of ten years of the date on which the present Agreement enters into force. The supply of products and services each year shall be limited to so much in yen as shall be equivalent to thirty million United States dollars ($30,000,000), at present computed at ten billion eight hundred million yen (Y10,800,000,000); when the supply of any one year falls short of this amount, the remainder shall be added to the amount for the next and subsequent years. However, the maximum amount supplied for any one year may be increased by agreement between the Governments of the High Contracting Parties.
(b) Long-term and low-interest loans up to so much in yen as shall be equivalent to two hundred million United States dollars ($200,000,000), at present computed at seventy-two billion yen (Y72,000,000,000), which are requested by the Government of the Republic of Korea and which will be covered by procuring the products of Japan and the services of Japanese people necessary for implementing the enterprises to be decided upon in accordance with arrangements to be concluded under paragraph 3 within a period of ten years of the date on which the present Agreement enters into force. These loans shall be extended by the Overseas Economic Cooperation Fund of Japan, and the Government of Japan shall take the necessary measures to enable the Fund to secure the funds for equal annual loans. The aforesaid supply and loans must serve the economic development of the Republic of Korea.
2. There shall be established a Joint Committee composed of representatives of the two Governments as an organ for consultation between them, with the power to

make recommendations on matters concerning the implementation of the present Agreement.

3. The two Governments of the High Contracting Parties shall take measures necessary for the implementation of this Article.

Article 2

1. The High Contracting Parties confirm that the problems concerning property, rights, and interests of the two High Contracting Parties and their peoples (including juridical persons) and the claims between the High Contracting Parties and between their peoples, including those stipulated in Article IV(a) of the Peace Treaty with Japan signed at the city of San Francisco on September 8, 1951, have been settled completely and finally.

2. The provisions of this Article shall not affect the following (excluding those which become the objects of special measures taken by either of the High Contracting Parties prior to the date of the signing of the present Agreement).

(a) The property, rights, and interests of the people of either High Contracting Party who have ever resided in the territory of the other High Contracting Party in the period between August 15, 1947, and the date of the signing of the present Agreement; and

(b) The property, rights, and interests of either High Contracting Party and its people, which were acquired or brought under the control of the other High Contracting Party in the course of ordinary contacts after August 15, 1945.

3. As a condition to comply with the provisions of paragraph 2 above, no claims shall be made with respect to the measures relating to the property, rights, and interests of either High Contracting Party and its people which were brought under the control of the other High Contracting Party on the date of the signing of the present Agreement, or to all the claims of either High Contracting Party and its people arising from the causes which occurred prior to that date.

Article 3

1. Any dispute between the High Contracting Parties concerning the interpretation or the implementation of this Agreement shall be settled primarily through diplomatic channels.

2. Any dispute which cannot be settled under the provision of paragraph 1 above shall be submitted for decision to an arbitral commission of three arbitrators; one to be appointed by the Government of each High Contracting Party within a period of thirty days from the date of receipt by the Government of either High Contracting Party from that of the other High Contracting Party of a note requesting arbitration of the dispute; and the third to be agreed upon by the two arbitrators so chosen or to be nominated by the Government of a third power, as agreed upon by the two arbitrators within a

further period of thirty days. However, the third arbitrator must not be a national of either High Contracting Party.
3. If, within the periods respectively referred to, the Government of either High Contracting Party fails to appoint an arbitrator, or the third arbitrator or the third nation is not agreed upon, the arbitral commission shall be composed of one arbitrator to be nominated by the Government of each of two nations respectively chosen by the Government of each High Contracting Party within a period of thirty days, and the third arbitrator to be nominated by the Government of a third power decided upon by agreement between the Governments so chosen.
4. The Governments of the High Contracting Parties shall accept decisions rendered by the arbitral commission established in accordance with the provisions of this Article.

Article 4
The present Agreement shall be ratified. The instruments of ratification shall be exchanged at Seoul as soon as possible. The present Agreement shall enter into force as from the date on which the instruments of ratification are exchanged.

2. Contention of the Parties

A. *Summary of the Petitioners' Assertions*

(1) Japan's violation of the Petitioners' human rights in making them sexual slaves, also in violation of international treaties such as '1921 International Convention for the Suppression of the Traffic in Women and Children,' and the 'Forced Labour Convention' {ILO C29}, were not part of the Agreement. What was settled by the Agreement was the Korean government's diplomatic protection of its nationals; therefore, the individual reparations claim of the peoples against the state of Japan was not waived.

However, the state of Japan asserts that the reparations claim has been extinguished pursuant to Article 2(1) of the Agreement, thereby denying its duty of legal reparations towards the Petitioners. On the other hand, the Korean government recognized on August 26, 2005 that Japan's liability regarding the issue of Comfort Women was not extinguished by Article 2(1) of the Agreement; thus there remains a conflict of interpretation between the Republic of Korea and Japan.

(2) Article 3 of the Agreement provides for settlement of dispute through diplomatic channels or arbitration in the case of dispute between the two countries concerning the interpretation or the implementation of this Agreement. In doing so, the obligation to settle disputes related to the interpretation of the above Agreement is placed on the contracting parties themselves; therefore, the Korean Government has the

duty to act in order to settle the dispute related to the interpretation of the above Agreement.

(3) Furthermore, the Korean Government has the duty to act pursuant to the Preamble of the Constitution indicating the succession to the cause of the Provisional Republic of Korea Government, Article 10 declaring the human worth and dignity and the duty of the State to guarantee the fundamental human rights of individuals, Article 23 regarding the guarantee of the right to property, the administrative principle of confidence protection as the contracting party to the Agreement at issue, as well as rights of citizens not enumerated in the Constitution pursuant to Article 37(1), such as diplomatic protection.

(4) Yet the Korean Government has not taken specific measures, i.e., diplomatic protection or steps of dispute resolution, to effectively guarantee the rights of the Petitioners. This failure to take administrative action violates the provisions of the Constitution.

B. *Summary of the Respondent's Assertions*

(1) A constitutional complaint regarding the nonfeasance of administrative power is permitted where, in spite of the fact that the agent exercising the fundamental rights can petition an administrative act or the exercise of governmental authority based upon a duty to act that is derived from the Constitution and specifically defined for the agent of governmental authority, such duty has been neglected. However, the Petitioners have not clarified what fundamental rights were violated by nonfeasance of the Respondent. The agent of the unlawful acts toward the Petitioners and subsequent responsibility belongs to the Japanese Government rather than the Korean Government; and diplomatic acts permit wide discretion on the part of the government. Therefore, a specific duty of state to act in order to settle dispute pursuant to the Agreement cannot be recognized.

Further, the Korean Government has been endeavoring for the welfare of the Petitioners as much as is in its power, even continuously raising this issue in the international community. Therefore, it cannot be concluded that there was a failure to act according to the duty provided for in Article 3(1) of the Agreement.

(2) Diplomatic protection being claimed by the Petitioners refers to the diplomatic act or other peaceful means of resolution that a state employs for its nationals, pursuant to its intrinsic power in relation to the damage incurred by an unlawful act of another state under international law. This power is attributed to the state; it is not a right that an individual can claim against its own government. Therefore, it cannot be determined to be a fundamental right under the Constitution.

Furthermore, the state has wide discretion regarding when and how to exercise diplomatic protection. Interpretation of Article 3 of the Agreement does not obligate the contracting party to submit all disputes regarding the interpretation and implementation of the Agreement to the arbitration panel. Therefore, the selection of method of dispute settlement pursuant to the Agreement should be determined in consideration of national interest; there is no legal duty to take specific diplomatic measures.

3. Background to the Case

Prior to making a decision on the case, we will first take a look at the background to this case and the overall circumstances.

A. *Circumstances at the Time of the Conclusion of the Agreement and Subsequent Process of Compensation*

(1) After the liberation of Korea, the Military Governor of the U.S. Army Forces in Korea declared Ordinance 33 on December 6, 1945, pursuant to which title to all Japanese property, private or public, within Korea would be vested in the Military Government of Korea. All such Japanese property was transferred to the Korean Government pursuant to the Initial Financial and Property Settlement Agreement between the U.S. and the Republic of Korea, which was effective on September 20, 1948 after the establishment of the Government of the Republic of Korea.

(2) In the San Francisco Peace Treaty concluded between the Allied Powers and Japan on September 8, 1951, the right to demand compensation was not granted to the Republic of Korea; rather, it provided in Article 4(a) that, in areas gaining independence from Japanese rule, "the disposition in Japan of property of such authorities and residents, and of claims, including debts, of such authorities and residents against Japan and its nationals, shall be the subject of special arrangements between Japan and such authorities." Article 4(b) stated, "Japan recognizes the validity of dispositions of property of Japan and Japanese nationals made by or pursuant to directives of the United States Military Government in any of the areas referred to in Articles 2 and 3."

(3) Pursuant to the aims of Article 4(a), the Republic of Korea and its people, and the state of Japan and its people, in order to settle the property debts, held the first Korea-Japan summit meeting on February 15, 1952, following a preliminary conference of October 21, 1951. Since the start of such meetings for the normalization of diplomatic relations between the two nations, there have been regular sessions and scores of preliminary, political, and subcommittee conferences, resulting in four side agreements including the Agreement in this case of June 22, 1965; Fisheries Agreement; Agreement

between the Republic of Korea and Japan concerning the Legal Status and Treatment of the Korean Residents in Japan; Agreement concerning Cultural Assets and Cultural Cooperation between the Republic of Korea and Japan.

(4) According to the 'Commentary to the Claims' submitted by the Respondent, the Korean Government, at the time of the first Korea-Japan Conference (Feb. 15 ~ Apr. 25, 1952), proposed the 'Outline of the Property and Claims Settlement Agreement between Korea and Japan' (hereafter "the eight items"). The items were: 1) Return of old books, art work, antiquities and other national treasures, map originals, and silver and gold; 2) Repayment of liabilities of the Japanese Government towards Chosun Government General as of August 9, 1945; 3) Return of the money transferred from Korea after August 9, 1945; 4) Restoration of property in Japan, belonging to organizations whose headquarters or main offices are in Korea as of August 9, 1945; 5) Restitution of the claims of Korean organizations or natural persons against Japan and its people of their Government bonds, public bonds, Japanese bank notes, outstanding receivables of the drafted Koreans, and other claims; 6) Legal recognition of stocks of Japanese organizations or any other securities possessed by Korean organizations or natural persons; 7) Restitution of faults arising from the above property or rights claims; 8) Return and payment of the above must commence immediately after the establishment of the Agreement and be terminated within at least six months.

(5) The first conference fell through due to Japan's property claims against Korea in response to the eight items claimed above. The continued differences regarding the following issues of Dokdo and the Peace Line, and the improper remark of the Japanese representative Kubota (久保田), stating that "Japan's 36 years of rule over Korea was beneficial to Korea," in addition to the political situations of both states delayed any practical discussion regarding the claims until the 4th Korea-Japan conference.

(6) It was not until the 5th Korea-Japan conference (Oct. 25, 1960–May 15, 1961) that actual discussion over the eight items took place. Japan's position regarding the eight items was as follows: Regarding item 1, the removal of silver and gold were done under lawful procedures, and therefore Korea has no legal basis for their return. Regarding items 2, 3, and 4, the property over which Korea can claim possession is limited to that following the declaration of Ordinance 33 of the Military Governor of the U.S. Army Forces in Korea on December 6, 1945. Regarding item 5, Japan strongly opposed Korea raising issues of compensation for personal injury and demanded that Korea provide thorough evidence, e.g., specific drafting, drafted numbers, and other evidentiary material. The discussion over the first five of the eight items continued in this manner in the Rights Committee at the 5th Conference until it was suspended by coup d'état on May 16, 1961. This only confirmed the fundamental differences in perception and failed to actually close the gap between their positions.

(7) Once the 6th conference resumed on October 20, 1961, a political approach was sought, since detailed discussion of the claims was time-consuming and a resolution was still remote. Following the meeting of Chung Hee Park and Ikeda on November 22, 1961, Korea's demand and Japan's offer was informally exchanged at the meeting of the foreign ministers in March of 1962. As a result, the difference between the two countries was identified, with Korea demanding $700 million of pure repayment and Japan offering a $74,000 payment and $200 million loan.

(8) In response, Japan first proposed to raise the sum by utilizing economic cooperation in the form of grants and loans in exchange for abandoning the right to claims. This proposal was made because, should the pure repayment on the claims issue take place, it would not only require a complicated analysis of the legal and factual relevance, but it would also reduce the amount by limiting its applicability to the area below the 38th parallel. In that case, Korea would not be able to consent to it. Korea first responded by saying that, while it ought to receive pure repayment as compensation for the claims, it would broaden its perspective and seek to settle the issue with repayment and grants. Korea then modified its position by proposing that, within the boundaries of settling the claims, the payment would take the form of pure repayment and grants, without indicating the precise amount for each category.

(9) Afterwards, Kim Jong-pil, chief of the Korean Central Intelligence Agency, met with Japanese Prime Minister Ikeda and twice with Japanese Foreign Minister Ohira. At the second meeting with Foreign Minister Ohira on November 12, 1962, the two agreed principally to an agreement to be proposed to the two governments regarding the settlement sum, its categories, and conditions. Following a process of adjustment, Foreign Ministers Lee Dong-won and Siina agreed to the "Agreement between Korea and Japan concerning the Settlement of Claims and Economic Cooperation" at the 7th Korea-Japan Conference on April 3, 1965. And on June 22, 1965, the Agreement was concluded, under which Japan would make payments to Korea in the form of grants and loans without specifying the category. The Agreement provided that the problems concerning property, rights, and interests of the two Contracting Parties and their peoples (including juridical persons), and the claims between the Contracting Parties and their peoples, were settled completely and finally.

(10) The Korean Government then passed the 'Act on the Management and Usage of Settlement Funds' on February 19, 1966 (repealed by Law no. 3613 on Dec. 31, 1982) to provide a legal basis for private compensation among grants. Then on January 19, 1971, it passed the 'Act Concerning Reporting of Civil Claims against Japan' (repealed by Law no. 3614 on Dec. 31, 1982) and received requests for compensation. However, requests were limited to those deceased after forced conscription by the Japanese and to holders of civil claims, i.e., private bonds or bank accounts that came under debate

during the conference as civil claimants against Japan. Finally, the 'Act Concerning Compensation of Civil Claims against Japan' (repealed by Law no. 3614 on Dec. 31, 1982) was passed on December 21, 1974, pursuant to which a total of KRW 9,187,693,000 was paid out from July 1, 1975 to June 30, 1977.

(11) The issue of Comfort Women was not discussed at all over the duration of the normalization conferences leading up to the conclusion of this Agreement, nor was it included in the eight items listed above. Even after the conclusion of the Agreement, the issue was not included in the compensation pursuant to legislative measures.

B. *Raising the Issue of Comfort Women and Its Progress*

(1) With the launching of the Korean Council for the Women Drafted for Military Sexual Slavery by Japan on November 16, 1990, and the public press conference of former Comfort Woman Kim (deceased December 1997) in August 1991, the issue of Comfort Women was finally raised in earnest.

(2) The Japanese Government had denied all responsibility, issuing statements that suggested that Comfort Women were "prostitutes" brought along by private businessmen following the army. However, when Yoshimi Yoshiaki (吉見義明), then professor at Chuo University, discovered six official documents in January of 1992 that uncovered the military's direct role in drafting Comfort Women, Japan had to drastically change its position.

(3) With the appearance of the victim, the discovery of related documents, and public awareness both domestically and abroad, the Japanese Government began conducting a fact-finding study on the issue. In July 1992, it announced its first results, recognizing government involvement in the issue of Comfort Women, but asserting that there was no evidence of the military's role in forcing women into slavery. On August 4, 1993, together with its second report, it acknowledged the involvement of the Japanese military and authorities, as well as the forced drafting and fatigue duty. Chief Cabinet Secretary Yohei Kono released a statement recognizing the grave violation of their human rights and expressing apologies.

(4) Comfort stations were first established by the Japanese navy as a measure to prevent instances of rape that resulted in the contraction of venereal diseases and engendered opposition of the local people during the 1932 Shanghai Uprising. With a mass dispatch of soldiers to China in the Sino-Japanese War beginning in July 1937, the Japanese army began to set up comfort stations in the conquered areas. The number of stations increased after the Nanking Massacre of December 1937. Besides providing a "mental consolation" to the soldiers, comfort stations were installed in order to pacify

the soldiers' discontent, to stir up morale, and to prevent desertion as the war dragged on. Their purpose was also to prevent the leaking of classified information by "hiring" women from colonies who could not speak Japanese.

From 1941, and during the course of the Asia-Pacific War, Japan installed comfort stations in their conquered territories in Southeast Asia and the Pacific. As identified in official documents, comfort stations were installed in regions invaded by Japan, e.g., Chosun, China, Hong Kong, Macau, and the Philippines. The number of Comfort Women is estimated to have been between 80,000 and 100,000, with some estimates reaching 200,000. 80% of the women were from Chosun, while others came from the Philippines, China, Taiwan, and the Netherlands.

(5) The Korean Government passed the 'Act on Livelihood Stability for Sexual Slavery Victims Drafted for the Japanese Imperial Army under the Japanese Colonial Rule (Law No. 4565)' on June 11, 1993, which began to provide the Comfort Women with living subsidies. However, the Japanese Government maintained that compensation for Comfort Women was already settled by the Agreement, and thus it could not take any new legal measures. On August 31, 1994, it announced that, in view of its moral responsibility for the seriously stained honor and dignity of the Comfort Women, it would deliver individual compensation or resettlement funds from humanitarian grounds and would seek to establish an Asian Women's Fund at the private level (rather than the government level).

(6) The Comfort Women and support groups in Korea, Taiwan, etc. perceived the substance of the Asian Women's Fund to be an evasion of the responsibilities of the Japanese Government. They declared their objections early on towards the Fund, which viewed the Comfort Women as objects of humanitarian philanthropy rather than just compensation. When its demand to suspend the activities of the Asian Women's Fund was refused by the Japanese Government, the Korean Government paid out to the victims a lump sum of KRW 43,000,000, an amount equivalent to that which Fund was to grant. The sum came from the government budget and private donations, under the condition that the recipients would not receive any money from the Asian Women's Fund.

(7) On December 6, 1991, Kim and 9 other Comfort Women filed a lawsuit against Japan for compensation of the victims of the Asia-Pacific War. Unfortunately, the case was closed when the Japanese Supreme Court rejected their appeal on November 29, 2004. During the trial, the Tokyo High Court held that, while the Plaintiffs may possibly have obtained compensation based on the duty of occupational safety, in addition to the unlawful acts themselves, all claims were extinguished pursuant to Article 2(3) of the Agreement regarding properties, rights, and claims. In the Pusan Comfort

Women and Women's Labor Corps Members Apology and Compensation case filed on December 25, 1992, the Plaintiffs were partially successful at the trial court level. However, this decision was overturned on appeal and ultimately nullified by the Supreme Court on March 25, 2003. Even the Comfort Women Apology and Compensation case filed on April 5, 1993 by Japanese-Korean Shindo Song was ultimately rejected by the Supreme Court on March 28, 2003.

(8) Certain documents from the Korea-Japan summit meeting of February 13, 2004 were publicized, pursuant to a release order from the joint government-civic committee issued on August 26, 2005. In these documents, the Korean Government announced that the Agreement in this case was aimed at resolving the financial and civil debt/credit relationship between Korea and Japan based on Article 4 of the San Francisco Peace Treaty. Regarding the "crimes against humanity," where state authorities like the Japanese Government may be involved (i.e. Comfort Women issue), the Korean Government also announced that Japan's legal responsibility had not been resolved because the claims cannot be deemed to have been settled by the Agreement.

Two resolutions were passed that called for the resolution of the Comfort Women issue, one from the U.S. House of Representatives and one from the Working Group for the 2008 Universal Periodic Review of the U.N. Human Rights Commission. However, as seen below, the Japanese Government responded to these resolutions by asserting that the issue was already fully settled through (1) an apology made in Kono's statement, (2) the settlement of legal issues through the Agreement in this case, and (3) the activities of the Asia Women's Fund.

(9) Such attitude and the measures taken by the Japanese Government were not welcomed by victims or by the international community. The U.N. Sub-commission on Prevention of Discrimination and Protection of Minorities (hereinafter "Sub-commission on Minorities") has been continuously studying the issue of Comfort Women. On January 4, 1996, its first report, titled "Coomaraswamy Report," confirmed that the human rights violations inflicted upon the forcefully drafted Comfort Women of World War II were clearly violations of international law. The report also made six recommendations for Japan, including: state compensation, punishment of those responsible, release of all documents preserved by the government, formal written apology, and amendment of textbooks. On April 19, 1996, the report was adopted at the 52nd U.N. Human Rights Commission.

On August 12, 1998, the Sub-commission on Minorities presented and adopted a second report from the Special Rapporteur Gay McDougall, which supplemented the above Coomaraswamy Report in calling for legal compensation by Japan and the punishment of those responsible. The "McDougall Report" had four objectives: (1) it clearly identified the comfort stations as examples of sexual slavery, emphasizing its enforced nature by calling them rape centers" or "rape camps;" (2) it asserted that the search of any living war criminals in emphasizing the punishment of those responsible; (3) it proposed an active intervention on the part of the U.N. (e.g. requesting reports from the Government of Japan at least twice a year detailing the progress that has been made; cooperation between the U.N. High Commissioner for Human Rights and the Government of Japan to punish those responsible and establish a panel to determine adequate compensation); and (4) it emphasized that these steps should be taken as quickly as possible in light of the advancing age of the Comfort Women.

(10) A movement began to delete the Comfort Women issue from textbooks and to modify Kono's statement during the conservative Koizumi and Abe administrations. In response, individual states began to deal with the situation more directly, as seen below.

On July 30, 2007, the U.S. House of Representatives unanimously adopted the Comfort Women Resolution, which mainly stated that: (1) the Government of Japan should formally acknowledge, apologize, and accept historical responsibility in a clear and unequivocal manner for its Imperial Armed Force's coercion of young women into sexual slavery, known to the world as 'Comfort Women', during its colonial and wartime occupation of Asia and the Pacific Islands from the 1930s through the duration of World War II; (2) clearly and publicly refute any claims that the sexual enslavement and trafficking of the 'Comfort Women' for the Japanese Imperial Armed Forces never occurred; and (3) educate current and future generations about this horrible crime, while following the recommendations of the international community with respect to the Comfort Women.

This act was followed by the adoption of Parliamentary resolutions in the Netherlands House of Representatives (November 8, 2007), Canada House of Commons (November 28, 2007), and the European Parliament (December 13, 2007), all calling for a formal apology from the Japanese Government, an acknowledgement of historical and legal responsibility, compensation for the victims, and education of future generations regarding the atrocity committed to more than 200,000 women forcefully drafted as Comfort Women.

(11) On June 12, 2008, the U.N. Human Rights Council, in its periodic review of Japan's human rights, formally adopted the Working Group Report carrying recommendations and inquiries of individual states regarding the issue of Comfort Women. On October 30, 2008 in Geneva, the U.N. Human Rights Committee also presented the evaluation report related to human rights in Japan and, for the first time, recommended the Japanese Government acknowledge legal responsibility for the Comfort Women issue and apologize in a manner acceptable to a majority of the victims.

(12) In Korea, a Resolution calling for formal apology and compensation for the restoration of the honor of Comfort Women was passed in the plenary session of the National Assembly on October 27, 2008 by a vote of 260 to 1. Starting with Daegu Metropolitan Council, from July 2009 through March 2011, 46 local councils nationwide have adopted resolutions urging the settlement of the Comfort Women issue. Furthermore, on December 11, 2010, the Korean and Japanese Bar Associations pronounced a joint statement regarding the issue, which (1) confirmed that the inconsistent interpretation and response by the two Governments regarding the substance and scope of the complete settlement provision of the Agreement interferes with determining an adequate remedy for the victims and aggravates mistrust; and (2) confirmed that legislation for the resolution of the Comfort Women issue, including an apology and monetary compensation, must be promptly processed by the Japanese Government and its Congress. These resolutions and statements urged the resolution of the issue by the Japanese Government through legislation before more victims pass away, demanding more aggressive diplomatic policies, even towards the Korean Government.

4. Judgment of the Elements

...

B. *Respondent's Duty to Act*

If there is no duty to act for government agent, this constitutional complaint becomes illegitimate. Therefore, we will now analyze whether this duty to act exists for the Respondent in this case.

The Agreement in this case is a treaty that was concluded and promulgated under the Constitution; therefore, pursuant to Article 6(1), it has the same effect as domestic law. However, Article 3(1) of the Agreement states, "Any dispute between the High Contracting Parties concerning the interpretation or the implementation of this Agreement shall be settled primarily through diplomatic channels." Paragraph 2 also provides, "Any dispute which cannot be settled under the provision of paragraph 1 above shall be submitted for decision to an arbitral commission of three arbitrators; one to be appointed by the Government of each High Contracting Party within a period of thirty days from the date of receipt by the Government of either High Contracting Party from that of the other High Contracting Party of a note requesting arbitration of the dispute; and the third to be agreed upon by the two arbitrators so chosen or to be nominated by the Government of a third power as agreed upon by the two arbitrators within a further period of thirty days. However, the third arbitrator must not be a national of either High Contracting Party."

According to the above dispute resolution clause, should there be a conflict in the interpretation of the Agreement between Korea and Japan, the respective governments are to seek resolution first through diplomatic channels and then through arbitration.

We will discuss whether this falls under the above situation where "the government agent's duty to act is specifically provided for in the law".

Petitioners, who were forcefully recruited, sexually abused, and forced to live the life of Comfort Women by the Japanese filed for reparations against the state of Japan. Japan, however, has denied compensation to Petitioners, asserting that such claims have been entirely extinguished by the Agreement in this case. Yet, the Korean Government has taken the position that the claims of the Petitioners were not settled by the Agreement and thus continue to exist; therefore, a dispute has arisen between Korean and Japan regarding the interpretation of the Agreement.

Article 10 of the Korean Constitution states, "All citizens are assured of human worth and dignity, and have the right to pursue happiness. It is the duty of the State to confirm and guarantee the fundamental and inviolable human rights of individuals." Here, human worth is the greatest constitutional value and state norm, binding all national institutions and signifying that the state has a duty to realize human worth. Therefore, human worth is not only a limit to state power, a mechanism by which individuals are protected from state violations, but it is also a 'task of state power,' for which the state bears the duty to protect its citizens when their human worth is threatened by third persons.

The Constitution further provides in Article 2(2) that "It is the duty of the State to protect citizens residing abroad as prescribed by law." Regarding this duty to protect citizens abroad, the Constitutional Court has already recognized that a state's duty to protect its citizens abroad is derived from the Constitution holding, "Pursuant to the State's duty to protect citizens residing abroad provided in Article 2(2) of the Constitution, the protection that citizens receive while residing abroad signifies support in the legal, cultural, educational and other domain that is specifically determined by law in political consideration of a state's citizens and its practice of diplomatic protection. This guarantees proper treatment in all areas as provided for by treaties, other international conventions and laws of the residing state." (Constitutional Court, Dec. 23, 1993, 89 Heon-ma 189, KCCR 5-2, 646).

Now, the Korean Constitution states in the Preamble that it upholds "the cause of the Provisional Republic of Korea Government born of the Independence Movement of 1 March 1919." Although it may have occurred before the Constitution was drafted, the duty to restore the damaged human worth and value of the victims forcefully recruited as Comfort Women to lead a tragic life with all dignity and value obliterated, the violation which occurred during the Japanese colonization when the state could not carry out its most basic responsibilities of protecting the lives and safety of its peoples, is one of the most fundamental duties of the Provisional Government that continues for the Government today.

Taking the above constitutional provisions in light of Article 3 of the Agreement, the Respondent has a duty to seek dispute resolution pursuant to this Article, based on a constitutional demand to protect and to help realize the reparations claim of nationals, whose human dignity and value were gravely violated by the systematic and continued criminal acts of Japan. Without the performance of this duty, there is the possibility of the Petitioners' fundamental rights being gravely violated; thus, the Respondent's duty to act is one deriving from the Constitution and from specific provisions in the law.

Furthermore, though the Korean Government has not engaged in any acts to directly violate the fundamental rights of the Comfort Women, it cannot be denied that the Respondent has the specific duty to act in order to remove the reason for any malfunction. The realization of the victims' reparations claim against the state of Japan and the restoration of their human worth and value has come to the current state of impairment because the Korean Government has not clarified the substance of the claims, but rather used the vague term "all claims" in the Agreement

C. *Nonuse of Governmental Authority*

Respondent claims that the Korean Government has decided among many diplomatic methods, seeking to settle the dispute through "diplomatic channels" and giving financial support and compensation to the victims on its own rather than demanding monetary reparations from Japan. Instead of financial compensation, the Korean Government has demanded the Japanese Government to cooperate in a more important and fundamental issue of thorough fact-finding, a formal apology and statement of regret, implementation of a proper account of history for educational purposes, etc., and to continually raise the Comfort Women issue in international society. Korea claims that this was a proper exercise of the wide diplomatic discretion granted to the Government in the dispute resolution measures articulated in Article 3(1) of the Agreement; therefore, it is not a nonuse of governmental authority.

However, the nonuse of governmental authority that is at issue in this case is the failure to pursue Article 3 dispute resolution measures in order to settle the conflict in the interpretation concerning whether the Agreement extinguished the reparations claims of Comfort Women against Japan; therefore, diplomatic measures that have neglected the issue of reparations claims do *not* fall within the scope of performance of its duties. Furthermore, from the perspective of restoring Petitioners' worth and value as human beings, having Japan acknowledge its wrongdoing and bear legal liability is an issue altogether different from the Korean Government providing funds for social security; therefore, providing partial living support for the victims cannot be considered performance of the duty to act.

Based on the assertions of the Respondent, the Korean Government has had a policy of not demanding monetary reparations from the Japanese Government since 1990s. Even after the full disclosure of documents related to the Korea-Japan Agreement, it responded to a query on April 10, 2006 saying, "Because of the potential to develop into an exhaustive legal argument with Japan, we will not take measures against the

Japanese Government regarding this issue." It has also declared repeatedly in submissions made after the filing of this case that it would not take any measures regarding disputes related to the interpretation of the Agreement in this case.

The Korean Government, as observed earlier, declared through the decision of the joint government-civic committee on August 26, 2005 that the Comfort Women issue has not been settled by the Agreement. It would be difficult to interpret this as being a dispute resolution measure taken pursuant to Article 3 diplomatic channels. Even if it were hypothetically so, such efforts to settle the dispute ought to continue; and if there are no other diplomatic channels through which to settle the dispute, then arbitration should be sought pursuant to Article 3 of the Agreement. Because the Respondent has neither directly made reference to the Comfort Women issue since 2008, nor made any particular plans to settle the issue, we cannot find that it has performed its duty either way.

D. *Conclusion*

Although there was a duty to act deriving from the Constitution, the Respondent has not performed the duty, thereby potentially violating the fundamental rights of the Petitioners. Therefore, we will now analyze the main issue to determine whether the Respondent's failure to claim violates the rights of the Petitioners and thus the Constitution.

5. Judgment on the Main Issue

A. *Existence of Dispute over the Interpretation of the Agreement in This Case*

(1) Article 2(1) of the Agreement states, "The High Contracting Parties confirm that the problems concerning property, rights, and interests of the two High Contracting Parties and their peoples (including juridical persons) and the claims between the High Contracting Parties and between their peoples, including those stipulated in Article IV(a) of the Peace Treaty with Japan signed at the city of San Francisco on September 8, 1951, have been settled completely and finally." In Article 2(g) of the Agreed Minutes, it states that the "the complete and final settlement stated in Article 2(1) of the above regarding the problems concerning property, rights, and interests of the two states is included in the 8 items of Korea's claim against Japan proposed by Korea in the Korea-Japan Conference (a.k.a 8 items); and it has been confirmed that no other claims can be made regarding the same."

(2) With regard to the interpretation of Article 2(1) of the Agreement, as observed earlier, the Japanese Government and the Judiciary were of the position that the reparations claims of the Korean people, including the Comfort Women, against the state of Japan were encompassed by the Agreement and, with its conclusion and implementation, were either waived or terminated. On the other hand, the Korean

Government declared through the decision of the joint government-civic committee on August 26, 2005 that issues concerning crimes against humanity such as that of the Comfort Women where state authorities, i.e., the government were involved were not settled by the Agreement, and therefore the Japanese Government still bears liability.

(3) The Respondent has repeatedly confirmed throughout the process of this constitutional complaint evaluation that, while Japan asserts that the reparations claims of the Comfort Women were extinguished by the Agreement, Korea has asserted that the reparations claims were not included in the Agreement. This difference of position falls within the scope of a "dispute" under Article 3 of the Agreement.

Also in the reference materials submitted on June 19, 2009 after the pleadings, it has made assertions based on the premise that a dispute exists over the interpretation of the Agreement in this case, stating that "the Korean Government has decided among many diplomatic methods, in seeking to settle [the] dispute through "diplomatic channels," ... [and] that this was a proper exercise of the wide diplomatic discretion granted to the Government that is included in the dispute resolution measures provided for in Article 3(1) of the Agreement."

(4) Therefore, there is clearly a difference between Korea and Japan in the interpretation of Article 2(1) of the Agreement as to whether the reparations claims of the Comfort Women is included in the claim against Japan, which falls under the "dispute" of Article 3.

B. *Dispute Resolution Procedures*

Article 3(1) of the Agreement states, "Any dispute between the High Contracting Parties concerning the interpretation or the implementation of this Agreement shall be settled primarily through diplomatic channels." Paragraph 2 provides for resolution through arbitration if disputes cannot be settled pursuant to paragraph 1. In other words, at the time the Agreement was concluded, these provisions anticipated a dispute in the interpretation and fixed dispute resolution principles and procedures, while setting the subject of these acts as the contracting states themselves.

Thus, now that the above dispute has occurred, the Respondent ought to resolve the issue through diplomatic channels pursuant to the dispute resolution procedures of Article 3; and it ought to submit the case to an arbitration panel after having attempted such settlement.

Therefore, we will now discuss whether the nonfeasance of the Respondent in not pursuing such dispute resolution procedures violated the fundamental rights of the Petitioners and is therefore unconstitutional.

C. *Whether Respondent's Nonfeasance Violates Fundamental Rights*

(1) Distinction from Precedents

In the case claiming that the nonfeasance or failure to request arbitration pursuant to Article 3(2) of the Agreement was unconstitutional (Constitutional Court, Mar. 30, 2000, 98 Heon-ma 206 Unconstitutionality of the Non-performance of arbitration request case), the Constitutional Court held: "Whether observed from the structure or content of Article 3 of the Agreement in this case or from the particularity of this diplomatic issue, the scope of governmental discretion is quite extensive in utilizing diplomatic channels or submitting the case to arbitration order [in] to settle dispute of the interpretation and implementation of the Agreement. Thus, the mere fact that the two contracting states of the Agreement have not been engaged in effective diplomatic exchange for a long time does not automatically place a duty on the government to submit the case to arbitration in its relationship with the Petitioners, the family of drafted Japanese-Koreans that were wounded. It is likewise difficult to assume that the Petitioners are automatically granted the right to request the government to submit the case to arbitration. Even based on the states duty to protect its citizens abroad (Constitution Article 2(2)) or the duty to protect individual human rights (Constitution Article 10), we cannot recognize the specific duty of the government to submit the dispute between Korea and Japan concerning the interpretation and implementation of the Agreement in this case to a particular methodology of arbitration, nor the Petitioners' right to claim this."

The above decision was about whether the Respondent had the duty to seek "dispute resolution by submission to arbitration" pursuant to Article 3(2) of the Agreement. The issue raised was whether, in spite of the provision in Article 3(1) calling for primary dispute resolution through diplomatic channels, a duty for the Respondent to seek "dispute resolution by submission to arbitration" pursuant to Article 3(2) could be immediately drawn.

The key issue in this case, however, is whether the Respondent bears the responsibility to seek dispute resolution pursuant to Article 3 paragraphs (1) and (2). Since paragraph (1) provides for resolution through a broad range of diplomatic channels, and at the current state in which the dispute has risen between the two states concerning the interpretation of the Agreement, the issue is whether the Respondent, first of all, has the duty to seek resolution through diplomatic channels, and second, when resolution cannot be reached, whether it has the constitutional duty to submit the case to arbitration.

In other words, the issue in this case is not whether the Respondent has the "duty to select a particular method" in order to resolve the dispute regarding the interpretation of the Agreement in this case, but rather whether it has the "duty to do the diplomatic acts according to the provisions of the Agreement in order to resolve the dispute regarding its interpretation." Thus, the question is distinguishable from the above case.

(2) Respondent's Discretion

Diplomatic acts goes beyond the relationship between a state and its people where a single set of values and rules are shared within a single state; rather, these acts deal with the relationship between two states of differing values and rules in the international environment. Undeniably, it is an area where wide discretion is granted to the government in determining its policy, taking into account the circumstances and nature of the dispute, the political situation domestically and abroad, international law, and universal practices.

However, the fundamental rights of the Constitution limit all state powers; and administrative powers, pursuant to the same duty to protect such rights, must also be exercised in a manner that can effectively guarantee fundamental rights. This area of diplomatic acts cannot be entirely exempt from judicial review. With regard to diplomatic acts affecting the fundamental rights of particular citizens, if nonperformance of a duty to act specifically provided for in the law is determined to be a clear violation of the duty to protect fundamental rights under the Constitution as observed earlier, it must be declared unconstitutional as an act violating fundamental rights. Ultimately, the Respondent's discretion cannot but be limited to the scope of rights granted to state institutions, after considering as a whole the importance of the violated fundamental right, the urgency of the threat of violation, the possibility of remedying the fundamental rights, and whether the decision to act would indeed be against national interest.

(3) Whether the Fundamental Rights were Violated by Nonfeasance

(A) *Importance of the Violated Fundamental Right*

The harm to Comfort Women, having been caused by the enforced mobilization and sexual slavery by the state of Japan and its military, is a unique harm, for which other precedents cannot be found.

The unique nature of the harm to Comfort Women was confirmed not only by the international community but also by the Japanese courts. The U.N. NGO report of the International Commission of Jurists on September 2, 1994 and the Report of the Special Rapporteur on violence against women or "Coomaraswamy Report" of the U.N. Commission on Human Rights published on February 6, 1996 defined the harm as "military sexual slavery." In the report of Gay McDougall, Special Rapporteur on Systematic Rape, Sexual Slavery and Slavery-like Practices during Armed Conflict, published on August 12, 1998, the acts forced upon Comfort Women were equated to "crimes against humanity." The resolution passed by the U.S. House of Representatives in July 2007 called "the 'Comfort Women' system of forced military prostitution by the Government of Japan ... unprecedented in its cruelty and magnitude, ... in one of the largest cases of human trafficking in the 20th century." In the Judgment of April 27, 1998 by the Shimonoseki Branch of the Yamaguchi Prefectural Court, Japan recognized the National Diet Members' failure to carry out their duties towards the Comfort Women and thus ordered compensation, stating that the "system was a manifestation of sexism and racism of the time which severely violated the dignity of women and profoundly damaged racial pride."

Regarding the widespread crimes against humanity committed by the state of Japan, the reparations claims of the Comfort Women is not only a property right guaranteed by the Constitution, but its realization also signifies the *a posteriori* restoration of their dignity, value, and personal freedom that were ruthlessly and continuously violated. Therefore, hindering the realization of these reparations claims is not limited to the property rights issue under the Constitution, but it is also directly related to the more fundamental violation of their worth and value as human beings (*See* Constitutional Court, July 31, 2008, 2004 Heon-ba 81, KCCR 20-2 A, 91, at 100–101).

(B) *Urgency of the Remedy of the Violated Fundamental Right*

From 1991 until recently, three cases before Japanese Courts filed by the Comfort Women have been rejected for various reasons, including that their reparations claims were extinguished by the Agreement in this case.

Now it has become next to impossible to seek judicial remedy of the Comfort Women through the Japanese Courts or to expect a voluntary apology or remedial measures by the Japanese Government. It has been over sixty years since the end of the Second World War, during which these women were forced by Japan to become military sex slaves, and it has been over twenty years since the victims began their suits against the government of Japan.

As of March 13, 2006, 125 of the 225 survivors to whom the 'Act on Livelihood Stability for Sexual Slavery Victims Drafted for the Japanese Imperial Army under the Japanese Colonial Rule' applied were still living. Even during the process of trial, many passed away, leaving 75 registered survivors alive as of March 2011. The Petitioners of this case originally numbered 109, but 45 have passed away during the trial, leaving 64 survivors living. Furthermore, the current living Comfort Women have all advanced in age, so that any further delay in time may make it impossible to restore the historical injustice and the violated human worth and value of these Comfort Women by realizing their reparations claims.

(C) *Possibility of Remedying the Fundamental Rights*

The Respondent asserts that it was in consideration of the uncertainty of the results from arbitration that the Korean Government promised economic support and compensation for the Comfort Women, and in exchange did not demand monetary reparations from Japan.

Even if the violated fundamental right was gravely important and the threat of violation imminent, if there were no possibility of remedy, it would be difficult to recognize Respondent's duty to act. However, it is not only in instances of perfectly guaranteed remedies that the duty to act would be recognized. Rather, a *possibility* of remedy would be sufficient to establish a duty; and if the victims were willing to take the risk of their reparations claims against the Japanese Government being ultimately rejected, then the Respondent must sufficiently take into consideration the intentions of the victims.

The Draft Articles on Diplomatic Protection, adopted by the U.N. International Law Commission in 2006 and proposed to the General Assembly, provides a recommended practice in Article 19. Under this practice, a state that is entitled to exercise diplomatic protection should give due consideration to the possibility of exercising diplomatic protection, especially when a significant injury has occurred. The state should also take into account, wherever feasible, the views of injured persons regarding whether to resort to diplomatic protection along with the reparation to be sought.

In this case, the Petitioners are seeking the performance of the Respondent's duty to act through this appeal; therefore, the intentions of the victims are most certainly clear. When considering the process leading up to the conclusion of the Agreement in this case as observed earlier, its surrounding circumstances, as well as movements both domestically and abroad demanding formal acknowledgement, apology, and compensation by the Japanese Government for the appalling, unprecedented violations of these women's human rights, the Respondent should not eliminate at the outset the possibility of Japanese compensation when pursuing dispute resolution pursuant to Article 3 of the Agreement.

(D) *Whether It is against Important National Interests*

The Respondent claims that it is difficult to perform the specific duty asserted by the Petitioners because, should it take dispute resolution measures pursuant to Article 3 of the Agreement and demand monetary compensation from the Japanese Government at the same time, it would result in exhausting legal arguments or discomfort. However, even considering the nature of diplomatic acts—requiring strategic decisions based on an understanding of international politics—it is difficult to consider that vague and abstract reasons like the "possibility of developing into exhausting legal arguments" or "diplomatic discomfort" can either be valid grounds for neglecting a remedy for the Petitioners facing a grave threat to a violation of their human rights or a national interest that must be seriously considered.

Rather, having the Japanese Government fulfill its legal obligations towards the victims through efforts toward a shared understanding of the historical facts of the past, thereby deepening mutual understanding and trust between Korea and Japan and their peoples, and taking this as a historical lesson to prevent such tragedy from recurring, would be the way to build a genuine relationship between Korea and Japan, while at the same time, corresponding with truly important state interest.

(E) *Conclusion*

Respondent's nonfeasance in this case has violated an important constitutional right of the Petitioners.

D. *Section Conclusion*

In light of Articles 10, 2(2), and the Preamble of the Constitution, as well as the wording of Article 3 of the Agreement in this case, the Respondent's duty to seek dispute resolution is a duty to act derived from the Constitution, which is specifically provided for in the law. Considering the possibility of grave violations of the Petitioners' fundamental rights, including their worth and dignity as human beings and their property rights, as well as the urgency and possibility of remedy, we cannot hold that the Respondent had the discretion not to perform this duty. We also cannot find that the Respondent, up to the present, has performed its duty to seek dispute resolution procedures pursuant to Article 3 of the Agreement in this case.

Ultimately, such nonfeasance of the Respondent violates the Constitution and the fundamental rights of the Petitioners.

6. Conclusion

As this appeal has merit, it will be admitted; and aside from the concurring opinion of Justice Cho, Dae-Hyeon in section 7 below, and the dissenting opinions of Justices Lee, Kang-Kook; Min, Hyeong-Ki; and Lee, Dong-Heub in section 8 below, all other participating Justices unanimously decide as stated in the Order.

7. Concurring Opinion of Justice Cho, Dae-Hyeon

Petitioners are victims who were forcefully drafted by the Japanese to live as Comfort Women, thereby having reparations claims against the state of Japan. They assert that these reparations claims cannot be exercised because of the 'Agreement between the Republic of Korea and Japan Concerning the Settlement of Problems in Regard to Property and Claims and Economic Cooperation' (hereafter 'the Claims Agreement'). The Petitioners' Constitutional complaint claiming violation of their reparations claim cannot be denied merely because the existence and scope of reparations claims have not been confirmed by judicial procedures.

The State must confirm and guarantee the reparations claims of the former Comfort Women against the state of Japan as their fundamental right (latter part of Article 10 of the Constitution). The Korean Government, however, concluded the Claims Agreement on June 22, 1965 after receiving $300 million in grants from Japan. It confirmed that that the problems concerning property, rights, and interests of the two states and their peoples have been settled completely and finally, and agreed that no claims could be made regarding these rights.

The Japanese Courts have concluded that because of this Claims Agreement, the Petitioners cannot claim compensation against the state of Japan regarding the Comfort Women.

Views have been divided as to whether the Petitioners' reparations claims against the state of Japan have been extinguished by the Agreement. If indeed the Claims Agreement extinguishes the Petitioners' reparations claims against the state of Japan, then the State that possesses the duty to guarantee the property rights of the Petitioners has concluded a treaty that extinguishes those very rights. Even if the Claims Agreement does not extinguish the Petitioners' reparations claims against the state of Japan, the Petitioners' exercise of that right is being hindered by the Agreement. Therefore, it is fair to conclude that the Republic of Korea bears the duty to pursue diplomatic negotiations or arbitration procedures against Japan pursuant to Article 3 of the Claims Agreement, in order to resolve the unconstitutional situation in which the Claims Agreement is hindering the Petitioners' exercise of reparations claims against the state of Japan.

As long as the Claims Agreement concluded between the Republic of Korea and Japan hinders the exercise of the Petitioners' reparations claims against the state of Japan, such treaty can been seen as violating the fundamental rights of the Petitioners. However, if the treaty were understood as the Korean Government's efforts to compensate the people's claims against Japan, using the $300 million from the Japanese Government to comprehensively settle the claims resulting from Japan's colonial rule, then it is difficult to assume that such treaty is in violation of Article 37(2) of the Constitution. Even if it were to be so interpreted, however, we cannot conclude that the Government of the Republic of Korea does not bear the duty to compensate citizens who can no longer exercise reparations claims against Japan after the conclusion of the Claims Agreement, under which the Republic of Korea received $300 million from Japan in exchange for the settlement of all reparations claims by the people against the Japanese Government.

After receiving $300 million from Japan, the Republic of Korea passed the 'Act on the Management and Usage of Settlement Funds' on February 19, 1966, which compensated only the deceased among the conscripted and failed to include Comfort Women as Petitioners. On June 11, 1993, it passed the 'Act on Livelihood Stability for Sexual Slavery Victims Drafted for the Japanese Imperial Army under the Japanese Colonial Rule' to pay out a lump sum and monthly subsidies for livelihood stability, in addition to granting preferential leases for rental housing, subsidies, medical benefits, and nursing services. Yet, it is difficult to conclude that the compensation was sufficient to satisfy the Petitioners' reparations claims against the state of Japan.

Thus, it must be declared that the Republic of Korea not only has the duty to eliminate the unconstitutionality of the Claims Agreement by pursuing diplomatic negotiations or arbitration procedures against Japan pursuant to Article 3, but that it also bears the duty to completely compensate the Petitioners for the loss suffered from no longer being able to exercise their reparations claims against the state of Japan because of the Claims Agreement.

Because it is highly unlikely that the obstacle to the Petitioners' exercise of their reparations claims against Japan will be removed by diplomatic negotiations or arbitration procedures—in fact, there is sincere concern that it will give the Petitioners false hope resulting in frustration and despair—the Republic of Korea bears an even greater duty to compensate the Petitioners' reparations claims against Japan *in full.* Furthermore, because the Petitioners have all advanced in age, the state's compensation measures for the Petitioners must be urgently implemented.

8. Dissenting Opinions of Justices Lee, Kang-Kook; Min, Hyeong-Ki; and Lee, Dong-Heub

Unlike the majority opinion, we cannot conclude based on the wording of the Constitution or any other constitutional principles that 'the Respondent has the duty to pursue dispute resolution measures under Article 3 of the Agreement in this case for the Petitioners.' Therefore, because we consider the Petitioners' constitutional complaint in this case to be illegitimate, we state our following dissenting opinion.

A. The Constitutional Court Act Article 68(1) provides that any person whose basic rights have been violated may file a constitutional complaint for the exercise of governmental power, or for the non-exercise of the same. Therefore, a constitutional complaint regarding the nonfeasance of administrative power is permitted where, in spite of the fact that the agent exercising the fundamental rights can petition an administrative act or the exercise of governmental authority based upon a duty to act that is derived from the Constitution and specifically defined for the agent of governmental authority, such duty has been neglected. (*See e.g.* Constitutional Court, Sept. 16, 1991, 89 Heon-ma 163, KCCR 3, 505, 513; Mar. 30, 2000, 98 Heon-ma 206, KCCR 12-1, 393, 401).

Further, it has been settled by this Court that the above phrase "duty to act, derived from the Constitution, is specifically defined for the agent of the governmental authority" includes several situations: where the duty to act is provided for the actor of governmental authority in the wordings of the Constitution; where the duty to act for the actor of governmental authority can be derived from the interpretation of the Constitution; and where the duty to act for the actor of governmental authority is specifically provided for in the law (*See* Constitutional Court, Oct. 28, 2004, 2003 Heon-ma 898, KCCR 16-2B, 212, 219).

We must bear in mind, however, that the specific duty to act provided in the wording of the Constitution, its interpretation, or the law must be a duty towards 'the citizen who is the agent exercising the fundamental right.' Only then can they file a constitutional complaint for the non-exercise of the administrative power that violated their rights, being one "whose basic rights guaranteed under the Constitution have been violated, due to the neglect of the duty of the agent exercising governmental authority, based upon which the agent exercising the fundamental rights can petition an administrative or governmental act."

The majority opinion considers together Articles 10 and 2(2) of the Constitution, the Preamble's language of "upholding the cause of the Provisional Republic of Korea Government born of the March First Independence Movement of 1919," and the wording of Article 3 of the Agreement in this case that holds that "the Respondent's duty to act is derived from the Constitution, an instance in which the duty is specifically provided for by the law" and that the specific duty of the Respondent is "to pursue dispute resolution measures under Article 3 of the Agreement in this case." We will discuss in more detail whether this interpretation is valid.

B. First of all, 'a specific duty to act deriving from the Constitution' cannot be drawn from the wordings or the interpretations of Articles 10 and 2(2) and the Preamble of the Constitution. Among the constitutional provisions regulating the rights and obligations of the State and its peoples are those that specifically and clearly provide the people with their basic and other rights. However, there are also provisions that are open, abstract, or declaratory, requiring a constitutional interpretation or specific ordinance to generate a binding right or obligation between the State and its people. Article 10, which provides the 'duty of the State to confirm and guarantee the fundamental and inviolable human rights of individuals,' and Article 2(2), which provides the 'duty of the State to protect citizens residing abroad as prescribed by Act,' both fall under the latter category. In other words, these articles merely provide a general and abstract duty of the State to guarantee and protect the basic rights of its people. The provisions themselves do *not* establish a duty on the part of the State to take any specific action for its people. Likewise, the Preamble's phrase "upholding the cause of the Provisional Republic of Korea Government born of the March First Independence Movement of 1919" defines the guiding ideology and principles concerning State tasks and the formation of order, standardizing people's agreement on the State's basic order of values. While it has a normative effect—providing guidelines for making and interpreting ordinances as the highest norm—it alone cannot generate a State's specific duty to act for its people.

Similarly, the fact that Articles 10 and 2(2) and the Preamble do not generate a specific duty to act or a citizen's right to claim such duty to act has already been settled by this Court (*See* Constitutional Court 2000.3.30. 98 Heon-ma 206, KCCR 12-1,

393, 402–403; 1998.5.28. 97 Heon-ma 282, KCCR 10–1, 705, 710, regarding Articles 10 and 2(2); *see also* Constitutional Court 2005.6.30. 2004 Heon-ma 859, KCCR 17–1, 1016, 1020–1021 regarding the Preamble).

Thus, no matter how grave or urgent the violation of the fundamental rights of the Petitioners in this case is, Articles 10 and 2(2) and the Preamble to the Constitution alone cannot generate the State's specific duty to act for the Petitioners. It is only when there exists a 'law providing for the specific duty to act' as a medium that the State's specific duty to act for the Petitioners can be recognized.

C. We will now discuss whether the dispute resolution procedure provided for in Article 3 of the Agreement establishes 'a specific duty to act is provided for in the law,' from which a 'duty deriving from the Constitution' can be drawn.

(1) First, "the duty to act specifically provided for in the law" should be interpreted as referring to situations in which it is provided that the "State bears a duty to act in a particular manner for its people." This is because a constitutional complaint regarding the nonfeasance of administrative power is permitted where, in spite of the fact that the agent exercising the fundamental rights can petition an administrative act or the exercise of governmental authority based upon a duty to act that is derived from the Constitution and specifically defined for the agent of governmental authority, such duty has been neglected. (Constitutional Court, Mar. 30, 2000, 98 Heon-ma 206, KCCR 12-1, 393). Thus, the specific duty to act as provided in the law must be "substantive which grants the right to demand the performance of a particular duty to act to the people, or the agent exercising the fundamental rights." This is a prerequisite for recognizing the possibility of a violation of fundamental rights, or at least a causal relationship, between the violation of one's fundamental rights and the State's failure to perform a specific duty to act like the above.

In general, if there are provisions granting a specific right to the people, either in legislation passed by the National Assembly or in the administrative laws, these may be considered situations in which a 'specific duty to act is provided in the law.' Up to the present, constitutional complaints filed before this Court regarding the non-exercise of administrative powers mostly concerned the issues of whether the State's particular duty towards the petitioners was established through domestic legislation, and whether there was nonfeasance of that duty. In legislation at issue, a specific duty to act was recognized: (1) when the duty at issue involved a restrictive act of the administrative power; or (2) when the duty involved a discretionary act that has been interpreted as a restrictive act in cases of conspicuous violations of fundamental human rights. (regarding the former, *see* Constitutional Court 1998.7.16. 96 Heon-ma 246, KCCR 10–2, 283 and 2004.5.27. 2003 Heon-ma 851, KCCR 16–1, 699; regarding the latter, *see* Constitutional Court 1995.7.21. 94 Heon-ma 136, KCCR 7–2, 169). Conversely, if the legislation provided for a purely discretionary act of the government office, then a specific duty to act for the petitioner was not recognized (Constitutional Court 2005.6.30. 2004 Heon-ma 859, KCCR 17-1).

However, where the contracting parties have provided for the specific substance and procedure of dispute resolution in treaties and other diplomatic documents, as in this case, such documents are prepared on the premise that each contracting party would bear the responsibility towards the other party; so, even if certain obligations are provided for, only the contracting state can only make demands to the other contracting state. Therefore, in order to be able to demand that one's own government ought, in turn, to "demand or carry out the rights and duties against another state pursuant to a treaty," the respective treaty must have specific provisions "granting the right to its people to make such demands." As long as such explicit wording is not stated in the treaty, the mere reason that the treaty deals with the rights of the people does not give rise to a right to demand one's own government take procedural measures as determined by the treaty.

The Agreement in this case concerns the "property, rights, benefits, and claims" between the two states or between the Japanese Government and people of another state or between the peoples of the two states (Article 2(1) of the Agreement). The wording is so general and abstract that it is unclear whether the issue of Japan's obligation to compensate Comfort Women like the Petitioners in this case is included in the above Agreement. As a result, a "dispute" has occurred between the two states regarding the interpretation and implementation of the Agreement in this case regarding the rights of the Petitioners. However, as long as the Agreement in this case does not vest in the people a right to demand pursuit of the dispute resolution procedures in Article 3, a mere relationship to the fundamental rights of the Petitioners cannot give rise to a specific right to demand that their government comply with the dispute resolution procedures in the above treaty.

Therefore, pursuant to the substance of the Agreement in this case, a specific duty of the State to act cannot be found, as the majority has concluded, because there is nothing in the Agreement granting people the right to demand that the government pursue the dispute resolution procedures in Article 3. Nor can the above duty to act be recognized from Articles 10 and 2(2) of the Constitution or its Preamble. Therefore, even considering the Agreement in this case together with the above provisions of the Constitution, the State's specific duty to act for the Petitioners in this case cannot be deduced.

(2) Next, in light of the substance of Article 3 of the Agreement, what the majority refers to as the "duty to do the diplomatic acts according to Article 3 of the Agreement in order to resolve the dispute regarding its interpretation" cannot be deemed a "duty" to perform a "specific" act.

(A) Article 3 of the Agreement in this case provides, "Any dispute between the High Contracting Parties concerning the interpretation or the implementation of this Agreement shall be settled primarily through diplomatic channels (paragraph 1)." "Any dispute which cannot be settled under the provision of paragraph 1 above shall be submitted for decision to an arbitral commission . . . within a period . . . from the date of receipt by the Government of either High Contracting Party from that of the other High Contracting Party of a note requesting arbitration of the dispute (paragraph 2)." Neither provision is stated in an "obligatory" manner: that diplomatic channels "must" be sought in case of dispute, or that, if such measures are at a standoff, arbitration "must" be sought. The wording "settled primarily through diplomatic channels" cannot be interpreted as anything more than a promise between the two contracting states to resolve issues diplomatically. "Submission for decision to an arbitral commission" likewise is done when "a note requesting arbitration" is received; yet, there is no wording that may be interpreted as having an "obligatory" element in requesting arbitration. Ultimately, nowhere in Article 3(1) or (2) is there anything that can be interpreted as a duty to seek diplomatic resolution or subsequent arbitration procedures when diplomatic channels are insufficient.

The majority opinion, however, makes no mention of such doubts in interpretation. Rather, based only on the gravity of the violated fundamental rights of the Petitioners and the urgency of the need to remedy the violations, it held that "it cannot be said that the Respondent has the discretion not to perform such duty to act." There is a big gap in logic: taking language from a treaty between states that has no obligatory effect at all and interpreting it as an "obligatory" provision enforceable upon the Respondent, the government of the contracting state, merely because the citizens affected by it are in a dire situation.

Rather, it is proper to see, in form and substance, that the act of pursuing the dispute resolution procedure in Article 3 of the Agreement is a "discretionary act" of the two contracting parties. In the Constitutional complaint based on Article 3—in which the drafted Japanese-Korean soldiers wounded in battle claimed that the State had a specific duty to submit the dispute regarding their compensation claim against Japan to arbitration—this Court interpreted it as being a discretionary act. The court held as follows:

> Article 3 of the Agreement in this case provides that any dispute between the two states concerning the interpretation or the implementation of this Agreement shall be settled primarily through diplomatic channels, and that any dispute which cannot be settled shall be submitted for decision to an arbitral commission when requested by the Government of either Contracting Party. "Whether observed from the structure or content of Article 3 of the Agreement in this case or from the particularity of this diplomatic issue, the scope of

> governmental discretion is quite extensive in utilizing diplomatic channels or submitting the case to arbitration in order to settle a dispute concerning the interpretation and implementation of the Agreement." Thus, the mere fact that the two contracting states of the Agreement have not been engaged in an effective diplomatic exchange for a long time does not automatically place a duty on the government to submit the case to arbitration based on its relationship with the Petitioners, the family of drafted Japanese-Korean soldiers that were wounded. It is likewise difficult to assume that the Petitioners are automatically granted the right to request that the government submit the case to arbitration (Constitutional Court, Mar. 30, 2000, 98 Heon-ma 206, KCCR 12-1, 393, 402).

The majority opinion distinguished the above case on the premise that it was a constitutional appeal based on the nonfeasance of the "duty to submit the case to arbitration" of Article 3 paragraph 2 while bypassing the "duty of diplomatic resolution" of paragraph 1. According to the majority, this case differs in that it raises the issue of the "duty to pursue dispute resolution procedures based on the entire Article 3." This, however, is a misinterpretation of the purpose of the above precedent. The reason that a specific duty to act was not recognized in the first case was because, as observed above, the Court viewed the "diplomatic resolution" or "submission to arbitration" pursuant to Article 3 as being a discretionary measure, not an obligation.

(B) Even if the "diplomatic resolution" or "submission to arbitration" provided in Article 3 were obligatory in nature, it would be difficult to find that this Article establishes a "specific" duty to act.

The duty to resolve disputes through diplomatic channels merely refers to the general, abstract standard of the duty of the State, analogous to the State's duty to guarantee basic rights, the duty to protect its citizens abroad, the duty to inherit and develop tradition and to promote national culture, the duty to endeavor towards welfare development for the physically disabled and others, the duty to protect public health, etc. Such general and abstract duties of the State are not "specific" duties to act. Therefore, even if they are clearly stated in the Constitution, these duties does not transform into "specific" duties of the State, of which citizens may directly demand their performance. If a citizen cannot demand the performance of duties by the State based on statements explicit in the *Constitution*—the basic norm regulating the normative relationship between a State and its people—how much less can the people, not even party to the agreement, demand the performance of a duty provided for in a *treaty*—a norm of lower status than the Constitution—by interpreting it as a "specific" duty to act.

Further, it is difficult to provide an objective standard to evaluate the agent or method, the degree of performance and completion of "the duty of diplomatic resolution." As the determination of whether the duty has or has not been performed is an issue of highly diplomatic field, it may be subject to judicial review by the Constitutional Court but requires judicial restraint pursuant to the principle of separation of powers. In light of the delicate diplomatic relations between Korea and Japan, whose exchange and cooperation must continue despite the gravity of issues like the Comfort Women, it is difficult to find a clear-cut standard by which to make determinations in this case (i.e. how much diplomatic effort is required to constitute 'performance;' whether diplomatic efforts discontinued after 40 years equates to 'non-performance;' whether efforts that are unsatisfactory to the Petitioners automatically equates to 'non-performance;' when the duty to submit the case to arbitration arises; etc.) The issue then is whether such a 'diplomatic' duty becomes a 'specific' duty, which the people can demand the State to perform. The Constitutional Court cannot vaguely impose a duty on the Government to 'make diplomatic efforts' merely based on treaty language without first determining whether the duty is specific enough. This imposition by the Court becomes a greater issue when it threatens to violate the principle of separation of powers by usurping the constitutional authority of the executive branch over policymaking and the execution of political and diplomatic acts."

D. Conclusion

Thus, based on the Constitution, Articles 10 and 2(2) and the Preamble, as well as Article 3 of the Agreement in this case, we cannot find that a specific duty of State to act for the Petitioners in pursuing dispute resolution procedures as determined by Article 3 exists. Therefore, the constitutional claim brought by the Petitioners, claiming that their fundamental rights were violated by the nonfeasance of the Respondent failing to pursue the above dispute resolution procedures, is illegitimate and must be rejected.

When considering the dire situation of the Petitioners, deprived of their lives as human beings after being forcefully recruited by Japan as Comfort Women and yet unable to obtain a humane apology from the perpetrators, any Korean citizen would sympathize with them and sincerely desire that the Korean Government would do all in its power for them. However, the Constitutional Court makes decisions based on the Constitution and the law; thus, no matter how important the party's situation is to the State or how desperate the situation is for the individual, this Court cannot overstep the Constitution, regulations of the law, and relevant constitutional principles. If a legal mechanism cannot be discovered in the Constitution, the law, or any other constitutional principles in order to remedy the fundamental rights of the Petitioners, then we can only conclude that the resolution of their legal status depends on the political authorities. As such, the Constitutional Court cannot force a resolution upon the Respondent without overstepping the limitations of the Constitution, the law, and its interpretation. This is the constitutional limit that must be preserved by the Constitutional Court, based on the principle of separation of powers.

Justices Lee, Kang-Kook (Chief Justice); Cho, Dae-Hyeon (No signature due to resignation); Kim, Jong-Dae; Min, Hyeong-Ki; Lee, Dong-Heub; Mok, Young-Joon; Song, Doo-Hwan; Park, Han-Chul; Lee, Jung-Mi

CHAPTER 3

International Legal Issues Arising from a Divided Nation

1 Introduction

Though Korea was liberated from Japanese colonialism at the conclusion of World War II, the Korean peninsula was in a precipitous state which eventually saw the division of the country. The immediate post World War II environment saw the rise of the Cold War period which pitted the Soviet Union and China against the United States in Northeast Asia. Following Japan's retreat, the U.S. occupied Korea from 1945–1948, with objectives of "imposing their own vision of modernity... based on democratic principles, promoting Korean culture and nationalist ideology, and, most important, establishing a Korean political system compatible with the pursuit of America's international objectives." Finally, in August 1948, the Republic of Korea was established; and although U.S. troops were originally scheduled to depart in mid-1949, Korea ended up becoming a protectorate of the U.S. following the Korean War.

While the Korean War was technically a civil war, not only was it fought out with foreign participation on both sides but it was also the first war fought under the flag of the United Nations. Estimated casualty for Korea is some 46,000 deaths and 100,000 wounded, while the figure for North Korea ranges around 215,000 killed, 303,000 wounded and over 101,000 captured or missing. The Chinese are estimated to have lost 400,000, 486,000 wounded, and over 21,000 captured. Still many more from other countries were killed, wounded or missing. Beyond these military casualties, the Korean War was one with the highest percentage of civilian death in any wars of the twentieth century with the lowest estimate at above two million. The war ended on July 27, 1953 with the signing of the armistice by the military commanders of both sides which sought to "insure a complete cessation of hostilities and of all acts of armed force in Korea until a final peaceful settlement is achieved..." That settlement has yet to be achieved.

2 Maritime Border

2.1 *The Maritime Boundaries of North Korea in the Yellow Sea*

The Democratic People's Republic of Korea (North Korea) signed the Law of the Sea Convention in 1982, but has not yet ratified it. Its claims to

© KONINKLIJKE BRILL NV, LEIDEN, 2016 | DOI 10.1163/9789004315754_006

maritime zones are somewhat obscure, and it has not entered into formal maritime delimitations with its neighbors. According to a Russian author, North Korea claimed a 12 nautical-mile territorial sea by a resolution of its cabinet ministers on March 5, 1955. On Aug. 1, 1977, North Korea's People's Army claimed a security zone apparently extending to "the boundary line of the economic zone in the West Sea [Yellow Sea]," i.e., to the median line separating North Korea's EEZ from that of China. The coordinates governing this security zone have never been provided, but within this area, military ships and planes are prohibited, and nonmilitary ships and planes (other than fishing vessels) must obtain prior approval before navigating in this region. Some scholars have observed that North Korea has apparently claimed the large West Korea Bay along its western coast as a historic bay, even though this body of water does not appear to meet the usual requirements needed to support such a claim.

North Korea has thus sought to "territorialize" the waters off of its western coast, and Ji Guoxing has explained that this "military warning zone has stricter restrictions [on navigational activities] than the territorial sea." Others have characterized the North Korean claim as "unprecedented." Korea, Japan, and the United States have protested the declaration of this zone.

Along its southern coastline just west of the Demilitarized Zone, North Korea has protested the use of the unilaterally-declared Northern Limit Line as a maritime boundary, and argues that the maritime boundary in that area should be drawn without regard to the five small Korean islands that hug North Korea's coastline. This area has been an area of continued and increasing tension.

2.1.1 The Maritime Boundary between China and North Korea

North Korea claimed a 200-nautical-mile exclusive economic zone on June 21, 1977, and said in its decree that in areas too crowded for a full 200-mile zone its claim was "to the half-line of the sea in those waters." This awkward phrase "half-line of the sea" apparently is meant to be interpreted as referring to the median or equidistance line, as becomes clear by a statement made by the North Korean delegate to the United Nations Conference on the Law of the Sea in 1975: "the boundary of the economic zone or patrimonial sea between adjacent or opposite States should be determined by consultation in accordance with the principle of an equidistant line or a median line." One prominent commentator has observed that natural prolongation becomes "meaningless" in the maritime delimitation between North Korea and China, because "[w]hatever the geophysical structure of the seabed between North

Korea and China may be, it does not play any role in the delimitation of the continental shelf nor of the economic zone since the distance between the two states is less than 400 miles."

In any event, China apparently does not assert natural prolongation with regard to its delimitation with North Korea, and "China upholds an equidistant line as the demarcation between [it and North Korea]." China seems to take this approach because the silt line prolongation theory would "give almost the entire [bay] to North Korea." Ji Guoxing has explained that "[t]he two regimes of EEZ and continental shelf stipulated in the LOS Convention are also applicable in the Yellow Sea," adding "[h]owever, as China, North Korea and South Korea are in the same continental shelf, as the width of the Yellow Sea is around 360 nm, the two regimes might be considered to be incorporated in the delimitation." The delimitation, he explained, should therefore be undertaken "[i]n accordance with the principles of equity and proportionality," whereby "various relevant factors and specific circumstances such as the length of the coastlines, the sediments, population, fishing, etc., need to be taken into consideration." Applying these factors, Ji notes that the Chinese coastline is substantially longer than North Korea's, measuring 688 kilometers to North Korea's 414 kilometers, a ratio of 1 to 0.6. China's historic fishing activities in the northern Yellow Sea should also be a factor, Ji explains, as is "the effect of [China's] Haiyang Island lying 43 nm off the Liaodong Peninsula," and thus "China would have substantially more continental shelf vis-à-vis North Korea."

Experts are unclear as to exactly where the maritime boundary begins in the north "because no treaty has been found which delimits the boundary between" the two countries. As explained in the introductory section above, North Korea claims a military exclusion zone that covers its entire EEZ up the median line. China has engaged in oil exploration on its side of the median line in the Bay of Korea. China and North Korea "signed an agreement on joint development of offshore oil resources in some parts of the northern Yellow Sea" on December 24, 2005, and have cooperated in carrying out this agreement.

2.1.2 The Maritime Boundary between North and South Korea

Little progress has been made in negotiating a maritime delimitation between the two Koreas in the Yellow Sea, because they are still technically at war and are deeply divided about many topics. Because many Koreans view reunification as inevitable, and thus do not accept the legitimacy of "two Koreas," it is difficult to examine the maritime border from a dispassionate objective stance. But the Korean people have been divided into separate kingdoms and competing regions during many historical epochs, and it is possible that the current division of the Korean peninsula will continue. It is useful, therefore, to examine the issues related to maritime delimitation as means of reducing one area of tension between the North and South.

On August 15, 1945, Japan surrendered to Allied forces and relinquished its control over the Korean peninsula, and on that same date General Douglas MacArthur unilaterally issued General Order Number One for the Japanese surrender, which included the decision that Korea was to be divided between Soviet and U.S. spheres of influence at the 38th parallel. After five years of big-power disputes regarding governance and unification, on March 25, 1950, North Korea sent seven combat divisions of the North Korean People's Army across the 38th parallel, leading to three years of fierce combat. On July 27, 1953, after a loss of an estimated 1,330,000 lives, an armistice agreement was signed that recognized a Demilitarized Zone separating the two states at roughly the same shared boundary that had existed prior to the war.

Is North Korea now a legitimate "state" or a rogue entity without international status? The constitutions of both North and South Korea each stipulates that it is the sole legitimate government for the entire Korean peninsula, and each has tried to envelop the other. The South's strategy in recent years has been to achieve unification gradually, by a policy of "construction first and unification later." By developing faster than the North, the South sought to become strategically more important to the world. The North, on the other hand, has proposed a confederated government, but the confederation "hinged on the complete change of the political and legal order of the ROK [Republic of Korea], which was tantamount to calling for the surrender of the ROK." These diplomatic strategies were reflected in the North and South's respective attempts to become members of the United Nations. The South wanted its own seat, while the North wanted a rotating seat shared by each nation. Neither country supported the other's proposal, and each application was vetoed year after year by the ally of the other Korea on the Security Council. Finally, when it became clear that Korea was going to pursue a U.N. seat on its own, North Korea acquiesced and applied for separate membership to the United Nations as well, and on September 17, 1991, both North and South Korea were accepted separately as member nations of the United Nations.

Following U.N. admission, President Roh, Tae-Woo orchestrated North-South High-Level Talks and signed the Basic Agreement on Reconciliation, Non-Aggression, and Cooperation of Exchanges. In that agreement, signed December 13, 1991, the two parties recognized the existence of each other's governing bodies, acknowledged each other's different systems, and recognized each side's autonomy in domestic affairs, without recognizing each other as independent states.

Later, during the Sunshine Policy of President Kim, Dae-Jung, who was elected on December 18, 1997, the Korean government encouraged other nations to establish diplomatic ties with both North and South Korea, and today most countries have diplomatic relations with both Koreas. Realistically, therefore, the two Koreas have to be treated as separate international "states."

2.1.3 The Northern Limit Line (NLL)

The United Nations Command and the North Korean army established a Military Demarcation Line on land at the time they signed the Inter-Korean Armistice Agreement on May 27, 1953, but did not extend it into maritime areas. The seaward extension, which became known as the Northern Limit Line (NLL), was drawn by U.N. Commander General Mark Clarke on August 3, 1958, and is a line that is roughly equidistant between the North Korean coastline and five tiny Korean islands (Paengnyongdo, Taechongdo, Sochongdo, Yongpyo-Yolto, and Udo, which, taken together, contain five square miles of land) that hug the North Korean coast but are controlled by and claimed by Korea. Its purpose was to prevent a clash between military vessels and aircraft of both sides, and seems originally to have been designed to prevent Korean naval vessels and aircraft from going north. It has been challenged by North Korea ever since, because it was declared unilaterally and because North Korea views it as an infringement on its sovereignty and its legitimate access to the sea. Because the NLL is not mentioned in the Armistice Agreement itself, its status and that of the waters around it remain contentious.

Korea acknowledges that the NLL declaration was not officially part of the agreement that marked the cessation of hostilities between the two countries, but argues that the NLL has become the *de facto* border because (1) North Korea did not object to the NLL until October 1973; (2) North Korea implicitly recognized the NLL several times; and (3) the 1991 Basic Agreement stipulates (in Article 11) that "the South-North demarcation line and areas for non-aggression shall be identical with areas that have been under the jurisdiction of each side until the present time" and that the Protocol on Non-Aggression states (in Article 10) that "the South-North sea non-aggression demarcation line shall continue to be discussed in the future. Until the sea non-aggression demarcation has been settled, the sea non-aggression zones shall be identical with those that have been under the jurisdiction of each side until the present time." Korea thus argues that the NLL cannot be unilaterally challenged or discussed except in a comprehensive agreement to bring permanent peace to the Korean peninsula, and Korean conservatives view alterations to the NLL as a violation of the Korean Constitution which requires the government to maintain the integrity of the nation's borders. Korean resistance to creating a joint development zone encompassing territory on both sides of the NLL is based partially on the concern that such an agreement would nullify the line and cede territory to North Korea. The United States concurs that the 1992 Basic Agreement between North and South Korea stipulates that both Koreas must respect the line until a new agreement can be reached.

North Korea counters that when the NLL was drawn, the U.N. command did not inform Pyongyang, which neither acknowledged nor accepted it. It argues that the NLL illegally restricts its access to the open sea and should be redrawn further to the south to more closely reflect the land demarcation between the two countries. North Korea asserts that it has challenged the line on many occasions during the past 55 years, particularly as the value of the blue crab catch in the area has become more apparent. It also argues that its vessels have regularly fished in the waters claimed by the South, and that since March 1955 it has claimed under customary international law a 12-nautical-mile territorial sea from its coast, which extends well south of the NLL. Because the NLL hugs the North Korean coastline, Pyongyang claims that it unfairly gives too much ocean space to Korea.

The NLL has served a useful purpose as a line of military control and should continue in place until the two Koreas can reach agreement to end their state of war. But if the two Koreas were to normalize their relations, and accept each other as independent countries, the NLL would probably not stand as a legitimate maritime boundary under the "equitable principles" that apply to maritime delimitations, because the NLL denies North Korea legitimate access to its adjacent sea areas and is contrary to the principle of "non-encroachment." Further, according to legal precedents and international practice, islands do not have an equal capacity with land masses to create maritime zones, nor do they command equal strength with an opposing continental area or land mass. This conclusion has been reached most dramatically in the 2009 decision between Ukraine and Romania, where the ICJ completely ignored Ukraine's Serpents' Island in the delimitation of the maritime boundary between the two countries in the Black Sea.

Using the "enclave" approach introduced in the *Anglo-French Arbitration*, a territorial sea (which probably should be less than 12 nautical miles because the islets are so close to the North Korean coast, as discussed in the next section) would be drawn around the five Korean islands, but the islands themselves would be ignored in drawing the main maritime boundary. Also, it appears that the NLL was drawn too close to the south side of the Onjin peninsula.

In sum, all recent decisions of the ICJ and arbitral tribunals have reflected two fundamental principles of international law: (1) large land masses trump smaller islands in terms of the generation of maritime zones and (2) each state must have at least some access to adjacent coastal waters. The NLL is inconsistent with these principles. Korea's contention that it is automatically entitled to a 12-nautical-mile territorial sea from its five small islands in this area also seems inconsistent with precedents in other crowded geographical areas, as explained in the next section.

2.1.4 The Breadth of the Territorial Sea

A central issue in the maritime boundary dispute between the Koreas is the breadth of territorial sea that should be drawn around Korea's five small islands adjacent to North Korea's southwestern coast. Korea appears to be aware of this problem, because "the straight baseline on the west coast of South Korea was drawn up to Soryung Do, an island south of the five West Islands," and "[a]s a consequence, the limit of Korea's territorial sea remains vague in waters off those five islands."

Article 3 of the Law of the Sea Convention allows countries to claim territorial seas of 12 nautical miles, but in some congested ocean areas, countries have claimed smaller territorial seas in recognition of the legitimate interests of their neighbors. In the Aegean Sea, for instance, Greece and Turkey have claimed territorial seas of six nautical miles, in order to preserve navigational freedoms and permit some shared use of this sea. Other examples where states have agreed to establish territorial seas of less than 12 nautical miles around islands that are in cramped locations or are on the "wrong" side of the median line include the Venezuelan island of Isla Patos (between Venezuela and Trinidad & Tobago), the Abu Dhabi island of Dayyinah (between Abu Dhabi and Qatar), and the Australian islands in the Torres Strait (between Australia and Papua New Guinea), all of which have been given only three nautical miles of territorial sea. Another intriguing example is found in the 1984 agreement between Argentina and Chile, where these two countries limited their territorial sea claim *in relation to each other* to three nautical miles, but claimed 12-nautical-mile territorial seas with regard to all other countries.

A relevant geographical analogy can be found in the Gulf of Finland, where the Russian port of St. Petersburg sits at the eastern end, wedged in between Finland in the north and Estonia in the south. Finland has claimed a 12-nautical mile territorial sea generally, but has limited its claim to three nautical miles in the Gulf of Finland to enable Russia to have a corridor for unimpeded access to the Baltic Sea.

A similar situation exists in the straits between Japan and Korea, where Japan—which asserts a 12-nautical-mile territorial sea in general—claims only a three-nautical mile territorial sea in the Soya Strait, the Tsugaru Strait, the eastern and western channels of the Tsushima Strait, and the Osumi Strait. Both Korea and Japan have limited their territorial-sea claims around the land areas adjacent to the Korean Strait to three nautical miles, in order to permit unimpeded passage through this area. Similarly, Belize has defined its territorial sea as extending 12 nautical miles from its coast, but has limited the claim to only three nautical miles between the mouth of the Sarstoon River and Ranguana Caye in order to give Guatemala a corridor for unimpeded transit into the Caribbean Sea, pending further negotiations.

These varied examples illustrate that the 12-nautical-mile territorial sea is not universally claimed. Countries have been flexible in asserting such claims in order to accommodate the interests of their neighbors—and free passage in general—through congested areas. It would seem, therefore, that it would inappropriate for Korea to insist on its right to claim 12-nautical-mile territorial seas around its five small islands off of North Korea's coastline.

One approach to consider, on a temporary or permanent basis, would be to establish a joint fishing area in the area around the NLL. This approach has been discussed, but the two countries have been unable to agree on the area that would be encompassed by such a zone.

2.1.5 Recent Developments

North and South Korean relations improved somewhat after the first Inter-Korean Summit in 2000, and the two countries worked together for a time on economic programs aimed at stimulating economic growth in North Korea and reducing tensions. But although the two Koreas have made repeated attempts to find a politically acceptable solution that would reduce or eliminate the risk of armed conflict in the area around the NLL, negotiations relating to this boundary have not achieved a successful outcome. The most obvious solution short of reunification would be to create a joint development zone around the NLL jointly managed by the two countries, but both sides have resisted compromise on this issue.

In September 1999, North Korea unilaterally announced that it had redrawn the line, extending its purported control over waters that are rich fishing grounds for crabs. Korea has not ceded its claim to the waters, however, and incidents have been common, including violent clashes between the two navies during the crab season in June 1999 and June 2002.

In June 2004, North and South Korean leaders agreed to take certain steps to reduce confrontation in the NLL region, including tightly controlling military vessels and stopping propaganda broadcasts around the NLL. The two sides agreed to have their navies share the same radio frequency, setting up a hotline between the military headquarters, and share information on illegal fishing activities by "a third country," namely China. Rather than facilitating enforcement along the NLL, however, North Korea may have encouraged Chinese poaching in the disputed area. According to a 2005 Korean intelligence report, North Korean patrol boats regularly escort Chinese fishing vessels into the disputed area south of the NLL in exchange for a portion of their illegal catch. That report also accuses North Korea of regularly underreporting the number of illegal Chinese fishing vessels in the area, which Korea estimates to be between 150–200 vessels per day, with this figure rising sharply during the crabbing season.

Shortly after these 2004 talks, North Korea began accusing the South of increasing its military presence around the NLL. Later that year, Korea changed military operation rules by requiring boats to refrain from firing warning shots at North Korean patrol vessels and fishing boats. This change came after North Korea protested warning shots being fired at its patrol vessels, despite both sides agreeing to use the same radio frequency and flagging methods. These changes did little to calm the situation as North Korea continued to claim that the South's patrol boats had crossed the NLL.

In May 2006, Korea proposed holding high level military talks that included the possibility of a Joint Fishing Zone around the NLL. Korea's offer was rejected a few days later, however, because North Korea held to the position that any change in the West Sea (Yellow Sea) must be accompanied by a redrawing of the NLL. With the opening of June blue crab season came more North Korea accusations that the South was crossing the NLL. The North claimed that the South made over 120 intrusions into its maritime territory, a claim that Korea has denied.

In late July 2007, the two countries held general-level military talks on reducing the possibility of clashes in the Yellow Sea, but the talks fell apart over the issue of the NLL. North Korea indicated that the failure to make any headway meant that it would not participate in similar talks with high-ranking military officers for a long time. Despite that assertion, the issue was again up for discussion at the Inter-Korean Summit in August of that year.

The timing of the impromptu summit was questioned by some in the Grand National Party as being a political ploy on the part of then President Roh to increase his party's chances of success in the December 2007 elections. Some critics argued that this move would cede Korea's sovereign territory (even though the NLL was not part of the official Armistice Agreement that ended fighting between the two countries). The second round of talks scheduled for October 2007 roused heated internal debate between conservative and liberal parties over how vital the NLL was to security and whether or not it could be redrawn. Although the talks were aimed at addressing more than just the Yellow Sea dispute, many conservatives called upon President Roh to postpone them until after the December elections. Then-presidential-nominee Lee, Myung-Bak of the conservative Grand National Party (GNP) indicated that he supported the Inter-Korean Summit but felt it should be limited in scope.

The outcome of the summit was viewed by some as one-sided, giving North Korea many concessions in the way of economic incentives while securing very little for Korean interests. The summit dealt with denuclearization of North Korea, repatriation of Korean POWs, as well as the establishment of the West Sea Special Zone for Peace and Cooperation. This "Peace Zone" plan had three parts: establishing a common fishery zone, creating a special economic zone, and allowing joint use of the Han River Estuary. The Han River at this location marks the border between North and South Korea and has been closed to private vessels. The Peace Zone plan would create a right of passage through the NLL from the Han River Estuary to Haeju, a North Korean harbor city roughly 70 km from the DMZ. Haeju would in turn be developed as an open port for international trade. Another term of the Summit Agreement was to allow North Korean vessels to pass through the NLL, and thus to have direct access to the Yellow Sea. The more specific details, such as the size of the zone, its exact location, the number of ships allowed, and a concrete management plan were to be worked out between the two sides at the defense minister talks in October 2007. Further meetings were scheduled before the Korean presidential elections to hammer out the details of the Agreement, with the hope that a joint development zone would reduce tension in the West Sea area and stimulate economic ties between the two countries.

During the 2007 election campaign, candidate Lee, Myung-Bak continued his criticism of the summit's outcome, and President Roh started a heated internal debate when he stated that the NLL was not a territorial line or part of the Armistice Agreement and should not be considered a "territorial concept." Because it had been unilaterally drawn by the United Nations Command, without the agreement of either of the two Koreas, it was not technically part of any official Korean delimitation, even though it had been in place since 1953. Roh's statement may have been an attempt to circumvent a constitutional challenge to the Summit Agreement by the Grand National Party, because the Korean Constitution specifically prohibits ceding territory to the North. Importantly, the Armistice Agreement does provide that the two Koreas may create a joint fishing zone in the Yellow Sea.

By late November 2007, attempts to implement the West Sea Summit Agreement plan had stalled despite offers by Korea to create a zone that spanned both sides of the NLL. One paper reported:

> Korea offered to designate a few joint fishing areas near the NLL with the fishery zones taking up equivalent areas on both sides of the line. North Korea, however, insisted four joint fishing areas should be created south of the NLL, which it recognizes as the legitimate sea border between the two Koreas. The NLL, drawn up by the U.S.-led United Nations Command at the end of the 1950–53 Korean War, has served as the de facto sea border. Seoul maintains a firm stance that a redrawing of the line cannot be a matter of discussion, which it sees as a territorial concession. The sides will continue discussing the matter at the next generals' talks, Korea's Defense Ministry officials said.

The talks did make headway in tourism and other areas, but the discussions on the Joint Fishing Zone did not make progress.

Although the summit was a minor success, it was not enough to keep the Grand National Party's nominee Lee, Myung-Bak from winning the presidential election. Almost immediately, the President-elect's officials expressed a "negative view" of the Agreement made at the Inter-Korean Summit. Comments by Lee's spokespersons reflected the GNP's view that the fishing zones south of the NLL would make the line meaningless and be a threat to Korea's security. Lee also stated that joint ventures that placed most of the economic burden on Korea might be halted until the economy picked up.

Lee's proposals went beyond making adjustments to recent agreements. He suggested that the Ministry on Unification be abolished, transferring its duties to the Foreign Ministry and that the Sunshine Policy be ended. The Sunshine Policy was an attempt by Korea during the presidencies of Kim, Dae-Jung and Roh, Moo-Hyun to encourage the North to give up its nuclear weapons program and become more open in exchange for food and economic aid. Lee's plan to do away with the Ministry on Unification could not be accomplished because it required the support of Parliament which was controlled by a more liberal coalition, but since that time, the conservative Grand National Party has regained the parliamentary majority.

After the inauguration of President Lee, Myung-Bak, efforts to improve relations between the two Koreas stalled. The new President made internal military changes that reflected his stance that the integrity of the NLL should be maintained. North Korea accused the South of violating the NLL by repeatedly sending its warships across the line, and frequently repeated its demands to have it redrawn. Korean officials have denied any such violations and have reiterated their commitment to maintaining the line.

3 Maritime Conflicts

3.1 *Lethal Maritime Conflicts between North and South Korea: Any Role for International Law?*

The purpose of this section is to look at the relationship between the Republic of Korea (Korea) and the Democratic People's Republic of Korea (North Korea) and to observe how Korea has responded to lethal maritime conflicts that involve itself and North Korea to determine what role, if any, international law has played in resolving these conflicts between the two states. Here, the lethal conflicts encompass situations that involved the deaths of Korean civilians or soldiers subject to maritime jurisdiction. The purpose in focusing on this particular type of conflict is to observe how Korea responded to North Korea when the circumstances involved relatively high stakes both in domestic and international terms and triggered international legal obligations that exist under the U.N. Charter, namely Articles 2(3) and 2(4) which provide that, "All Members shall settle their international disputes by peaceful means in such a manner that international peace and security, and justice, are not endangered;" and that "All Members shall refrain in their international relations from the threat or use of force against the territorial integrity or political independence of any state, or in any other manner inconsistent with the Purposes of the United Nations."

... It appears that Korea would have had a very strong incentive to utilize international law and its mechanisms for dispute resolution. As far Korea's domestic political circumstances are concerned, a failure to respond to North Korea would lead to intense public criticism that there was no justice for Korean deaths while an aggressive military response to Northern action might trigger war and destroy Korea's vibrant economy. Thus, the use of international law and its mechanisms to sustain peace should be an attractive option to Korea in light of the difficult domestic and international political circumstances facing it. Therefore, if mainstream international lawyers like Harold Koh are correct, assuming Korea has embraced international law and its processes, then Korea's actions should demonstrate at least a consistent willingness to utilize law and its corresponding mechanisms in its dealings with North Korea.

However, if Goldsmith and Posner are correct, then Korea's use of international law would be dependent on national self-interest and presumably would demonstrate a lack of faith in actively utilizing an international legal system that lacks enforcement particularly in relation to the conduct of an outlaw state like North Korea that has demonstrated little or no regard for international law. One might find then Korea's reaction to the North's conduct primarily dependent on a calculation of relative costs and benefits to employing international law and its mechanisms for enforcement and dispute resolution and observe a pattern of use that correlates directly to state interest.

3.1.1 Transnational Legal Process

In his explanation of why states obey international law, Harold Koh builds on the earlier work of his mentors, Abram and Antonia Chayes who championed the concept of the international legal process. It describes a process in which states exist within a complex web of treaty relationships whereby:

> ...[N]ational actors seek to promote compliance not through coercion but, rather, through a cooperative model of compliance, which seeks to induce compliance through interactive processes of justification, discourse, and persuasion. Sovereignty... no longer means freedom from external interference, but freedom to engage in international relations as members of international regimes. "The New Sovereignty" thus comprises not territorial control or governmental autonomy, but "status—the vindication of the state's existence as a member of the international system." Now, the impetus for compliance is not so much a nation's fear of sanction, as it is fear of diminution of status through loss of reputation.

This "managerial" approach sees treaty regimes as "managing an interactive, dialectic process of justificatory discourse, in which norms are invoked, interpreted, and elaborated in a way that generates pressure for compliance." Ultimately, member states internalize these legitimate norms in view of a state's relations with other states and the dynamics at the domestic level in terms of appealing to local constituencies towards compliance.

While generally agreeing on the general approach of the Chayeses, Koh notes that the fear of losing a state's international reputation when it comes to non-compliance with a treaty term assumes that the interpretation of the term in question is mutually accepted by the state parties. Accordingly, if a state violates a treaty term and the interpretation of that term is unchallenged, then the reputation of the breaching state diminishes within the legal community. However, Koh observes that the interpretation of treaty norms is not necessarily definitive because treaty regimes are not necessarily given the authority to make the definitive interpretation of the treaty norms. There are other actors and institutions that are able to give meaning to treaty terms and thus, there is more room for states to act in relation to treaty norms.

Koh also takes issue with the Chayes' omission of a more descriptive account of how exactly states internalize treaty norms into their domestic legal systems that give rise to compliance. According to Koh, it is exactly that "transnational legal link" between the international legal system and a state's domestic legal structure that shapes the "managerial process of interstate bargaining at the global level" that will mold the national interest of the state towards compliance. As he states:

> These institutional habits lead nations into default patterns of compliance.... When a nation deviates from that pattern of presumptive compliance, frictions are created. To avoid such frictions in a nation's continuing interactions, national leaders may shift over time from a policy of violation to one of compliance. It is through this transnational legal process, this repeated cycle of interaction, interpretation, and internalization, that international law acquires its "stickiness," that nation-states acquire their identity, and that nations come to "obey" international law out of perceived self-interest. In tracing the move from the external to the internal, from one-time grudging compliance with an external norm to habitual internalized obedience, the key factor is repeated participation in the transnational legal process. That participation helps to reconstitute national interests, to establish the identity of actors as ones who obey the law, and to develop the norms that become part of the fabric of emerging international society.

The transnational legal process perspective can be seen in the overall development in the theoretical approaches to the compliance question. It goes beyond viewing obedience to international law resulting from purely exogenous factors to highlighting the complexity of workings of both exogenous and endogenous forces that pull states towards compliance with international law. However, this perspective has been criticized along with other non-instrumental approaches as either being naïve or idealistic or failing to give a "realistic" account for state behavior in relationship to law.

3.1.2 Law and Economics Approach

Unlike Koh's process approach to understanding international law compliance, Goldsmith and Posner put forward an instrumentalist perspective that is focused on the realist assumptions that states are the primary actors in the international system and that they act upon national self-interest on the basis of rational choice. However, rather than affirm the existence of global anarchy and deny the existence of international law as many political realists do, this law and economics approach views the existence of international rules solely dependent upon endogenous factors such as the preferences of the government and not on the basis of an exogenous normative framework. Simply put, the existence of international law does not emanate from morals, principles, or norms; but rather international rules find their basis, existence, justification, and compliance from repeated rational state action that maximizes state interest.

In doing so, they adopt important assumptions made by realism and put forward the view that international law does not have the capacity to constrain state behavior to the extent that mainstream international lawyers have consistently put forward. Their view of customary international law bears this point out. While predominant approaches treat international law as having a normative character that exits beyond the state, Goldsmith and Posner challenge that basic assumption by using four game theory models (coordination, coincidence of interest, cooperation, and coercion) to why states comply with treaties and customary international law. Thus, as they lay out case studies to demonstrate through the application of these models to international law, they claim to show that the conventional understanding of compliance through the principle of *pacta sunt servanda* in the context of treaties and *opinio juris* with respect to customary international law do not really provide a satisfactory account for why states obey these rules. They posit that states appear to submit to international law as result of their state interest. As they put it:

> International law emerges from states' pursuit of self-interested policies on the international stage. International law is, in this sense, endogenous to state interests. It is not a check on state self-interest; it is a product of state self-interest.... international law does not pull states toward compliance contrary to their interests, and the possibilities for what international law can achieve are limited by the configurations of state interests and the distribution of state power.

3.1.3 Role of International Law

To determine whether the transnational legal process approach or the law and economics perspective provides an accurate model to understand state compliance with international law, case studies are necessary to test the rigor of these theories. Both Koh and Goldsmith/Posner offer up specific cases that support their respective positions. In both instances, the issue of obedience to international law is framed in the context of state action in relation to compliance with treaties and customary international law. In that context, it is important to distinguish the different types of state action/inaction or conduct that is the basis to determine whether states comply with international law. Here, the issue is raised as to what methodological approach should be utilized to assess compliance or non-compliance. Much in the way of evidence for determining international law compliance has come in the way of applying qualitative as opposed to quantitative research methodologies in figuring out what role international law plays in state behavior. Thus, in attempting to determine whether states comply with international rules, there has been a strong reliance on using qualitative methods such as case studies and historical references to state action in the form of treaty making or other actions of international legal import. In that regard, as Goldsmith and Posner observe in the context of evaluating the existence of customary international law, there is a potential selection bias whereby the state practice that is utilized to justify its existence is "usually based on a highly selective survey of state practice that include only major powers and interested states."

Another problem arises in pursuing social inquiry on the question of compliance is the work to establish a causal nexus between state action and obeisance to international law. The issue presented is whether the action undertaken by the state directly results from complying with international law. This problem is clearly demonstrated in the context of establishing customary international law and the element of *opinio juris* or the sense of legal obligation. As Brownlie notes, this "psychological element" is decisive in separating whether an action of the state is mere usage or consistent with an international legal obligation. Insofar as it is considered the subjective element of customary international law, skeptics point out that there is no real objective basis to determine whether a state is motivated to act or to refrain from acting because of some felt obligation. Others point out that states never act on the basis of obligation, but solely from national interest.

Conscious of these specific challenges, the assessment measure in this section of determining the role of international law with respect to Korea's response to North Korean acts of violence is limited in scope. The assumptions being made are at one end, the use of international law as part of the official rhetoric of a state's response to an incident between itself and another state without more is indicative of a relatively weak role of international law. While it might show a public commitment to international law, the mere reference to international law in public statements can be inconsequential and indeed self-serving. The idea here is that states regularly invoke statements making reference to international law by indicating that another state is in violation while making no commitment to abide by the rules as expressed in the idiomatic expression, "Do as I say, not as I do." In this sense, states utilize international law as part of the ordinary rhetoric in condemning the actions of another state. Yet without additional legal action undertaken by the victim state in light of the violation of international law, it would seem to endorse the underlying position taken Goldsmith and Posner that states only use international law in light of their national interest. Here, the use of international as political rhetoric involves very little in terms of cost with very little investment in terms of outcomes. While not every violation of international law need be acted upon by the victim state, the absence of further action in light of consistent violations of international rules appears to support the conventional realist wisdom that states will not utilize the international legal system in circumstances where the political or security stakes are high.

On the other end, the assumption is being made that a resort to using international legal mechanisms such as referring a case to an international judicial body demonstrates a potentially strong role of international law for the victim state. Here, the state not only shows a commitment to use international rules, but it is also willing to risk "losing the case" by submitting the matter to adjudication. As lawyers are keenly aware, the submission of a case effectively leaves the result out of one's control and in the hands of another, a third party adjudicator. If the presumption is that the state acts in its own national self-interest and has a strong incentive to manage disputes own its own terms, then sending a dispute for resolution to a third party might be strong evidence of the "normative pull" or the exogenous character of international law. It would seem to demonstrate a measure of faith in and commitment to the international legal processes despite the apparent substantial cost of losing.

Also consistent with this sense of compliance, the referral of a situation as mandated by international law to a third party institution such as the U.N. Security Council would also be indicative of a strong role of international law within the context of the state. Especially in relation to violent conflicts between states, Chapter VII of the U.N. Charter sets out the terms for collective security where the members of the U.N. would join together in order to stop an aggressor state. Accordingly, the Security Council is endowed with in Article 24 of the Charter "the primary responsibility for the maintenance of international peace and security," and that members of the U.N. "agree that in carrying out its duties under this responsibility the Security Council acts on their behalf." Under Article, 25, "The Members of the United Nations agree to accept and carry out the decisions of the Security Council in accordance with the present Charter." Such decisions of the Security Council can include the use of force. Particularly in relation to outlaw states that are engaged in violence, victim states presumably have recourse not only to a political solution, but a legal one in light of collective security as mandated by the U.N. Charter. In that regard, the focus on the reaction of states to violence by outsiders offers a unique insight into the attitude of the state in question towards international law and the role it plays in shaping its response to acts of violence.

Yet, depending on one's presuppositions about the nature of international law, observations of the same events can lead to different conclusions. For the law and economics set, geopolitically smaller states tend to use the international legal process as an instrumentality against bigger states since international law allows weaker states to offset the power of big states. Therefore, given this potential ambiguity in interpreting the motivation for the positive use of international legal mechanisms, at the very least, a consistent pattern of non-use in the face of violent conflict would tend to show a relatively small role of international law in the victim state.

3.1.4 Violent Maritime Conflict between the Two Koreas

The ongoing maritime conflict between North and South Korea and the attempts to manage the various disputes between the two countries are useful points of comparison to evaluate the efficacy of the transnational legal process and law and economic perspectives of international law. While Korea is a "bigger" country than the North in terms of its economic size, military sophistication, and international reputation, it faces severe geopolitical constraints because of the relative size of North's military and the resultant high cost to its economy and well being subject to North Korean provocation. If the international legal system has a normative quality to it, then one might expect Korea to be willing to use international law and its dispute resolution processes in a variety of contexts including situations where the circumstances were severe. However, if, as according to Goldsmith/Posner, international law were a merely a product of state interest, then Korea would use international law and its processes only when it was in its own interest to do so.

An evaluation of the role of international law in Korea's response to North Korea's maritime provocation is complicated because the relations between North and South cannot be seen simply in the context of relations between two independent states at a time of peace. The formal relationship between the two countries is defined by the armistice that was concluded at the end of the Korean War. Because the armistice is not a peace treaty, both countries are technically in a state of war even though at the same time, many in the South cannot fathom a return to all out armed conflict. It is quite difficult to assess on the ground whether the situation Korea finds itself in is a time of war or peace. Adding to this confusion is the perspective taken from the Korean Constitution that provides in Article 3 that the territory of Korea includes the entire Korean peninsula. This leads to the conclusion that the North Korean government is illegitimate and is in illegal occupation and thus the conflict with the North is entirely an internal matter.

Yet despite this domestic legal understanding in the South, both countries are members of the United Nations and North Korea is considered to have legal personality under international law as a legitimate state. This apparent tension that exists between the internal political and legal perspective of Korea towards the North as an outlaw state, and the realities of North Korea's international legitimacy have not hampered both countries abilities to interact with each other as independent states.

3.2 *The Cheonan Incident: A Perspective from International Law and Politics*

March 26, 2010 is when the tragic sinking of the Korean corvette, *Cheonan* occurred. The vessel sank near the Northern Limit Line (NLL), the disputed maritime border between the two countries in the Yellow Sea on the Korean side killing 46 sailors. News of the ship's sinking dominated coverage from the Korean news media for weeks and included videos of anguished relatives of the young men who lost their lives. At the time, President Lee, Myung-Bak vowed to find the cause of Cheonan's sinking. In a show of restraint, there was no immediate indication from the Korean government as to who was to blame though there was widespread speculation that the sinking was caused by North Korea. Calling for a thorough investigation, the Korean government commissioned the Joint Civilian-Military Investigation Group comprised of investigators from Korea, the United States, Australia, the United Kingdom and the Kingdom of Sweden. On May 20, 2010 the group issued its final report and laid responsibility for the attack on *Cheonan* solely with North Korea. It concluded that the "'*Cheonan*' was sunk as the result of an external underwater explosion caused by a torpedo made in North Korea." The reaction of the Korean government was swift. In his speech to the Korean people several days later on May 24, President Lee enumerated specific steps his government would take in response to the incident which included closing off Korean waterways to North Korean vessels along with halting all inter-Korean trade with the notable exception of Korean business activities in the North Korea city of Kaeseong.

Beyond the measures taken by the Korean government, President Lee also indicated that he would refer the matter to the Security Council with the hope that the member states of the United Nations would hold North Korea accountable. Additionally, in a show of resolve against the North, working in consultation and cooperation with the United States, the two countries conducted a series of joint naval exercises in the East Sea/Sea of Japan. Nevertheless, despite the efforts of the Korean administration to "internationalize" the incident by attempting to secure a Security Council resolution and to involve U.S. naval forces to pressure North Korea, there appears to be no tangible payoff in Korea's attempt to magnify the incident. In fact, Korean efforts seemed to have backfired.

On November 23, less than seven months after the *Cheonan* incident, North Korean artillery shells exploded on Yeonpyeong Island just south of the NLL, not far from the site where *Cheonan* sank, leaving 4 Koreans dead and 19 injured. Korea counterattacked with shelling of its own, which according to the Korean media largely missed their intended targets. Soon afterwards, consistent with its response to the sinking of *Cheonan*, Korea responded with stern words and naval drills. President Lee declared in a nationally televised address on November 29 that "Now is the time we have to demonstrate our determination with actions rather than many words." From November 28 to December 1, the Korean navy conducted joint naval drills with the USS George Washington carrier fleet in the Yellow Sea.

The domestic and foreign policy decisions made by the Korean government in response to these attacks reveal the failure of the present administration to appreciate the complexities of inter-Korean relations which includes the outstanding maritime border issue over the NLL. Needless to say, the relationship between North and South is complicated. It cannot be viewed simply from a political or legal perspective. In fact, it could be said that both North and South have been relatively successful in avoiding all out armed conflict through the use of dispute management mechanisms that were put in place after the signing of the armistice. This ability to keep a relative peace shows that inter-Korean relations have a special nature unlike those between other states and that inter-Korean issues should be approached in a sensitive way. However, the Lee administration's handling of *Cheonan* and Yeonpyeong incidents reveal an inability to appreciate this special relationship and has brought to the surface a number of unsettled issues that have seemingly confounded the administration's response. These include the question of state recognition of North Korea by the South, along with the related conflict of law between the Korean Constitution and international law, and the South's foreign policy position on dispute settlement. With no apparent resolution of these issues or clear direction on how to approach these open questions, the administration has pressed forward leading towards a series of mistakes, miscalculations, and missed opportunities on the domestic and international fronts complicating the administration's position on dealing with the North.

3.2.1 Mistakes, Miscalculation, and Missed Opportunities: Back to the Cold War?

With respect to the *Cheonan* incident, an examination of the domestic actions taken by the Korean government reveal parallels with the administration's response towards the candlelight vigils that took place in reaction to the decision to resume U.S. beef imports at the beginning of Lee, Myung-Bak's presidency. The administration failed to exercise leadership to shore up public opinion on the issue before it mandated its policies. The result has been a deepened ideological gap and doubt within a key segment of the Korean populace because of a lack of transparency in the decision-making process and insufficient explanations given to the public on what precipitated the policy decision. The National Bureau of Audit (the Korean equivalent to the United States' Government Office of Accountability) which examined the government's handling of incident found that the initial briefing provided by the Korean military concealed and manipulated crucial evidence and the timeline of events that led up to the sinking of *Cheonan*. While it is quite understandable for the Korean government keep certain information classified, the kinds of mistakes that were made in this case resulted in a crisis of confidence in the government's handling of the investigation and the subsequent conclusions that were released by the international investigation. There are a significant number of Koreans who still believe in various conspiracy theories that argue essentially that the Lee administration with assistance from the United States sank *Cheonan* in an effort to shore up public support before crucial local elections last year and to justify the administration's hard line policies toward the North.

On the international front, the administration faced a similar attitude among key neighbors, namely China and Russia, who expressed doubt as to North Korea's culpability. Given the Lee administration's efforts over the years to strengthen strategic ties with the United States, it is not surprising that China and Russia were wary of Korea's efforts to lay blame on the North. Despite this obvious position, the Korean government failed to adequately engage both members of the "Permanent Five," to ensure widespread support for Korea's international effort to punish North Korea. Both China and Russia were left off of the Joint Civilian-Military Investigation Group whose conclusions were called into question by both nations. It was under these circumstances that Korea sought to bring the *Cheonan* incident to the Security Council seeking a resolution that would clearly lay state responsibility of the tragedy on North Korea.

This begs the question of what gave the Korean government the apparent confidence to bring this matter before the Security Council? More specifically, why did Korea think that China and Russia would be sympathetic to its cause? Economic relations between Korea and China and Russia have improved in quantity and quality, but that does not mean that security issues will be affected by improved economic relations. Most notably, despite the magnitude of the incident, the South was unable to get an actual resolution put up for a vote due to the strong initial opposition from China. The resulting presidential statement from the Security Council failed to even mention North Korea specifically by name. While it provided that "the Security Council condemns the attack" and that it "underscores the importance of preventing further such attacks or hostilities against the Republic of Korea," it essentially does nothing as both North and South claimed victory after it was issued. The North argues that the statement shows that the South failed to prove that it was the culprit for the sinking while the spin from the South is that it shows that the international community is steadfast in its condemnation of North Korea.

All of this reveals that the Korean government did not have clear minimum standards in terms of the kind of outcome it desired from its efforts at the Security Council. The failure to get a clear statement attributing responsibility to North Korea has only fueled domestic conspiracy theories that the Korean government and the United States were somehow responsible for the tragedy. In short, the Korean government desired to show the North that there was a price to pay for attacking *Cheonan*; however, its effort to bring the international community to punish North Korea resulted in failure and has put the Korean government in the uncomfortable position of having no apparent exit strategy. It reveals a naivety on the part of the South as to the realities of the regional political dynamics at play. By putting forth a resolution in the Security Council which would force China and Russia to reveal their hands on North Korea was hasty and unwise and has threatened Korea's immediate future relations with both countries.

With the course of action set by the Lee administration, the Korean peninsula continues to replay the Cold War bipolar order where the dominance of two hegemonic forces in Northeast Asia largely determined international relations in the region. Where Moscow once was, Beijing has now filled the vacuum created by the collapse of the Soviet Union. The administration's approach in this situation pits China, along with North Korea and Russia on one side against the United States, Japan, and Korea on the other. In doing so, it creates a sense that the administration failed to manage and take control of the crisis on its own terms by setting a course of action that has essentially taken the political initiative out of Korean hands and passing it on to the United States which has the risk of further escalating an already delicate situation. At the time, the United States indicated that it would seize North Korean bank accounts in foreign banks that the Treasury Department has kept under surveillance. While asserting that it has authority to do so under Security Council Resolution 1874 which was adopted in June of 2009, the timing of this effort seemed to suggest that the United States was signaling that the freezing of North Korean assets was due to the *Cheonan* incident. The curious timing of this action leads to the appearance that the United States is using the matter as a pretext for further action against North Korea.

3.2.2 Losing China?

The end result of such an approach is that Korea has likely lost an opportunity to engage the one state that has the most influence over North Korea, China. What is particularly troubling is the Lee administration's miscalculated efforts to force China's hand on North Korea. To achieve a Security Council resolution condemning North Korea requires the support or neutrality of the Permanent Five. The administration failed to fully engage China and Russia leaving both off the international team investigating the cause of the sinking of *Cheonan*. China's public skepticism of the results of the international investigation despite the seemingly overwhelming evidence of North Korean culpability and their apparent opposition to Korea's efforts to secure a Security Council resolution reveals that the Korean government failed to take into account China's strategic interests in supporting North Korea.

By referring the case to the Security Council, the Korean government gave over any diplomatic initiative and control it had in managing its relations with North Korea. By effectively ignoring one hegemon, China, and involving another, the United States, Korea is no longer in a position to independently deal with North Korea on its own terms. This has further complicated the development of an exit strategy that might have been contemplated by the South. A far better approach would and continues to be for the South to take the initiative to deal bilaterally with the North on the serious issues that directly impact both sides and are the obvious source of conflict, namely, the problem of the Northern Limit Line.

3.2.3 A Way Forward: Abandon the Cold War Paradigm and Take the Initiative

If the goal of the Korean government is to hold North Korea responsible for the 46 innocent lives lost on *Cheonan* and to respond effectively to the attack on Yeonpyeong Island, it must not only better appreciate the realities of a post-Cold War Northeast Asia where economic relations with China are separate from security considerations in the region, it should also give priority to taking the initiative to settle the outstanding boundary issue over the NLL. Despite the fact that the Lee administration has taken a decidedly harder line against the North in an about face from the "Sunshine Policy" pursued by his predecessors in the Blue House, Korea should address the territorial and boundary issues that contextualize the sinking of *Cheonan* and the shelling of Yeonpyeong. Because the sinking of *Cheonan* and the shelling of Yeonpyeong occurred near the NLL, and from the North Korean perspective, within its maritime border, any movement towards resolution will require both sides to resolve this outstanding territorial and boundary issue. Prior to the sinking of *Cheonan*, both sides have lost sailors and ships in 1999 and 2002 due to naval skirmishes near the NLL with each side claiming that the other was in violation of the maritime border. Failure to deal with this contentious maritime border issue will likely lead to future violent conflict which risks further escalation on the peninsula.

Korea also needs to give proper weight to the critical role that China and Russia play in the region and especially in matters of importance to Korea. In this regard, it appears that Korea's economic prosperity and dependence on the United States has caused it to neglect the relative political importance of China and Russia. Seoul must put aside the outdated strategy of pitting former Cold War allies and enemies against each other. Over the years, Korea has sought to engage China through closer economic ties, yet Korean policymakers have seemingly forced China into the position of having to choose between improved relations with Korea or risk destabilizing the North which could lead to thousands if not millions of North Koreans to flee across its largely unmanaged border between the two countries. China chose to side with the North maintaining the Cold War paradigm.

Korea missed an opportunity to deal with North Korea over *Cheonan* on its own terms by seeking an unlikely Security Council resolution and partnering with the United States in pressuring the North through joint military drills which it also did in response to the North's attack on Yeonpyeong. To regain the initiative, the Korean government should put a halt to its current policy and begin to find ways to resolve the conflict over the sinking of *Cheonan* and the shelling of Yeonpyeong on the basis of understanding the complex nature of inter-Korean relations. Simply put, Korea should not treat *Cheonan* and Yeonpyeong as international legal issues that pit one sovereign state against another and making use of hegemonic forces. By doing so, Korea further complicates an already complex relationship and may lose the chance to constructively resolve the issue on a bilateral basis.

The Lee administration should focus on developing its policies over these issues with an aim to deal with the North directly as opposed to the strategy it has adopted which has sought to increase pressure on the North through the international community and the United States as proxies. That policy has failed and only emboldened the North. Instead, the Korean government must be more willing to exercise the leverage it has over North Korea. In 2009, inter-Korean trade amounted to $1.6 billion USD which represents 32.8% of North Korea's total trade volume and only 0.24% for Korea. The Kaesong Industrial Complex situated in North Korea where Korean companies have established industries employing North Korean workers accounted for 75.5% of inter-Korean trade in 2010. Clearly, North Korea needs Kaesong more than the South. The government could severely restrict Korean business activities at Kaesong thereby reducing the amount of foreign capital available to the North. In his address to the Korean people on May 24, 2010, President Lee hinted that possibility when he indicated that "Matters pertaining to the Kaesong Industrial Complex will be duly considered, taking its unique characteristics into consideration." However until now, the only Korean action that has been taken regarding Kaesong has been to prevent new Korean investments from entering and reducing the number of Korean employees at the site. The Lee administration must give serious weight to shutting down Kaesong in response to these violent North Korean attacks.

3.2.4 Conclusion

Korea must be able to deal with North Korea on its own terms given the unique relationship that exists between the two countries. By placing its bet on the passage of a Security Council resolution that it ultimately failed to secure in regards to the *Cheonan* incident and ratcheting up the military pressure on North Korea in response to Yeonpyeong, the South's ability to find ways to seek justice for the innocents who lost their lives in both attacks has been compromised. The vague wording of the presidential statement from the Security Council and the uncertain legal status of the statement itself left no international legal basis upon which South Korean could take further actions against the North. Indeed, the silence of the statement as to state responsibility creates the impression that the international community takes no stance as to North Korea's culpability. To further complicate the matter, the involvement of the United States has brought about concern and skepticism from China which is widely recognized to have the most leverage over North Korea. The Lee administration needs to abandon its present course of merely declaring stern words and conducting joint naval drills with the U.S. and should seize the opportunity to play a more active in role in settling the NLL issue on a bilateral basis. The future of inter-Korean relations and justice for those who perished is at stake.

4 Law of the Sea

4.1 *North Korea and the Law of the Sea*

To date, there has been minimal research published regarding North Korean perspectives on the law of the sea. It is because the North Korean materials on the law of the sea are not made public. For the West, only some translated versions of literature from the Soviet Union that introduced North Korea's position to the law of the sea have been available. Despite the difficulty in accessing the relevant North Korean materials such as its legislation on the law of the sea, this section will try to briefly introduce them. To this end, dealing with the North Korean baseline system, and its regime of territorial sea and exclusive economic zone, this section will review North Korea's peculiar application and interpretation of the law of the sea. However, due to the difficulty in accessing primary sources, this section is focused on a review of available literature on public international law published in North Korea.

North Korea is one of the signatory states which has yet to ratify the 1982 U.N. Convention on the Law of the Sea. Although the Convention is not binding upon North Korea, it should be noted that it bears the obligation not to defeat the object and purpose of the Convention as prescribed in Article 18 of the 1969 Vienna Convention on the Law of Treaties. Therefore, the Convention may provide us with significant guidelines in assessing North Korean perspectives as written in its literature. The review in this section will show us how well North Korea takes advantage of the relevant provisions of the 1982 U.N. Convention on the Law of the Sea in the conflicts with its neighboring States to accomplish the goals of its marine policy.

4.1.1 Baseline System and Historic Bays

Internal waters of North Korea comprise of bays, estuaries and ports, and waters enclosed by straight baselines. It is not known which baselines North Korea has adopted as its general baselines, as between normal or straight ones. However, North Korea's claim to historic bays may imply that it adopted the straight baseline system. Defining historic bays as "bays historically recognized as internal waters of a coastal State by reason of economic interests, military purposes and geographical features," North Korea has asserted that the East Korea Bay and the Gyeongsung Bay in the East Sea (Sea of Japan; hereinafter referred to as the East Sea), and the West Korea Bay, and the Ganghwa Bay in the Yellow Sea fall within historic bays, and that, in particular, the East and the West Korea Bays are "those with characteristics of historic security and fishing areas". Considering that the North Korean coastlines are mostly comprised of the coastlines of the bays, it can be presumed that North Korea adopted straight baselines as its general baselines. It has been observed that the line followed a Soviet practice of drawing a 108-mile straight baseline enclosing the Peter the Great Bay in 1957. The lengths of the lines between the natural entrance points of each of the West and the East Korea Bays are far more than twenty-four nautical miles, and their indentation is smaller than the area of semi-circle having the diameter of the line. Moreover, the lines depart to an appreciable extent from the general direction of its coast. Therefore, North Korea's claim to historic bays is devised to justify the establishment of what are in fact excessive straight baselines enclosing those bays, because the bays do not satisfy the criteria of juridical bays required by international law.

The two straight baselines enclosing the East Korea Bay and the Gyeongsung Bay were officially made known to the world when North Korea proclaimed military boundary zones as well as 200-mile economic zones in 1977. However, there have been no articles or reports that indicate that North Korea has asserted that the West Korea Bay is also a historic bay.

4.1.2 The Territorial Sea and Its Navigational Regimes

When the tragic Pueblo incident took place in 1968, at some 40 miles from the nearest North Korean land territory, western writers assumed that North Korea already claimed a 12-mile belt of territorial sea. The assumption was warranted because a publication issued in 1970 by the Soviet Navy would assert that North Korea set the breadth of the territorial sea at 12 miles by Resolution No. 25 of the Cabinet of Ministers of 5 March 1955.

With regard to the implications of the territorial sea regime, North Korea asserts that the regime has three fundamental interests: 1) protecting national security from imperialistic invasion, 2) enhancing economic wealth of its nationals, and 3) developing maritime carriage. The three-mile limit of the territorial sea, though adhered to by state practice in the 1950s, was never universally accepted. At the First and Second U.N. Conferences on the Law of the Sea in 1958 and 1960, the international community failed to agree upon the outer limit of the territorial sea. Therefore, North Korea might have been considered as a "persistent objector" to the three-mile limit rule. However, this does not mean that its 12-mile claim must have been opposable to the States that were proponents of the three-mile limit (except China, which declared a 12-mile limit in 1958), until the 12-mile limit achieved the status of customary international law as mandatory maximum limit for the territorial sea.

With regard to the legal status of foreign ships in North Korea's territorial sea, its government prohibits all activities related to photographing, survey, research and mapping as well as exploration of marine resources. In addition, North Korea set up a stringent navigational regime in its territorial sea. North Korea asserts that foreign warships in particular do not enjoy the right of innocent passage, arguing that military equipment in warships themselves constitute threats to security of a coastal State. Therefore, foreign warships are not authorized to pass through North Korea's territorial sea without prior approval from the North Korean government or prior agreements among the States concerned. Moreover, even in a case when an approval is given, North Korea requires that the passage of the ships shall be under the control of North Korea's Navy or Coastguard.

In this regard, it is noteworthy to review the policies of neighboring States on navigational regime for foreign warships. China once declared that foreign warships would be requested to obtain advance approval from or give prior notification to a coastal State for the passage through its territorial sea. However, since the Chinese Law on the Territorial Sea and the Contiguous Zone which came into force before the date of the declaration stipulates that foreign warships must obtain permission from the Chinese government to enter its territorial sea, prior notification is not sufficient for passing through the Chinese territorial sea. In contrast, Korea, another coastal State of the Yellow Sea, requires foreign warships or government ships that are operated for non-commercial purposes to give a prior notification to the Korean government when passing through its territorial sea. Although the legitimacy of both the approval and the notification requirements have been debated among international lawyers, it appears prudent for foreign warships to comply at least with prior notification requirement in the context of regional peace and security when intending to visit or pass through the territorial seas of the coastal States of the Yellow Sea.

4.1.3 Military Boundary Zone and Exclusive Economic Zone Regimes

North Korea's Central People's Committee proclaimed a 200-mile economic zone by way of the decree of 21 June 1977. The decree stipulates that North Korea's economic zone extends up to 200 miles from its baselines or up to median/equidistance line in the sea areas where a 200-mile limit cannot be established. This may imply that in the Yellow Sea where the breadth of the sea areas is not beyond 400 miles, North Korea considers the median/equidistance line as an interim maritime boundary with China. It has been also observed that North Korea proclaimed military boundary lines in order to protect the rights enjoyed in its economic zones. While the 50-mile limit from its baselines is proclaimed as a military boundary line in the East Sea, the maritime delimitation line of economic zones is proclaimed as a military boundary line in the Yellow Sea.

North Korea's proclamation of military boundary zones could not gain any support from its neighboring States. Even China must have been in a troubled position in approving the proclamation, and as a consequence it remained silent on the proclamation. The troubled position may come from the conflicting implications that would be implicit in the support of the proclamation: such support may consolidate the legitimacy of the Chinese Military Warning Zones that have existed for more than two decades at that time, but on the other hand it may affect the Chinese adherence to the principle of natural prolongation in delimiting continental shelves or exclusive economic zones with its neighboring States.

North Korea's military zone regime is focused on the constraints that it imposes on the navigation of foreign vessels and the flight of foreign aircrafts in and over the zones. In the military boundary zone the navigation and the flight of foreign warships and aircrafts are prohibited, but civilian ships (excluding fishing boats) or civilian aircrafts are allowed to navigate or fly only with appropriate prior agreement or approval.

Reportedly, in order to enforce the decree effectively, North Korea enacted the "Regulation on the Economic Activities of Foreigners, Foreign Vessels and Aircrafts in the Economic Zones of Democratic People's Republic of Korea," on 2 August 1978. However, the text of the Regulation has not been made public. Since general international law accepts the freedom of flight over and navigation in exclusive economic zones, it is necessary to ask what constraints are imposed upon the flight of aircraft by this regulation and navigation of vessels. In this regard, it should be noted that a North Korean textbook reads that "foreign vessels and aircrafts may navigate and fly in accordance with normal navigation and flight rules under the condition that they respect the legal status of the exclusive economic zone of a coastal State." Although it is not clear what the term "normal navigation and flight rules" means, it may be assumed from this textbook passage that formally North Korea does not impose any excessive constraints on the flight over and navigation in its economic zones (unlike in its territorial sea), if the flight and navigation is not directly related to economic use of its economic zones.

The same assumption, however, may not apply to the 50-mile military boundary zone in the East Sea. Moreover, as the entire economic zone of North Korea in the Yellow Sea falls within its military boundary zone, the assumption presumably is totally inapplicable in the Yellow Sea. Particularly in peacetime, therefore, the constraints established in its military boundary zones may not be tenable, because they ignore the freedom of flight and navigation enjoyed by other States in the exclusive economic zones of North Korea.

It is not known whether North Korea has proclaimed its continental shelf. However, North Korea may be presumed to consider it unnecessary to regulate its continental shelf, because its economic zone regime includes the sub-soils of the zones.

4.1.4 Navigational Regime in Straits Used for International Navigation

Under the 1982 U.N. Convention on the Law of the Sea, the regime of transit passage applies to "straits used for international navigation between one part of the high seas or an exclusive economic zone and another part of the high seas or an exclusive economic zone." However, North Korea's perspective on the strait regime seems different from that of general international law and of the 1982 Convention. The major difference lies in the treatment of the straits connecting an enclosed sea and an ocean. The literature in North Korea argues that the navigational regime for such straits should be established differently from that for the straits connecting one part of the high seas and another part of the high seas. As the coastal States of an enclosed sea have special interests in the regime, it adds that the regime for straits connecting one part of an enclosed sea and another part of the high seas should grant more favorable rights to the coastal States of the enclosed sea. For examples of straits, the literature illustrates the Bosporus and Dardanelles straits in the Black Sea, and the straits in the Baltic Sea. This perspective may be interpreted as the reiteration of the former Soviet Union's position as asserted in regard to those straits.

Geographically, North Korea is not a coastal State embracing any straits located in the Yellow Sea and the East Sea. Despite political tensions with South Korea and Japan, North Korea's commercial vessels can pass through the routes set up in the Jeju and the Korea straits. Although it is controversial whether the Jeju strait falls within the definition of strait used for international navigation, the official position of the South Korean government is that it is not a strait which the regime of transit passage applies to. However, apart from the controversies over its legal nature, South Korea allowed North Korean commercial vessels to pass through a route in the Jeju strait set up by the "Amendment and Supplement agreement to implement and comply with the North and South Koreas Agreement on Maritime Transportation."

Japan and South Korea defined the breadth of their territorial seas as 3 miles in the Korea strait, thereby unintentionally creating a high seas corridor in the strait. Therefore, in the high seas corridor of the Korea strait, North Korean vessels enjoy freedom of navigation. The high seas corridor plays a significant role of protecting the national security of Japan and South Korea. Under the regime of transit passage, North Korean submarines may transit submerged throughout the Korea strait between the bordering coastlines without being required to navigate on the surface or to show their flag. However, in the current situation, they are required to do so when passing through the territorial seas in the strait because the regime of innocent passage applies thereto. The legitimacy of the high seas corridor has never been officially contested, but the U.S. government has alluded to support for the regime of the corridor by stating that if the navigational and hydrographic characteristics for safe navigation are present, then the regime in the Korea strait is permissible in accordance with Article 36 of the 1982 U.N. Convention. Taking full account of such advantage in security, Japan has set up a narrow territorial sea less than 12 miles in its other straits such as La Perouse, Osumi, and Tsugaru straits.

4.1.5 Perceptions of the High Seas Regime

North Korea takes a negative view on the military use of the high seas. It harshly criticizes any test activities of nuclear weapons in the high seas, and even names the military use of the high seas as "piracy." Moreover, North Korea ignores the complete immunity from the jurisdiction of any State other than the flag State that is enjoyed by warships on the high seas, by asserting that if the crew or passengers aboard warships or State-owned vessels use force against any vessels navigating on the high seas, all the States have the right to stop, inspect and seize the vessels. North Korea tries to find the justification for its rejection of the immunity in the concept of piracy, but it seems to be an untenable view when taking into account Articles 101 and 102 of the 1982 U.N. Convention.

As to the right of hot pursuit prescribed in Article 111 of the 1982 U.N. Convention, North Korea also admits it as an internationally recognized right of coastal States. However, the literature in North Korea remains silent as to when the right ceases. The silence seems intentional, when considering the nature of its military boundary zones.

North Korea's tendency to interpret arbitrarily the international law of the sea is prominent with regard to the high seas regime, but in matters of maritime safety it attempts to abide by international standards. For instance, North Korea concluded with China the "Agreement on the Rescue of Ships and Aircrafts in Distress at Sea and Cooperation for Lifesaving" in

July 1956, and acceded to the 1974 International Convention for the Safety of Life at Sea and its Protocols. Article 7 of the "Agreement on Maritime Transportation between North and South Koreas" also regulates cooperation for rescue and emergency measures in marine accidents.

4.1.6 Maritime Delimitation

There are two contending viewpoints with regard to the primary principle of maritime delimitation; one is comprised of those who adhere to equidistance with an exception for special circumstances, and the other is those who favor equitable principle. The two viewpoints were fully represented in the debates in the meetings (UNCLOS III) that led to adoption of the U.N. Convention; but the provisions related to maritime delimitation in the 1982 U.N. Convention are in favor of the equitable principles, since they state that the maritime delimitation between States with opposite or adjacent coasts shall be effected by agreement on the basis of international law, as referred to in Article 38 of the Statute of the International Court of Justice, in order to achieve an equitable solution.

It is hard to estimate in which camp North Korea stands. However, there has been one interesting event which suggests North Korea's preference for the equidistance method in maritime delimitation. As noted above, the decree of 21 June 1977 proclaimed that the economic zone of North Korea would be set to median/equidistance line in the sea areas where 200-mile limit cannot be established. The literature in North Korea also supports the preference to equidistance method in delimiting exclusive economic zones, by stating that "using equidistance line, coastal States shall resolve the delimitation of economic zones through negotiation." In addition, the literature commented that equidistance lines are frequently used for the delimitation of territorial seas, continental shelves and economic zones. On the other hand, it deserves attention that the literature also admits that equidistance line is not a unique method to delimit economic zones, by stating that in state practice historic status of the relevant sea areas and security interests may be considerably taken into account as special circumstances which may shift the equidistance/median line.

4.1.7 Conclusion

As reviewed above, the incompatibility of North Korea's perspectives on the law of the sea with general international law and the 1982 U.N. Convention on the Law of the Sea consists mainly in its establishment of excessive straight baselines and military boundary zones. The fact that the drawing of its baselines has not been made public may be a serious threat to maritime safety as well. The best way for North Korea to safeguard the rights to use its territorial sea, continental shelf, and exclusive economic zone is to ratify the 1982 U.N. Convention and to abolish its military boundary zones. More practically speaking, North Korea is recommended at least to give due publicity to the charts of its baselines or the lists of geographical co-ordinates of points, specifying the geodetic datum of the lines required in Article 16 of the 1982 U.N. Convention, in order for other States to ascertain the position of the lines. In addition, North Korea has resisted the fact that most provisions of the Convention have clearly achieved the status of customary international law, and thus it is difficult to make good use of its situation as that of a legal vacuum, remaining outside the Convention regime. Since numerous provisions of the Convention have achieved the status of customary international law, it would be better to voice its rights and interests inside the Convention regime. The efforts to invite North Korea to ratify the Convention and to abolish the zones may look too visionary, but the international community should try its best to persuade North Korea to do so in the long run. To abolish its military zones would be welcomed by the international community as a great gesture of peace, and it would remove uncertainty in applying international norms of the sea in the sea areas adjacent to North Korea.

5 Safety of Navigation

5.1 *South Korea and the Safety of Navigation: Uncertainty Derived from Undefined Fences*

The sea plays an important role for Korea's economy and security, and thus, making good order at sea is a vital priority for the country. South Korea has maritime disputes with Japan over the Dokdo and with China over the Ieodo, which has so far led to little progress in maritime boundary delimitation negotiations between Korea and these two countries.

In terms of security, Korea is technically still at war with North Korea since hostilities during the Korean War were only halted by an armistice agreement in 1953. In particular, the issue of North Korea's nuclear weapons program, as well as the unresolved dispute over sea boundaries between the two countries in the West Sea present serious challenges to peace and stability on the Korean Peninsula. After naval skirmishes in the West Sea in 1999, 2002 and 2009, tensions have escalated recently following the sinking of a Korean navy corvette, the *Cheonan*, in March 2010. Additionally, Korea's participation in the Proliferation Security Initiative (PSI) has been met with verbal threats of war by North Korea.

5.1.1 North Korea's Military Demarcation Zone

In 1977, North Korea established the Military Demarcation Zone (MDZ) up to 50 n.m. in the East Sea and up to the limits of EEZ in the West Sea. By prohibiting any fishing activities by foreign vessels within the MDZ, the area was established not only for simple security benefits but also to protect economic benefits as was clearly stated. Its exclusive nature in limiting even the principle of free navigation by civilian vessels has been strongly criticized for being without precedent in the international society.

At the General Officer talks that followed the West Sea Engagement of June 15, 1999, North Korea proposed a new maritime boundary. On March 23, 2000, North Korean Navy Command declared a "navigation order" regarding the five islands in the West Sea, according to which passage is permitted in specified waterways past the Korean islands of Paengnyongdo and Yonpyongdo.

There first needs to be a precise understanding of the purpose behind establishing the MDZ. The MDZ, as a by-product of the Cold War, is being emphasized of its security benefits; however, its complex nature including economic benefits makes it difficult to persuade North Korea to make concessions easily. An analysis of their position through various meeting records at the 3rd U.N. Law of the Sea conference shows their extreme misunderstanding of the international order and explains why it could not but establish MDZ.

Then Korea can seek to persuade North Korea by emphasizing real economic benefits. At the above conference, North Korea showed a lack of flexibility in approaching the two issues of security and economic benefits by directly and overly connecting them, as generally evident in socialist states. North Korea also strongly criticized that joint development of marine resources was a representative case of imperialist mentality. Recently, however, a change in their practical re-evaluation of the issue was evident, especially in the agreement with China to jointly develop offshore oil fields of 2005. Yet, to induce North Korea to abandon the MDZ would likely make things difficult at the negotiations; therefore, there needs to be a persuasion strategy that would help North Korea to separately perceive the issues of economic benefits and security issue. Korea could also seek to alleviate the exclusivity of MDZ by proposing Joint Marine Scientific Research Zone, Joint Fishing Zone and Joint Resource Development Zone, etc., which will be discussed further below.

5.1.2 Passage Order

Because Korea's transition into the peace regime has not occurred but rather technically remains in armistice, the reality is that a passage regime meeting international standards cannot be maintained. When considering the quantity of goods being transported, the passage routes and traffic volume, the full implementation of a peacetime regime of UNCLOS will result in greater benefits for North Korea rather than the South.

In relation to the passage order, potential key issues that may arise are: 1) passage order regarding the unilateral declaration of 5th degree West Sea, 2) passage within the MDZ, and 3) the passage of North Korean commercial vessels through the Jeju strait, though all of these still have greater benefit for North Korea.

One way to deal with this issue is to make trade-offs. The unilateral declaration of North Korea at the 5th parallel is clearly an attempt to demilitarize the NLL without having transitioned into the peace regime, which is not only a threat to security but is also directly connected to the territorial issue. Therefore, no trade-off is possible in this regard. However, there needs to be a flexibility that could somewhat make concessions between passage through the MDZ and passage of North Korean commercial vessels through the Jeju strait. From an economic cost-benefit analysis, however, the trade-off does not seem so beneficial to the South; therefore, there needs to be a systematic cost-benefit analysis regarding maritime navigation.

5.1.3 Territorial Sea Baselines between South Korea and North Korea

The West Sea sufficiently meets the criteria for drawing straight baselines pursuant to international customary law or UNCLOS. In spite of this, however, there has been hesitation in drawing territorial sea baselines in the adjacent waters (including straight baselines) in order to prevent provocation of the tense relations between the North and the South. In case of enclosed seas or semi-enclosed seas, however, both states have been rather aggressive and competitive in establishing straight baselines in order to secure extensive maritime jurisdiction.

For the two Koreas facing China and Japan, there lies not only a need for mutual cooperation for national interest following unification, but also of mutual response towards China and Japan, which North Korea needs to be reminded of. The establishment of baselines as an international matter has already been dealt with in the North Sea Continental Shelf cases; so even if the North and the South were to mutually cooperate to this end, diplomatic conflict with China and Japan will be inevitable. In other words, confirmation and proclamation of baselines, in spite of diplomatic frictions, will definitely have the effect of prior occupation in maritime delimitation negotiations with China and Japan. Therefore, there is a need to reach concessions in the near future.

If the two Koreas were to be united, the islands to the north of the 5th parallel in the West Sea can be connected with the southern islands to form a straight baseline, useful for securing a wider maritime jurisdiction. Unfortunately, the

North and South are currently divided, and it is difficult to find precedents where islands belonging to different states were connected to establish baselines. In applying international law, the concession regarding the connection of islands around 5th parallel for straight baselines has a great potential to provoke China; thus cooperation with North Korea requires precaution. Further, should the unification of the two Koreas occur, at the 5th parallel, islands such as Paengnyongdo, Taechongdo and Sochongdo scattered along the coast may also be connected for drawing straight baselines. Thus, there needs to be caution regarding this possibility as well.

5.1.4 Establishment of Various Joint Zones

Regarding the establishment of joint fishing zones as part of economic cooperation between the North and South, there already exists an agreement in principle; however, issues such as NLL and the range of the zone have prevented it from being actualized. With regard to the establishment of other joint zones, as mentioned above, there needs to be examination of three functional zones—Joint Marine Scientific Research Zone, Joint Fishing Zone or Joint Resource Development Zone—which will need to be modified with time.

As observed earlier, North Korea has strong tendency to equate economic benefits with security. Therefore, a progressive development beginning with discussions regarding a Joint Marine Scientific Research Zone with relatively less economic benefits, ultimately building up to the establishment of a Joint Resource Development Zone, would be desirable.

With regard to a Joint Marine Scientific Research, it is not absolutely necessary that a zone be established. Therefore, there is the advantage that it will be free from issues like the NLL. There can also be emphasis at the civilian level, i.e., transfer of marine scientific technology or technical support issues, making it a form of cooperation with much less political burden. Running parallel to this, the issue of marking of the East Sea can be considered in the mutual exchanges among civilian or academic groups.

Joint Fishing Zones and Joint Resource Development Zones are directly connected with the NLL of the West Sea. Thus, both West and East Seas ought to be dealt together as a package deal; and in negotiating the zones, the South should seek to include parts of the MDZ and areas below the NLL. Joint Resource Development Zones in developing gas or oil appears impractical when considering the current situation of the two Koreas and North Korea's energy security issues in relation to their dependence on China.

The general understanding is that development of oil fields is directly connected to energy security. Therefore, considering that there are very difficult international political barriers to North Korea selecting Korea as its partner,

Korea will need to focus on building trust. Therefore, starting negotiations with the above mentioned Joint Marine Scientific Research in order to build mutual trust should take precedence.

5.1.5 Boarding of North Korean Sailors on South Korean Ships

Currently, ships of Korean nationality have been hiring foreign sailors for relatively cheaper wages to reduce labor cost. Thus, there needs to be an examination of the practical benefits and legal issues arising from the possibility of North Korean sailors boarding Korean ships.

First of all, there needs to be a thorough economic evaluation of how the boarding of low-wage North Korean sailors would contribute to the cost cutting of the shipping industry. Under the current UNCLOS, the nationality of vessel follows the principle of the exclusivity of the flag State, under which the State under whose flag the ship sails may exercise jurisdiction over ships in the high seas. There are many exceptions to this principle, however; thus, Korea must take greater caution when taking on board North Korean sailors. In particular, should North Korean sailor board ships of Korean nationality, there lies the possibility of increased security searches by the U.S. due to the PSI. It is not likely that such security searches will occur on the high seas under current international law practices. Even if the possibility exists, it should not be an issue as long as the ship's registration documents are thoroughly prepared while in operation. However, when entering the territorial waters or port facilities of states voluntarily participating in the PSI, one can sufficiently foresee enhanced security searches. Therefore, the hiring of North Korea sailors should be considered successively, starting from destination states not participating in the PSI.

5.1.6 Status and Passage Regime of the Jeju Strait

The Jeju Strait is a strait situated between the southern mainland and Jeju Island. The distance from the northernmost point of Jeju Island at 34 N (Chuja-myun Daeseo-ri) to Haenam of Jeolla-namdo is 47 n.m. (87 km), and to Mokpo is 76.5 n.m. (141.6 km) and from Jeju's main island to its Isle of Chuja is 25 n.m. (48 km). There are many small islets scattered throughout the Jeju Strait with depth averages around 70m with its deepest point at 140m. With straight baselines connecting the surrounding islands of Geomundo, Yeoseodo, Jangsoodo, Jeolmyungseodo, and Soheuksando as the starting point, the waters towards the mainland constitute internal waters, while the waters towards Jeju Island constitute the territorial sea. The Jeju Strait is often utilized for international navigation between one part of the high seas or an exclusive economic zone and another part of the high seas or an exclusive economic zone.

With three coastal borders, Korea's urgent tasks are to strengthen its economic power through overseas trade and national security through securing marine power, e.g., safety of sea routes and navigational channels. Being at the center of Northeast Asia's oceans, Korea holds an important economic, military and strategic value in connecting Northeast Asian sea routes to the world. Recently, in particular, in addition to the island disputes among states surrounding these waters, there has been increased competition over maritime jurisdiction and resources. Thus marine order and defense of sea routes are directly related not only to national survival but also to regional peace and security.

In relation to the safety of sea routes in Northeast Asia, the straits that are of strategic value are the Korea Strait and Jeju Strait. Though the width of the Korea Strait is merely 23.5 n.m., the limitation of territorial seas by Korea and Japan has created high seas or an EEZ passage way in it which has made issues regarding passage of military vessels and submarines less problematic. On the other hand, the Jeju Strait is entirely included within the territorial waters of Korea, which gives it a different geographical and hydrographical status and therefore a different international legal status. The Jeju Strait is part of Korean waters, but it is a strait between one part of the high seas or an exclusive economic zone and another part of the high seas or an exclusive economic zone and is thus utilized as an international strait for international navigation of vessels. Still, opinions vary as to which navigational regime would apply under the UNCLOS.

If the Jeju Strait can be seen as a "normal" international strait used between one part of the high seas or an exclusive economic zone and another part of the high seas or an exclusive economic zone of the Yellow Sea, the East China Sea and the East Sea, then transit passage under the UNCLOS would apply, which in turn would significantly limit the regulatory authority and jurisdiction exercised by Korea as a littoral state. Korea would further be required to acknowledge the right of foreign aircraft to enter the airspace above the strait. However, if it is seen as a strait with "a route through the high seas or through an EEZ of similar convenience," then it would become an international strait permitting innocent passage rather than transit passage of the UNCLOS article 38(1).

Therefore, disputes can be prevented by creating specific regulations regarding the passage of military vessels and submarines in Korea's Territorial Sea Laws and its Implementation Orders through a clear indication that the Jeju Strait is one to which innocent passage applies. While the issue of North Korean vessels is complex requiring further examination, there needs to be clear policies that not only distinguish between civilian and government vessels but also clearly indicate the guidelines for the passage of North Korean vessels through the Jeju Strait.

Judicial Decisions

(1) *Is the U.N. Membership of ROK and DPRK a Mutual, Tacit Consent?*

Constitutional Court [95 Heon-ga 2] Decision issued October 4, 1996.

Following the decisions of this court in 89 Heon-ga 113 (Decision of April 2, 1990) and 90 Heon-ga 11 (Decision of June 25, 1990), Republic of Korea (Korea) and the Democratic People's Republic of Korea (North Korea) simultaneously joined the United Nations (U.N.) on September 17, 1991. The two governments, on December 13 of the same year, signed the Inter-Korean Basic Agreement, which subsequently entered into force. Taking into consideration their effect on the above decisions, the simultaneous membership cannot be deemed to have given effect to the mutual acknowledgement of statehood of South and North Korea. Neither does the conclusion and entry into force of the Inter-Korean Agreement indicate an abandonment on the part of the North of its plans of communist revolution towards the South; and as provocations along these lines continue to this day, the mere situational changes mentioned above do not evidence a fundamental change of logical or realistic circumstances upon which the decisions were reached. Even today, no other changes calling for a different conclusion can be acknowledged.

(2) *Legal Nature of the Inter-Korean Basic Agreement*

Constitutional Court [89 Heon-ma 240] Decision issued January 16, 1997.

On December 13, 1991, Government officials of South and North Korea signed the Inter-Korean Basic Agreement (Agreement towards Reconciliation, Non-Aggression, Exchange and Cooperation between South and North Korea), which entered into force on February 19, 1992. However, as this Agreement was concluded "[r]ecognizing that their relationship, not being a relationship between states, is a special one constituted temporarily in the process of unification (preamble)," the Agreement has the nature of a Joint Statement or Gentlemen's Agreement that promises to faithfully carry out the agreements between the authorities of South and North Korea (*See* Supreme Court [98 Doo 14525] Judgment issued July 23, 1999).

(3) *Territorial Clause of the Constitution and the Status of North Korea*

Supreme Court [90 Do 1451] Judgment issued September 25, 1990.

Article 3 of the Constitution states, "The territory of the Republic of Korea shall consist of the Korean peninsula and its adjacent islands." Under law, no other state agencies in conflict with the sovereignty of the Republic of Korea can be recognized (Judgment

© KONINKLIJKE BRILL NV, LEIDEN, 2016 | DOI 10.1163/9789004315754_007

issued by this court on Sept. 28, 1961, 4292 Hyeong-sang 48). Though North Korea exists as an independent sovereign state in international society, and our Government has used the title of North Korean Head of State to propose summit meetings with the North, this is not evidence that North Korea is not an anti-government organization violating the territorial sovereignty of the Republic of Korea …

(4) *Status of North Korea's Military Government*

Military Supreme Court [4281 Heong-sang 10] Judgment issued March 24, 1948.

It is obvious that two legal systems cannot exist within the territory of one nation; and even if a part of the territory is temporarily occupied by the military of another state, or that the state in its entirety is occupied by two or more military groups, this does not mean that the country becomes divided into two or more independent states. Therefore, even though our country has been conquered by the U.S. and U.S.S.R., and the South and the North now have differing legal systems, this is not evidence that the North is not part of our homeland. Thus it follows that the Soviet army note as forced currency in North Korea is regarded as a banknote under Criminal Act article 149, and the Claimant's arguments are unacceptable.

CHAPTER 4

The Development of the Law of the Sea in Korea

1 Introduction

Korea is surrounded on three sides by water; towards the west is the West Sea (Yellow Sea), to the south is the Korea Strait, and to the east is the East Sea (Sea of Japan). It relies on the oceans for it economic livelihood and well-being including fisheries and inbound and outbound sea freight traffic which has been crucial to Korea's rapid economic development as an export-oriented economy. Consequently, sea lane safety and the securing of passageways has been necessary for Korea to sustain its economic growth through foreign trade and securing sea power for national security. Situated at the center of the Northeast Asian Seas, the waters surrounding Korea are important from an economic, military, and strategic perspective. More recently, intensified competition for maritime jurisdiction and marine resources among the Northeast Asian states together with island sovereignty disputes have made the issues of maritime order and safety of sea lanes a vital concern, directly relevant to state survival, as well as to the peace and safety of the region.

2 Fisheries

2.1 *Korean Response to Changes of the International Legal Framework for Fisheries in the Northeast Asian Seas*

Three Northeast Asian states; China, Japan, and Korea ratified the 1982 United Nations Convention on the Law of the Sea (UNCLOS) soon after it entered into force in 1994, meaning that they became parties to UNCLOS. Therefore, with respect to the fisheries in the sea areas around these states, adjustments have been made in their relations in accordance with UNCLOS.

According to the UNCLOS provisions on exclusive economic zones (EEZ), the East China Sea, the Yellow Sea, and the East Sea/Sea of Japan, which are surrounded by the three states, North Korea, and Russia, should be divided into EEZs for each coastal state. This would leave no high seas between the EEZs, as the breadth of these seas is not longer than 400 nautical miles. However, as with EEZ issues elsewhere, it is not easy to reach an agreement on the EEZ boundary delimitations between these states, and consequently they

© KONINKLIJKE BRILL NV, LEIDEN, 2016 | DOI 10.1163/9789004315754_008

have chosen to conclude provisional arrangements to deal with the fisheries problems in these seas.

The changes to the international fisheries order in this region, brought about by UNCLOS and the adoption of bilateral fisheries agreements of the three states, has made it so that they cannot exploit fisheries resources in this region as freely as before. Additionally, in return for recognizing exclusive jurisdiction over EEZs, more responsibilities are imposed on them as coastal states with regard to the conservation of living resources. The parties are well aware of these increased restrictions on fisheries and the greater responsibility for the conservation of living stocks, and are taking necessary measures to cope with changes in the fisheries environment in the region.

The Korean government has taken various measures to manage Korean fisheries. Some measures include licensing fisheries, clean-up of fishing grounds, restrictions on fishing periods and mesh size, and temporary closures of fishing areas. However, when Korea was going to conclude a multilateral fisheries agreement with Japan and China, it was pointed out that Korea should reform its marine fisheries structure and also reorganize its fisheries industry to accommodate management of living resources. In this light, the two most important measures taken by the Korean government are the reduction in number of fishing vessels and the introduction of the Total Allowable Catch (TAC) system.

2.1.1 Reduction in Number of Fishing Vessels

Around the mid-1980s, fishing grounds for Korean fishermen deteriorated seriously and marine resources began to deplete rapidly. Accordingly, the amount of fish caught by marine fisheries began to decrease after it peaked in the early 1990s. Rising labor costs and oil prices caused many difficulties to fisheries management in Korea. Faced with this situation, the Korean government decided to carry out its plan for the reduction of fishing capacity to enable Maximum Sustainable Yield (MSY) in fisheries.

The Special Measures for Agriculture and Fishery Development Act Law No. 6223 para. 1 No. 1 (Kor.) provides that, for the sake of fisheries structure reorganization, the Minister of Maritime Affairs and Fisheries has the authority to devise policies and assistance measures adjusting the number of fishing vessels to protect living marine resources and to increase fisheries' competitiveness. Article 52 of the Fisheries Act Law No. 6656 para. 1 No. 2 (Kor.) also provides that, for the adjustment of fisheries, the number of fisheries vessels can be limited by Presidential Order. On the basis of these provisions, in 1993, the Marine Fisheries Structure Reorganization Plan was made. Under this plan, 13 kinds of marine fisheries vessels and unlicensed vessels, including surrounding net, long bag set net, stow net vessels and bottom trawl vessels, were chosen as the objects of reduction. These were the kinds of fisheries that were thought to deplete living resources and expected to experience hardship when the marine products market opened to the foreign fisheries industries. For the reduced vessels, 100 percent compensation for the vessels' residual value was given from national funds. Fishermen who abandoned fisheries as their businesses were compensated 50 percent of three years' average revenues from national funds.

The continuously changing fisheries environment and necessity of international regulations reduction (to be explained below) compelled the general reduction plan to be revised three times. Originally, it was planned that from 1994 to 2001, 6,673 fishing vessels (104,000 in tonnage) should be reduced, using approximately $203 million from the budget. However, due to the poor results, it was decided in 1995 that this plan should be extended to 2004, and the number of vessels to be eliminated changed to 7,133 (130,000 in tonnage), using $286 million. This plan was changed one more time in 1996. Finally, through the culmination of three revisions to the plan, the target of vessel elimination curtailed sharply from 6,673 vessels to 2,990, though the budget for ship owners taking compensation swelled from $203 to $820 million. The assumption is that the original plan and its first revision were made on unrealistic assumptions.

In addition to the general reduction explained above, in 1999, the Korean government prepared another track for the reduction in number of fishing vessels to accommodate its fishing capacity with respect to the narrowing of fishing grounds that was, and would be, brought into force by the multilateral fisheries agreements with Japan and China. This special track of reduction has been called "international regulation reduction," as it was made inevitable by the conclusion of "international" fisheries agreements between Korea and neighboring states. In 1999, the Korean government enacted the Special Act for the Assistance of Fishermen and the Like in Accordance with the Conclusion of Fisheries Agreements and for the Fishery Development Law No. 7207. Basically, this law is to be applied to the fishermen whose fisheries activities were restricted by agreements concluded by Korea with another state or states. However, it is provided that this law is specially applied to the fishermen whose fisheries activities were restricted by fisheries agreements between Korea and Japan or between Korea and China. On the basis of the law, the Korean government was to buy fishing vessels and fishing gear from the fishermen who decided to quit fisheries, and dispose of them. In addition, about

90 percent of the three years average revenues, as aforementioned, are to be paid from national funds. The "international regulation reduction" that continued from 1999 to 2002, is now finished.

Compared to the general reduction, the planned international regulation reduction is a far more concentrated one. Though the planned numbers of reduction are almost the same between general reduction and international regulation reduction, the budget allotted for the latter exceeds that of the former by approximately three times.

Generally speaking, the effects of the reduction of fishing vessels in preserving living resources cannot be estimated with precision due to so many variables. Nevertheless, it is estimated that the reduction in number of fishing vessels by the Korean government did not yield the expected effect of restoring living resources. The reasons for this undesirable result are as follows:

- Even though a fishing vessel is eliminated, when the license for a fishery is not terminated, the license enters into an idle state and after some years revives again and increases fisheries efforts;
- The fish stocks not caught by eliminated vessels are still cropped by other types of fishery vessels; and
- Vessels engaging in illegal fisheries are excluded from the object of reduction and are still at work depleting marine resources.

At present, another program to reduce the number of fishery vessels is being implemented in Korea. On a budgetary basis of $492 million, 6,300 coastal fishery vessels are to be eliminated from 2004 to 2008. In the first year of the program (2004), 653 coastal fishery vessels and 72 off-shore fishery vessels were eliminated.

2.1.2 Total Allowable Catch System

Introduction of the Total Allowable Catch (TAC) system is another most conspicuous feature of fisheries policies taken by the Korean government under the influence of UNCLOS and bilateral/multilateral fisheries agreements. In order to implement Article 61 and other relevant provisions of UNCLOS, and to preserve living resources within its EEZ, Korea decided to adopt a TAC system. Article 54-2 of the Fisheries Act Law No. 6656 para. 1 provides that the Minister of Maritime Affairs and Fisheries, the mayors, or the governors of provinces have the authority to decide the TAC when they recognize the necessity to do so in order to preserve and manage marine living resources. It is also provided that, in deciding the TAC, the primary concern should be the state of object species as a resource.

Upon the legal basis of the Fisheries Act, the TAC Deliberation Committee sets up the tentative TAC and the plan for the management of the TAC. The tentative TAC and plan for management are then transferred to the Central Marine Products Adjustment Committee, a deliberating and advisory organization for the Minister of Maritime Affairs and Fisheries. This Committee then finally decides the TAC. In the process of deliberation and decision of the TAC by the two committees, the National Fisheries Research and Development Institute provides scientific assessment of the resources that are the objects of TAC. Once the TAC is decided, 70 percent of it is allotted to the metropolitan cities and provinces, and the mayors and governors of these cities and provinces again allot the TAC to individual fishermen. The reserved 30 percent of the TAC is allotted to individual fishermen when they have exhausted more than 80 percent of the originally allotted TAC.

The TAC system was implemented on a trial basis in 1999, and after two years, it was implemented in its entirety.

2.1.3 Problems to be Solved

The TAC system implemented in Korea is estimated not to have brought the expected result of preserving and recovering marine resources. The reasons for this poor outcome are as follows:

- As pointed out above, TACs of many species have exceeded their ABCs;
- The TAC system is not properly linked with other traditional methods of fisheries control. In preserving and recovering living resources, relying only on the TAC may cause a "race-to-fish" scenario, which is the very competitive fishing among fishermen to exhaust the allotted TAC ahead of others; and
- The scientific estimation of the amount of living stocks is still imprecise. Presently, five different levels of data are used to figure out ABC and TAC. However, because the necessary data for the determination of ABC and TAC are not well enough accumulated, ABC and TAC of most species are decided on the basis of low-level data.

2.2 *Fisheries in the East China Sea and the Issue of Law Enforcement in the EEZ: Korean Perspective*

The main issue of this section is whether it is possible to apprehend Chinese fishing vessels engaged in fishing near the "Intermediate Zone" south of Jeju between Korea and Japan. The waters south of Jeju is an area where the EEZ claims of Korea, China and Japan overlap. Unfortunately, there is no agreement among the three states concerning its delimitation, and only domestic law and bilateral treaties exist. These are taken into consideration because international law provisions, such as UNCLOS, are unclear. Different boundary zones have been delimited between Korea & Japan and Korea & China in the waters south of Jeju. Under these agreements, the Korea-Japan Agreement applies to issues between Korea and Japan, while the Korea-China Agreement applies to issues between Korea and China. One key characteristic of these agreements is that in areas of overlapping Intermediate Zones, domestic laws do not apply to the nationals of the bilateral partner state. Beyond such zones, law enforcement is possible but may give rise to complex issues of diplomatic relations. Thus, the basic principle for Korea is: where there are separate agreements with foreign states, the agreement applies; but where no such agreement exists, law enforcement is refrained beyond the median line with the other state.

2.2.1 Domestic Law Considerations

Fishing activities conducted by foreigners within Korea's EEZ is regulated by the "Act on the Exercise of Sovereign Rights on Foreigners' Fishing, etc. within the Exclusive Economic Zone." The waters over which the above Act is applicable is determined by the EEZ Act (Art. 2(1)). EEZ Act Article 5 states, "The Republic of Korea shall not exercise its rights in its EEZ under Article 3 in the area beyond the median line between the Republic of Korea and relevant states unless agreed separately between the relevant states and the Republic of Korea." The EEZ Act also provides in Article 3(2), "Where agreement with foreign states exist, the agreement shall apply." Therefore, the Fisheries Agreements with China and Japan takes precedence in application. In short, from domestic law perspective, where there are separate agreements with foreign states, the agreement applies; but where no such agreement exists, law enforcement beyond the median line is refrained.

2.2.2 International Law and Diplomatic Considerations

UNCLOS Article 73 provides for the enforcement of laws and regulations of coastal states in the EEZ, but this is premised on the existence of boundary delimitations between states with opposite or adjacent coasts. UNCLOS Article 74(3), which provides for the EEZ delimitation between states with opposite or adjacent coasts, states, "… the States concerned … during this transitional period, shall make every effort … not to jeopardize or hamper the reaching of the final agreement." Thus, in such intermediate zones where delimitation has not been made, the geographical limits of justified law enforcement for each coastal state is unclear. As unilateral enforcement of law in the intermediate zone can result in objection or dispute with another state, consideration of the practices of surrounding states and the potential countermeasures of the adverse state is necessary in actual enforcement.

2.2.2.1 *Bilateral Agreements Concerning the Waters South of Jeju*

2.2.2.1.1 Korea-Japan Fisheries Agreement (effective January 22, 1999)

Article 9(2): Among the zones surrounded by the following lines, paragraph 3 of Annex I will apply to the zones north of the southernmost parallel of Korea's EEZ.

Annex 1(3): Contracting parties will cooperate pursuant to the following provisions in order to prevent marine biological resources from being threatened by excessive exploitation in the zones determined by Article 9(2) of this Agreement.

Annex 1(3)(A): Each Contracting State will not apply its relevant domestic laws towards nationals and fishing vessels of the other Contracting State within this zone.

Agreed Minutes Article 2: With regard to the establishment of the zone in Article 9(2) of the Agreement, the Korean Government intends to cooperate with the Japanese Government not to damage the fishery relations Japan has built with third states in certain zones of the East China Sea. However, this should not be understood as being harmful to the position of Korea concerning such agreements concluded by Japan with third states.

Article 4: Both Governments, based on this Agreement as well as other fisheries agreements that have been or will be concluded by each state with third states, intend to pursue specific measures to maintain harmonious fishing order in the East China Sea through the Korea-Japan Joint Fisheries Commission established by Article 12 of this Agreement and other similar joint commissions to be established by agreements with third states.

2.2.2.1.2 Korea-China Fisheries Agreement (effective June 30, 2001)

Article 9: Unless there are specific agreements between the Contracting Parties, the current fishing activities will be maintained in a certain area north of the parallel where the northern portion of the Provisional Measure Zone designated by Article 7(1) is situated, and in the area to the south of the Transitional Zone designated by Article 8(1); and domestic laws regarding fisheries will not be applied to the nationals and fishing vessels of the other Contracting Party.

2.2.2.1.3 China-Japan Fisheries Agreement (effective June 1, 2000)

Agreed Minutes Article 2: The current fishing activities in part of the East China Sea north of the Provisional Measure Zone (North latitude 30° 41'N) will be respected.

2.3 *The Legal Assessment of the Illegal Fishing Activities of Chinese Fishing Vessels: A Focus on Detention of Foreign Vessels*

On April 20, decisions were issued in two cases concerning Chinese sailors engaged in illegal fishing activities. In one case, a Korean Coast Guard officer was stabbed to death in December 2011 in the process of detaining an illegal Chinese fishing vessel. The trial court, Incheon District Court—Criminal Division, handed down a 30 year prison term and fine of 20 million won to the captain of the Chinese vessel, *Luwenyu* no. 29, who was responsible for the stabbing. The other sailors and the captain of another Chinese vessel, *Lihaoyu*, were sentenced between 18 months to 5 years in prison for interfering with the detention. The other case occurred in November 2011 where, in the process of detaining a Chinese fishing vessel that had intruded upon Korean territorial waters northwest of Chujado of Jeju to engage in fishing activities, Chinese sailors wounded 5 Korean Coast Guard officers, inflicting upon them injuries that required 2–7 weeks of recuperation. The Jeju Regional Court, an appellate court, affirmed the decision of the trial court—which sentenced the Chinese captain to one year and other two sailors to 14 months—and dismissed the appeals. The two cases show a strong determination on the part of the judiciary to deal with the systematic and violent resistance to the prevention of illegal fishing.

This section is a legal analysis of the detention of foreign vessels engaging in illegal fishing. It first looks at the international and domestic regulations concerning illegal fishing, and then proceeds to discuss the issues of security and immediate release following arrest.

2.3.1 International Law Provisions Concerning the Prevention of Illegal Fishing Activities

2.3.1.1 *UNCLOS Provisions*

2.3.1.1.1 Regulation of Fishing in the Territorial Seas

The United Nations Convention on the Law of the Sea (UNCLOS) grants to the coastal states the right of fishery regulation concerning foreign vessels within their territorial waters and the EEZ. A state's territorial jurisdiction reaches to its territorial waters, thus a state certainly has all rights of regulation concerning fishing of foreign vessels. Provisions directly on point are UNCLOS Articles 2 and 3. Article 2(2) provides, "This sovereignty extends to the air space over the territorial sea as well as to its bed and subsoil"; and paragraph (3) states, "The sovereignty over the territorial sea is exercised subject to this Convention and to other rules of international law." Paragraph (3) takes into consideration the fact that the exercise of sovereignty within the territorial waters over the right of innocent passage and flag state jurisdiction of foreign vessels may be partially restricted by international law. However, the regulation of fishing within territorial waters, in particular, is considered to be an inherent right of the coastal states; thus restrictions in general are not placed unless specifically provided for in bilateral agreements.

2.3.1.1.2 Conservation and Usage of Fisheries Resources in the EEZ

The Exclusive Economic Zone (EEZ) newly implemented by the 1982 Convention bears a *sui generis* character. Within this zone, the coastal state has "sovereign rights for the purpose of exploring and exploiting, conserving and managing the natural resources, whether living or non-living," as well as "jurisdiction as provided for in the relevant provisions of this Convention with regard to ... installations and structures [and] marine scientific research." However, all States enjoy the freedoms of navigation and overflight traditionally recognized in the high seas and other internationally lawful uses of the sea related to these freedoms. In this regard, the EEZ is a unique zone bearing the characteristics of both territorial waters and high seas.

Fishing activities within the EEZ concerns the conservation and utilization of living resources and thus falls within the exclusive jurisdiction of the coastal state. The coastal state has the authority to regulate the fishing activities of foreign vessels within its EEZ through domestic laws. UNCLOS more specifically provides for the conservation and utilization of living resources in Articles 61 and 62.

Article 61 concerning the conservation of living resources provides for the coastal state to determine the allowable catch of the living resources in its exclusive economic zone, as well as the proper conservation and management measures to prevent over-exploitation, to maintain or restore populations to produce the maximum sustainable yield, and to take into consideration the effects on species associated with or dependent upon harvested species. Article 62, which can be deemed the foundational clause for fishing regulations, provides for the utilization of living resources and can be summarized as follows: First, optimum utilization of the living resources must be achieved without prejudice to article 61.

Second, a coastal state determines its capacity to harvest the living resources; but where the coastal state does not have the capacity to harvest the entire allowable catch, it shall, through agreements or other arrangements, give other states access to the surplus of the allowable catch. Because the Convention says that the coastal state "shall ... give other States access," it is obligated under law to grant such access when the conditions are met.

Third, in giving access to other states, the relevant factors to be considered are inclusive. The examples given by the Convention include the significance of the living resources of the area to the economy of the coastal state concerned and its other national interests, the rights of land-locked or geographically disadvantaged states, and the need to minimize economic dislocation in states whose nationals have habitually fished in the zone or which have made substantial efforts in research and identification of stocks.

Fourth, the laws and regulations of the coastal state concerning the regulation of fishing must be consistent with this Convention. As examples that may be included in the laws and regulations, UNCLOS provides for 11 items including licensing of fishermen, licensing of fishing vessels and equipment, determining the species which may be caught, and fixing quotas of catch, regulating seasons and areas of fishing, the types, sizes and amount, etc.

2.3.1.1.3 Enforcement of the Laws and Regulations of the Coastal State

As seen above, UNCLOS allows the coastal state to pass laws and regulations to conserve and to utilize the fishery resources within its EEZ. The coastal state would certainly endeavor to ensure that such laws are followed; and where fishing activities of foreign vessels are in violation of such laws, it would seek proper restrictions pursuant to the law. However, because UNCLOS has separate regulations concerning the enforcement of the laws, the coastal state is obligated to comply with its provisions in the enforcement of its laws. With regard to the enforcement of laws and regulations of the coastal state, Article 73 provides as follows: First, the coastal state may, as long as the laws and regulations adopted by it for the conservation and utilization of living resources is in conformity with this Convention, take measures such as boarding, inspection, arrest and judicial proceedings, as may be necessary. This derives from the sovereign rights that a coastal state has over its EEZ; Second, where the vessels and their crews have been arrested for their violation of the laws and regulations of the coastal state, they must be promptly released upon the posting of reasonable bond or other security. Thus, delay in their release for various reasons in spite of the posting of bond or security violates the Convention. This issue will be discussed further. Third, paragraph 3 provides that penalties for violations of fisheries laws and regulations of the coastal state are possible, but they may not include imprisonment or any other form of corporal punishment. Several things must be carefully considered in relation to this. First, the point is that this clause provides that corporal punishment "may not [be] include[d]," an expression which requires careful interpretation because it uses the word "may" having a degree of permissiveness unlike the word "shall" of strict, legally binding force. Thus, strictly speaking, interpretation may be possible asserting that imprisonment does not immediately constitute a violation of the Convention for which the state bears liability. However, the same clause also provides that where states have agreed, corporal punishment may be imposed; therefore, in its context, in spite of the word "may," it would be proper to interpret the clause as prohibiting corporal punishment without an agreement to the contrary. Next is that confiscation is possible as a form of punishment by the coastal state without the consent of the related state. In other words, confiscation of the fishing vessel and its catch is possible if provided by law. Lastly, such restrictions of enforcement measures apply to the EEZ; thus, if the illegal acts of foreign fishing vessels occur within the territorial waters of the coastal state, corporal punishment will be possible even without the above restrictions of the Convention.

The EEZ is a unique zone bearing the characteristics of both territorial waters and high seas. With regard to the economic utilization of living resources such as fisheries, the coastal state has sovereign rights and can thus exercise jurisdiction over the EEZ similar to that which is exercised in its territorial waters. The UNCLOS only places certain restrictions on the adoption and enforcement of laws on conservation and utilization of living resources. Thus, the coastal state needs to comply with such provisions of the Convention in apprehending and punishing illegal fishing activities of foreign vessels within its EEZ.

2.3.1.2 *Punishment Provision and Scope of Executive Jurisdiction under the Korea-China Fisheries Agreement*

The Korea-China Fisheries Agreement (Agreement) was signed on August 3, 2000 and entered into effect on June 30, 2001. The Agreement was concluded before the maritime boundary delimitation between the two states was settled, and thus has a provisional measure zone similar to that of the Korea-Japan Fisheries Agreement. On both sides of this zone were established transition zones which, pursuant to the clause providing for their absorption into the EEZ of the respective states four years after the Agreement enters into force, have now become part of the EEZ of Korea and China. Thus the current Agreement, similar to the Korea-Japan Fisheries Agreement, provides that within the Provisional Measure Zone, the Korea-China Joint Fisheries Committee decides the conservation and management measures, while the coastal state exercises exclusive jurisdiction within its EEZ.

2.3.1.2.1 Authority within the Provisional Measure Zone

The Korea-China Fisheries Agreement provides that, concerning the conservation and reasonable utilization of marine living resources within the

Provisional Measure Zone, both states take conservation and quantitative management measures pursuant to the decision of the Joint Fisheries Commission. This Commission is comprised of 1 representative appointed by each state and a number of other members; and Korea and China host annual conferences in turn. The main task of the Commission is to negotiate with other states about the following and to make recommendations to the respective governments: (a) allowable type and amount of catch and other specific conditions for the nationals and vessels of the other state; (b) maintenance of fishing order; (c) status of marine living resources and their conservation; (d) and fisheries cooperation between the two states. It should be noted that this Commission only has the authority to negotiate regarding these specific areas and to make recommendations to the governments, but that it does not have actual authority to make binding decisions and to enforce them.

The coastal state cannot exercise jurisdiction over vessels of the other state within the Provisional Measure Zone. In other words, Korea can only take management and other necessary measures against Korean nationals and ships; and when it has discovered Chinese nationals or ships violating the decisions of the Commission, it can only call them to attention and notify the Chinese Government of the fact and circumstances. Though, at this point, the Chinese Government is required to respect this notification and to report back to the Korean Government after having taken necessary measures, it would be difficult for this to have actual binding effect. The Agreement does not provide for vessels of third states such as Japan entering the Provisional Measure Zone to fish, but it would be possible to interpret such case as permitting the exercise of jurisdiction for both states. This is because in the absence of a boundary delimitation with regard to the EEZ, the Agreement grants fishing jurisdiction to both states within the entire Provisional Measure Zone. In other words, the coastal state can exercise fishing jurisdiction over third state vessels even beyond the provisional median line.

2.3.1.2.2 Authority within the EEZ

The area towards the coast of Korea within the Provisional Measure Zone is Korea's definite EEZ; and in this zone, as determined by UNCLOS, it can exercise sovereign rights over living resources. The Agreement also regulates a few more specific details. First, both states must determine and notify every year the type and quota of fish that may be captured, as well as fishing season, areas and conditions that can be granted to the nationals and vessels of the other state within their EEZs. At this point, both states must consider relevant factors such as the state of living resources within its EEZ, its fishing capacity, traditional fishing activities, fishing in the restricted zones, etc. Second, the nationals and the vessels of each state must comply with the relevant laws of the other state while fishing in the EEZ of the other state. Third, where the vessels and their crews have been arrested for their violation of the laws and regulations of the coastal state, they must be promptly released upon the posting of reasonable bond or other security. In case of violation of fishing laws in the EEZ, UNCLOS prohibits the imposition of corporal punishment such as imprisonment "in the absence of agreements to the contrary by the States concerned." Because the Agreement does not state agreements to the contrary, corporal punishment cannot be imposed with regard to fishing activities within the EEZ.

2.3.1.2.3 Dispute Resolution Provisions in the Agreement and Its Application

A key feature of the Korea-China Fisheries Agreement distinguishing it from other fisheries agreements is that it does not specifically provide for dispute resolution. This is particularly noticeable in that even the Korea-Japan Fisheries Agreement that was referenced for this Agreement contained a dispute resolution clause. The Korea-Japan Fisheries Agreement, concluded in November 1998 and entering into effect in January of 1999, contains a relatively detailed provision concerning dispute resolution procedures in Article 13—first requiring the two states to seek negotiation when in dispute over the interpretation and application of the agreement, and then requiring submission to an arbitration panel when unresolved.

However, the Korea-China Fisheries Agreement also contains a general provision stating that "Nothing in this Agreement shall be interpreted to prejudice the position of either Contracting Party with regard to any matters of the law of the sea." Thus, any dispute arising from the interpretation and application of this Agreement will need to be resolved pursuant to this provision and general international legal principles concerning dispute resolution.

2.3.2 Major Korean Legislation Regarding Policing of Illegal Fishing Activities

2.3.2.1 *Exclusive Economic Zone Act*

Upon becoming state party to the UNCLOS on January 29, 1996, the Republic of Korea enacted the Exclusive Economic Zone Act (EEZ Act) on August 8 of the same year. Under this law, the Republic of Korea declared an EEZ up to 200 n.m. In accordance with UNCLOS and the EEZ Act, Korea is now able to exercise diverse jurisdiction over the EEZ. However, due to the fact that the distance between Korea and China and Korea and Japan is less than 400 n.m., it is inevitable and has already been noted that the EEZ between the three nations overlap. Consequently, the boundary delimitations have yet to be clearly established. Concerning those areas with undetermined boundaries, Korea's EEZ Act states that in such areas, Korea shall not exercise jurisdiction in the areas that are beyond the median line between the two countries "unless agreed otherwise." The median line refers to the virtual line that is equidistant from the baselines of the two countries involved.

Because of this provision, Korea's exercise of jurisdiction over the Provisional Measure Zone between Korea and China that are beyond the hypothetical median line may pose a problem. Now, the EEZ Act also states "unless agreed otherwise"; and the Provisional Measure Zone is a special zone that has been agreed upon by the Agreement, which is a separate set of agreements. Therefore, in accordance with the Agreement, the interpretation is then possible that concerning fishing activities, Korea has jurisdiction over the entire Provisional Measure Zone. However, because the Agreement only deals with items related to fisheries, the EEZ Act is applied to the exercise of jurisdiction over activities such as marine scientific research, piracy, and marine terrorism; and Korea will only be able to exercise jurisdiction up to the hypothetical median line.

2.3.2.2 *Fishery Resources Protection Act*

The Fishery Resources Protection Act (FRP Act) designated the jurisdiction of fishery resources protection zone with coordinates, according to which the waters on the North Korean side were also included, while including only a part of the Provisional Measure Zone. The waters that come under the Korean EEZ in accordance with the Agreement have also been included in the jurisdiction zone; therefore, based on the FRP Act, Korea has no issue in exercising jurisdiction in its EEZ. The FRP Act legislates that those who wish to engage in fishing in the fisheries jurisdiction zone should be approved by the Minister for Food, Agriculture, Forestry and Fisheries. Any individual who conducts fishing activities without approval will face up to three years in prison or a fine of up to KRW 500,000 and will have his or her fishing boat, equipment, catch, and farmed goods and products confiscated. Additionally, the FRP Act invests criminal investigation rights to the "officers and enlisted men on duty on naval fleet" and that "judicial police affairs shall be conducted by a public official appointed by an executive order." It should be noted here that although the FRP legislates up to three years of imprisonment and fines for violation, the Agreement contains no such provision. In addition, given the fact that UNCLOS prohibits corporal punishment, it appears difficult to strictly enforce the FRP Act in case of minor violations committed by foreign vessels.

2.3.2.3 *Act on the Exercise of Sovereign Rights on Foreigners' Fishing, etc. within the Exclusive Economic Zone*

2.3.2.3.1 Regulations on Foreigners' Fishing

The Fisheries Law and the Fishery Resource Management Law can be called the two fundamental Korean statutes on fisheries. However, these two laws are not applicable to foreigners' fishing activities; instead, the "Act on the Exercise of Sovereign Rights on Foreigners' Fishing, etc. within the Exclusive Economic Zone" (hereafter "Act on Foreigners' Fishing within the EEZ") is applied. Consequently, the fishing activities by Chinese fishing boats within Korea's EEZ are subject to the Act on Foreigners' Fishing within the EEZ.

The Act on Foreigners' Fishing within the EEZ defines "fishery" as "activities of catching, gathering, or farming marine animals and plants." Furthermore, it defines "fishing activities" as "all activities related to the following: fishery or fishery-related exploration/gathering, storage/preservation/processing of catch, transport of catch or any byproducts from catch, supply of articles necessary for ships, and any other fishery-related acts as regulated by order of the Ministry for Food, Agriculture, Forestry and Fisheries." In other words, the Act on Foreigners' Fishing within the EEZ has a very comprehensive regulation of fishing activities that includes even the storage/preservation/processing/transport of catch and supply of articles necessary for ships.

The Act prohibits foreigners or foreign ships from transferring or receiving any catch or byproducts that have been obtained by other ships within the EEZ. It also prohibits the direct raising of the catch in Korean ports. These restrictions can be understood as a method to secure effective means of controlling the amount of allowable catch and to protect the Korean fish market.

2.3.2.3.2 Authority of Judicial Police Officers

According to the Act on Foreigners' Fishing within the EEZ, a judicial police officer may order a foreign ship to stop if it is suspected of committing the following illegal fishery activities: (a) if convicted of activities that violate this Act and any other orders, restrictions, or conditions as regulated by this Act, (b) if convicted of activities that violate the fishery agreement signed with the Republic of Korea and any other orders, restrictions, or conditions as regulated by the agreement. Consequently, should there be any illegal activities defined by the Agreement, the judicial police officer may issue a stop order. If a foreigner has violated any orders, restrictions, or conditions set by the Act on Foreigners' Fishing within the EEZ, the Minister for Food, Agriculture, Forestry and Fisheries may order a suspension of all fishery activities within the EEZ up to one year or the Minister may also revoke fishery licenses.

2.3.3 Issues Related to Security and Prompt Release of Ship and Crew Members

2.3.3.1 *Relevant Korean Regulations and Enforcements*

Concerning security and prompt release, UNCLOS Article 73(2) stipulates that "Arrested vessels and their crews shall be promptly released upon the posting of reasonable bond or other security." Also on the issue, the Act on Foreigners' Fishing within the EEZ and its enforcement ordinance provide detailed protocols.

The judicial proceedings for foreign ships that have violated the Act on Foreigners' Fishing within the EEZ shall be conducted by a prosecutor and a judicial police officer. The prosecutor or judicial police officer may execute necessary measures such as stop order, embarkation, inspection, and arrest for the ship, the captain of the ship and any other violators who have violated any order, restriction, or condition as stipulated in the Act on Foreigners' Fishing within the EEZ. The judicial police officer shall report to the prosecutor on any measures he or she has taken. Except in emergency cases, the judicial police officer shall act under the direction of the prosecutor. When the prosecutor takes any of the measures aforementioned or receives a report from the judicial police officer, he or she shall immediately notify of the following to the captain or any other violator:

1. Intention of releasing the captain, crew, ship, and any other confiscated goods when security or document that guarantees provision of security has been submitted to the prosecutor in accordance with the ordinance of the Ministry of Justice;
2. Amount of security.

Upon receiving the security as noted above or the document that guarantees its provision, the prosecutor must promptly release the captain, any other crew, and any confiscated goods without delay. The amount of security shall be decided in accordance with the criteria set by executive order and shall be decided by the prosecutor depending upon the violation and other extenuating circumstances.

In case the security falls under any of the following two categories, it shall be reverted to the National Treasury one month from the day of designation.

1. When the captain or any other violator have been required by the prosecutor or the court to make appearance but does not show on designated day and place;

2. When the captain or any other violator have been required by the prosecutor or the court to submit the returned goods but does not submit the goods on designated day and place.

However, if an appeal is made within three months of the designated day when the violator should make an appearance on a specified day or will submit confiscated goods, then the security will not revert to the National Treasury. If, however, the captain or any other violator does not show up or submit the confiscated goods on the specified day that was appealed, then the security shall be reverted to the National Treasury the very next day. If by protocol the collateral has been reverted to the Treasury between one month and three months after the day of designation, then the already reverted collateral will be returned. Additionally, if before the security is reverted to the National Treasury, the declared fines are paid and custody of security is no longer necessary, the prosecutor shall return the security.

2.3.3.2 *UNCLOS Regulations and ITLOS Judgments for Prompt Release of Ship and Crew*

Regarding the prompt release of ship and crew, Article 292 of UNCLOS recognizes the compulsory jurisdiction of international courts such as the International Tribunal for the Law of the Sea (ITLOS). Currently, in accordance with UNCLOS Article 298, both the Republic of Korea and China have declared to be exempt from submission to the compulsory jurisdiction of ITLOS. Therefore, without the consent of the two states, the cases related to the following may not be brought before ITLOS: disputes regarding maritime boundary delimitations, disputes on military activities, disputes on sovereignty or other rights related to jurisdiction, and disputes related to the Security Council of the U.N. exercising assigned functions. However, issues related to the prompt release of ship and crew is not restricted by this provision. Therefore, one needs to note carefully that such issues may be dealt with at any time before the ITLOS.

The policy on the prompt release of ship and crew is a policy unique to UNCLOS. It is frequently used considering that the first incident that was brought before ITLOS had to do with prompt release. On prompt release, UNCLOS provides in Article 292:

1. Where the authorities of a State Party have detained a vessel flying the flag of another State Party and it is alleged that the detaining State has not complied with the provisions of this Convention for the prompt release of the vessel or its crew upon the posting of a reasonable bond or

other financial security, the question of release from detention may be submitted to any court or tribunal agreed upon by the parties or, failing such agreement within 10 days from the time of detention, to a court or tribunal accepted by the detaining State under article 287 or to the International Tribunal for the Law of the Sea, unless the parties otherwise agree.

2. The application for release may be made only by or on behalf of the flag State of the vessel.
3. The court or tribunal shall deal without delay with the application for release and shall deal only with the question of release, without prejudice to the merits of any case before the appropriate domestic forum against the vessel, its owner or its crew. The authorities of the detaining State remain competent to release the vessel or its crew at any time.
4. Upon the posting of the bond or other financial security determined by the court or tribunal, the authorities of the detaining State shall comply promptly with the decision of the court or tribunal concerning the release of the vessel or its crew.

The flag state of the vessel may file the application for release only when 1) the authorities of a state party have detained a vessel flying the flag of another state party and 2) it is alleged that the detaining state has not complied with the provisions of this Convention for the prompt release of the vessel or its crew upon the posting of a reasonable bond or other financial security. The court or tribunal to which the question of release from detention can be submitted should, as a rule, be a court or tribunal that the parties have agreed upon. If such agreement has not been reached within 10 days from the time of detention, then the question of release may be submitted to a court or tribunal accepted by the detaining state under article 287 or to ITLOS. At that moment, the detaining state can be said to be given the discretion to decide which court or tribunal the question should be submitted to. Such application for release may be made only by or on behalf of the flag state of the vessel.

The court or tribunal that has received the application for release shall handle it without delay and prejudice to the merits of any proceedings against the vessel, its owner or its crew in an appropriate domestic forum. The authorities of the detaining state remain competent to release the vessel or its crew at any time. The court or tribunal can determine the bond or other financial security. Upon the posting of the bond or other financial security determined by the court or tribunal, the authorities of the detaining state shall comply promptly with the decision of the court or tribunal concerning the release of the vessel or its crew. As has been described thus far, this policy serves the purpose to "promptly" handle the problem of the arrest of a vessel and its crew. Therefore, if the detaining state delays compliance with the decision of the court or tribunal without any justifiable reason, then the state is in violation of UNCLOS.

2.3.3.3 *ITLOS Judgments: Prompt Release and Reasonable Bond*

Up to present, the following nine prompt release cases have been submitted to ITLOS pursuant to article 292 of the UNCLOS.

(1) *The M/V "Saiga" Case* (*Saint Vincent and the Grenadines* v. *Guinea*, 1997)
(2) *The "Camouco" Case* (*Panama* v. *France*, 2000)
(3) *The "Monte Confurco" Case* (*Seychelles* v. *France*, 2000)
(4) *The "Grand Prince" Case* (*Belize* v. *France*, 2001)
(5) *The "Chaisiri Reefer 2" Case* (*Panama* v. *Yemen*) (2001)
(6) *The "Volga" Case* (*Russian Federation* v. *Australia*, 2002)
(7) *The "Juno Trader" Case* (*Saint Vincent and the Grenadines* v. *Guinea-Bissau*, 2004)
(8) *The "Hoshinmaru" Case* (*Japan* v. *Russian Federation*, 2007)
(9) *The "Tomimaru" Case* (*Japan* v. *Russian Federation*, 2007)

Among these cases, *The "Grand Prince" Case* was dismissed for lack of jurisdiction because Belize was not the flag state of the vessel at issue in the case; *"Chaisiri Reefer 2" Case* was held to be a nonsuit because of Yemen's release of vessel; and the *"Tomimaru" Case* was not decided on pursuant to Article 292(3) due to the decision of the Supreme Court of the Russian Federation. Thus, the remaining six of the nine cases actually dealt with the issue of "reasonable bond or other financial security."

One issue dealt in these cases was the issue of whether there is a time limit in the filing of an application by the flag state for the prompt release of the vessel being detained. In the *"Camouco" Case*, Panama claimed that France had filed its application more than three months after the detention of the *Camouco*; and because France had failed to act promptly, the Tribunal had to dismiss the case. The Tribunal held that the flag state was not required to file an application at any particular time after the detention of a vessel or its crew as long as the allegation made in the application was well-founded. Thus, the flag state may, as long as its vessel and crew are being detained, request their prompt release at any time.

More importantly, the core issue among the prompt release cases was how to determine what a "reasonable" bond or other security is. The detaining state—of the vessel and crew—often seeks to set a bond (security) as high as possible, while the flag state of the detained vessel and crew claims that the amount is excessive. Among the six cases that actually dealt with this issue, the Tribunal in all cases, except for the *M/V "Saiga" Case* in which the government of Guinea Bissau did not set the bond, refused to accept the claims of both the detaining states and the flag states.

ITLOS stated in the *"Camouco" Case* that a number of factors including the gravity of the alleged offences, the penalties imposed or imposable under the laws of the detaining state, the value of the detained vessel and of the cargo seized, were relevant in an assessment of the reasonableness of bonds or other financial security.

Regarding the gravity of the alleged offences, in the *"Hoshinmaru" Case*, a criminal case was instituted by Russian Federation against Japan for "illegal fishing with grave damages." Japan claimed that the bond of 22,000,000 rubles was excessive because the violation was not a grave one and that the amount of the bond should not exceed 8,000,000 rubles. The Tribunal determined the reasonable bond to be 10,000,000 rubles, holding that the offense committed by the Master of the *Hoshinmaru* should not be considered as a minor offence or an offence of a purely technical nature. The Tribunal also held that although a violation of the rules on reporting may be sanctioned by the detaining state, it is not reasonable that a bond should be set on the basis of the maximum penalties which could be applicable to the owner.

ITLOS also took into consideration the value of the confiscated vessel and cargo in determining the bond. The confiscated cargo, from the perspective of the detaining state, can be considered an "illegal catch" from its EEZ or "goods stolen" from state property. This then can raise the issue of whether it is reasonable to estimate the "illegal catch" or "goods stolen" in setting the bond. In the cases submitted to the ITLOS, the detaining states confiscated all cargo.

3 Maritime Safety and Security

3.1 *Korea's Maritime Challenges and Priorities*

The sea plays an important role for Korea's economy and security, and thus, making good order at sea is a vital priority for the country. . . .

3.1.1 The Proliferation Security Initiative

Proliferation of weapons of mass destruction, their delivery systems, and related materials remains a major challenge for the international community.

Given the volatile situation on the Korean Peninsula and North Korea's withdrawal from the Six Party Talks in 2009 as well as the country's stated intention of carrying on with its nuclear weapons program, Korea is facing a difficult challenge in terms of its response to North Korean export of such materials by sea. The issue continues to be a priority and its membership in the Proliferation Security Initiative should be seen in this light.

Immediately following North Korea's second round of nuclear tests in May 2009, Korea decided to become a member of the Proliferation Security Initiative (PSI) after having sent observers to PSI exercises in the past as a like-minded country. A previous North Korean nuclear test in October 2006 had not led to Korean participation in the PSI due to concerns about the risks of renewed military confrontations with North Korea and the fact that an agreement with similar effects as the PSI already existed between the two countries, namely the Agreement on Maritime Transportation between the South and the North.

As a consequence of the increased tensions between the two Koreas in the wake of the sinking of the *Cheonan* in March 2010, the Korean government in June 2010 announced its intention to join the Operational Experts Group (OEG), the steering committee of the PSI, by the end of 2010. In addition, Korea hosted a PSI workshop for Asia-Pacific member countries in October 2010. These steps indicate that Korea is preparing to play a key role in sharing intelligence regarding North Korea with the other PSI members and further underline that anti-proliferation remains a key priority for Korea.

3.2 *The Legal Framework of Maritime Security in East Asia: A Comparative View*

In the post-Cold War era, international disputes have taken on a new and distinctive character. During the Cold War, an ideological confrontation between the U.S. and U.S.S.R. along with conventional threats to security from nuclear weapons maintained a balance of power. In the post-Cold War era, while conventional security threats have decreased, they has been replaced by nonconventional threats of regional, ethnic, religious and resource disputes, terrorism and piracy.

Another trend to note is that disputes during the Cold War era, which mostly occurred on land, has begun to shift to the seas. Various aspects of maritime disputes, i.e., maritime resources, sea lanes of communication, maritime delimitation and maritime security, which were submerged during the Cold War era, are now beginning to be revealed in conflicts, with low-intensity maritime disputes deepening. With inter-state conflicts growing particularly more acute in Northeast Asia regarding interests in the oceans, e.g., maritime territorial sovereignty and maritime resources, there is the possibility of these conflicts turning into high-intensity disputes.

Together with these issues, non-conventional maritime security threats, i.e., maritime terrorism and piracy that has been on the rise since the 9/11 terrorist attack, are becoming significant threats to the international trade order and free navigation. To deal with such non-conventional maritime security threats, the international community, under a U.S. led initiative in its capacity as the world's largest economy, is strengthening the existing international legal regime and concluding new agreements to strengthen worldwide cooperation for their implementation.

Unfortunately, the United Nations Convention on the Law of the Sea (UNCLOS), which provides the basic framework for this new maritime order, is revealing many imperfections and limits in supporting the international efforts to respond to the needs of maritime security. Its provision on piracy in particular is much too limited and thus divorced from reality, and it contains no provisions regulating maritime terrorism. Further, while there are increasing concerns over the proliferation of weapons of mass destruction (WMD) through the seas, it is difficult for the conventional international legal framework that emphasizes freedom of navigation to respond to these newly arising threats to security. This has led to the international community to either form new maritime security regimes apart from the UNCLOS which has been driven by the U.S. following the events of 9/11 or to strengthen existing ones.

With such changes in international maritime security and the emergence of new threats, it became necessary for the three northeast Asian states of Korea, China and Japan, which are overwhelmingly dependent upon seaborne trade, to examine their legal systems that would support their participation in a new maritime security regime and their subsequent domestic implementation.

This study compares and evaluates how the global maritime security regimes for the confrontation of piracy, port and vessel security, and maritime terrorism are being accommodated by the legal systems in Korea, China and Japan, as well as how the legal groundwork for the implementation of such maritime security regimes is being laid out.

3.2.1 Vessel and Port Security

3.2.1.1 *Amendment of the SOLAS Convention*

In the wake of the 9/11 terrorist attack in 2001, the international community developed comprehensive security regulations entitled the International Ship and Port Facility Security Code (ISPS Code) to strengthen the security of ship and port facilities. The ISPS Code refers to international rules for the security of vessels and port facilities as adopted at the state party conference on December 12, 2002, enhancing the 1974 Convention for the Safety of Life at Sea (SOLAS) resolutions Part A (Mandatory) and Part B (Recommended).

At the 22nd general meeting of the IMO held in November of 2011, a mere two months after 9/11, the conference of contracting governments to the 1974 SOLAS Convention was decided to be held in December of 2002 to develop measures for port and vessel security, and commissioned the Maritime Safety Committee (MSC) to prepare the preliminary draft of the amendment to the Convention. The MSC prepared the draft from the period of February to December of 2002, and in December, 113 government representatives met in London for the Diplomatic Conference on Maritime Security and unanimously voted to adopt the amendment to the SOLAS Convention. The amendments to the SOLA Convention adopted at the conference can be summarized as follows:

- Chapter 5 was amended to require all ships of 300 gross tonnage and upwards but not more than 50,000 (not including oil tankers and passenger ships) to be fitted with the Automatic Identification System (AIS); while passengers ships engaged in international voyage and cargo ships of 300 gross tonnage and upwards, as well as mobile offshore drilling units and ships built after 2008 were required to be fitted with Long-Range Identification and Tracking (LRIT) system;
- Chapter 11-1 (Special measures to enhance maritime safety) was amended to require that i) all passenger ships of 100 gross tonnage and upwards and cargo ships of 300 tonnage and upwards should be marked with its Ship Identification Number (SIN), ii) port State control on operational requirements, and iii) placement of Continuous Synopsis Record (CSR);
- Chapter 11-2 (Special measures to enhance maritime security) was added to i) enshrine the ISPS Code for specific provisions regarding vessel and port security, ii) require all ships to be provided with the Ship Security Alert System (SSAS), and iii) regulate the state control of ships in port such as the refusal of entry;
- Adoption of the ISPS Code as an annex.

While the SOLAS Convention regulates standards for the construction, equipment and operation of ships for the safety of persons on the sea, the ISPS Code seeks to identify and prevent any acts that threaten the security of ships and port facilities through the cooperation of the workers on ships or in port facilities. Because the two differ in legislative purpose and scope of application, there were limitations for the SOLAS Convention to accommodate the ISPS Code in the first place. Expanding the ISPS Code to include port facilities, regardless, was made possible by the consensus reached regarding the need to strengthen maritime security and to establish a new international maritime security regime in the wake of 9/11 and address the increased threats of maritime terrorism. In addition, although the establishment and amendment of international conventions generally take several years, the "tacit acceptance" procedure of the 1974 SOLAS Convention that allowed an amendment voted by two-thirds of the member states to automatically take effect in six months if there is no particular opposition within a year also played a significant role in placing the ISPS Code within the Convention. The aggressive effort of the U.S. to push ahead, led by the U.S. Coast Guard, was another factor that helped quickly conclude the legislative process; and finally, on July 1, 2004, the amendment took effect.

3.2.1.2 *Contents of the ISPS Code*

The ISPS Code, as an annex to the amendment of the SOLAS Convention, is comprised of 19 articles, divided into mandatory provisions in Part A and recommended provisions in Part B. Though the provisions of Part B are not mandatory, considering that they must be referenced in establishing and understanding security regulations, they ought to be seen as equally mandatory as Part A in reality. This is because Part A provides the basic framework for the security system and instructs the referencing of specific provisions in Part B.

The ISPS Code is applicable to i) all passenger ships, ii) cargo ships of 500 gross tonnage and upwards, iii) mobile offshore drilling units, and iv) port facilities utilized by ships engaged in international voyage. Key responsibilities include i) setting the security level by each government and providing adequate guidelines, ii) conducting approval and evaluation of national ships and port security plans, as well as security check-ups of foreign ships, and communicating security related information to the IMO, iii) appointing ship security officers (SSOs) onboard and establishing self-security evaluation plans to be approved by the administration (flag) state, after which international ship security certificates (ISSCs) are placed onboard, iv) appointing (shipping) company security officers (CSOs), and v) as for the port state, having in place port facility security measures based on the security level and appointing port facility security officers (PFSOs).

3.2.2 Accommodation by Domestic Law and Its Evaluation

Following the full implementation of the ISPS Code, as of January 2011, 1004 Korean flagged vessels obtained the security certificates; and 28 trade ports utilized by ships of international voyage became their targets. The government in 2003, due to time constraints prior to the Convention's entry into force, legislated and implemented the Regulation regarding Security of Ships and Port Facility through public notice by the Ministry of Maritime Affairs and Fisheries. Because the domestic accommodation of the ISPS Code was a legislative matter directly related to the rights and duties of citizens, however, the legal status of the public notice to implement such duties was inadequate. Thus, in August of 2007, the legal grounds were strengthened by the enactment of the Security of Ships and Port Facilities Engaged in International Voyage Act.

This law provided for: i) the setting of security level of ships and port facilities engaged in international voyage (Articles 5 & 6); ii) appointment of a general security officer and ship security officer by the owner of the ship engaged in international voyage (Articles 7 & 8) and the acquisition of international ship security certificates (Articles 11 & 12); iii) port state control of foreign ships based on the possession of international ship security certificates (Article 19, para. 1); iv) the duty to communicate ship security information 24 hours prior to the entry of foreign ships into a port of the Republic of Korea and the ensuing power to limit movement, request modification, investigate ship or refuse entry (Article 19, paras. 4 & 6); v) appointment of a port security officer by the owner of the port facility and the implementation of a security evaluation (Articles 23 & 24) and so on.

3.2.3 Maritime Terrorism under International Law

As can be seen in the cases of the hijacking of *Achille Lauro* in Egyptian waters in 1985, the attack on the U.S. destroyer U.S.S. *Cole* while anchored in Yemen in 2000, and the attack of the French oil tanker *M/T Limburg* in 2002, maritime terrorism against ships is becoming a reality.

Today, where the majority of the worldwide import/export goods are transported over the sea, even a temporary shutdown of major sea lanes of communication due to maritime terrorism can greatly affect the world economy. Yet states face difficulty in determining political priorities and securing the necessary means due to the shifting objects of maritime terrorism such as ships, ports, maritime infrastructures, and limited anti-terrorism resources. Further, a precise definition of maritime terrorism cannot be found in international law, which could result in confusion regarding counter-maritime terrorism policies, in international cooperation and the exercise of jurisdiction over terrorists.

The concept of maritime terrorism can be clarified when compared with that of piracy. As can be observed in the *Achille Lauro* case, there are religious beliefs or political ideologies behind maritime terrorism, while piracy seeks private, economic gain. Despite this distinction, however, maritime terrorism and piracy often have mixed goals; and the two are fundamentally similar in that they are both illegal acts committed on the seas thereby threatening the safety of navigation and incurring much damage to persons and property.

The UNCLOS only provides for acts of piracy as mentioned above. The two conditions necessary for piracy, namely i) on the high seas or places outside the jurisdiction of any state and ii) the two ship rule requiring the attacking ship and a victim ship is inadequate in that it cannot cover instances like 9/11 on the oceans where a passenger or crew hijacks the ship and utilizes the vessel as a weapon to attack port facilities.

Further, unlike piracy cases where any state discovering or successfully suppressing acts of piracy can exercise jurisdiction, maritime terrorism, which does not satisfy the elements of piracy, raises unresolved issues of the existing framework international law such as the elements of the crime, transfer of suspect, and exercise of jurisdiction. To prevent maritime terrorists from going unpunished due to the lack of jurisdiction under international law, the international community adopted the Convention for the Suppression of Unlawful Acts against the Safety of Maritime Navigation (SUA Convention) in March 1988 to extend the scope of jurisdiction.

3.2.4 Legislative Accommodation of the SUA Convention and Its Evaluation

The main purpose of the SUA Convention is to prevent unlawful acts threatening safe navigation and to ensure that appropriate action is taken against persons committing unlawful acts against ships. The adoption of the SUA Convention was directly influenced by the hijacking of the luxury Italian cruiser *Achille Lauro* on October 7, 1985. Following this incident, on December 9 of the same year, U.N. General Assembly resolution 40/61 instructed the IMO to examine adequate measures against maritime terrorism committed against ship and crew. As a result, On March 10, 1988, the SUA Convention was adopted, entering into force on March 1, 1992. As of 2016, there are 166 state parties. The IMO also adopted The Protocol for the Suppression of Unlawful Acts against the Safety of Fixed Platforms Located on the Continental Shelf which was not included in the SUA Convention.

After 9/11, to prevent ships from being utilized for terrorist purposes or for the transport of WMD, under the leadership of the U.S., the 1988 SUA Convention was reevaluated. As a result, the IMO adopted the Protocol of 2005 to the Convention for the Suppression of Unlawful Acts against the Safety of Maritime Navigation. The amended SUA Convention (Articles 1 & 16), the 2005 Protocol to the SUA Convention (Articles 17 & 24) and their annexes were combined to form the Convention for the Suppression of Unlawful Acts against the Safety of Maritime Navigation, 2005 (2005 SUA Convention).

The 1988 SUA Convention defines "offence" as i) destruction or damage to a ship or its cargo, ii) an act of violence likely to endanger the safe navigation of the ship, iii) acts of violence against a person on board, iv) attempt, incitement or threats of the above acts and so on. The same Convention recognizes the varying jurisdictions of flag state of the victimized ship, the state in which the crime occurred, the nationality of the suspect or victim, state of residence for persons without nationality and so on. By establishing jurisdiction and facilitating the transfer of criminals, the focus was on preventing situations in which criminals would go unpunished for lack of jurisdiction.

However, in a changing security environment along with heightened terrorist threats, issues have been raised as to the difficulty of applying the 1988 SUA Convention to cases in which ships are utilized as means for terrorism or for transporting terrorist supplies such as WMD. The 2005 SUA Convention created new provisions to bolster such weaknesses.

First, Article 3*bis* was newly added to include within the scope of "offences" i) intimidating a population, or to compel a Government or an international organization to do or to abstain from any act, ii) uses against or on a ship or discharging from a ship any explosive, radioactive material or BCN (biological, chemical and nuclear) weapon, iii) discharges, from a ship, oil or other hazardous or noxious substance, iv) transports on board a ship any explosive or radioactive material. Second, the 2005 SUA Convention also added a boarding and inspection provision in 8*bis* to prevent terrorism. Where the requesting Party has reasonable grounds to suspect that the ship or a person on board the ship has been, is or is about to be involved in the commission of an offence, it may request the flag state to board and inspect the vessel, at the point which the flag ship may authorize the request or refuse and conduct the boarding and inspection with its own law enforcement. Third, in relation to the extradition of criminals or judicial assistance, the contracting state cannot refuse the extradition request on the basis of determining the act to be a political crime.

3.2.4.1 *Korea*

Korea became party to the 1988 SUA Convention in May 2003; and to domestically accommodate the Convention and its Protocol, enacted the Punishment for Damaging Ships and Marine Structures Act (Punishment for Damage Act) the same year to expand jurisdiction to acts committed by foreign nationals against Korean ships and marine structures outside Korean territory. It also provides for the process of transfer of criminals and defines specific acts of the crime.

More specifically, it provides for: i) the punishment of foreign nationals for criminal acts committed against ships and marine structures outside of the territory of Korea (Article 3); ii) the captain's transfer of a criminal to a SUA Convention state party pursuant to the approval of the Minister of Justice (Article 4), and iii) includes unlawful acts such as murder or infliction of injury upon persons on ship or marine structures and hijacking of ship, damage to ship and others, installation of dangerous objects, delivery of false information, threats, and so on (Articles 5 & 13).

3.2.4.2 *Evaluation*

Maritime terrorism is a transnational crime, whose preparation, implementation and impact go beyond the boundaries of a state. Thus, complex international legal issues are at play in the investigation of the crime of terrorism and the punishment thereof.

The 1988 SUA Convention provides for the extension of jurisdiction and the duty to extradite criminals to facilitate the punishment of persons committing maritime terrorism. In light of the increased potential for terrorism on the seas using ships or transport of terrorist related goods in the wake of 9/11, the amended 2005 SUA Convention, in particular, added new provisions defining offenses to include the transport of BCN and related substances, as well as the inspection of suspicious vessels.

The current 2005 SUA Convention has not entered into force until July 28, 2010 due to a lack of state parties which appears to be partially due to the newly added provisions and their potential to infringe upon state sovereignty. Another reason may also be that the state parties of the SUA Convention, who are actively participating, may undergo searches or inspection necessary for the prevention of the transport of WMD over the seas by the WMD Proliferation Security Initiative (PSI).

However, in spite of the fact that the PSI that began under the initiative of the U.S. involves military action, it is taking place outside the framework of the U.N.; and the fact that the participating states are relatively few in comparison to the member states of the U.N. has raised criticisms regarding its justification under international law. Taking these points into consideration, the SUA Convention—currently with 166 member states—will contribute more significantly to the prohibition of the proliferation of WMD and terrorism than that of PSI, which is more loose in terms of international legal justification or binding force as a treaty, especially after the 2005 SUA Convention is in force.

3.2.5 Conclusion

The domestic accommodation and implementation of international treaties regarding piracy and maritime security of the three Northeast Asian states of Korea, China and Japan have been described above. As states are entirely dependent upon seaborne trade, securing the safety of the sea lanes of communication has become part of their respective national agendas. Thus, these countries are putting great efforts into securing safe passage of their ships from pirates who disturb maritime trade order and interfere with the free passage of vessels, as well as to provide security measures for their major national port facilities and marine structures.

Although threats of maritime terrorism are increasing, the lack of a unified definition under international law such as through the UNCLOS, SUA Convention and so on, in addition to the differing domestic systems for punishment of terrorists could cause confusion in cooperating towards distinguishing maritime terrorism from piracy and punishing them. Further, the 2005 SUA Convention seeks to prevent the transport of unlawful WMDs over the seas, while the PSI system has to still overcome the challenge of strengthening its justification under international law.

The national criminal justice systems that were developed before piracy became an international issue did not realize the need for legislating to punish acts of piracy against their respective vessels in foreign waters. Thus, it follows that today, the criminal procedures for domestically punishing pirates arrested in foreign waters such as Somalia ought to be supplemented. Also, in relation to this, just as the International Criminal Court exists to punish crimes against humanity, the establishment of an international anti-piracy tribunal solely in charge of punishing pirates which is being raised by the international community, should be actively evaluated.

Korea, China and Japan, which are connected by the oceans, need to construct a close regional cooperative system for maritime security. Furthermore, in response to piracy and maritime terrorism in waters beyond their national territory and to secure the safety of the sea lanes of communication which is of mutual benefit, there is a need to cooperate for a balanced justice system to deal with and punish acts that threaten the safety of the oceans.

4 Maritime Cooperation

4.1 *Protection of the Sea Lanes in the Jeju Waters and Maritime Cooperation in Northeast Asia*

Having entered the globalized 21st century, the safety and protection of sea lanes have become a major concern among littoral states of the Northeast

Asian seas both from military and non-military perspectives. The economic development strategies of these states are highly dependent upon foreign trade, which are mostly conducted over the sea. The strategic interests of the U.S., Russia, China and Japan, as well as that of the divided states of North and South Korea in Northeast Asia have become more sensitive and more focused than any of the other regions of the world. Competition and confrontations among the states in the region have often been heightened by the issues of sea lane protection and safety. The semi-enclosed nature of the Northeast Asian seas have further pushed the relationship among these states into a more acute tension, in particular concerning the expansion of maritime jurisdiction and the continuing sovereignty dispute over islands, especially following the entry into effect of the U.N. Convention on the Law of the Sea (UNCLOS) in 1994.

Today, it is difficult for any single state to independently secure the oceans and sea lanes as they cover a very extensive area. Thus, securing the oceans and sea lane safety through marine cooperation is becoming a very important state agenda not only on a global scale but also at the regional level. In spite of regionalism spreading around the world, however, the disparate and divergent factors among states in the Northeast Asian region are very visible, from which confrontations and conflicts still continue to arise.

Based upon this background, this section first evaluates the importance of protecting Northeast Asian sea lanes and the strategic value of the Jeju Sea around the Jeju Strait and Ieodo waters. This section then proposes the formation of a regional marine cooperation system at the maritime governance level for sea lane security.

4.1.1 Significance of the Northeast Asian Seas and Sea Lanes

4.1.1.1 *Definition of the Northeast Asian Seas*

Northeast Asia refers to the region of Asia that includes Korea, Japan and China while a broader definition includes the Northeastern region of China, Mongolia and far eastern Russia. "Northeast Asian Seas" refer to the waters around which these Northeast Asian states are situated as coastal states. The waters surrounded by the eastern coast of the Asian continent beginning at the Korean Peninsula to Singapore in the South, and a line of islands from the Japanese archipelago, the Ryukyu Islands, Taiwan, and the Philippines to Borneo and Sumatra of Indonesia is generally called the China Sea. This is then divided by the Taiwan Strait as the boundary, with the northern side being called the East China Sea and the southern side the South China Sea. The East China Sea is generally referred to as the Northeast Asian Seas. More specifically, with a line drawn from the southern point of the Korean Peninsula to the Yangtze River as a reference point, the Northeast Asian Seas can be divided into the Yellow Sea (West Sea) lying between the Korean Peninsula and the Eastern coast of China to the north; East China Sea in a narrower sense between Taiwan and the Korean Peninsula to the south; the East Sea between the Korean Peninsula and Japan; and the Sea of Okhotsk between Eastern Sakhalin of Soviet Union and Kamchatka Peninsula. Among these four seas included in the Northeast Asian Seas, the Sea of Okhotsk has been considered an inland sea of Russia; but the other three seas have been at the center of major activities and interests of the surrounding states.

With the Northeast Asian waters at the center, Korea lies adjacent to or across major powers such as Japan, China, Taiwan, and Russia, while maintaining a distinctive relationship with North Korea as a divided state. The U.S. is not a state around the Northeast Asian seas *per se*, but due to the cooperative military relationships with Korean and Japan, concluded through the "Mutual Defense Treaty between the Republic of Korea and the United States of America" and the "Security Treaty between Japan and the United States of America," it has become an indirect marginal state with very important political and military interests in Northeast Asian waters. Thus, it can be said that there are 7 states (areas) which include Korea, Japan, North Korea, China, Russia, Taiwan and the U.S. surrounding the Northeast Asian seas (region).

The Northeast Asian seas have been utilized as major sea lanes for trade and military purposes by the littoral states and major maritime powers, and they have long received much international political and economic attention. The East China Sea is an important body of water situated at the intersection of sea lanes of communication connecting the East Sea and the Yellow Sea to the north, the South China Sea and the Philippine Sea to the south, and the Pacific Ocean to the east. And because it is surrounded by states of competitive or hostile relations, i.e., Korea, China, Taiwan, Japan, Russia and the U.S., conflict can arise at any time.

The Northeast Asian seas have become a major stage of activity for the U.S. and Russian navies, as well as China and Japan. From the American perspective, the Northeast Asian seas are recognized for their strategic importance not only in maintaining a maritime military presence but also in safeguarding sea lanes to hold the southward advance of the Russian navy in check. For Japan, China and Korea that are oriented towards ocean-going navies, the Northeast Asian seas are recognized for their strategic importance for state security. There are also many choke-points, which include the Jeju Strait, the Straits of Korea, Tsushima Strait, Taiwan Strait, Tsugaru Strait, Soya Strait and Tatar Strait, the strategic value of which have received attention for their essential location in the Northeast Asian sea lanes.

4.1.1.2 *Current Northeast Asian Sea Lanes and Their Significance*

Strictly speaking, Sea Lines of Communication, also abbreviated as SLOC, referred to the concept of supply lines or munitions vessel, "the maritime routes which connected operation forces and the base of operations, along which supplies and augmentation forces would be transported." The same definition was often utilized in a non-military context, thus causing confusion with Sea Lanes of Communication. SLOC today, or sea lanes, encompass "lanes of marine transport for commercial and military purposes."

With regard to economic development, the importance of sea lanes has long been recognized. As Sir Walter Raleigh, during the reign of Queen Elizabeth of England in the 16th century, stated, "For whosoever commands the sea commands the trade; whosoever commands the trade of the world commands the riches of the world, and consequently the world itself." It has been historically proven that a state which has control over the sea or had the power to effectively rule the oceans became a rich and powerful state that prospered. Admiral Mahan emphasized principles of maritime strategies early on as a foundation for national development; and based on this strategy, England the U.S. have built great maritime military strength to become maritime states which lead the world.

Maritime military strength, or sea power having this as a core element, has become the foundation for national development and a basic factor for measuring national power today. States that possess sea power, for the safety of their own sea routes, passively utilize the vast SLOCs while more actively attempting to focus and demonstrate their sea power in the oceans in order to support their allies, eliminate opposing forces within the region and to neutralize the interventions of other states.

No state today can be self-sufficient, self-supporting, and independent economically; rather we live in a system of an international division of labor and cooperation where resources and products must be traded. In particular, the explosive increase of the world population today and the increase in the demand for resources, as well as the accompanying rise in the exchange of goods and services, make the usage of sea lanes for maritime trade inevitable. In order to safely transport goods necessary for survival, e.g., oil, food, raw materials or military goods to one's own country, not only during peaceful times but also in times of emergency, there rises the need to protect sea lanes. The oceans also bear important economic value as a treasure trove of biological and mineral resources. It would not be an overstatement to say that together with maritime trade, securing the safety of sea lanes for the exploration and exploitation of marine resources is now becoming an important agenda not only for individual states but for the international community as well.

There are varying different explanations regarding the distribution of the sea lanes in the Northeast Asian seas. One view provides that among the regular line of traffic utilized by foreign trade vessels of Korean nationality, there are eight sea lanes including the Korea-Japan route, Southeast Asian route, North American route, Middle Eastern route, European route, Australian route, African route, and Middle and South American route. Another view discusses 3 Korea-Japan routes and 4 Korea-Southeast Asia-Middle East route for a total of seven sea lanes. A third view notes the Northern route connecting the North American region and the Siberian region, the Korea-Japan route connecting Japan, the Korea-China route connecting China, and a Southern route connecting Southeast Asia-Middle East-Europe, for a total of 4 sea lanes. Lastly, there is a view that describes a Korea-China route passing through the West Sea directly to the East Coast of China; a southwestern route passing through the East China Sea and leading to Southeast Asia, the Middle East, Europe and Africa; a southeastern route passing around the Japanese archipelago or the strait and leading to North, Middle and South America; and a Korea-Japan route passing through the East Sea and the Korea Strait and leading to Japan, for a total of four major sea lanes.

The strategic significance of the North American route has been highly evaluated not only from an economic perspective but also from that of the Korea-U.S. alliance and military cooperation. The Korea-China route has been greatly growing in trade volume since the establishment of Korea-China relations. The Middle East route is one that has been receiving much attention because of its instability due to oil transport and conflicts in the region. The Korea-Japan route, besides its significance in itself, is important because Korea transports oil from the Persian Gulf along the same route up to the East China Sea. Considering that it must pass through the Japanese sea lane, there certainly is a close connection. Furthermore, the Korea-Japan route is more important in that any hindrance to the Japanese route can directly affect the safety of Korean routes. The Southeast Asian route connecting Korea to Southeast Asia passes southeast of Jeju Island and the Ryukyu Islands of Japan, passing through the Bashi Strait between the Philippines and Taiwan, or the Taiwan Strait between China and Taiwan, finally arriving at the South China Sea. In order to enter the Indian Ocean from the South China Sea, vessels must pass by the widespread islands of the five ASEAN states—the Philippines, Indonesia, Malaysia, Thailand and Singapore.

4.1.1.3 *Significance of the Northeast Asian Sea Lanes*

Geographically, Korean foreign trade cannot but be dependent upon air and sea lanes, especially because maritime trade constitutes almost all of all foreign trade that is conducted by Korea. Thus, securing the safety of sea lanes is an absolute necessity for national development. It is also an absolute requisite for state survival, not only in times of peace but also in national emergencies. Nearly the entire trade volume of Korea is dependent upon trade coming through the Northeast Asian Sea Lanes. Having followed an outward-oriented development strategy from the 1960's, Korea has emphasized foreign trade as a mechanism for economic development. Korea's achievement as a maritime power—the world's 11th largest economy, 10th in maritime trade volume, foremost in shipbuilding capabilities, and 5th in handling containers—was attributable to the sea lanes connecting Korea to the world. Seventy-three percent of Korea's GDP is dependent upon foreign trade, and 99.7% of the entire trade volume is being transported over the sea. With the scale-up in transport volume and extended distances, in addition to lower transport costs, the importance of shipping and ports and the need for sea lane safety will be greatly emphasized in the future.

As a littoral state to the East Sea, the Yellow Sea and the East China Sea, and being situated where it can control the Korea Strait (a critical route for Russia's entry into East China Sea); and the Jeju Strait (a traffic point connecting the Yellow Sea and the East China Sea); as well as the outer sea lanes, Korea has historically been subject to attacks by great powers that have an interest in maritime traffic. Korea is surrounded by seas in which the navies of the major maritime powers co-exist despite the fact that these powers have engaged in intense confrontations. The Russian Pacific Fleet, the U.S. 7th Fleet, as well as the Japanese and the North Korean Fleets are afloat all the time in the East Sea, while in the Yellow Sea, there are the Chinese, North Korean and U.S. Fleets, and in the south, there are the U.S., Russian, Chinese, Japanese and Taiwanese Fleets in the East China Sea. Trade and military supplies are transported through these sea lanes with these fleets afloat. Thus, the Northeast Asian sea lanes have great significance for Korea from a military, strategic and economic perspectives. More recently, with the regrouping of maritime order and the heightening of conflict concerning the expansion of maritime jurisdiction and marine resources, the importance of safety and defense of sea lanes have gained more attention.

4.1.1.4 *Strategic Value of the Northeast Asian Sea Lanes and the Jeju Sea*

Jeju Island is situated at the southernmost point of the Korean Peninsula. It is not only at the center of the triangle connecting the Chinese mainland, the Korean Peninsula and the Japanese archipelago, but it is also located at the center of the Northeast Asian sea lanes surrounded by these states. The waters surrounding the Jeju Island is often called the Jeju Sea, which includes the Jeju Strait and the East China Sea in a narrow sense of the term, while what is called the "Ieodo Waters" south of the Jeju Island is part of the East China Sea. From a geographical perspective, the Jeju Island and Strait lie at or around a major point of the sea lane through which Korea advances not only to the Korea-Japan route and Korea-China route but also to Southeast Asia, the Middle East, Europe and other regions. Because of its geopolitical location, Jeju Island has long been evaluated among states of the Northeast Asian Sea region as bearing strategic value as key position for peace, security, economic, and other cooperation.

The Jeju Strait is a strait situated between the southern mainland and Jeju Island. The distance from the northernmost point of Jeju Island at 34° N (Chuja-myun Daeseo-ri) to Haenam of Jeolla-namdo is 47 nm (87 km), and to Mokpo is 76.5 nm (141.6 km) and from Jeju's main island to its Isle of Chuja is 25 nm (48 km). There are many small islets scattered throughout the Jeju Strait with depth averages around 70m with its deepest point at 140m. With straight baselines connecting the surrounding islands of Geomundo, Yeoseodo, Jangsoodo, Jeolmyungseodo, and Soheuksando as the starting point, the waters towards the mainland constitute internal waters, while the waters towards Jeju Island constitute the territorial sea. The Jeju Strait is often utilized for international navigation between one part of the high seas to an exclusive economic zone and another part of the high seas to an exclusive economic zone.

4.1.2 Legal Status and Strategic Significance of the Jeju Strait

4.1.2.1 *Definition and Types of "International Straits"*

In order to discuss what legal status the Jeju Strait has under international law, and in particular whether it satisfies the conditions necessary for international straits, we first need to discuss the U.N. Convention on the Law of the Sea (UNCLOS) provisions concerning the conditions and types of (international) straits. International law regarding the oceans, or the Law of the Sea, has regulated the passage regime in the straits used for international passage; and the UNCLOS, also referred to as the Constitution of the Oceans, adopted in 1982 and entering into effect in 1994, categorizes such straits with regard to the passage regime into the following six types:

1) UNCLOS Article 37 "straits which are used for international navigation between one part of the high seas or an exclusive economic zone and another part of the high seas or an exclusive economic zone" to which "transit passage which shall not be impeded" applies;

2) Article 38(1) "strait [that] is formed by an island of a State bordering the strait and its mainland, [where] there exists seaward of the island a route through the high seas or through an exclusive economic zone of similar convenience with respect to navigational and hydrographical characteristics" to which "innocent passage without suspension" applies;
3) Article 45(1)(b) "straits used for international navigation between a part of the high seas or an exclusive economic zone and the territorial sea of a foreign State" to which "innocent passage without suspension" applies;
4) Straits to which the passage regime under the Convention does not apply, but Article 36 "strait [where] there exists through the strait a route through the high seas or through an exclusive economic zone of similar convenience with respect to navigational and hydrographical characteristics";
5) Article 35(C) "straits in which passage is regulated in whole or in part by long-standing international conventions in force specifically relating to such straits";
6) Article 311(2) straits whose passage regime is regulated by "other agreements compatible with this Convention and which do not affect the enjoyment by other States Parties of their rights or the performance of their obligations under this Convention" though not long-standing.

4.1.2.2 *Evaluation of the Passage Regime of International Straits*

The UNCLOS included 12 provisions regarding straits in Articles 34 to 45, which greatly differ from the provisions of the 1958 Convention on the Territorial Sea and Contiguous Zone [hereinafter "Territorial Sea Convention"]. The Territorial Sea Convention can be distinguished from the freedom of passage in the high seas in that it only regulates innocent passage in the territorial seas. The UNCLOS, on the other hand, not only provides for innocent passage and passage regime in archipelagic waters but also regulates transit passage that applies to certain types of international straits.

The transit passage regime was a product of a compromise between the proposal of major maritime powers such as the U.S. and the former Soviet Union which demanded absolute freedom of navigation in international straits that become part of the territorial seas of the littoral states with their expansions up to 12 nm, and that of the strait states claiming that only the traditional innocent passage regime must continue to apply to territorial waters. The U.S., Soviet Union, and other maritime powers that desired to secure freedom of navigation and naval mobility sought a separate strait passage regime rather than that of innocent passage. The littoral states that had continued to expand their jurisdiction over the oceans by expanding their territorial waters and the establishment of economic zones, however, had supported the innocent passage regime applicable to territorial waters. Ultimately, both sides compromised and agreed to acknowledge the increased ocean jurisdiction of the littoral states, while implementing the transit passage regime guaranteeing the "free passage and normal navigation" of ships and aircrafts for certain types of international straits.

UNCLOS, in implementing "transit passage" as a passage regime for international straits, limits the straits to certain types to which this regime applies. According to the Convention, transit passage applies to straits used for international navigation between a part of the high seas or an exclusive economic zone and the territorial sea of a foreign state. Seas where such passages are freely conducted, or in straits connecting two seas where the law of the high seas are applicable, the right of transit passage is guaranteed for military vessels and other non-commercial government vessels. Additionally, transit passage refers to "the exercise of … the freedom of navigation and overflight solely for the purpose of continuous and expeditious transit of the strait" through the zones where transit passage is recognized. With regard to submarines which are required to navigate on the surface and to show their flag in innocent passage, whether passage under the surface is permissible in transit passage is disputed.

4.1.2.3 *Legal Status of the Jeju Strait and the Passage Regime*

Among the waters surrounding Korea, in light of their strategic significance, Jeju and the Korea Straits give rise to issues with passage of foreign, especially military, vessels. While the width of the Korea Strait is a mere 23.5 nm, Korea and Japan have both limited their territorial seas to 3 nm. Therefore, these waters include a passage route through the high seas or an EEZ. The Korea Strait is not an international strait to which the transit passage pursuant to Article 36 of UNCLOS would apply. Rather, within the territorial waters of the two states, only the traditional innocent passage applies; and for the high seas or EEZ, freedom of passage is guaranteed for vessels and aircrafts.

In contrast, the Jeju Strait, as observed earlier, is a strait formed by the Korean mainland and Jeju Island, and is therefore entirely included within the territorial waters of Korea. This geographical, hydrographical characteristic of the Jeju Strait gives it a different international legal status. First of all, the Jeju Strait connects parts of the high seas or EEZ, thereby fulfilling the geographical element of an international strait. Second, it is utilized for international navigation, which grants it an international legal status, although further determination is necessary as to whether transit passage is applicable under the UNCLOS.

First, we shall examine the geographical characteristics of the Jeju Strait. The Jeju Strait is formed by the Korean mainland and the island of Jeju. The distance from Jeju's northernmost point to Haenam of Jeollanamdo on the Korean mainland is 47 nm. However, due to the straight baselines formed by the islets in between, the distance between Jeju's baselines and these straight baselines is less than 24 nm. Thus, the Jeju Strait in its entirety is included within the territorial waters of Korea. If the Jeju Strait had no other characteristic but was utilized for international navigation between one part of the high seas or EEZ to another part of the high seas or EEZ in the Yellow Sea, the East China Sea or the East Sea, it would be an international strait to which transit passage would apply. However, if there exists "a route through the high seas or through an EEZ of similar convenience," transit passage would not be applicable to the Jeju Strait pursuant to Article 38(1) of the UNCLOS.

In truth, there is no clear guideline as to what this "route through the high seas or through an EEZ of similar convenience" means or who determines the existence of such a route; therefore, there is much debate—and potential for dispute—regarding this issue. The general opinion is that the Jeju Strait is a strait utilized for international navigation but has the navigational, hydrographical characteristic of "a route through the high seas or through an EEZ of similar convenience" towards the ocean at the same time. Therefore, the transit passage of UNCLOS does not apply to the Jeju Strait, but rather innocent passage without suspension. It follows that in the Jeju Strait, only innocent passage of vessels is acceptable and not the passage of aircraft in the airspace above the strait, and "submarines and other underwater vehicles [that] are required to navigate on the surface and to show their flag." Further, "[t]here shall be no suspension of innocent passage through such straits." This writer is of the opinion that this fact—that transit passage does not apply to the Jeju Strait but rather innocent passage without suspension—ought to be clearly indicated in Territorial Sea Laws of Korea and their Implementation Orders in order to prevent unnecessary debate or dispute.

If the Jeju Strait does not fall under transit passage and must therefore guarantee innocent passage without suspension for all foreign vessels, passage of foreign military vessels or non-commercial government vessels must also be allowed pursuant to the UNCLOS, which would give rise to discrepancies in the application of Korea's 1996 Law on Territorial & Adjacent Waters (Territorial Sea Laws) Article 5 and the Implementation Order Article 4. The reality under UNCLOS is that all vessels including military vessels must be guaranteed innocent passage through territorial waters of litttoral states. However, Article 5(1) of Korea's Territorial Sea Laws provides that when foreign military vessels or government vessels of non-commercial purposes seek to pass through territorial waters, they must give prior notice to the proper authorities pursuant to an Executive Order. Article 4 of the Implementation Order further provides that pursuant to Article 5(1), the following must be notified to the Minister of Foreign Affairs and Trade three business days prior to its passage.

Innocent passage of foreign government vessels including military vessels is a right guaranteed by UNCLOS. Therefore, should a littoral state require prior notification or authorization, the lawfulness of this requirement can be determined by the effect on the right of passage of foreign vessel in light of the purpose of the UNCLOS. Prior authorization is practiced on the premise that the passage could be denied and is therefore unlawful; prior notification, on the other hand, seeks to allow passage on the premise of prior notification. Therefore, as long as it does not contradict international law, a state may regulate the activities of foreign vessels within its territorial waters; and in light of the rights of littoral states to take actions to prevent non-innocent passage, it appears that this may co-exist with UNCLOS passage regimes. There are views, however, arguing that depending upon the interpretation, Korea's Territorial Sea Laws could categorize Korea as a state regulating the passage of foreign vessels within its territorial waters. There would be no practical benefit to such categorization.

Because the Jeju Strait is included in Korea's territorial waters, the very requirement of prior notification under Article 5 can be an issue. However, Article 4 of the Implementation Order, with regard to the passage of foreign military vessels, recognizes an exception to the requirement in case where there is no high sea included in the strait used for international navigation. Therefore, in this case, the Jeju Strait, which is used for international navigation, can avoid debate or dispute regarding the implementation of the prior notice system.

4.1.2.4 *Passage of North Korean Vessels through the Jeju Strait*

Article 5 of the Territorial Sea Laws provides, pursuant to the innocent passage of UNCLOS, that foreign vessels that do not threaten the peace and order of the Republic of Korea or its national security may pass through the territorial waters. This gives rise to the issue of whether North Korean vessels—military or non-commercial government vessels, can pass through ROK waters since North Korea is currently in a state of armistice with Korea and would presumably threaten Korea's national security and whether the innocent passage of any and every North Korean vessels can be refused.

This actually occurred in June 2001 when four North Korean merchant vessels including *Cheongjin II* entered the Jeju Strait. At the time, Korea did not allow North Korean vessels to enter the territorial and adjacent waters; thus, a Korean naval corvette and patrol killer medium (PKM) demanded the immediate exit of these vessels. As the first attempt of such passage through the Jeju Strait since the armistice, this incident generated much debate regarding the legal status of the Jeju Strait and the adequacy of the government response. Korea has permitted innocent passage of other foreign vessels over the years but had prohibited North Korea from doing so pursuant to its rules of operation. This contributes to the attitude that innocent passage cannot apply to North Korea because the two countries are maintaining a ceasefire and technically are still at war. However, there still has been much debate as to whether the ceasefire relationship should be judged as being in war rather than being at peace, and whether prohibition of passage should continue for both government and civilian vessels even though the ceasefire has continued since 1953.

Since then, North and South, with the purpose of materializing the spirit behind the June 15 Declaration, agreed to the Inter-Korean Marine Agreement and its annexes at the 14th Ministerial Meeting in 2004 that would guarantee the operation of vessels in sea routes connecting Incheon, Gunsan, Yeosu, Busan, Ulsan, Pohang and Sokcho ports in the South and Nampo, Haeju, Goseong, Wonsan, Heungnam, Cheongjin and Najin ports of the North. At the 15th Ministerial Meeting in June 2005, it was agreed that civilian vessels of the North could pass through the Jeju Strait; and in August, an amendment/supplementary agreement was reached that would add the Jeju Strait sea route to the previous Marine Agreement annexes. In one sense, this shows that there has been a change in the perception of North Korea, from that of an enemy state to a partner in cooperation and exchange. Even so, however, exclusion of the issue of passage of North Korean military vessels and non-commercial government vessels show that the fundamental attitude has not changed.

As part of its May 24 response to North Korea's attack on the Korean corvette *Cheonan* on March 26, Korea prohibited the entry of North Korean vessels into Korean territorial and adjacent waters, thereby returning to the pre-August 2005 situation. As such, the Jeju Strait is an area where North-South Korean relations can easily and clearly be observed and playing an important role in Korea's national security.

4.1.3 Legal Status and Significance of the Ieodo Waters

4.1.3.1 *Location and Legal Status of Ieodo*

"Ieodo" is situated at the center of the East China Sea, precisely at 125 degrees 10 minutes 57 seconds east longitude and 32 degrees 07 minutes 23 seconds north latitude. It is a "submerged rock or reef," the peak of which is 4.6 m below sea level, and lies 149 km (81 nm) southwest of Korea's Marado, 276 km (149 nm) west of Japan's Torishima and 245 km (133 nm) northeast of China's Tongdao.

Ieodo is a major fishing ground in East China Sea due to the joining of Kuroshio current moving north and the cold current of the Yellow Sea moving south, as well as the coastal waters of the Chinese mainland, resulting in an abundant habitat for various types of fish, e.g., mackerel, croacker, anchovy, bream, pollack, etc. The ocean floor around Ieodo, furthermore, forms part of the continental shelf that is presumed to contain useful mineral resources. Above sea level, it lies at the pathway of major typhoons, making it a key location for marine scientific research and meteorological observation, i.e., changes in marine environment, as well as the establishment of bases for rescue operations and fisheries support at the same time. Lastly, the waters surrounding Ieodo have been recognized by states around the Northeast Asian seas not only as a major SLOC but also as a primary maritime zone for military and strategic activities.

Ieodo is not an island under UNCLOS but a mere underwater reef. However, because the name Ieodo, often known as Parangdo, includes the Korean word "do" or island, it is highly likely that those who do not know can misconstrue it to be an actual island. Ieodo is marked as Socotra "Rock" in international charts; however, even the word "rock" under UNCLOS refers to a very small island which is always lying above sea level. Thus, even the name Socotra Rock can lead to misconceptions regarding its true nature. "Ieodo" does not bear the status of an island under provisions of the UNCLOS. Therefore, any claim of sovereignty over Ieodo or efforts to make it a base point for establishing maritime jurisdiction zones, i.e., territorial seas, EEZs and continental shelf, as well as expanding maritime jurisdiction, are without legal effect.

4.1.3.2 *Significance of the Ieodo Waters and the "Ieodo Issue"*

The Korean government recognized the significance of Ieodo and the surrounding waters by constructing an Ocean Research Station which has been in operation since 2003. The Ieodo Ocean Research Station is a fixed structure in jacket form, located about 700 m south from Ieodo, and 41 m in depth. Its upper portion is approximately 1320 square meters, consisting of a cellar deck for equipment and facility installations, a main deck for living quarters and laboratories, and a helideck for rescue operations equipment and human transport.

The Chinese government in 2000 and 2002, raised objections through diplomatic channels concerning Korea's construction of the Ocean Research Station; and through its Foreign Ministry briefing stated that "Suyanzao" (the Chinese name for Ieodo) was a reef situated where Korean and Chinese EEZs overlap and that any unilateral acts of Korea on Ieodo had no legal effect. While the Chinese representative mentioned that because Ieodo was an underwater reef, there was no territorial sovereignty dispute between Korea and China, he also emphasized that China wanted to settle the maritime jurisdiction issues through conversation. Recently, China also unreasonably demanded, by sending its state vessels, that two Korean vessels—tugboat and barge—stop the unpermitted recovery within its EEZ of a 50,905-ton bulk carrier that sank 0.8 km southwest of Ieodo.

The "Ieodo Problem" is not a "sovereignty issue" under international law of the sea, nor is it a simple "maritime jurisdiction issue." China's raising of the Ieodo issue is a visible example of China's movement towards expanding its maritime jurisdiction in the East China Sea, while at the same time, it is evidence that China's Northeast Project is simultaneously being geared towards the Northeast Asian seas. In that sense, the Ieodo issue is not only an international legal issue related to the law of the sea, but also a complex international issue with international political implications in which China is unreasonably asserting its views in order to expand its influence in the Northeast Asian seas. It exists as a potential issue that may possibly lead to acute confrontations and conflicts between Korea and China regarding the maritime order and security in the region.

4.1.4 Peace and Marine Cooperation in Northeast Asia

With the UNCLOS entering into effect in 1994, there have been many indications of a change in the maritime legal order. The UNCLOS allows the extension of territorial seas and adjacent zones up to 12 and 24 nm respectively and continental shelf up to 350 nm, while regulating the new EEZ regime that can extend up to 200 nm. In this manner, the UNCLOS guarantees the quantitative and qualitative expansion of the maritime jurisdiction of littoral states. At the same time, regarding the high sea resources that have traditionally been developed and exploited freely pursuant to the principle of "freedom of the high seas," the concept of the deep seabed was newly implemented by naming the deep sea-bed and minerals as common heritage of mankind to be placed under joint international management and exploitation. The UNCLOS further provides for the formation of maritime order through an enforced dispute resolution system. The UNCLOS system, by expanding jurisdictional waters in order to allow littoral states to secure marine resources and to implement a powerful system of dispute resolution and restrictions, appears to signal the return from the current "freedom of the seas" to the age of "distribution of the oceans."

Today, the navigation of ships and aircrafts in the high seas, the EEZ and the air above them are guaranteed; however, issues concerning the freedom of military activities of foreign vessels in the EEZ of littoral states, and non-military issues, i.e., development and exploitation of marine resources, marine scientific research, maritime environment conservation, are becoming the sources of international maritime disputes. Also in the Northeast Asian seas, there are many islands under sovereignty dispute such as Japan's "Four Northern Islands" (Etorohu, Kunashiri, Habomai, Shikotan), Diaoyutai (also known as the Senkaku Islands), and Dokdo, causing an increase in the diplomatic and military confrontations among the interest states. The sovereignty issue of the islands themselves has significant negative effect, not only on the peace and stability of Northeast Asia, but also in the formation of maritime order and settlement of relevant disputes. Recently, there have been many disputes in the Northeast Asian seas regarding EEZ delimitation and fisheries jurisdiction, while confrontations regarding marine pollution and environmental conservation have also been building.

4.1.5 Changes in Marine Security Policy of Northeast Asian States

Recently, threats to the maritime security of states around the Northeast Asian seas that had been dormant are newly arising as issues between them. Amidst the confrontation between Japan and China that has been continuing concerning the Senkaku Islands and the sinking of the corvette, *Cheonan*, and shelling of Yeonpyeong Island in 2010 between the Koreas, there has been a movement among states around the Korean Peninsula and the Northeast Asian seas to establish strategies for strengthening national maritime security against real and potential threats. There is a desperate need to form an international cooperation system and common security that would also secure the safety of SLOC for the safe international transportation of the states' strategic interests.

Meanwhile, in addition to the Proliferation Security Initiative (PSI) which seeks to prevent the proliferation of nuclear weapons and WMDs, the Container Security Initiative (CSI) has been implemented by the initiative of the U.S. Customs and Border Protection, triggered by the 9/11 incident in 2001. There also have been the adoption of the Convention for the Suppression of Unlawful Acts Against the Safety of Maritime Navigation (SUA Convention) of 1988 and 2005, a movement to strengthen the SUA Convention Regime that seeks to suppress acts such as maritime terror threatening the safety of maritime navigation.

However, the possibility cannot be ignored that the trend of the increasing sea power of the Northeast Asian states has acted as a factor contributing to the disputes. One particular feature related to the increasing sea power of

Northeast Asia is that while the sea power of the U.S., Russia, and other former maritime powers have been diminishing, the powers within the region such as China and Japan, as well as Korea and Taiwan, have begun to become stronger. China, in particular, is pursuing an ocean-going navy by modernizing it. The characteristics of the strengthening of Northeast Asian sea power in China, Japan and others, are: 1) emphasis in large scale and cutting edge technology reflecting the "Military Revolution Project;" 2) improvement and expansion of submarine powers; 3) fleet building and expansion of states within the region. Such increases in the sea power of Northeast Asian states can be seen as reflecting "a shift in defense priorities" emphasizing the importance of sea power on a global scale in the aftermath of the Cold War.

The strengthening of the sea power of Northeast Asian states reflects their awareness of the need for securing maritime deterrence and the attempt to limit the maritime activities of other states; thus, competition for increased sea power is expected to become more conspicuous in relation to securing the safety of major international straits. Since these states in the region are highly dependent upon trade by seas, securing the safety of sea lanes is directly related to the transportation of goods which is also directly connected to national economy and survival. Thus, as long as this significance is recognized, the strengthening of their sea power and maritime police force is expected to continue. If all the heightened capacity of sea power were to be mobilized within a limited area, the possibility of accidental confrontations resulting from misunderstanding and misjudgment will become higher; while the expansion of the scope of naval activity, e.g., securing islands that are under dispute and EEZ surveillance will also likely increase the probability of confrontation.

4.1.6 Northeast Asian Sea Lanes Security and Marine Cooperation System/Regime

Fundamentally, all states must possess police and military power sufficient to protect its own peace and security. The security of major Northeast Asian sea lanes including the Jeju Strait must also be based on such inherent safety/security capacities. This sea power is absolutely necessary not only to secure the safety of straits and sea lanes and to protect maritime sovereignty in times of war or crises, e.g., maritime terrorist acts resulting from issues of maritime jurisdiction or island sovereignty, or armed confrontation between states, but also to effectively maintain maritime safety and regulate unlawful acts, e.g., illegal acts of piracy or fishing, or maritime speculation in areas of high maritime traffic or fishing activities. Only when such sea power can secure its own maritime security can it then actively participate in multilateral cooperative systems.

A Northeast Asian maritime cooperative system must meet certain criteria for the advancement of security and cooperation for peace within the region. The need to construct such a peace or security cooperation framework and its possibility can be found in the change of the international order observable in the post-Cold War era. Unlike the Cold-War symbolized by confrontation of two sides based on ideological differences, the post-Cold War international order is demonstrating an entirely different characteristic. With the increasing variety of concerns, the traditional issue of military security in international politics has relatively weakened in proportion. This is based on the increase of issues transcending state borders such as the protection of the marine environment since the collapse of the Cold War. Such change in the security environment raises the need for transnational, comprehensive maritime cooperation rather than competition and confrontations among states.

The concept that is gaining more attention today than "joint security" is "cooperative security." Cooperative security refers to ending the confrontational relationship among the military regimes of each state and reaching a security objective through a cooperative relationship that is fundamentally compatible. The main thrust is in inducing a cooperative intervention of interested states not by physical threats or coercion but by an institutionalized process and consent. "Cooperative security" differs from "joint security" in that it actively pursues, for the prevention of war, institutionalized measures that have been consented to by all parties making it difficult to mobilize for invasion.

Those emphasizing opportunistic factors assert that such a change in the international order is also appearing in Northeast Asia—that military confrontation in the region has also weakened due to the end of the Cold War, replaced instead by economic and environmental factors. However, the international environment in the post-Cold War era may have these positive factors, there also are new sources of international conflict, together with uncertainties of the future. There are much more complicated geopolitical factors at play in the Northeast Asian region compared to other regions. The competitive relationship among the four major powers surrounding Northeast Asia—the U.S., China, Japan, and Russia—is still very fierce and complicated; thus even the formation of mutual trust is difficult prior to the institutionalization of cooperation. Ironically, these very issues have heightened the need for a maritime security cooperative regime.

4.1.7 Building a Northeast Asian Maritime Cooperation Regime

In order for Korea to effectively protect and to secure its maritime security in the sea lanes surrounding the Jeju Strait and Ieodo waters, it is obvious that it must above all be equipped with a sufficient level of sea power and an adequate maritime police force. Furthermore, a system allowing close, joint operations between the navy and the coast guard needs to be built As mentioned above, actualizing sea lane protection and maritime security agendas by building a cooperative regime among states of the Northeast Asian seas may be one valid approach. Thus, Korea must strengthen its cooperative activities together not only with North Korea, Japan, China, and Russia but also the coastal states of the Pacific, i.e., U.S. and Canada, actively responding to changes in the international maritime order in order to elevate its stature as a maritime power.

The first task necessary in achieving the goal of sea lane security and maritime cooperation through such a regional, multilateral cooperative regime, is building mutual political and military trust among states in the region. North and South Korea, the U.S. and North Korea, as well as Japan and North Korea, have yet to establish diplomatic relations, which is more pressing than anything else. Formation of a trust relationship between Korea and China by improving mutual understanding is urgent. Ultimately, only upon such a foundation can trust in military relations be possible upon which maritime cooperation could be built, transforming the Northeast Asian seas long known as "Sea of the Cold War" to "Sea of Peace."

There also is a need to strengthen the regional cooperative regime regarding fisheries and other uses of the oceans in the East Sea, East China Sea, and the Yellow Sea that is surrounded by Korea, Japan, Taiwan, Russia, and North Korea. This area bears the characteristics of semi-enclosed seas and requires close regional cooperation in the management and distribution of resources, even biological resources. Thus, efforts toward establishing a joint rule and cooperation system concerning the baseline regime, maritime delimitation, marine scientific research, continental shelf development, management of fishery resources, cooperation regarding fisheries, prevention of marine pollution and environmental protection, sea lane safety and protection, and maritime policy and dispute resolution is urgent.

The current fishery order in the Northeast Asian seas is regulated by the fisheries agreements concluded between each of the three states of Korea, China, and Japan. As a result, there are instances in which the establishment of areas such as the waters south of the Jeju Island is overlapped by three independently concluded agreements, e.g., Korea-Japan Fisheries Agreement, Korea-China Fisheries Agreement, and China-Japan Fisheries Agreement. This urgently requires a joint management and regulation system among the three states. Being situated at the center of the Northeast Asian seas, Korea faces a variety of maritime issues and is greatly concerned with securing sea lane safety. Therefore, it is important that Korea fully understand the security and economic facets of maritime issues and not only seek to improve the maritime security environment of the region, but also actively participate in the discussions to form a more secure maritime order.

Various conflict factors exist in the Northeast Asian seas in relation to island sovereignty and sea lane safety. Thus, institutionalized options for peaceful mediation or resolution of maritime disputes and cooperation are necessary through regional peace and security dialogues among governments such as through the ASEAN Regional Forum or the Northeast Asia Security Dialogue, as well as the Council for Security Cooperation in the Asia Pacific, and JEJU Forum at the civilian level.

4.1.8 Conclusion

With regard to the safety of Northeast Asian sea lanes, Korea has two straits—Korea Strait and Jeju Strait—that can be recognized for their strategic value. While the width of the Korea Strait is a mere 23.5 nm, Korea and Japan have both limited their territorial seas to 3 nm. Therefore, these waters include a passage route through the high seas or an EEZ and thus the potential for issues concerning the passage of military vessels or submarines is not very high. In contrast, the Jeju Strait can be distinguished geographically and hydrographically in that it is entirely included within the territorial waters of Korea, thereby having a different international legal status. Though the Jeju Strait itself is part of Korea's territorial waters, it connects parts of the high seas or EEZ, thereby giving it the status of an international strait. However, opinions are divided as to which passage regime is applicable to it under the law of the sea.

If the Jeju Strait is a "normal" international strait utilized for international navigation between one part of the high seas or EEZ to another part of the high seas or EEZ in the Yellow Sea, the East China Sea or the East Sea, it would be an international strait to which transit passage would apply, which would significantly limit the scope of regulation and jurisdiction that could be exercised by Korea as its littoral state. Korea would also have to bear the burden of permitting right of flight over the area by foreign aircrafts. However, many agree that there exists "a route through the high seas or through an EEZ of similar convenience" beyond Jeju Island, making it an international strait to which "innocent passage" rather than "transit passage" which applies pursuant to Article 38(1) of the UNCLOS.

Thus, there is a need to clearly indicate this as such to prevent unnecessary conflict in the Territorial Sea Law and the Implementation Orders, through specific provisions applicable to military vessels and submarines, that the Jeju Strait is a strait to which continuous, "innocent passage" of ships is applicable. Passage of North Korean vessels is another issue requiring thorough evaluation, but there is a need to distinguish between military and non-commercial government vessels from civilian ships and to determine policies regarding their passage through Korean territorial waters such as the Jeju Strait based on clear theoretical foundations.

As for the Ieodo waters, if a hypothetical "median line" is drawn between Korea and Japan, Ieodo lies much closer to Korea than China. Because there is no particular reason to rule out the "median line" standard, Ieodo and its surrounding waters can be seen as belonging to the EEZ of Korea even before finalizing the boundary delimitation between Korea and China. Thus, Ieodo and the seabed of its surrounding waters become part of the Korean continental shelf or EEZ seabed which Korea can freely develop and exploit. China, however, is seeking to exercise rights equal to Korea in Korea's EEZ jurisdiction by claiming that the Ieodo waters are located in an area where both states can freely operate pursuant to the current Korea-China Fisheries Agreement. China is particularly interested, not only the fishing issue but also in resource development in the EEZ and continental shelf; therefore, it has been continuously raising issues with Korea's installation and operation of the Ocean Research Station on Ieodo. In order to establish Korea's jurisdiction over Ieodo waters, as well as maritime security and order, there is a need to strengthen its international legal arguments against China and to devote its efforts to building a maritime cooperation system based on mutual benefits for both states.

For Korea to effectively protect the Northeast Asian SLOCs including the Jeju Strait and Ieodo waters, it must first of all secure a sufficient level of sea power and maintain an adequate maritime police force. At the same time, it ought to actively search out options to realize maritime security and sea lane protection issues through international maritime cooperation through strengthened exchange and cooperation with other states surrounding Northeast Asian seas such as Japan and China. It must strengthen international cooperation not only with Japan, China, Taiwan, and Russia, but also with the coastal states of the Pacific such as the U.S. and Canada in order to prevent an escalation of sea power. It also needs to improve its diplomatic efforts and national power to actively participate in the establishment of a cooperative maritime security system in Northeast Asia.

5 Maritime Boundaries

5.1 *Intertemporal Law, Recent Judgments, and Territorial Disputes in Asia*

Asian colonialism has produced many unresolved conflicts that have divided parts of the region since the end of World War. Japan continues to claim sovereignty over the Southern Kurile Islands/Northern Territories (Kurile

Islands) against Russia (formerly part of the Soviet Union); over the Pinnacle Islands/Senkaku Islands (Senkaku Islands)/Diao-yu-tai (or Tiao-yu-tai) against the People's Republic of China (China) and the Republic of China (Taiwan); and over Liancourt Rocks/Dokdo/Takeshima (Liancourt Rocks) against Korea. Resolutions to these territorial disputes are impeded by the deep-rooted historical bitterness between Japan and its neighbors.

In addition to the territorial disputes over the aforementioned islands, competing claims over the Spratly Islands (by China, Malaysia, Philippines, Taiwan, Vietnam, and Brunei), Paracel Islands (by China, Vietnam, and Taiwan), New Moore/South Talpatty/Purbasha Island in the Bay of Bengal (by Bangladesh and India), Kashmir (by China (Aksai Chin), India (by Jammu and Kashmir), and Pakistan (by Azad Kashmir and Northern Areas)) still impact international relationships in these regions. Other key issues deserving attention include the division of Korea into two ideologically opposed states as well as the so-called Taiwan Straits issue, which influences the bilateral relations between China and Taiwan.

Almost all Asian countries are involved in territorial and boundary disputes with their neighboring countries. Regional stability in Asia is still heavily influenced by the legacy of colonialism and is partly dependent on the outcome of ongoing territorial disputes in which former colonizing countries take part as disputants.

Although the claimants for ownership of the disputed territories often rely on ancient historical sources for support, much of the uncertainty surrounding territorial disputes is a by-product of the post-World War II boundary decisions and territorial dispositions. The controversies in question did not arise as independent territorial disputes within East Asian countries, but are reflections of the legacies of post-war decision-making.

The ongoing territorial disputes in Asia involve intertwined political and legal issues. This is particularly so given that historical facts were not regarded as major factors in the post-World War II territorial dispositions in Asia. Although it is not always easy to dichotomize politics and law in specific territorial disputes, it is also impossible to reach a conclusion as to the strength of the competing claims based solely on international legal principles and sources. Therefore, this section will address the very nature of the disputed territories in Asia using relevant customary international law relating to territorial acquisition and loss.

5.1.1 The General Rules of International Law on Territorial Acquisition and Loss

When territorial and boundary disputes issues came to the surface in Asia, the biggest challenge was to determine how to resolve these disputes using the international law that was developed and formulated in this area, rather than the European/Western international law.

No rule of international law exists prescribing a single mode for the acquisition and loss of territory. Customary international law provides traditionally recognized modes of territorial acquisition and loss, which have been developed through decisions and awards of international judicial and arbitral bodies. States can acquire territory through five traditional methods: discovery and occupation, cession, accretion, conquest, and prescription. The seven traditional ways of losing territory in international law are: abandonment (or dereliction), relinquishment (or renunciation), cession, operations of nature, subjugation, prescription, and revolt.

Important factors relevant to establishing sovereignty over specific territories include: (1) a state's activities over a given region displayed in an actual, continuous, peaceful, and sufficient manner; (2) displays of sovereignty which may take different forms according to the character of the territory in question; (3) the evidence produced by both claimants as to the exercise of functions of state and governmental authority by acts generally indicative of sovereignty; and (4) the relationship between the states' activities to the claim and the possession of the territory in question.

5.1.1.1 *Intertemporal Law and the Territorial Disputes in Asia*

Intertemporal law raises questions about what legal rules to apply to particular disputes at particular times. The claims of parties to disputed territory must therefore be evaluated using the international law and the prevailing legal standards in existence at the "critical date" when the disputes are and the issue must be discussed within the context of the critical date.

Other questions that must be explored within the context of the critical date include: (1) whether, at the material time, legal concepts or a legal regime on territorial acquisition existed in Asia; (2) and more importantly, assuming that such a regime existed, what role, if any, should it play in the resolution of the disputes in question; (3) and, if such a regime existed, what impact do subsequent factual and legal developments have, especially if the areas in question have been subject to significant factual and legal changes over the years?

Again, this section will not attempt to determine which country has the stronger claim to the disputed but rather will focus on the legal implications of the territorial and boundary disputes in Asia at the material times.

It is debatable whether Asian history shows an essential difference between Asian legal concepts and the principles of general international law regarding the modes of acquiring and losing territory. Two possible interpretations exist.

On the one hand, one study of Chinese practice of acquiring and losing state territory, has pointed out that:

Close study of the records of imperial China's foreign relations does not support the thesis that China in the past always dictated the terms of its relations with other states, as suggested by the traditional "tributary system" model. Rather, this record reveals a complex mixture of rules and practices, some reflecting the hierarchal presuppositions of the tribute model, others representing ad hoc working compromises between China and other countries. Yet another category of rules and practices appears to have been grounded in shared notions of fairness, equality, reciprocity, and mutual respect for "territorial sovereignty." Indeed, Qing boundary rules and cases spanning more than one hundred years indicate that substantive equality and reciprocity, coupled with Sinocentric hierarchy in form, were the dominant characteristics of the border control system, at least with regard to Qing relations with Korea, Vietnam, Siam and Burma.

On the other hand, from the Chinese perspective, the Western practice of putting everything in black and white is not all-important. "Based on the long history of Chinese administrative geography, the Chinese had their own way to demarcate legitimate political space and marine space in the East China Sea. In particular, the Chinese created the Sinitic world order by networking their investiture-tributary system to demonstrate the Chinese way of hegemony during traditional periods." For the Chinese, history, geography, and actual circumstances have combined to make their ownership of certain territories a reality; thus, they had frequented these territories uninterrupted and unchallenged by other countries for centuries.

Prior to the 18th century, discovery alone sufficed to entitle states to establish and maintain sovereignty over the specific territories under rules of international law. According to the principle of intertemporal law, the evaluation and determination of historic titles must be made in light of the rules of international law which were in force at the time such title was allegedly acquired. It is also debatable, however, whether claims of sovereignty in Asia can be judged by norms developed in Europe, particularly since the general understanding of how to establish a valid claim to territory has been established through decisions and awards by international judicial and arbitral bodies many centuries later, mainly in the early 20th century. Accordingly, evaluating Asian countries' claims of sovereignty over the specific territorial and boundary disputes would depend, as pointed out earlier, on whether legal concepts or legal regimes on territorial acquisition existed at the time in Asia, and the implications of such concepts and regimes for the resolution of the disputes over the specific territorial and boundary disputes in contemporary times.

5.1.2 The Authority and Legal Basis for Territorial Dispositions

There is no uniform rule of international law defining any single manner for cession of territory. Territorial dispositions are generally matters of considerable importance to the various nations concerned, and most nations would doubtless desire that the disposing document be of substantial dignity, namely, a treaty. Because territorial questions are often threats to peaceful international relations, methods that result in an unequivocal settlement are desirable. For these reasons, cession by a peace treaty is the common manner of disposing territories of a defeated state.

Power of disposition, limited or unlimited depending on circumstances, however, is often given by the defeated state in the treaty without naming the recipient. In those cases in which this method has been used, two circumstances are generally present: (1) the disposition is not agreed to by all concerned at the peace conference; (2) some action must be taken outside the peace conference before definitive disposition can be agreed to by those concerned, such as a plebiscite on the establishment of a mandate through international organizations such as the League of Nations.

Brownlie has explained that, "on a number of occasions a group of leading powers, perhaps in association with a large number of other states, have assumed a power of disposition although the legal bases of such a power were problematical." Under the subheading of "Disposition by Joint Decision of the Principal Powers," Brownlie mentions:

> After the defeat of the Central Powers in the First World War, and the Axis Powers in the Second World War, the leading victor states assumed a power of disposition, to be exercised jointly, over the territory of the defeated states.... States losing territory as a consequence of dispositions in this wise might, and often did, renounce title by the provisions of a peace treaty to the areas concerned, but the dispositions were assumed to be valid irrespective of such renunciation and the recipients were usually in possession prior to the coming into force of a peace treaty. The existence of this power of disposition or assignment is recognized by jurists, but they find it difficult to suggest, or to agree upon, a satisfactory legal basis for it. Some translate political realities into legal forms by supposing that the community of states has delegated such a power to the 'principal' or 'great' powers....

Where renunciation confers a power of disposition to another state or a group of states, legal weight is given to such right of disposal. With regard to the power of disposition over renounced territory, it has not been the practice of states to give due consideration to the historical interests of the state that has been dispossessed of the subject territory. According to the law of succession, "when by cession or otherwise, a part of a state's territory is transferred to another, a succession to certain rights and obligations associated with the transferred territory occurs." Therefore, it seems that the successor state's right to title, whether such title was acquired directly from renunciation or indirectly through disposition, shall be equal to that of the relinquishing state and shall continue to prevail over other rights in its territory.

There may also be a circumstance where a state relinquishes territory without expressing its intention as to who is to have title to, or the power to dispose of, the territory. The question then is whether the sovereign title of territory should automatically vest in the state that maintains the best sovereign claim, or whether the territory should be disposed of by collective powers. If the territory is to be disposed of by collective dispositive powers, it seems equitable that those powers give adequate consideration to any existing claims held by a previously dispossessed state.

5.1.3 Precedents for the Blanket Renunciation of Territory in Peace Treaties and Their Implications

In the treaties discussed below, territory was relinquished without explicit stipulation as to the disposition of sovereignty over the territory, either ultimately or intermediately. The relinquishing country simply renounced its sovereignty over the territory without conveying it to any other country. Thus, questions arose regarding the status of these territories. Under these circumstances, another power may acquire sovereignty: (1) through war and the results of war; (2) by occupation as defined in international law under a claim of right; and (3) by an international agreement among the interested powers. In the 18th and 19th centuries, Europe and its foreign territories were carved up successively through these processes.

It thus became customary to provide for the blanket renunciation of territory and the cession of territory to specific countries in peace treaties. The extent to which previous treaties provide a precedent for the 1951 San Francisco Peace Treaty will be discussed in the examples that follow.

The Treaty of Paris of 1814, concluded between the victorious allies and defeated France, defined the new French boundaries. A sweeping renunciation of territory was inserted in Article III: "France on her part renounces all rights of Sovereignty, Suzeraineté, and of possession, over all the Countries, Districts, Towns, and places situated beyond the Frontier above described, the Principality of Monaco being replaced on the same footing on which it stood before the 1st of January, 1792."

The Treaty of 1814, like the Japanese renunciation in the San Francisco Peace Treaty, did not make the renunciation specifically in favor of any particular power or powers. This treaty, like the 1951 San Francisco Peace Treaty, contained three further provisions indicating the ultimate disposition of considerable portions of territory relinquished by France: "The States of Germany shall be independent, and united by a Federative Bond. Switzerland, Independent, shall continue to govern herself. Italy, beyond the limits of the Countries which are to revert to Austria, shall be composed of Sovereign States." However, unlike the San Francisco Peace Treaty and its subsequent circumstances, additional and more detailed dispositions of the renounced territories were later made by Allied Powers in the definitive Treaty of Paris of 1814, the Final Act of the Conference of Vienna, and other subsequent treaties among the allies.

The Treaty of Peace of 1898 between the United States and Spain also contained a territorial clause on blanket renunciation. Regarding the disposition of Cuba, Article I of this treaty reads:

> Spain relinquishes all claim of sovereignty over and title to Cuba. And as the island is, upon its evacuation by Spain, to be occupied by the United States, the United States will, so long as such occupation shall last, assume and discharge the obligations that may under international law result from the facts of its occupation, for the protection of life and property.

The history of negotiations of this article reveals that the Spanish delegates originally proposed that Spain "relinquishes her sovereignty over the Island of Cuba, transferring it to the United States Government, which accepts it, in order that they may in turn transfer it at the proper time to the Cuban people, upon the conditions established in this treaty." The United States negotiators rejected this proposed language because the United States disclaimed any disposition or intention to exercise sovereignty over Cuba. The language that was finally accepted provided for Spain's renunciation of sovereignty over Cuba, but did not specify to whom that sovereignty was to be transferred, directly or indirectly. Thus, although a provision was made for the United States to act as an occupying power over Cuba, the issue of Cuban sovereignty was left unresolved.

The two treaties cited above are analogous to the 1951 San Francisco Peace Treaty in their provisions for renunciation of territory by the vanquished. Neither of these treaties contained an explicit and adequate stipulation as to the disposition of sovereignty over the relinquished territory. For both the Treaties of 1814 and 1898, political understandings or expressions among the victors were designed to provide for the disposition of sovereignty over all the relinquished territories, and these intentions were accepted without challenge. Thus, the concept of "*terra nullius*" did not arise, despite the existence of a gap in title between the renunciation and the final acceptance of the new *status quo*.

On the other hand, in the 1919–1920 peace treaties, the cession of territory to specific countries was executed, country by country, by means of "political clauses". In the Treaty of Versailles, for example, Germany turned its colonies over to the principal Allied Powers. There was no individual cession of territory, and no case of a territory having an ambiguous status.

5.1.3.1 *Eritrea-Yemen Arbitration and Article 16 of the Treaty of Lausanne*

In the Treaty of Peace concluded at Lausanne on July 24, 1923 (Treaty of Lausanne), Turkey specifically renounced the Dodecanese Islands and Castellorizzo in favor of Italy, but renounced all other territories without explicit stipulation. Likewise, the Treaty of Peace with Italy signed at Paris on February 10, 1947, provides that: "[t]he final disposition of these possessions [the Italian colonies] shall be determined jointly by the Governments of the Soviet Union, of the United Kingdom, of the United States of America, and of France, within one year from the coming into force of the treaty. . . ."

It is instructive, in this respect, that in the recent Eritrea-Yemen Arbitration, the tribunal devoted a significant portion of its award to the determination of the import of Article 16 of the Treaty of Lausanne, which is to the effect that:

> Turkey hereby renounces all rights and title whatsoever over or respecting the territories situated outside the frontiers laid down in the present Treaty and the islands other than those over which her sovereignty is recognized by the said Treaty, the future of those territories and islands being settled or to be settled by the parties concerned.

On the demise of the Ottoman Empire, were the disputants, not being parties to the Treaty of Lausanne, at liberty to treat the islands as *terra nullius* and therefore subject to occupation? In this regard, Eritrea argued that because Article 16 did not transfer the islands to any particular state and did not specify any particular procedure for conveying ownership of the islands, their ultimate disposition was left to the general principles of international law for territorial acquisition.

The tribunal took the view that the islands could not be so treated on account of Article 16 of the Treaty of Lausanne. The arbitrators held that: "[it] is not unreasonable to conclude that what was envisaged was a settlement of the matter in the future by all those having legal claims or high political interest in the islands, whether Treaty of Lausanne High Contracting Parties or not." Accordingly, the territories over which Turkey renounced title "did not become *terra nullius*" and "[s]overeign title over them remained indeterminate pro tempore." Such indeterminacy could be resolved by the "parties concerned" at some stage in the future, by present (or future) claimants *inter se*. Therefore, the territories "did not become ... open to acquisitive prescription by any State, including any of the High Contracting Parties ... [n]or did they automatically revert (insofar as they had ever belonged) to the Imam [of Yemen]."

The tribunal emphasized that under Article 16, the question of sovereignty over the islands in dispute remained indeterminate until the "parties concerned" made the appropriate determination. There is no indication in the award, however, as to when, if any, such a determination was made. Neither is there any indication that, in the view of the tribunal, the treaty had fallen into desuetude. Additionally, except in the case of Italy, which renounced any rights and interests that accrued to it under the Treaty of Lausanne pursuant to the Treaty of Peace with Italy of 1947, the tribunal did not mention any denunciation of the Treaty of Lausanne by the "parties concerned".

The Imam was not a party to the Treaty of Lausanne, thus in a technical sense, the treaty was *res inter alios acta* as to Yemen. If title had been with Yemen at that time, the parties to the Treaty of Lausanne could not have transferred title elsewhere without Yemen's consent. The title, however, as indicated above, remained with Turkey. Boundary and territorial treaties made between two parties are *res inter alios acta* vis-à-vis third parties. But this special category of treaties also represents a legal reality that necessarily impinges upon third states, because they have effect *erga omnes*. If state A passes its title to territory to state B, then state C is legally without purpose to invoke the principle of *res inter alios acta*, unless its title is better than that of state A. In the absence of such better title, a claim of *res inter alios acta* is without legal import.

How and why does the Treaty of Lausanne "have effect *erga omnes*"? As a nonparty to the Treaty of Lausanne, was Yemen not at liberty to assert a claim contrary to that of the "parties concerned"? The tribunal held that nonparties were not at liberty to treat the islands independently from the Treaty of Lausanne after the demise of the Ottoman Empire. If, as the tribunal held, treaties such as the Treaty of Lausanne operate *erga omnes*, could the exercise of governmental authority by the disputants, with knowledge of the indeterminate status of the islands, be a basis for a sovereignty claim over those islands? The exercise of governmental authority by the disputants should not, in such circumstances, have been treated as a basis for sovereignty claims. As a matter of fact, although the tribunal dismissed Eritrea's argument to that effect, the islands became *terra nullius*. The tribunal's basis for award based on the exercise of the functions of governmental authority by the disputants, is analogous to a treatment of the islands as *terra nullius*.

If, as far back as 1947, Italy had ceased to be a "party concerned," how could Eritrea, which claimed to have inherited title from Ethiopia which in turn, inherited title from Italy, become a "party concerned" within the ambit of Article 16 of the Treaty of Lausanne? If the tribunal made its determination solely on the strength of the exercise of the functions of governmental authority, without reference to the Treaty of Lausanne, there would be no basis for the statement that the disputants were the remaining "parties concerned." What became of the so-called *erga omnes* effect of the Treaty of Lausanne? How could the actions of disputants qualify as evidence of the exercise of state and governmental authority when they had knowledge of the existence of the treaty, and gave it *erga omnes* effect? At best, the tribunal could have avoided criticism of its ultimate decision that the islands were *terra nullius* if it had based its decision on the acquiescence of the "parties concerned" to the acts of the disputants on the islands. The tribunal failed to make that connection and instead raised the acquiescence argument only in terms of the relationship between the disputants.

What the tribunal should have done in the circumstance was to hold that the Treaty of Lausanne had no relevance to the case and confined itself to the evaluation of the evidence of the exercise of governmental authority, disregarding the subsisting indeterminate status of the islands. According to Riesman:

> The Tribunal's construction of Article 16 of the [Treaty of Lausanne] is the basis for the rejection of Eritrea's central argument. But if that provision suspended resolution of the question of sovereignty disputes over the islands, such that Italian actions did not constitute effectivités, when did Article 16 become caducous? If Article 16 is still in force, then the concurrence of all concerned parties (whoever they may be) is required for the settlement of the issue of sovereignty over the Red Sea islands or, alternatively, is required for the submission of the question to a third party. However, the parties to the Lausanne Treaty did not concur in the

compromis, and it is not certain that all other concerned parties were consulted or even notified. Thus, the Tribunal's construction of Article 16 raises questions about the integrity of the Tribunal's own jurisdiction. This problem might have been obviated if the parties had elected to place the dispute before the International Court of Justice (ICJ), which has limited competence to deal with the procedural challenge of essential third parties.

5.1.3.2 *Case Concerning Maritime Delimitation and Territorial Questions between Qatar and Bahrain and the British Decision of 1939*

In *Qatar v. Bahrain*, which concerned disputes between the two states over Zubarah, Hawar Islands, and Janan Island, the ICJ concluded that Bahrain had sovereignty over the Hawar Islands. Although Bahrain claimed, in support of its argument, that "its sovereignty over the Hawar Islands has been exercised continuously and uninterruptedly over the last two centuries and has been acknowledged by the inhabitants of the islands, and Qatar has never exercised any kind of competing authority over the islands" the ICJ considered only the British decision of 1939 throughout its reasoning, and this 1939 decision virtually served as the sole basis of the judgment.

Likewise, the ICJ found that Qatar had sovereignty over Janan Island including Hadd Janan, on the basis of the British Government's decision in 1939 on the question of sovereignty over Janan Island, as interpreted in 1947. Although the British Government concluded that Hawar Islands belonged to Bahrain and not to Qatar, no remarks were made regarding Janan Island, nor was it specified which islands were to be considered "Hawar Islands." Qatar, on its part, referred to the letters dated December 23, 1947, drafted in identical terms and sent by the British Political Agent in Bahrain to the Rulers of Qatar and Bahrain, in which the sea-bed between the two states was delimited by the British Government. In those letters, Janan Island was not regarded as being part of the islands of the Hawar group. The ICJ thus concluded that the British Government's 1947 letter provided an authoritative interpretation of the 1939 decision and its results.

5.1.4 Conclusion

Notable decisions and awards by international judicial and arbitral bodies for formulating the relevant international law relating to territorial acquisition and loss include: *Islands of Palmas Arbitration, Clipperton Island Arbitration, Legal Status of Eastern Greenland Case, Minquiers and Ecrehos Case, Western Sahara, Case concerning the Land, Island and Maritime Frontier Dispute*

(El Salvador v. Honduras Case), Eritrea-Yemen Arbitration, Case concerning Kasikili/Sedudu Island, Case concerning Maritime Delimitation and Territorial Questions between Qatar and Bahrain, Land and Maritime Boundary between Cameroon and Nigeria, Sovereignty over Pulau Ligitan and Pulau Sipadan, and the very recent decision in *Frontier Dispute (Benin/Niger)*.

The general understanding of territorial disputes in international law has developed through decisions and awards by international judicial and arbitral bodies, and these cases generally involve either colonizing countries or colonized/newly independent countries. Consequently, none of these cases parallels the situation of the cases involving both colonizing countries and colonized/newly independent countries. In other words, cases involving former colonies and former imperial powers did not count as major factors in formulating the relevant international law relating to territorial acquisition and loss. Thus, it is debatable whether the general rule of international law on territorial disputes can be applied, without modification, to the specific cases which cannot clearly fit into those general terminologies and categories.

In such circumstances, it is imperative to clarify the relevant norms of international law and develop new norms to address the very nature of the territories in dispute. This will be critical for formulating a broader framework for the appreciation of the nature of territorial disputes in Asia.

Although the main purpose of intertemporal law is to strengthen legal security in international relations, it is criticized that intertemporal law is "a mere political handmaiden to the politics of power of the imperial states who set out on a worldwide conquest of territory," and that it has been used "to legitimize" blind acceptance of past manipulations of a legal system that was created by, dominated by and imposed by imperial states upon the rest of the world." International law has operated in historical periods to validate the acquisition of territory by states regardless of the intentions of colonized states. Earlier formulations of general principles of international law for territorial acquisition upheld the imperial empires that led to the current political configuration of the Asia, and beyond.

5.2 *Territorial Disputes and Delimitation Issues between Korea and Its Neighbors*

5.2.1 Naval Skirmishes in the West Sea (Yellow Sea) and the Cheonan Incident

Although the NLL has never been accepted by North Korea there had not been any violent clashes until June 1999 when several North Korean naval vessels crossed the NLL and opened fire against Korean warships leading to an armed skirmish. Similar naval incidents occurred in 2002 and 2009 resulting in several

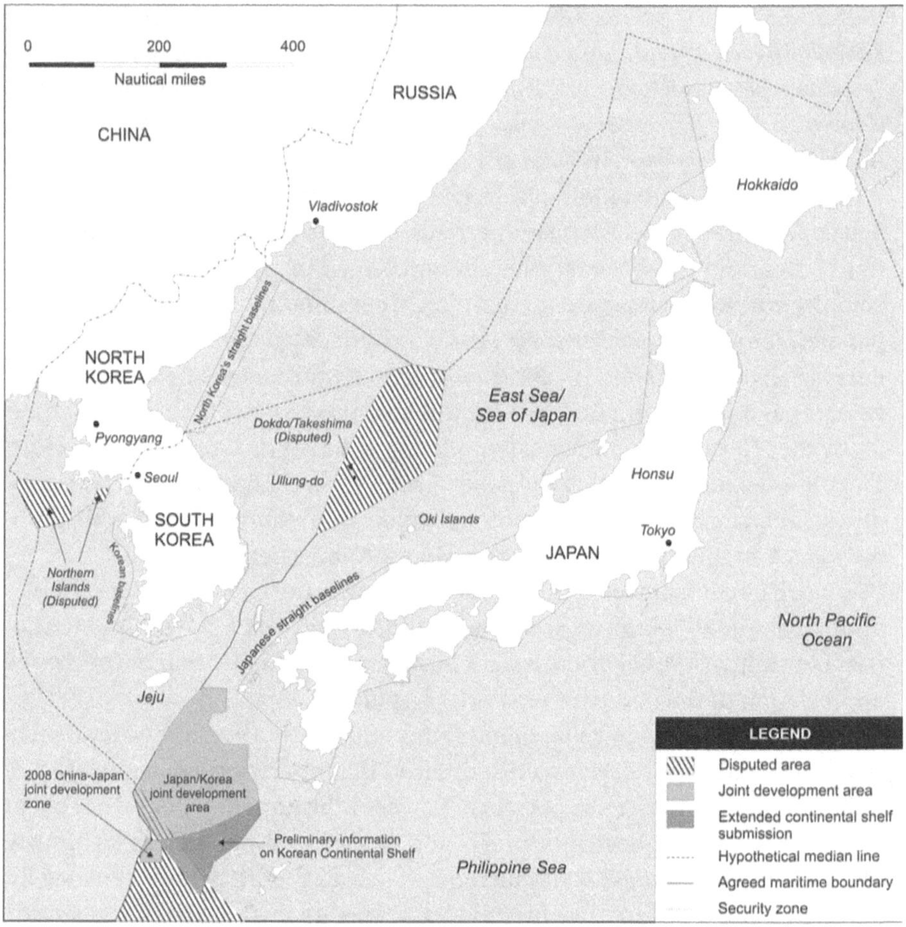

* *This map originally appeared in Seokwoo Lee and Hee Eun Lee (eds.),* Dokdo: Historical Appraisal and International Justice *(Brill/Martinus Nijhoff Publishers, 2011), p. xi.*

dead and wounded sailors on both sides. In addition, North Korea has drawn its own demarcation line which is located south of the NLL. After the skirmish in November 2009, the North Korean Army reiterated that it considered this the only valid border and that it would be defended with merciless military measures.

On 26 March 2010, the Korean corvette, the *Cheonan*, sank near Baengnyeong Island on the Korean side of the NLL resulting in the death of 46 sailors out of a total crew of 104. To determine the cause of the sinking, the Korean government established the "Joint Civilian-Military Investigation Group" consisting of Korean experts as well as international experts from Australia, Sweden, the

United Kingdom, and the United States. The result of the investigation was released on 20 May 2010 where it was concluded that the sinking of the *Cheonan* was the result of an explosion caused by a torpedo made in North Korea and fired by a North Korean submarine. North Korea, however, has denied having played any role in the sinking of the *Cheonan*.

Based on the findings of the international investigation team, Korea on 4 June 2010 referred the issue of North Korea's role in the sinking of the *Cheonan* to the U.N. Security Council seeking a resolution condemning North Korea. On the international front, however, the Korean administration has faced an unfavourable attitude among key neighbours, namely China and Russia, who have expressed doubt as to North Korea's culpability for the sinking of the *Cheonan*.

All the Korean government was able to show for its efforts at the United Nations was a presidential statement from the Security Council which made no mention of North Korea at all. The effect of such a statement to provide international legal justification for any subsequent Korean actions against North Korea is doubtful as it does not rise to the level a binding Security Council resolution. To add insult to injury, North Korea claims that the statement of the Security Council absolves it from any responsibility at all and provides a propaganda coup for the Kim Jong-Il regime. While there may have been some in the Korean government who desired to show North Korea that there was a price to pay for sinking the *Cheonan*, Korea's effort to bring the international community to punish North Korea has resulted in failure and has put the Korean government in the uncomfortable position of having no apparent exit strategy. On November 23, 2010, North Korean artillery crossed the NLL, landing on Korea's Yeonpyeong Island, causing deaths and substantial destruction.

5.2.2 Maritime Delimitation Between Korea and China in the Yellow Sea

The West Sea/Yellow Sea is a semi-enclosed body of water measuring about 520 nautical miles from north to south and about 380 nautical miles from east to west. The total area covered by the Yellow Sea is 400,000 square kilometers, with an average depth of 55 meters, and a maximum depth of 125 meters. This section focuses on the unresolved maritime boundary between Korea and China, which have both ratified the 1982 United Nations Law of the Sea Convention. Article 57 of the Law of the Sea Convention authorizes each coastal state to declare an exclusive economic zone (EEZ) of 200 nautical miles from the coast or "from baselines from which the breadth of the territorial sea is measured," but because the Yellow Sea is less than 400 nautical-miles wide, none of the coastal states can declare full zones and their claimed EEZs overlap. The extent of the overlap is exacerbated by arguably-excessive straight baselines that have been claimed by the coastal countries.

Because the Yellow Sea is rich in natural resources, with the capacity for year-round fishing and an estimated oil reserve that may contain up to ten billion barrels of oil, it has been difficult for the coastal countries to agree on the maritime delimitation. Tension over these resources endangers security in Northeast Asia, and conflicts are likely to continue as long as the region's maritime boundaries remain unresolved. Korea and China have had an awkward relationship during previous centuries, but they are cooperating economically at present and it should be possible for these two important countries to reach an agreement on the maritime delimitation of the Yellow Sea.

Korea has maintained since the 1960 that the most equitable approach to the maritime delimitation in the Yellow Sea is to utilize the equidistance principle, whereby the exclusive economic zones of Korea and China would be delimited at the median line. This position is somewhat inconsistent with Korea's approach toward its boundary dispute with Japan in the East China Sea, where Korea argues for the natural prolongation approach, but Korea explains the difference by referring to the goal of delimitations, which are to reach an "equitable" result. China's approach toward delimitation also has its inconsistencies, because it favors the natural prolongation theory in the Yellow Sea dispute with Korea, but maintains that the equidistance line should divide its boundary with North Korea in the Gulf of Korea and with Vietnam in the Gulf of Tonkin. Perhaps most importantly, the natural prolongation approach does not appear to apply in any significant geographic way to the Yellow Sea, because (unlike the East China Sea, where the seabed drops off sharply at the Okinawa Trough, near the small Japanese islands) the Yellow Sea has a flat, shallow, and a relatively featureless sea floor throughout. The sediments do not shift dramatically from clay to sand, but instead makes a gradual transition and the sea includes areas where the sediments mix.

5.2.3 Maritime Delimitation and Territorial Disputes between Korea and Japan in the East Sea (Sea of Japan)

Korea regained its independence after World War II, but its sovereignty over Dokdo continues to be challenged by Japan, and the events, decrees, and agreements during and after World War II continue to be relevant to this controversy. Dokdo consists of two rocky structures and 32 smaller outcroppings in the East Sea that have a combined land area of 0.18 square kilometers. East Island (Dongdo) has a circumference of 1.9 kilometers and West Island (Seodo) has a circumference of 2.8 kilometers. These islets are located 88 kilometers (about 55 miles or 47 nautical miles) from Korea's Ullungdo and are about 158 kilometers (about 99 miles or 86 nautical miles) from Japan's Oki Islands. Korea's claim to Dokdo goes back many centuries and is based on contacts during many previous eras. Japan asserts, on the other hand, that Dokdo was *terra nullius* in 1905 and that Japan acted in accordance with international law in claiming and incorporating the islets into Japanese territory at that time. Korea viewed this initiative as part of Japan's aggressive and illegal expansionism whereby Japan established a protectorate over Korea in 1905 and then formally annexed Korea in 1910. After World War II, Korea re-established its occupation of Dokdo and has maintained a small contingent of marine guards on the islets during the past half century.

The delimitation of maritime boundaries between Korea and Japan in the East Sea (or the Sea of Japan) and the East China Sea also remains unsettled, except in the southern part of the continental shelf in the East Sea of Korea. Prompted by the need for the exploitation of oil on the continental shelf, Korea and Japan agreed to the joint development of the disputed continental shelf south of Jeju Island in 1974, in addition to the delimitation of the continental shelf in the Korea Strait. As with China and Japan, a disputed island, Dokdo (or Takeshima)—which is located 50 nm east of Korea's Ullung Island and 90 nm north-west of Japan's Oki Islands, and is currently under Korea's control—lies at the core of the dispute over maritime boundary delimitation between the two countries. Whereas Korea has argued that the EEZs of both countries should be divided along a median line between Ullung Island and the Oki Islands, Japan claims a median line between Ullung Island and Dokdo, arguing that Dokdo is its own island. Both countries' claims enclose Dokdo within their own EEZs. The recent standoff by the coast guards of the two countries over Japan's attempt to conduct a maritime survey in the disputed waters off Dokdo might represent the volatility of maritime issues between the two countries.

5.3 *Maritime Delimitation and Joint Resource Development in the East China Sea*

5.3.1 Maritime Delimitation and Joint Resource Development in the East China Sea

China's Exclusive Economic Zone and Continental Shelf Act declares an EEZ up to 200 nautical miles and provides that the continental shelf "comprises the seabed and subsoil of the submarine areas that extend beyond its territorial sea throughout the natural prolongation of its land territory to the outer edge of the continental margin, or to a distance of 200 nautical miles from the baselines from which the breadth of the territorial sea is measured where the outer edge of the continental margin does not extend up to that distance." Though there may be slight variation in terminology, it has generally accommodated the definition of continental shelf provided in article 76(1) of the UNCLOS. In cases of conflicting claims with other states, the law also provides that they "shall be settled, on the basis of international law and in accordance with the principle of equity, by an agreement delimiting the areas so claimed."

On the other hand, Japan's Law on the Exclusive Economic Zone and the Continental Shelf also provides for an EEZ and continental shelf up to 200 n.m. but provides that in cases of conflicting claims, it would reach to the median line from the baselines of each state.

In short, China claims a 200 n.m. EEZ and continental shelf and claims to resolve conflicting claims through "the principle of equity" while emphasizing natural prolongation. Japan likewise claims a 200 n.m. EEZ and continental shelf, but limits the boundary to the median line in case of conflicting claims. In other words, while Japan limits itself to the median line in overlapping areas, China only states that it would conclude agreements under the principle of equity so that its jurisdiction still reaches 200 n.m. under domestic law. Therefore, from the median line to 200 n.m. on Japan's side, there is an overlap of jurisdiction under the laws of both states, while only China has jurisdiction over waters on China's side of the median line. This is similar to the relationship between Korea and China. Korea's EEZ Law declares a 200 n.m. EEZ but delimits boundaries based on agreement with adjacent states. This alone appears to be the same as the relevant Chinese provision excluding the "principle of equity." However, Korean law also provides that the "exercise of jurisdiction" only reaches the median line. Thus, while the Korean EEZ Law states that its boundaries of conflicting areas are determined by agreement with another party in writing, the exercise of jurisdiction is limited to the median line in reality, which is similar in effect to Japan's law limiting the boundary to the median line.

In the East China Sea where the distance between the two coasts do not reach 400 n.m., there are several factors to consider for maritime delimitation between China and Japan. First is the effect of the Senkaku Islands, which is also the object if this study; second is the effect of the Okinawa Trough on the limits of the continental shelf. Also related is the theoretical issue of whether the natural prolongation of the land territory can apply within the 400 n.m. between the two coasts.

5.3.2 The Role of the Senkaku Islands on Boundary Delimitation

According to Article 121 of the UNCLOS, "Islands" that are not "[r]ocks which cannot sustain human habitation or economic life of their own" can generate not only territorial sea up to 12 n.m. but also its own EEZ and continental shelf. Therefore, if the Senkaku Islands were to be recognized as "islands," the state exercising sovereignty over the islands can also claim EEZ and continental shelf based on these islands.

The Senkaku Islands are comprised of five small islands and three reefs. These five islands, especially the main island of Diaoyu, reaches 3.5 km^2 in area with thickly wooded forests and fresh water. Thus, although it is currently uninhabited due to its geographical isolation, inhabitation is not impossible. Considering the abundant fishing grounds and underground resources, even independent economic livelihood appears possible. Thus, it is not too difficult to claim the Senkaku Islands as "islands." If the Senkaku Islands belonged to Japan, it could claim the equidistant line between China and Senkaku's coast as a boundary; but if China's sovereignty were to be recognized, China could claim as a boundary the equidistant line between the Senkaku and the Ryukyu Islands. According to a study, the area between the two equidistant lines reach up to 67,800 km^2; thus, the full recognition of Senkaku Islands in boundary delimitation would also signify the gain or loss of the same area.

An interesting point, however, is that neither China nor Japan is claiming maritime boundaries based on the Senkaku Islands. Presumably, Japan's position is due to the fact that even if it were to declare a median line between the Ryukyu Islands and China, the Senkaku Islands would still be part of its territorial waters; so it desires to avoid provoking China, which is fiercely fighting for sovereignty over the island, while also taking into consideration current international jurisprudence that does not fully recognize the effect of remote islands on maritime delimitation. On the other hand, China claims boundaries based on the Okinawa Trough, which is situated on Japan's side of the median line between the Senkaku and Ryukyu Islands and thus does not need to be claimed based on the Senkaku Islands. However, China's claims are based on natural prolongation of land territory, which is irrelevant to EEZ boundaries unlike the continental shelf.

5.3.3 Okinawa Trough

Adjacent to the Ryukyu Islands and running parallel, the Okinawa Trough is about 900 km in length and 36–150 km in width, encompassing an area of more than 100,000 km^2. Its depth reaches over 1000m; and considering that the average depth of the East China Sea is about 370m, it is geomorphologically distinct from the area.

According to the preliminary information submitted by China to the Commission on the Limits of the Continental Shelf (CLCS) on May 11, 2009, China determined four points of foot of the continental slope (FOS) and established the outer edge of the continental shelf at 20 to 38 n.m. from the FOS. Connection of these four points forms the continental shelf boundary claimed by China, the shortest distance from China's coast being 228 n.m. and the longest 277 n.m.

The claim to outer limits of the continental shelf made by China does not differ greatly from that of Korea. Korea submitted preliminary information to the CLCS on the same day as China, in which four points of FOS were determined to establish the outer limits that lie at the southern boundaries of the current Korea-Japan Joint Continental Shelf Development Zone.

Japan has not accepted the claims of China and Korea—that the Okinawa Trough should form the outer limits of the continental shelf. Instead, Japan claims that, because it is a mere dent in the natural prolongation of land territory, the boundary should be the median line between the coasts of the two states.

Though China formally made a submission to the CLCS in 2012, the Commission cannot consider the issue of the Okinawa Trough, because the East China Sea is an area of dispute concerning the sovereignty over and maritime delimitation around the Senkaku Islands. Even if the Commission were to consider the issue and make recommendations based on the findings, it would not affect the boundary delimitation between the two states. The Annex to the Rules of Procedure of the CLCS also provides that in case of land or maritime dispute, the Commission would not consider or qualify a submission without the prior consent of all states that are party to the dispute.

In short, even if the Okinawa Trough were deemed to be a geological break between China and Japan as claimed by China, under the current international legal system, delimitation would be difficult without the prior consent of Japan. Furthermore, what weakens China's claim is the fact that the distance between the two coasts does not reach 400 n.m. as further discussed below.

5.3.4 Limits of the Continental Shelf within 400 n.m.

UNCLOS defines the continental shelf in two ways in Article 76(1). It states that the continental shelf comprises the seabed and subsoil of the submarine areas that extend "throughout the natural prolongation of its land territory to the outer edge of the continental margin" or "to a distance of 200 nautical miles from the baselines" where the outer edge does not reach 200 n.m. In short, the Convention simultaneously provides for the natural prolongation criteria as well as the 200 n.m. distance criteria, the latter of which does not take geological and geographical factors into consideration. In the case of the East China Sea, the greatest width reaches 345 n.m.; and though the Okinawa Trough lies beyond 200 n.m. from China, it is situated less than 100 n.m. from Japan. Thus, China asserts the natural prolongation of land territory, while Japan asserts the distance criteria for determining the outer limits of the continental shelf. What then should be the standard for boundary delimitation?

As is well known, the International Court of Justice (ICJ) in the *North Sea Continental Shelf* Cases of 1969 supported the natural prolongation of land territory criteria, which influenced the conclusion of the Agreement between the Republic of Korea and Japan concerning Joint Development of the Continental Shelf. However, with the advent of the 1982 UNCLOS emphasizing an "equitable solution" of boundary delimitation, the natural prolongation criteria receded. In the same year, in the *Continental Shelf case between Tunisia and Libya*, the ICJ held that, of the two criteria given in Article 76 of the Convention, natural prolongation of the land territory is the main criterion and that the 200 n.m. is the basis of title for coastal states in "certain circumstances." Three years later, however, in the 1985 *Continental Shelf case between Libya and Malta*, the ICJ held that for boundary delimitation at a distance of under 200 miles from the coast and where the coasts of the parties is less than 400 miles, title depends solely on the distance from the coasts and that geological or geomorphological characteristics are immaterial. Such a decision of the ICJ signified that the distance criteria has replaced the geomorphological criteria except in cases of extending the limits of the continental shelf beyond 200 n.m., as identified in the dissenting opinion of Judge Oda.

Pursuant to the Libya/Malta case above, only the distance criteria should be applicable to the East China Sea, in which case China's assertion of the Okinawa Trough as the boundary would be rejected and Japan's assertion of the median line would become the boundary, although such boundary may be slightly altered according to "relevant circumstances." However, there are also critiques of the above decision. Professor Jianjun Gao categorizes the cases in which the distance between two states does not reach 400 n.m. into three situations. First is where the distance to the continental break does not reach 200 n.m. for both states; second, where there is no continental break; and third, where the distance to the continental break does not reach 200 n.m. for one side but exceeds 200 n.m. for the other. Professor Gao does not raise issues with the first two categories to which solely the distance criteria, particularly the median line principle, applies. Concerning the third category, however, he asserts that it is inconsistent for one state to apply the distance criteria and the geomorphological criteria to the waters beyond the 200 n.m. and therefore should only apply the geomorphological criteria. The Libya/Malta case where the maximum distance was 183 n.m. is an example of the first category, while China's case in the East China Sea is an example of the third category. In other words, in the latter example where the continental break lies beyond 200 n.m. from the coast, it would be inconsistent to apply the distance criteria up to 200 miles and the geomorphological criteria beyond it; therefore, only the geomorphological criteria should be applied. In asserting that the geomorphological criteria ought to be applied to the East China Sea where the distance from the Chinese coast to the Okinawa Trough exceeds 200 n.m., Professor Gao refers to the 1997 Maritime Boundary Treaty between Australia and Indonesia. This treaty differentiated between the boundaries of the EEZ and the continental shelf; although the limits of the continental shelf were set beyond 200 n.m. from Australia, in the areas adjacent to the Indonesian coast, the boundaries were set at the Timor Gap where there was the continental break.

In the third category, it is possible to be critical of Professor Gao's proposal since it only defends the position of states whose continental break lies beyond 200 n.m. and fails to take into consideration the position of states that do not reach 200 n.m. The issue in the third category then is whether, while one state asserts geomorphological criteria while the other asserts the distance standard and the two positions are incompatible, the application of geomorphological criteria alone can be seen as an "equitable solution" provided for in UNCLOS Article 83(1) and, even more importantly, conforms to the fundamental standards.

5.3.5 Conclusion

The major factors affecting the East China Sea delimitation between China and Japan depend upon the recognition of the effects of the Senkaku Islands and the Okinawa Trough. Even if the Senkaku Islands that are currently under an intense sovereignty debate are recognized as "islands" generating its own EEZ and continental shelf, neither China nor Japan currently assert boundary delimitation based on these islands. Therefore, the key factor in the delimitation between the two states is whether the Okinawa Trough can be seen as a continental break; and even if it were to be so, there still remains the issue of whether the geological concept of natural prolongation of land territory can be applied where the distance between the states does not reach 400 n.m. Unlike Japan's claim that the Okinawa Trough is a mere dent, the view that it should more properly be seen as a continental break appears predominant. Even so, there are strong doubts as to whether the geological criteria alone should be applied without consideration of distance where the distance does not reach 400 n.m, more so because the ICJ clearly held in the Libya/Malta case that the distance criteria is to be applied in such cases.

Furthermore, unlike the continental shelf, there is no room for application of geological concepts in the EEZ boundaries. Therefore, China's claim of the Okinawa Trough as a maritime boundary is ultimately asserting that the EEZ and the continental shelf require different boundaries. Although the

EEZ includes the seabed and subsoil, or the continental shelf, within 200 n.m., states may determine different boundaries for the upper waters and the seabed and subsoil as we can see in the delimitation between Australia and Indonesia. UNCLOS takes this into consideration in providing that "[t]he rights set out in this article with respect to the seabed and subsoil shall be exercised in accordance with Part VI."

While Japan claims the median line for both the EEZ and continental shelf, China's position does not seem so clear. In other words, though it claims the Okinawa Trough as the maritime boundary, China has not clarified whether this is limited to the continental shelf or whether it includes the EEZ. Because China's Exclusive Economic Zone and Continental Shelf Act, as well as UNCLOS Article 57 both prohibit the extension of the EEZ beyond 200 n.m., it is clear that the Okinawa Trough lying beyond 200 n.m. from the Chinese coast cannot be the boundary of its EEZ. Such obscurity is also evident in China's boundary delimitation with Korea, as it claims boundaries beyond the median line based on geological grounds; but it is questionable whether this can be applied to EEZs as well.

In conclusion, the maritime boundary has yet to be determined between China and Japan; and as the positions of both states still remain acute, any consensus in the near future looks difficult. In the midst of this, issues concerning the development of rich natural gas and oil resources were also raised. Resource development is intimately related to boundary delimitation; but as such delimitations cannot be waited for, there have been unilateral developments or joint developments sought after.

Though China and Japan are fiercely fighting for sovereignty over the Senkaku Islands, neither state claims maritime boundaries based on the islands. Currently, China claims the Okinawa Trough as the boundary based on the natural prolongation theory, while Japan claims the median line between the two coasts. This is because one asserts geological or geomorphological criteria while the other asserts a simple distance criteria where the distance between the two sides does not reach 400 n.m. In the 1985 *Continental Shelf case between Libya and Malta*, the ICJ held that in cases where the distance between two states does not reach 400 n.m., only the distance criteria applies. Whether this decision is clearly upheld in future decisions will greatly influence the delimitation between China and Japan.

Furthermore, if it is as China asserts, China will have to claim different boundaries for its EEZ and continental shelf because the Okinawa Trough lies beyond 200 n.m. from the Chinese coast. However, it is still unclear as to where China claims as the boundary of its EEZ. Even if it were to claim boundaries equal to its continental shelf pursuant to the principle of equity, this would be difficult to accept in light of the UNCLOS limiting the EEZ to 200 n.m., as well as Chinese law accommodating this provision.

Maritime delimitation between China and Japan has impacts on Korea as well. A portion of the central waters south of Jeju Island that is a part of the Korea-Japan Fisheries Agreement, and much of the Korea-Japan Joint Continental Shelf Development Zone, overlap with the Provisional Measure Zone of the China-Japan Fisheries Agreement. The 200 n.m. boundary claimed by China also overlaps with the median line asserted by Japan. Thus, because the claims of Korea, China, and Japan overlap in the northern part of the East China Sea, the three states must reach an agreement to determine a tri-point area. If such an agreement is difficult, a joint development zone with the participation of all three states could also be considered.

Though China and Japan agreed to joint resource development in 2008, the agreed zone was a very small area adjacent to the Korea-Japan Joint Continental Shelf Development Zone, and the points of agreement have not been implemented. China has been developing four oil fields including Chunxiao in its waters adjacent to the median line asserted by Japan. However, China also has been excluding the participation of Japan, while Japan has been strongly objecting to the unilateral development of oil fields by China. If indeed the oil fields on China's side are connected past the median line asserted by Japan, then China's unilateral development will infringe upon the potential sovereign rights of Japan, thereby violating international law.

6 Piracy

Despite continued vigorous efforts of the international community to eradicate piracy, such acts and the harm it has caused has been on the rise. The costs incurred are colossal. As one study shows, direct costs, i.e., the ransom demand for kidnapped sailors and vessels, insurance premiums, detour costs, procurement of defense equipment and the operation of the navy, in addition to indirect costs, i.e., losses in trade by neighboring states due to avoiding dangerous regions, as well as flight of foreign investment, add up to 7 to 12 billion USD annually. Together with such economic loss, piracy is becoming a grave threat to seaborne trade and to the right of humankind to freely make use of the oceans.

The most distinctive feature of piracy is the recent move of such activities from Southeast Asian waters near the Malacca Strait to the Gulf of Aden and near off the coast of Somalia. Prior to mid-2000's, the Malacca Strait and

Southeast Asian waters were the most vulnerable to pirate attacks; recently, however, piracy in the area has significantly decreased while the coast of Somalia and the African waters including the Gulf of Aden has emerged as the new center for such activities. This trend is evident by the fact that piracy cases in the Malacca Strait (including the Singapore strait) numbered 52 between 2006 and 2010, while off the coast of Somalia and the Gulf of Aden numbered 564 around the same time.

The decrease of piracy in Southeast Asian waters can be credited to the continued anti-piracy efforts of the littoral states. The coastal states of Malaysia, Indonesia and Singapore surrounding the Malacca Strait have endeavored to strengthen judicial assistance and cooperation such as through joint periodic naval and air force patrol and permitting foreign vessel entry into territorial waters when pursuing pirates.

Other countries within the area, especially Japan and Korea, concluded the Regional Agreement on Combating Piracy and Armed Robbery Against Ships in Asia (ReCCAP), which became effective in 2006, for the establishment of a multilateral anti-piracy regime and to provide equipment such as guard boats, as well as human and material resources for the eradication of piracy including training in the execution of maritime laws. ReCCAP establishes an Information Sharing Center, regulates cooperation in the arrest and extradition of pirates, and provides support and cooperation for anti-piracy capacity building. This agreement is also significant in that, unlike the declaratory nature of previous anti-piracy efforts, it provides for a binding multinational cooperative regime.

Korea, China and Japan, three Northeast Asian nations that are wholly dependent on sea lanes of communication for import-export commodities and energy transport, have been greatly endeavoring to secure the safety of the sea lanes of communication from pirates. The three states have also dispatched military vessels to actively participate in the international efforts to fight piracy in Somalia and to protect their vessels passing through Somalia and the Gulf of Aden.

Unfortunately, there have been several constraints to the flag state of the vessel or crew in their exercise of jurisdiction in transferring and trying the arrested pirates, as was evident in the transfer and trial of the pirates who hijacked the Malta-registered chemical tanker *Samho Jewelry* on January 15, 2010 in Somali waters.

International Law Provisions

General regulations regarding piracy are provided in the UNCLOS Article 101 which defines piracy as consisting of:

> (a) any illegal acts of violence or detention, or any act of depredation, committed for private ends by the crew or the passengers of a private ship or a private aircraft, and directed: (i) on the high seas, against another ship or aircraft, or against persons or property on board such ship or aircraft; (ii) against a ship, aircraft, persons or property in a place outside the jurisdiction of any State; [as well as] (b) any act of voluntary participation in the operation of a ship or of an aircraft with knowledge of facts making it a pirate ship or aircraft.

Piracy is a universal crime that seriously undermines the rights of all states to freely and peacefully use the oceans; therefore, any state seizing a pirate ship may exercise jurisdiction over it (Article 105). However, such seizures may only be carried out by military vessels or those on government service (Article 106).

With Somali pirates running rampant, the international community has been striving to fight piracy with the U.N. playing a central role. Through a sequence of Security Council Resolutions—1816 (June 2008), 1838 (Oct. 2008), 1846 (Dec. 2008), 1851 (Dec. 2008) and 1897 (November 2009)—the U.N. has been urging the participation of the international community and justifying measures taken against Somali pirates under international law. More specifically, it has called for: i) deployment of naval vessels and military aircrafts, ii) conclusion of agreements to facilitate investigation and prosecution of pirates, and iii) authorization of nations entering the territorial waters in pursuit of pirates.

6.1 *Korea's Maritime Challenges and Priorities—Piracy and Armed Robbery against Ships*

With more than 99% of Korean trade transported by sea, the Korean economy is dependent on secure global sea lanes of communication. Furthermore, as the country does not have any domestic production of oil, Korea is dependent on oil imports, 80% of which is transported from the Middle East through two of the world's major oil transit chokepoints, the Strait of Hormuz and the Straits of Singapore and Malacca. Any disruption of vessels carrying oil to Korea through these sea lanes of communication will have a potentially devastating effect on the Korean economy. At present, the biggest threat to trade and energy flows seems to be piracy and armed robbery against ships. Korea is actively engaged in regional and international efforts aimed at combating this problem.

Korea is a Contracting Party to the Regional Cooperation Agreement on Combating Piracy and Armed Robbery Against Ships in Asia (ReCAAP) and has provided funding and staff to the ReCAAP Information Sharing Center (ReCAAP ISC), which was officially launched in Singapore in 2006. To support the international efforts to combat piracy and armed robbery against ships in the Gulf of Aden and in the waters off Somalia, Korea joined the Combined Task Force 151 (CTF 151) in 2009.

The ability to dispatch naval vessels to operations in distant locations is the result of the Korean strategy to transform its navy from a coastal force into a blue water navy with capacity to protect Korea's global commercial interests and to contribute to maintaining peace around the world. As part of the "Defence Reform 2020", the Korean Navy will be reorganized into three Fleets, a Submarine Command, an Aviation Command and a Mobile Flotilla (reinforcement). The overall number of vessels will be reduced, but total capabilities will be upgraded with new-generation frigates and AEGIS destroyers.

6.2 *Republic of Korea v. Araye*

A recent decision of the Korean Supreme Court upheld the exercise of universal criminal jurisdiction over Somali pirates convicted of hijacking a Korean vessel in the Indian Ocean. This was the first Korean piracy prosecution and it revealed various procedural issues related to the prosecution of such crimes that remain to be resolved.

On January 15, 2011, Somali pirates hijacked the MV *Samho Jewelry*, a chemical carrier flying the Korean flag, on the high seas in the northern Indian Ocean near Oman. The pirates, after gaining control of the *Samho Jewelry* and its crew, appropriated and transferred to their mother ship approximately USD $12,000 worth of goods, including laptops, watches, cell phones, and shoes, and demanded ransom. However, a Korean naval task force, the Cheonghae Unit, headed by the destroyer *Choi Young*, had been tracking the *Samho Jewelry* and—as the pirates gave signs of preparing another hijacking—mounted a rescue operation on January 21. That effort ended in the deaths of eight pirates (including their leader) and the capture of five others. The crew was unharmed except for the captain, who had been seriously wounded by the pirates.

When the *Samho Jewelry* entered a Yemeni port, the Korean government sought to negotiate the transfer of the captured pirates to Yemeni judicial authorities for purposes of prosecution in Yemen or Kenya. As cooperation with those countries became difficult, the captives were returned to the custody of the Korean government and subsequently transferred to Korea on January 30. Upon arrival, the pirates were handed over to the South Regional Headquarters of the Korean Coast Guard, which had jurisdiction over Busan, where the Samho Shipping Company was located.

On February 7, after an investigation, the pirates were sent to the Busan District Prosecutor's Office, which indicted them on February 25 on eight counts of criminal acts related to piracy: forcibly taking the ship; forcibly taking property on the ship; forcibly operating the ship; demanding ransom to release the hostages; firing at soldiers; inflicting physical assault, threats, and bodily harm on the crew; using the crew as "human shields"; and firing on the captain. The pirates were additionally charged with maritime robbery and attempted murder, robbery and attempted murder, obstruction of justice (special operations) and infliction of injury, and violation of the Punishment for Damaging Ships and Sea Structures Act.

In March, following a conference with their court-appointed lawyers, all of the pirates with the exception of Abdullah Hussein Mahamud requested a jury trial. On April 11, 2011, having considered the requests, Busan District Criminal Court No. 5 decided to commence the jury trial on May 23. Mahamud's separate bench trial began on June 1.

At trial, the pirates claimed that their rights to due process had been violated, citing Article 12 of the Korean Constitution, since following their arrest, they had been transferred to Korea without a proper procedural basis. They also argued that they had not been arrested pursuant to a warrant and that a warrant was not issued during the transfer period; that they had not received any legal assistance; that due process had not been guaranteed when they were detained by the Korean Navy; and that despite physical assaults by the *Samho Jewelry*'s sailors during their arrest, the Korean military had made no effort to protect them. Because their presence in Busan was forced on them without due process, they challenged the court's territorial jurisdiction over the case.

All the defendants were convicted. The court ruled that, by virtue of the domestic Criminal Procedure Act, it had territorial jurisdiction over the case based on the current location of the defendants. Another key issue was the shooting of the captain, in particular determining who was responsible for that crime. On the basis of the testimonies of both pirates and crew members, the court found that only Mahomed Araye had fired at the captain. But whether the pirates as a group had colluded to shoot the captain was another question; all the pirates vigorously denied any such involvement. The court held that it was difficult to conclude that, in the midst of the rescue operation by the Cheonghae Unit, the pirates had conspired to kill the captain in retaliation for causing their imminent capture.

Araye, the pirate who had wounded Capt. Seok Hai-kyun, received a life sentence; the others were each sentenced to thirteen or fifteen years in prison. The court justified the imposition of these penalties (which were heavy by

Korean standards) by citing several factors: the distress inflicted on the victims and their families; the intolerable insult to a sovereign state of collectively and systematically attacking its military, which had been dispatched to protect Korean ships and participate in the international effort to safeguard maritime security; the "excessively selfish and greedy motive" of the defendants in seeking instant riches at the cost of lives; their "daring and indiscriminate scheme" in hijacking ships on the high seas and attempting an additional hijacking; and "the need to warn the Somali pirates" from venturing into waters where Korean ships frequently navigate.

Following the sentencing, both the defense and the prosecution immediately appealed, the former on grounds of excessive sentences and defendants' innocence of certain charges, and the latter on grounds of unreasonably lenient sentences (the prosecution had sought the imposition of capital punishment) and errors of law.

The Busan High Court, which considered the appeals, issued its decision in only three months, which was unprecedented in expeditiousness for a criminal case. It corrected several technical misapplications of law by the district court (which in the separate trial of Mahamud had improperly added the sentence from a lesser offense to the sentence it imposed on him for attempted murder and had omitted punishment for certain crimes committed by the other defendants). The High Court reviewed and accepted the trial court's jurisdictional and factual findings. Subsequently, the Supreme Court rejected the appeals of both the defense and the prosecution and upheld the revised sentences.

Among the issues the Korean courts considered, the most critical was whether the special forces of the Cheonghae Unit of the Korean Navy had the authority to arrest and confine the pirates. The jurisdiction exercised by the Cheonghae Unit in subduing the pirates may be grounded in international law in Article 105 of the United Nations Convention on the Law of the Sea (UNCLOS) and various Security Council resolutions, but the basis in domestic legislation was unclear.

Pursuant to its military orders to save the hostages aboard the *Samho Jewelry*, the Cheonghae Unit captured the pirates and confined them for nine days. Under Korea's Criminal Procedure Act, the legal authority to investigate and arrest lies with the public prosecutor. Judicial police officials such as investigators and police lieutenants conduct investigations under the instruction of the public prosecutor, and law enforcement officers such as police sergeants and patrolmen assist the investigation under the direction of judicial police officials. Because Korean criminal law does not grant judicial powers to military groups like the Cheonghae Unit, the defense claimed that the unit's exercise of judicial authority had been unauthorized.

The trial court did not accept these arguments. It held that although no specific provisions applied directly to the Cheonghae Unit's arrest and transfer of the pirates to the investigative bodies, it was proper to apply Korean criminal procedure to the case. Article 212 of the Criminal Procedure Act provides that "[a]ny person may arrest a flagrant offender without a warrant," while Article 213(1) states: "In cases where a person other than a public prosecutor or judicial police official arrests a flagrant offender, he shall immediately turn over the offender to a public prosecutor or judicial police official."

The court determined that the arrest made by the Cheonghae Unit at sea came under Articles 212 and 213. Finding the navy, dispatched under the National Assembly's consent as representing the government, to be "any person" under the statute was perhaps the only possible decision because of the legislative deficiency regarding the activities of the Cheonghae Unit.

This case was Korea's first trial on piracy. But it was not the first time that these pirates had hijacked a Korean ship. The previous incident took place in April 2010, and was only resolved 217 days later, when Samho Shipping paid a ransom of $9.5 million. This history explains, at least in part, why the Korean government decided to transfer the pirates on *Samho Jewelry* to Korea to undergo trial when their handover to other countries became infeasible. That background also contributed to the realization that a clear basis was needed in Korean law for bringing the perpetrators to justice. An even more significant factor was the recent "arrest and release" practice of states and the passive attitude of the Kenyan government regarding the trials of pirates captured by foreign states.

The basis for the personal jurisdiction of Korean courts over the *Samho Jewelry* pirates can be found in both international and domestic law. The international legal basis is provided by Article 105 of UNCLOS, Article 6 of the Convention for the Suppression of Unlawful Acts Against the Safety of Maritime Navigation (SUA Convention), and Article 5 of the International Convention against the Taking of Hostages. Korea has ratified all three. Article 6(1) of the Korean Constitution provides, "Treaties duly concluded and promulgated under the Constitution and generally recognized rules of international law shall have the same force and effect of law as domestic laws of the Republic of Korea." Thus, treaties, once ratified, do not require additional legislation for domestic application.

The jurisdictional basis in Korean domestic law resides in Article 6 of the Criminal Code, which explicitly provides for criminal jurisdiction when the victim is a Korean national ("passive personality" jurisdiction), as well as in Article 3 of the Law on Punishment for Damaging Ships and Sea Structures. The latter, in particular, was designed to implement the SUA Convention and therefore does not require the victim to be a Korean national. Article 3(3) of this law covers foreign nationals who have violated the SUA Convention and are within Korean territory. In the case at bar, the court applied the law pursuant to the above articles.

Nonetheless, although Korean law clearly provided a sufficient basis for the prosecutions, the Ministry of Justice submitted to the National Assembly a proposed amendment to the Criminal Code on March 25, 2011, clearly establishing universal jurisdiction (which was previously unknown in the Korean Criminal Code) and strengthening the country's ability to prosecute the most serious international crimes. The ministry explained that while both "international crimes violating the universal principle of human rights" and "international conventions seeking to regulate them" had increased, some "crimes committed by foreign nationals abroad... do not fall under... our criminal law even with mechanisms such as personal or territorial jurisdiction and protective jurisdiction." It cited this need and strengthening international cooperation as justifying the measure. The bill was forwarded to the Legislation and Judiciary Committee of the National Assembly on October 27, 2011, and currently remains pending.

While the amendment does not specifically define "universal jurisdiction," it provides in Article 7 that "[t]his law applies to foreign nationals having committed one of the following offenses outside the territory of the Republic of Korea." The article then enumerates an expansive list of the specific crimes to which universal jurisdiction would apply. It would also allow Korea as a state party to exercise universal jurisdiction under the SUA Convention by calling the crimes governed by it "punishable pursuant to treaties binding upon the Republic of Korea."

Commendably, the defendants received a quick and fair trial—four months from investigation to the trial court's verdict, and three months from the appeal to the High Court's decision—and each defendant was represented by two legal counsels (except Mahamud, who had one for his bench trial) even though the case involved accomplices. In addition, Somali interpreters were provided from abroad and defendants' human rights were guaranteed through criminal procedure and a jury trial.

But the case raised questions about the legitimacy of the arrests under international law, in particular whether the use of force by Korean naval forces and the subsequent confinement of the pirates conformed with Korea's international legal obligations. The traditional definition of piracy as provided under UNCLOS Article 101 refers to actions taken for private ends by the crew of a private ship; the laws of war (international humanitarian law), which apply to states or organized armed groups, do not necessarily apply to the suppression of such acts of piracy. The pirates' arrest by Korean naval forces can therefore be seen as equivalent to the arrest of flagrant offenders under domestic law; and the armed forces assume the role of police on the high seas where the governmental powers of any single state do not reach.

Yet the Somali pirates are difficult to categorize, as their systematic organization, taking up of arms, and ties to armed terrorist groups have complicated their character. Thus, it can be asked whether international humanitarian law can be applied to these pirates, just as it can be asked about terrorist groups like Al Qaeda.

Despite this lack of clarity, the use of armed force for the suppression of piracy is justified by UNCLOS Article 105. But such force is permitted for the purposes of arrest and capture only and does not justify the use of deadly force unless the conditions for self-defense arise, which would be evaluated under the standards of necessity, proportionality, and immediacy.

After their arrest in the Indian Ocean, the pirates were confined for nine days without the intervention of a court or legal counsel before being handed over to the Coast Guard, which had proper judicial authority to arrest them. Although domestic law provides for prompt requests for arrest warrants and other guarantees of due process, these restrictions did not apply because the court determined that the arrest had been made by "private individuals." As seen above, Article 213(1) of the Criminal Procedure Act requires that suspects arrested by someone other than the public prosecutor or an enforcement officer be "immediately" handed over to the authorities.

The Supreme Court, however, interpreted the word "immediate" generously. As used in Article 213(1), the Court ruled, it does not mean "to be adjacent in time to the point of arrest, but rather means 'not delaying handover or continuing confinement without justifiable reason'" (pp. 2–3). In considering the overall situation at the time, the Court held that the spatial and material limitations involved made the nine days spent in transferring the suspects after their arrest by the Cheonghae Unit inevitable, and that as a result their delayed handover and continued confinement cannot be seen as lacking justification. Unfortunately, the Court's decision can be interpreted as allowing indefinite confinement past nine days without a warrant as long as it is "inevitable due to spatial and material limitations."

This decision is problematic in that it appears to violate Article 9 of the International Covenant on Civil and Political Rights, to which Korea is a party and which is considered to be part of domestic law pursuant to Article 6(1) of the Constitution. Article 9 permits deprivation of liberty only in accordance with the law (Art. 9(1)); and it entitles detainees charged with criminal offenses to be brought before proper judicial authorities and tried within a reasonable time or released (Art. 9(3)), and all detainees to bring proceedings before a court so that a decision may be made without delay on the lawfulness of their detention (Art. 9(4)). Beyond resulting in the incarceration of the individuals responsible for the act of piracy against the *Samho Jewelry*, this incident led to the proposal of significant amendments to Korean law, incorporating and giving effect to the principle of universal jurisdiction for the most serious international crimes. At the same time, it has left unresolved some important procedural issues that are likely to be encountered in any future exercise of such jurisdiction over serious extraterritorial crimes involving Korean interests.

6.2.1 Korea and Piracy

Acts of piracy are punishable under the Criminal Act and Punishment for Damaging Ships and Marine Structures Act (hereinafter "Punishment for Damage Act"). It defines piracy in Article 340 as the forcible seizure of a ship or another's property after intruding upon a ship through the threat of collective force on the sea and includes that those having killed, caused injury or raped a person is punishable under the crime of maritime robbery. At the same time, acts of piracy in a broader sense, threatening the safety of maritime infrastructures on the continental shelf or on Korean vessels outside her territories, are punishable under the Punishment for Damage Act.

Because Korea does not have independent regulations punishing acts of piracy like the U.S. or Japan, issues were raised in the process of transferring and trying the *Samho Jewelry* pirates, together with the need to strengthen the legal grounds for the anti-piracy activities of the navy in the Gulf of Aden. To be more specific, because of the gap between the elements of maritime robbery provided for in the Criminal Act and the UNCLOS and its lack of clarity, there is a potential for confusion in the process of dealing with piracy as it is inevitably intertwined with international issues.

Issues that can be posited from the differing elements constituting the act of piracy under the UNCLOS and maritime robbery under the Criminal Act are as follows:

- First, the UNCLOS limits the purpose of piracy to "private ends," while no such restrictions exist under the Criminal Act;
- Second, acts of piracy under the UNCLOS must meet the two ship rule where one pirate ship commits an act against another ship, while no such rule exists under the Criminal Act;

- Third, the UNCLOS does not indicate whether the act of piracy must be committed by more than one person; thus it appears that even an act by one person can meet the elements necessary for the crime of piracy. The Criminal Act, however, requires a "collective force," which may be difficult to establish in the case of an act committed by a single person;
- Fourth, the UNCLOS includes acts of voluntary participation or of inciting or intentionally facilitating piracy while no such rule exists under the Criminal Act;
- Fifth, while the UNCLOS defines the location as "On the high seas, or in any other place outside the jurisdiction of any State," the Criminal Act only states "in the sea" thereby having no such limitation. While the UNCLOS limits the location to the high seas and places beyond the jurisdiction of any state, the International Maritime Organization (IMO) describes crimes committed within the jurisdiction of a state as sea robbery, thereby differentiating the two.

As mentioned earlier, several issues were raised due to the gap between domestic and international law, as well as the limitations of the domestic justice system, in the process of transferring and trying the *Samho Jewelry* pirates. Although the vessel was a Maltese flagged vessel, there were no issues regarding Korea's exercise of jurisdiction pursuant to the universal jurisdiction provision of UNCLOS Article 105. Rather, in the process of the trial, lawfulness was questioned regarding i) the arrest and transfer of the pirates by the navy, ii) request for the warrant after the arrest and transfer, and iii) the assistance of legal counsel.

First, with regard to the arrest of the pirates by the navy, Criminal Procedure Act, Article 213 (Delivery of Arrested Flagrant Offender) was an issue that was raised. It provides in paragraph 1 that "In cases where a person other than a public prosecutor or judicial police official arrests a flagrant offender, he shall immediately turn over the offender to a public prosecutor or judicial police official." Thus, there was much debate as to whether the 9 days it took for the pirates to be handed over by the navy—who were not judicial police officials—to the investigative institutions could be considered as being "immediate." Regarding this issue, the Busan District Court, in recognizing these circumstances such as the refusal of neighboring states to receive the pirates and the difficulty in finding flights for their transfer, held that "the nine days it took for the Cheonghae Unit to deliver the Defendants to Korea was inevitable due to spatial and material limitations" and therefore falls within the definition of "immediately."

The second issue raised was whether a warrant was requested within the time period provided in Criminal Procedure Act, Article 203–2(5) stating that where a flagrant offender arrested is sought to be detained, a warrant of detention must be requested within 48 hours. On this point, the Busan District Court cited Article 200-2(5) in holding that while the provision applies to situations in which a public prosecutor or judicial police official arrests a flagrant offender, and in special cases where the transfer to the investigative institutions following the arrest exceeds 48 hours as was in this case, it would be proper to view the above 48 hours as starting when the investigative institution receives the flagrant offender.

The third issue raised was the point at which the suspects should have received legal assistance. The Busan District Court held that the moment of receipt of the flagrant offender by investigative institution is when the right to legal counsel should be guaranteed.

While decisions of the court regarding the above points were generally reasonable, there continue to be points raised regarding the difficulty of equating the arrests made by the navy operating in the Somali waters as being executed by "private individuals," considering the fact that the arrest of pirates is an exercise of public power, premised on criminal punishment. With regard to the "immediacy" provision, there also needs to be modifications considering potential factors that might lead to a delay such as the political situation of adjacent states, bad weather conditions, the arrest of other pirates afterwards and so on. On the other hand, there are concerns that further breaking down the legal provisions would prove unfavorable because the arrest and treatment of suspects are inevitably unpredictable and unsteady as it is premised upon military operations against heavily armed pirates.

In spite of the forceful anti-piracy efforts of the international community, considering the continued increase of piracy in Somali waters, the possibility of future arrest and transfer of pirates to Korea cannot be ruled out. Further participation of the navy in international anti-piracy efforts to secure the safety of the sea lanes of communication is expected, and the same issues raised in the justice system in the *Samho Jewelry* piracy case can resurface. Thus, there needs to be a modification of the domestic law at least to prevent future controversies.

In this regard the following changes should be made: first, amendments should be included in the relevant provisions of the Criminal Act, Criminal Procedure Act, Punishment for Damaging Ships and Marine Structures Act, etc.; second, the Special Act regarding Judicial Actions in the Anti-piracy Operations of the Navy in Somali Waters should be enacted; and iii) a separate regulation in the judicial system for the purpose eliminating piracy should be made.

The Special Act regarding Judicial Actions in the Anti-piracy Operations of the Navy in Somali Waters was proposed as a bill in November of 2009, but there has not been any other significant developments. Similar to that of Japan, a separate regulation regarding the handling of pirates and their arrests can balance out the piracy provisions in UNCLOS and thus help settle the gap between domestic and international legal provisions. While it can also resolve the limitations exposed in the capture and trial process of the pirates, there still remains the burden of new legislation. Although the gravity of the issue of piracy was raised together with the need for separate legislation, the counter-argument that the current legal system is sufficient for judicial action was also given much weight.

Judicial Decisions

(1) *Judgment on the New Fisheries Agreement between Korea and Japan*

Constitutional Court [99 Heon-ma 139, 142, 156, 160 Consolidated] Decision issued Mar. 21, 2001.

(c) We will now examine whether the Agreement at bar, which has undergone the above process until its conclusion and entry into force, violates the territorial rights guaranteed by the Constitution because it not only violates the sovereignty and territorial rights of the people of the Republic of Korea in the territorial waters and the Exclusive Economic Zone (EEZ) but also abandons sovereignty over Dokdo that is part of our territory by including Dokdo in the intermediate zone between Korea and Japan.

First, in examining the relationship between the Agreement at bar and the EEZ, we can observe from the title, text and the annexes that this Agreement regards fisheries. Therefore, it has no direct relationship with the delimitation issues of the EEZ. This is confirmed in Article 1 of Annex 1 which provides, "The Contracting Parties shall continue to negotiate in good faith for an early delimitation of the exclusive economic zone."

Further, the distinction between the waters designated as EEZ and intermediate zone under this Agreement is that the former is adjacent to the littoral states; and even if a 200 nautical mile EEZ were to be designated, it would be determined in an area that would not raise further issues between Korea and Japan so that the littoral state may exercise sovereign authority over the fisheries in the EEZ (Article 7(1)). As for the latter, since it is not convenient to determine baselines of the territorial sea because the outer borders of the 200 n.m. EEZ of Korea and Japan overlap, a fixed zone was predetermined in order to permit fishing within the zone by people and ships of both countries by agreeing not to apply laws and regulations on fisheries to nationals and fishing vessels of the other Contracting Party in the zone (Annex I para. 2(a)). This intermediate zone extends from the East Sea to the East China Sea south of Jeju Island, over two points within the region (Article 9). This intermediate zone was determined by yielding certain distance inward from the outer limits of the EEZ on the part of each state rather than claiming the median line which each party is called on to adopt in the absence of an agreement. Therefore, it does not appear to be a unilateral surrender on the part of any one state nor that there was any significant loss of balance (*See* Exclusive Economic Zone Act art. 5(2) and Law on the Exclusive Economic Zone and the Continental Shelf of Japan art. 1(2)).

Next, we will consider the relationship of this Agreement to the territorial waters. In the U.N. Convention on the Law of the Sea, EEZ is defined as "an area beyond and

© KONINKLIJKE BRILL NV, LEIDEN, 2016 | DOI 10.1163/9789004315754_009

adjacent to the territorial sea" that "shall not extend beyond 200 nautical miles from the baselines from which the breadth of the territorial sea is measured" (arts. 55 & 57). Similar provisions exist in domestic laws of both Korea and Japan (*See* Exclusive Economic Zone Act art. 2(1) and Law on the Exclusive Economic Zone and the Continental Shelf of Japan art. 1(2)). Not only does the Agreement at bar not directly regulate the EEZ's, but even if EEZ's were to be designated, they would refer to areas beyond the territorial seas. This is also applicable to the intermediate zone within the scope of this Agreement; therefore, even if Dokdo were to be a part of the intermediate zone, it clearly does not influence the issue of sovereignty over Dokdo or that of the territorial waters.

(d) As examined above, Claimant's assertions that territorial rights regarding territorial waters of Dokdo and EEZ were violated by these treaty provisions are without merit.

(2) *Case Concerning Piracy*

Republic of Korea v. Araye (2011 Do 12927 Verdict, issued December 22, 2011 [Supreme Ct.])

Case 2011Do12927

Order
All appeals are dismissed.

Reasoning
The issues of the appeal are analyzed as follows.

1. Regarding the Issue of Violation of Territorial Jurisdiction

A. Criminal Procedure Article 4(1) states, "The territorial jurisdiction of the court shall be determined by the place of offense, the place of domicile, residence of the defendant, or the place where the defendant is presently located." The "place where the defendant is presently located" here refers to the location in which the defendant is at the time of the institution of public action, not only of voluntary selection but also one forced under due process of law.

While flagrant offenders may be arrested by any persons without a warrant (Criminal Procedure Act Article 212), if persons other than a public prosecutor or judicial police official (hereinafter "prosecutor and others") make such an arrest, he must be immediately turned over to the prosecutor and others (Criminal Procedure Act Article 213(1)). "Immediately" in this case does not need to be adjacent in time to the point of arrest, but rather means "not delaying the handover or continuing confinement without justifiable reason." Further, when the prosecutor and others arrest a flagrant offender or seek to confine him after they have taken delivery of the flagrant offender, a request for a warrant must be made within 48 hours of arrest. If a warrant is not requested for within the given period, the suspect shall be released (Criminal Procedure Act Articles 213-2, 200-2(5)). The reasoning behind the above legislation regarding the arrest of flagrant offenders—the decision to request a warrant within the limited time period and to require release if such request is not made—is not only in that there have been requests to protect human rights in prolonging detention without warrants, but also in order to guarantee reasonable time for the investigating institution to decide whether to request a warrant. Thus where a flagrant offender is arrested by persons other than the prosecutor and others, and the offender is delivered without unnecessary delay, the above 48 hours begin not at the time of arrest but rather at the time when the offender is delivered to the prosecutor and others.

B. According to the reasoning and findings of the trial court as upheld by the appellate court, the following facts can be found.

On January 21, 2011, on or around 06:00 hours, the Defendants were arrested by the soldiers of the Cheonghae Unit on the high seas 670 miles northeast of Garacad, Somalia for offenses including maritime robbery and were confined in isolation in Samho Jewelry (hereinafter "the vessel in this case"). The Cheonghae Unit sought to negotiate the transfer of Defendants to adjacent states such as Oman for various reasons, i.e., issues arising from long-distance transportation, procedural ease with which the Defendants could exercise their rights for their defense in locations close to their own country, and in the effort to maintain friendly relations with neighboring states pursuant to the U.N. Security Council resolutions calling for international action and cooperation regarding piracy in the waters near Somalia, etc. However, upon the refusal of the neighboring states for reasons, i.e., similar future requests from other states and lack of detention facilities, the Cheonghae Unit decided to transfer the Defendants to Korea. Afterwards, when it proved difficult in finding flights for them, the Defendants were transferred with the help of the United Arab Emirates on their private plane. They were transferred on Jan. 30, 2011, to the police officers belonging to the Southern Regional Department of the Korean Coastguard. Prior to the arrival of the Defendants in Korea, the Prosecution requested a warrant for the Defendants on or around 20:30 on January 29, 2011 at the Busan Regional Court. The court issued a warrant for questioning on or around 23:30 the same day; and following the suspect interrogation on or around 8:00 on January 30, 2011, a warrant for detention was issued around 10:40.

C. The trial court, based on the above facts, found that the arrest of Defendants as flagrant offenders by the soldiers of the Cheonghae Unit was an arrest made by persons other than the prosecutor and others; and considering the fact that it took 9 days for the Defendants to be transferred to Korea was inevitable due to spatial and material limitations, it could not be seen as having unreasonably delayed transfer or continued the arrest. After holding that the 48 hours provided for the requesting of the warrant began on or around 04:30 of January 30, 2011 when the police officers received the Defendants, the trial court further found that because the Defendants were confined pursuant to a warrant requested and issued within 48 hours since then, the Defendants were detained in the Busan Detention Center pursuant to lawful arrest, immediate transfer and lawful confinement. The trial court therefore held that it had territorial jurisdiction.

Based on the above principles and facts, the judgment of the trial court as upheld by the appellate court is reasonable; and we cannot find, as alleged by the counsel for Defendant Abdikhadar Aman Ali (hereinafter "Defendant Aman Ali") in his appeal, that there was a misapplication of territorial jurisdiction or of the arrest and detention of flagrant offenders in the Criminal Procedure Act.

2. Regarding Firing at the Soldiers and Attempted Murder & Maritime Robbery, etc.

A. Article 30 of the Criminal Act provides that "Co-Principals" is established by satisfying both subjective and objective elements of the intention to jointly commit the crime and the commission of the crime through functional control of the act based on such joint intentions. Thus, an accomplice who has not directly undertaken an act constituting the offense can still satisfy the above elements and bear responsibility as Co-Principle of the conspiracy. In order for an accomplice not directly implementing an act undertaking the offense to be recognized as a Co-Principle of the conspiracy, his status or role in the in the crime and his command or control over the process of the crime as a whole shall be taken into consideration to show that he is not a mere accomplice but rather maintains a functional control of the act through fundamental contributions towards the crime (See Supreme Court, issued Apr. 26, 2007, 2007Do235 Verdict). In this case, in light of the overall circumstances, i.e., the method and planning of the crime, the number of people involved and their dispositions; the particularity of time and place of the crime; the possibility of contact with others and the foreseeable reactions in the process of committing the crime; if in the process of committing the crime or achieving the purpose, the co-conspirators could foresee the commission of derivative crimes but failed to prevent or take appropriate measures in such regard; we can find that there was a tacit conspiracy regarding all the crimes and even functional control, even if there were no indications of intention regarding each of the derivative crimes. (See Supreme Court, issued Apr. 26, 2007, 2007Do428 Verdict; Supreme Court, issued Apr. 28, 2011, 2011Do284 Verdict).

B. According to the reasoning and findings of the trial court as upheld by the appellate court, the following facts can be found.

The pirates in this case, including the Defendants, conspired to threaten the vessel with weapons such as guns in order to overtake the vessel by force, to take the vessel and crew to Somalia as hostage, and to demand ransom for their release. The pirates in this case, under their leader and his second in command, acted systematically by dividing up their roles at various locations, i.e., sending an advance party for the hijacking of vessel, keeping watch over the hostages and the use of communication devices, control of the engine room, standing watch on the Wing Bridge, translation, cooking, etc. Following the hijacking, they knew that a military vessel of unidentified nationality was pursuing them; and they stood watch in shifts on the Wing Bridge with weapons such as machine guns to defend against anti-piracy operations by external forces. On January 18, 2011, during the navy's first attempt at a rescue operation, when the naval RIB boat kept approaching despite having sent out the crew confined in the steering house to the Top Bridge or Wing Bridge, the pirates in this case did not simply fire warning shots but rather fired direct shots at the RIB boat, thereby wounding three victims including Ahn, Byeong Joo.

Based on these facts, the appellate court found there to be a tacit conspiracy among the pirates including not only the armed efforts to push back the attempted rescue operations in the process of taking the hijacked vessel in this case to Somalia, but also the shooting of the naval RIB boat. The court further held that Defendant Awil Buraale (hereinafter "Defendant Buraale"), who fired at the RIB boat with a machine gun at the time, fired at the soldiers with the intent to kill pursuant to the above conspiracy and thus bears the liability of a Co-Principal regardless of whether Defendant Abdulahi Ali actually took part in the firing.

In light of the above principles and findings, the conspiracy of the pirates in this case including the Defendants, included the act of firing upon the soldiers; and the factual findings and judgment of the appellate court, in finding that such acts showed the intent to murder, was reasonable. Also according to the factual findings and the selected evidence of the appellate court, Defendant Abdulahi Ali contributed as a lookout with a rifle in hand, as well as keeping watch over the communication devices in the steering house pursuant to the division of tasks among the pirates. When considering the overall scope of the conspiracy and the circumstances of the crime, as well as the division of roles among those contributing to piracy, even if the above Defendant did not actually take part in the undertaking of the actual crime, he still becomes an accomplice to the above crime of Maritime Robbery and Murder through the functional control of the act through his fundamental contributions. There may be some inadequacies in the instructions of the appellate court, but the conclusion that the above Defendant bears the liability of a Co-Principal with regard to the crime is legitimate.

Ultimately, the factual findings and the judgment of the appellate court has not erred in misinterpreting the law regarding Co-Principals or misunderstood the facts as alleged by the counsels of the above Defendants in their appeal.

3. Regarding the Use of "Human Shield" and Attempted Murder & Maritime Robbery

The intent in the crime of murder does not require a purpose to kill or a planned intent to do so. Rather, it is sufficient if it could be foreseen that one's acts have the potential to cause the death of another; and while the subjective certainty of such occurrence is included, the crime may be established even if it is uncertain (See Supreme Court, issued June 24, 2004, 2002Do995 Verdict). In the circumstances of a co-conspiracy, if one of the conspirators escapes from the collusive relationship prior to the commission by the other conspirators, he no longer bears liability for their actions. To escape such a relationship, however, requires the dissolution of the functional control assumed by the conspirator. Thus, if the conspirator has actively participated in influencing the acts of the other conspirators, he cannot be seen as having escaped the relationship without having aggressively acted to stop the crime or otherwise effectively remove his influence from the implementation of the crime (See Supreme Court, issued Sept. 9, 2010, 2010Do6924 Verdict).

The appellate court found that following the navy's first attempted rescue operation, the leader of the pirates in this case instructed all the pirates to send out the crew that was being held hostage to the Wing Bridge should the naval attack resume; that pursuant to such orders, the crew including victim Seok, Hae-gyun was sent out to the Wing Bridge by one of the pirates once the second naval rescue operation began; and the Wing Bridge at the time was being showered with warning shorts of the navy. The appellate court further held that among the pirates, there was a prior conspiracy to utilize the crew as "human shields" should the navy renew their attempts to rescue them. They could foresee that sending out the crew to the Wing Bridge in the midst of naval fire could result in their deaths yet they disregarded that possibility, which could be recognized as negligent homicide; and thus, their act of murder began when they sent out the crew to the Wing Bridge. The court thus held that because the above acts were taken pursuant to a prior conspiracy, Defendant Buraale and Abdulahi Ali, in abandoning their guns and running away, could not have resulted in their escape from the collusive relationship.

In light of the above principles and findings, the factual findings and judgment of the appellate court were reasonable; and the court has not erred in misinterpreting the law regarding Co-Principals or misunderstood the facts as alleged by the counsels of the above Defendants in their appeal.

4. Regarding the Shooting of Seok, Hae-gyun and Attempted Murder & Maritime Robbery

A. Regarding the Defendant Mahomed Araye's (hereinafter "Defendant Araye") Reasons for Appeal

The appellate court held that factual findings and judgments made based on the selected evidence were sufficient to find that Defendant Araye shot Seok Hae-gyun with the intent to kill. In other words, ① Victim Seok, during the second rescue operation, was discovered in the steering house of the vessel with a gunshot wound that penetrated his left abdomen towards the right rib and causing a comminuted fracture to his left arm. In light of the degree of his injury and the circumstances, it is highly likely that Seok sustained the above gunshot wounds after having returned to the steering house from the Wing Bridge. ② Fragments of the AK rifles used by the pirates were discovered in Seok's left femoral region (left gluteal region). In light of the fact that the warning shots of the navy were raining down upon the Wing Bridge and steering house at the time, it is unlikely that the above fragments resulted from the stray bullets of the pirates' counterattack. ③ Unlike the other pirates in the steering house who were not armed or had disposed of them under their leader's orders, Defendant Araye had not obeyed the same but continued to be armed with an AK rifle in the steering house; and it was only after Seok was wounded and the navy's penetration was imminent that he fled to the cabin and disposed of his AK rifle around the stairs. ④ Kim Doo-chan and others that had taken refuge at the steering house with Seok witnessed Araye standing to the left of Seok with his gun; heard one of the pirates looked for Seok saying "captain, captain"; not too long after, heard a gunshot different from that of the navy; and after the arrest of the Defendants by the navy, Kim identified Defendant Araye as the one having shot at Seok.

When the reasoning of the appellate court is seen in light of its findings, its factual findings and judgment are reasonable; and it did not err in misunderstanding the facts as alleged by the counsel of the above Defendant in his appeal.

B. Regarding the Appeal of the Prosecution

(1) Regarding Defendant Araye

The final appeal is a post-appeal evaluation of the intermediate appellate decision. Thus, issues not raised at the intermediate appeal do not fall within the scope of the final appeal. If issues remain unraised at the intermediate appeal or the issues are not adjudged by the court by its own authority, they cannot be grounds for final appeal. (See Supreme Court, issued Jan. 27, 2011, 2010Do7947 Verdict).

The issue on appeal is that despite the fact that Prosecution indicted Defendant Araye as Co-Principal with other Defendants, the appellate court erred in independently finding him as having committed the crime alone. Unfortunately, it is clear that this has not been raised in the intermediate appeal and therefore cannot become grounds for the final appeal.

(2) Regarding other Defendants

The appellate court held that the conspiracy of the pirates in this case was in hijacking the vessel, forcing it to sail to Somalia, demanding ransom, and to achieve such purpose by eliminating hostages if there were hindrances. It also held that once the purpose was frustrated and their very survival could not be guaranteed, killing for the sake of revenge for having caused the frustration could not have been part of the conspiracy. The court further held that pirates other than the Defendant Araye at the time disposed of their weapons in the steering house under their leader's orders and gave up resistance by seeking refuge from the crossfire in the steering house or the cabin, thereby effectively ending the collusive relationship regarding the act of piracy. Defendants Buraale, Abdulahi Ali and Aman Ali, who had taken refuge for their own survival, could not have foreseen that Defendant Araye would have shot at Seok to kill him.

In light of the above principles and findings, the factual findings and judgment of the appellate court are reasonable; and it did not err in misunderstanding the facts as alleged by the counsel of the above Defendant in his appeal. The case cited for this appeal (Supreme Court, issued Jan. 13, 2011, 2010D09927 Verdict) has different facts and cannot be applied to this case.

5. Regarding the Claims of Unreasonable Sentences of the Defendants

Considering the various elements for sentencing, e.g., Defendants' age, dispositions, intelligence and environment, motivation, method and results of the case, and the circumstances of the crime after the commission, there is no remarkable reason to determine that the appellate court sentencing was excessively unreasonable.

6. Conclusion

All appeals are dismissed and ordered to comply with the opinion of the Supreme Court.

Justices:
Supreme Court Justice Lee, Sang-Hoon
Supreme Court Justice Chun, Soo-Ahn

Chief Justice:
Supreme Court Justice Yang, Chang-Soo

CHAPTER 5

Other International Legal Issues Affecting Korea

1 Migration

1.1 *Korean-Chinese, Migrant Workers, Marriage Immigrant Women, and the Refugee Act*

1.1.1 Introduction

"[T]he concept of globalization implies, first and foremost, a stretching of social, political and economic activities across frontiers such that events, decisions and activities in one region of the world can come to have significance for individuals and communities in distant regions of the globe." In particular, there is a transnational expansion of economic activities that not only push capital beyond its borders but also "cheap" labor from third world countries, especially women, resulting in the feminization of immigration and thus an increase in the migration of human resources. From the 70's construction boom in the Middle East up to the early 80's, Korea was an aggressive exporter of labor. However, passing through a high-growth period in the late 80's, it went from a source country to a destination country for labor and marriage immigrants. Since then, the percentage of foreign migrants and their stays in Korea increased, so that by the mid-2000's, Korea attained the status of an "immigration state" as designated by the United Nations. According to the statistics released by the Immigration Services of the Ministry of Justice in 2011, the number of foreign nationals residing in Korea reached its peak at 1.4 million (1,395,077). Among them, the number of long-term residents, excluding temporary stays and tourist visas, exceeded 1 million, reaching 2.2% of Korea's total population. In spite of this, in its 2004 World Economic Outlook, the International Monetary Fund stated that Korea would need to accommodate immigrants up to 35% of its population for it to be able to retain the current labor force until 2050. Along these lines, the continued administrative and legal systems and culture towards "others/outsiders" that the Korean society holds fast to should be transformed in a variety of different ways. However, the issue of "immigration" and "immigrants" in Korea bears a unique context that is distinct from western states. The historical experience of forced transfer and such during the Japanese colonization era, exclusive nationalism based on the Confucian traditions of East Asia, and gender bias grounded in the patriarchal

© KONINKLIJKE BRILL NV, LEIDEN, 2016 | DOI 10.1163/9789004315754_010

system, etc. are affecting the immigration policies and immigrant issues in Korean society.

This section will examine the human rights issues of overseas nationals, migrant workers, marriage immigrant women, with regard to their immigrant status. More specifically, the issues to be dealt with are: first, violation of equal rights of the Korean-Chinese (*Joseon-jok*) in their immigration process pursuant to the Act on the Immigration and Legal Status of Overseas Koreans (hereinafter "Overseas Koreans Act"); second, human rights violations in relation to immigration of unregistered migrant workers pursuant to the Act on the Employment, etc. of Foreign Workers (hereinafter "Employment Permit System Act") and Immigration Control Act; third, issues concerning the guarantee of residence permits for marriage immigrant women and recognition of dual nationality pursuant to the Immigration Control Act and Nationality Act; and lastly, review of the significance and limitations, as well as problems, of the recently enacted Refugee Act.

1.1.2 Issues Concerning the Immigration Status of Korean-Chinese (*Joseon-jok*)

1.1.2.1 *Significance of the Act on the Immigration and Legal Status of Overseas Koreans*

Korea's immigration policies concerning foreign nationals are regulated by the Immigration Control Act. However, Korean nationals overseas are separately regulated by the Act on the Immigration and Legal Status of Overseas Koreans (hereinafter "Overseas Koreans Act"). The Overseas Koreans Act implemented by the Kim, Dae-Jung administration in December 1999 provides preferential treatment for overseas nationals satisfying the criteria laid out by law by granting them similar legal status as that of nationals within Korea.

The concept of Overseas Koreans is an exceptional term not generally used by other countries. Other countries rather utilize the term "overseas nationals," which indicate those who, with voluntary intent, leave their original state and emigrate to another in order to reside there, while retaining the nationality of their originating state. Though they have left their state of nationality to their resident state, it is natural that they are granted immigration privileges equivalent to that of other nationals because they have retained their nationalities.

However, the Overseas Koreans Act defines Overseas Koreans more broadly than the definition generally used. Overseas Koreans Act Article 2(2) defines "foreign nationality Koreans" as those who have held the nationality of the Republic of Korea in the past, or even if they have not, include those who are lineal descendants of Korean nationals, thereby granting them extensive immigration and legal privileges pursuant to the Act.

1.1.2.2 *The Scope of "Foreign Nationality Koreans" Pursuant to the Overseas Koreans Act*

Then, just how far does the scope of "Koreans" extend? In the proposed draft of the Overseas Koreans Act of September 29, 1998, the definition of foreign nationality Koreans was "Among persons of Korean lineal descent and having acquired the nationality of a foreign country, those prescribed by Presidential Decree." However, with the submission of the Ministry of Foreign Affairs stating that such legislation of *jus sanguinis* violates principles of international law, that the international custom relating to such legislation follows the principle of past nationality, and that it may create diplomatic friction with China as it conflicts in part with China's integration policy towards its minorities, "foreign nationality Koreans" were defined in the final proposal as Koreans having emigrated abroad after the establishment of the Government of the Republic of Korea.

Arguments were made against this definition as having been created without a rational basis because, although Koreans having emigrated *before* the establishment of the Government of the Republic of Korea or Koreans having emigrated *after* the establishment were fundamentally the same "Koreans," the Overseas Koreans Act created an arbitrary standard of the holding of Korean nationality to grant immigration and legal status privileges only to those *after* the establishment of the government and excluding the same for those *before* its establishment. Further arguments were made that such an interpretation was a denial of the legitimacy of the Provisional Government of the Republic of Korea. Pursuant to these arguments, a constitutional petition was filed by Koreans forcefully transferred to Sakhalin prior to the establishment of the Government of the Republic of Korea as well as the Korean-Chinese. The Constitutional Court held in 2001 concerning the scope of Overseas Koreans limited to "those having emigrated abroad after the establishment of the Government," that "the establishment of the Government cannot be a rational basis for differentiating Overseas Koreans." Declaring the provision unconstitutional, it ordered the amendment of the provision by December 31, 2003.

Thus, the Ministry of Justice amended the scope of the Overseas Koreans Act from the previous "persons or their lineal descendants having emigrated abroad after the establishment of the Government of the Republic of Korea and, having lost the nationality of the Republic of Korea, have acquired the nationality of a foreign country" to persons, "prescribed by Presidential Decree, of those who, having held the nationality of the Republic of Korea or as their lineal descendants, have acquired the nationality of a foreign country," so that the discrimination no longer existed among emigrants depending upon their point of emigration. At the same time, the Enforcement Decree was also amended to define foreign nationality Koreans as "those who, having held the nationality of the Republic of Korea (including those who had emigrated abroad before the Government of the Republic of Korea was established), have acquired the nationality of a foreign country" and "those whose parent or grandparent of either side, having held the nationality of the Republic of Korea, have acquired the nationality of a foreign country."

On the one hand, during the amendment process of the Overseas Koreans Act after being found unconstitutional by the Constitutional Court, arguments were raised that granting immigration and legal status privileges to foreign nationals of Korean descent conflicted with the International Convention on the Elimination of All Forms of Racial Discrimination (hereinafter "ICERD") which Korea was a party to.

Having been ratified by the National Assembly and thus having the same effect as that of domestic law, ICERD article 5 provides for the "guarantee [of] the right of everyone, without distinction as to race, colour, or national or ethnic origin, to equality before the law ..." including rights to leave and return to a country, right of residence, right to own property, the right to free choice of employment, etc. The argument raised was that granting privileges to foreign nationals of Korean descent was equivalent to "preference based on race" in article 1(1) of ICERD; and the various privileges enjoyed by the Overseas Koreans under the Act ultimately fall under the scope of human rights, the discrimination of which is prohibited by article 6 of ICERD.

In the case of Korea, however, the formation of the concept of Overseas Koreans has a historical context different from that of other states. This is because the migration of Overseas Koreans was more often involuntary, unlike the voluntary emigration of most other countries. According to statistics, forced transfer during the forced Japanese occupation of Korea numbered between 1.2–1.6 million, while some scholars estimate the number to exceed 2 million. Japanese colonization of the Korean Peninsula had resulted in forced transfer policies and involuntary emigration by the Japanese government, resulting in countless numbers of involuntary emigrants. To consider as "preference based on race" the "deserving treatment" of persons of Korean descent inevitably residing abroad due to forced transfer against their humanity by the colonizing state is an imperialistic conception that seeks to present Japanese colonization and the subsequent forced migration as being "natural." Within this context and in relation to the historically unique circumstances of Korean-Chinese, the Constitutional Court held, "Rather than helping fellow Koreans who could not but leave the country due to its dismal historical situation, adopting lawfully discriminatory policies is a situation without precedent even in foreign countries. Thus, it is very difficult to recognize the legitimacy of the discrimination in this case from a humanitarian perspective, even apart from an ethnic perspective. The benefit that the government seeks to gather from the discrimination in this case is significantly smaller than the resulting pain and division among fellow Koreans." Within this historical context, granting special immigration status to Koreans that have been forcefully transferred and their descendants to allow their return to the homeland is based on the rationale of the non-normal circumstances of the colonization era during which the status of the sovereign state was deprived, while simultaneously restoring the rights of its citizens prior to colonization. In spite of this, the *de facto* status of Korean-Chinese and Korean-Russians (*Joseon-jok* and Koryeoin) have not improved due to the gap between the law and its implementation.

1.1.3 Issue of Immigration Status of Unregistered Migrant Workers

1.1.3.1 *Current Status*

According to the "Current Status of Foreigners with Employment Status" from the Ministry of Justice, there are a total of 595,098 migrant workers with employment permits in Korea as of December 31, 2011. Among them, persons with lawful status number 540,259, while persons without permits and thus considered illegal aliens number 54,839. Over 80%, of these persons (45,105) are workers having entered the country with unprofessional employment visas (E-9) under the EPS Act. This shows that the issue of unregistered immigrants in Korea lying at the heart of immigration problems is not unrelated to the EPS Act.

The total number of unregistered migrant workers discovered in 2011 numbered 92,970, among which 18,034 were forcefully removed, and 5,112 ordered or advised to depart. Every year, approximately 23,000 migrant workers are being deported out of the country.

Similarly, the migrant workers that have legally lost their resident status are in a dead zone of human rights in labor and daily life. The fact that among the 80 concerns and recommendations put forth by international human rights bodies since 1990's concerning the human rights situation of immigrants in Korea, 25 concerned the human rights of migrant workers, showing that the improvement of their human rights is an important task for our society.

1.1.3.2 *Uniqueness of Migrant Worker Issue to Korea*

For a long time, Korean society has shared the myth of a single ethnicity and thus a strong sense of identity of blood relations, resulting in an exclusive attitude towards different matters. This ethnic identity was only emphasized by the eras of violent change under Japanese colonization and the contemporary U.S. military government regime. As a result, the basic understanding of immigrants was that they were harmful to the purity of blood and social oneness, which lead to a widespread attitude of discrimination. At the same time, the Koreans' exclusive attitude towards others was dependent upon the economic status of the country from which the foreigner comes from, and this ultimately was not irrelevant to their "skin color." Koreans have an attitude towards others that is more exclusive towards those that are economically inferior or have darker skin. "Migrant workers" is a term referring not to whites from the U.S., Canada or Europe coming to teach English but is biased towards northeast, southeast and central Asians engaged in 3D labor. The concepts of upper circuit and survival circuit generally refer to the global migration route of MNC workers in fields such as finance for the former and unskilled workers in manufacturing for the latter; but in Korea, these have much relevance to skin color.

Such an understanding was also reflected in the immigration policies of the Korean government. The Ministry of Justice has been planning and carrying out operation plans since 1962, through which the ideologies behind such policies are evident. According to these plans, immigration control administration bears an international character as it is concerned with foreign nationals; and as the population concentration of Korea ranks 4th in the world, the government strongly promotes population and immigration control policies. Thus, the arrival of foreigners must come under strict regulations, and immigration policies should be set in consideration of "the effect if law breaking foreigners or unethical foreigners on the lives of the citizens." However, for a large population to survive in a limited area with limited resources, technologies of the advanced states must be brought in and the arrival of such skilled persons welcomed. It thus reveals the need to carry out immigration control by balancing the two conflicting interests of restraining the arrival and attracting foreigners.

Such an immigration policy became the root of the present-day regime which grants immigrant status by categorizing the immigrants into a hierarchy of those to welcome or to exclude based on the subject of their applicative policies. In other words, professional skills are actively embraced from the perspective of national interest and economy, while simple labor and illegal aliens were excluded as object of aggressive control/management. However, within this "rational" appearing decision lies a racist attitude as evident in the difference of skin color between professionals arriving through the upper circuit and the simple labor force arriving through the survival circuit. Thus, at the root of the government exclusion policies toward migrant workers and the unregistered workers that are subject to control are the combination of deeply rooted exclusive pure-blood and racist attitude of Korean society.

Based on these problems, issues that arise from Act on the Employment, etc. of Foreign Workers and the subsequent employment permit system, which have become the channel for the largest number of unregistered migrant workers in Korean society, will be discussed in the next section, as well as recommendations for the improvement of their human rights situations.

1.1.4 Issues Concerning the Employment Permit System Pursuant to the Act on the Employment of Foreign Workers

1.1.4.1 *Limitation of Employment*

The discussion regarding the implementation of the EPS began in 1995 and continued for 8 years until 2003, when the legislation was finally passed under the condition that it would be carried out in parallel with Industrial Trainee System. The EPS was implemented in order to resolve issues with the Industrial Trainee System, such as overstaying after the training period, and overdue wages and violence of the employers committed due to the vulnerability of those who overstay. By broadly categorizing the foreign labor force as professional skilled labor and simple labor, the system began to change in order to ease the accommodation of the latter. This system permitted employers seeking to hire foreign laborers to permit such employment, while issuing employment visas to foreigners seeking to be employed by such permitted employer for set periods. However, the resulting irregular status of foreigners having entered with these visas is a task yet to be tackled by the system.

Act on the Employment, etc. of Foreign Workers article 18 provides, "Any foreign worker may work as an employee for not more than three years from the date on which he/she enters the Republic of Korea." According to article 18(3), "Foreigners having been employed in Korea and have departed from the country, (except for foreign workers under article 12(1)) may not be re-employed under this Act within 6 months of the date of departure." This provision is understood to have been included in order to avoid the general side-effects of foreign workers such as long-term employment and stays, and to grant employment opportunities to numerous other foreigners seeking employment in Korea, by placing procedural restrictions such as limiting the permitted duration of employment activities to three years in principle and requiring passage of six months after departure before seeking reemployment.

It has long been argued and criticized that this three-year limitation is too short from the perspective of the actual parties involved. Thus, Act on the

Employment, etc. of Foreign Workers was amended several times to allow stays longer than three years in exceptional circumstances; but as recognition of such exceptions still is rather limited, the fundamental issue has not been addressed.

Further, article 25(4) limits the change of workplace of foreign workers to three times in three years, which makes the status of migrant workers unstable. Though various reasons exist in specific and individual cases which make such change inevitable, collectively limiting the number of possible changes of workplace violates the freedom of employment of migrant workers. In particular, leaving the final, third workplace ultimately means involuntary departure pursuant to the termination of resident status for the migrant worker, which entails the danger of being forced to work for low wages. In December 2011, the Act was amended to allow migrant workers to change workplaces without including it in the three permissible changes if there was no fault with the change; but in cases where the migrant workers are no longer able to work due to a workplace accident, this is still included within the three permissible changes.

This was also pointed out in the recommendations of the commissions of international human rights conventions, ratified by Korea. The ICERD commission, in its recommendation pursuant to the 13th and 14th periodic reviews submitted by Korea, expressed its concern for the widespread discrimination and abuse at the workplaces such as the non-renewable 3-year employment contracts, severe limitations in job changes, long working hours, low wages and dangerous working conditions. The Standards Committee of the ILO at the 98th session of June 2009 called for the relief/flexibility of the excessive restriction of freedom to change workplaces, as such appropriate level of flexibility and the subsequent reduction in the excessive dependence of migrant workers on their employers would help reduce their vulnerability.

Furthermore, as is evident in the title of this system (EPS), this law is focused on the employers and thus can be seen as already being premised on discrimination of foreign workers. In this context, there are experts that argue for a labor permit system focused on laborers rather than the employment permit system. These experts point out that under the currently active EPS, strict observance of contract term is applied regardless of the satisfaction of the workers with their workplaces so that their freedom of changing jobs is not guaranteed. With insufficient enforcement/binding force concerning non-performance of the employer such as the withholding of wages, foreign workers must withstand various disadvantages as such under the Industrial Trainee System, which results in unregistered aliens.

1.1.5 Human Rights Issues for Unregistered Migrant Workers

1.1.5.1 *Need for the Protection of Unregistered Migrant Workers under the Law*

The International Convention on the Protection of the Rights of All Migrant Workers and Members of Their Families (1990) widely protects the rights of unregistered migrant workers and their families, but Korea has not yet ratified this treaty. As a result, unregistered immigrants are excluded from legal and systemic protection of Korean society and thus placed in the dead zone of human rights protection. As observed in the statistics above, the field in which mass unregistered immigrants occur is through the Non-professional Employment (E-9) visa of the EPS system. The strengthening of the legal protection of unregistered migrant workers is ultimately the core of legal protection for all unregistered immigrants.

Prior to a discussion of this issue, it needs to be understood that the issue of unregistered migrant workers in Korea is a structural result of Korea's immigration policy and the needs in the labor market. Most of the foreigners seeking work in Korea through the EPS system must pay enormous costs to brokers in Korea for their immigration processing, due to which they bear huge debts when entering the country. Such debts become a direct cause for their escape from their contracted workplaces. The Working Visit System which targets Korean-Chinese and Koreans of the former Soviet Union is a system that allows their lawful entry into Korean without the intervention of brokers. When we consider that globalization is where social, political and economic decisions and activities in one region of the world can come to have significance for individuals and communities in distant regions of the globe, it is undoubtedly clear that this system triggered changes especially in the economy of Korean-Chinese frequently traveling to and from Korea and for those in their livelihood including the freedom to immigrate. Of course, the increased number of Overseas Koreans worsened their rights as laborers; which means that the Korean government does not pay for the social costs connected with the increasing number of foreign workers.

The inflow of migrant workers through the EPS system takes place according to state policy adopted pursuant to agreements individually made between the Korean government and other states. The Foreign Workforce Policy Committee under the Prime Minister reviews and adopts most of the policy regime such as Basic Plan for Foreign Workers, Work Type and Scale for Bringing in Foreign Workers, Designation and Cancellation of Foreign Worker Sending States, Businesses, Workplaces and Employment Scale that can Hire Foreign Workers, and Protection of Rights and Interests of Foreign Workers, etc. In spite of this, the fact that migrant workers brought in under such a regime planned by the state constitutes over 80% of the irregulars/unregistered within the country shows that there is a serious problem with the construct of the regime itself. Further, unconditionally categorizing these unregistered migrant workers as illegal aliens, subjecting them to forced deportation and other enforcement measures only places their already destitute lives in greater fear/suspense.

Thus the argument that resident status and legal protection should be distinguished and the latter provided to unregistered migrant workers is gaining support. Migrant workers have already lowered production costs with their low wages, and their services in the 3D labor play an important role in the industrial structure of Korean society. It is self-contradictory to label the unregistered as "illegal" and exclude them from protection of the law without acknowledging this reality.

When we observe other countries such as Spain, those countries utilize the term "irregulars" instead of unregistered or illegal immigrants in implementing policies to "regularize" them. Though irregular, once "registered" at the city hall where they reside, they are granted the privilege of free education and medical services, so that they have relatively more opportunities than other countries to enjoy rights of education and health. As we can observe in Spain and Italy, regularization rescues the irregular migrant workers from their destitute labor situations and reduces tax evasion occurring from illegal employment, so that overall, the central and regional governments increase their tax income, allowing an equal realization of higher quality welfare system. Others argue that the immigration control regimes of western states in this regard protect the internal market through priority measures for nationals and strict restrictions in the process of employment, so that the guarantee of rights to education and health for irregular immigrants is an independent regime. However, the current EPS allows the hiring of migrant workers only when domestic workers cannot be hired, so that the protection of the domestic labor market and protection of unregistered immigrants under the law actually conflict. Thus, expanding the legal protection of unregistered migrant workers is most urgent.

1.1.5.2 *Human Rights Violations in the Process of Law Enforcement of Unregistered Immigrants*

A survey revealed that most of the periodic law enforcement operations conducted jointly by the Ministry of Justice and the police force against unregistered immigrants were conducted without identification (37.4%), forcing entry without consent or permission (71.5%), by enforcement officers in civilian clothing (47.9%), at workplaces (43.0%) or place of residence (17.9%) en masse. 79.5% of the enforcement officers used handcuffs, while there were cases where police equipment, electric shock devices and net guns were used. Those arrested upon their visit to public offices numbered 4.9%. Among those arrested in public offices, 15.3% had visited the offices in order to report their injuries/harm/damages, while 14.5% were testifying or giving witness statements when their unregistered status were revealed. In particular, it was further revealed that some 100 migrant workers perished in the process of law enforcement after 2003, showing the urgent need for human rights friendly mechanisms.

Another big issue in the current Immigration Control Act of arrest—internment (confinement)—forced removal is that there is no control exercised by the courts over the process of physical confinement ("internment" under Immigration Control Act). Internment under the Immigration Control Act refers to the immigration control official administering activities taking into custody or impounding a person having a reasonable ground to be suspected of falling under persons subject to deportation at a foreigner internment room, foreigner internment camp or other places designated by the Minister of Justice. Although such internment measures are administrative measures equivalent to *de facto* confinement in nature restricting "personal liberty" under article 12 of the Constitution, the current laws do not include review by the court in the process prior to and after arrest and internment. Concerning the lack of court review with respect to "internment" measures taken after arrest, in particular, arguments have been raised that this violates article 12(6) of the Constitution. On the contrary, there are opposing arguments stating that the internment under the Immigration Control Act is an administrative act rather than one of criminal punishment and thus does not require a warrant.

However, the Habeas Corpus Act (enacted on Dec. 21, 2007, law no. 8724) was enacted recently in order to regulate physical confinement according to administrative measures, thereby clarifying that judicial relief procedures were still applicable to such confinement. However, the current Habeas Corpus Act excludes persons "in custody pursuant to the Immigration Control Act" from its scope of application. However, because the Constitution provides that anyone can petition review on the legality of custody to the court and because this is closely related to personal freedom, it is not a basic right under the Constitution guaranteed only to the citizens but a fundamental right guaranteed for all people. Thus, migrant workers subject to forced removal also fall within the scope of article 12(6) of the Constitution, and the provisions of the current 'Immigration Control Act' and Habeas Corpus Act are highly likely to be unconstitutional.

1.1.5.3 *Human Rights Violation of Foreigner Custody Facilities*

Internment facilities for foreigners are not, in principle, correctional facilities. Rather, it is a waiting area for custodial purposes and execution of forced removal in the context of administrative procedures. Thus, restricting freedom of persons within these facilities must remain at the bare minimum necessary for the execution of removal procedures. However, an observation of the current operation of the facilities show that living within the custody facilities is limited to the "main hall" (prison), and free movement within the facilities is impossible, so that it is very similar to general detention facilities in operation. Such operation also signifies that the custody facilities can be abused as one forcing quick removal by its punitive nature. This directly contravenes the U.N. recommendations stating that foreigners who are in custody and are not criminals should not be treated as such, and custody pursuant to reasons such as illegal stay should in no instance bear a punitive character.

Cases of human rights violations have also been discovered in the basic operation of internment facilities. According to the results of a status survey conducted following a fire incident at the foreigner custody facility in Yeosu in 2007, grave violations of human rights were being committed such as accommodation of persons exceeding the proper number; issues of custody period, form and environment; issues of physical examination and storage of possessions during the process of custody; meeting with legal counsel and restriction of visitations; restriction of correspondence and telecommunication; poor facilities, hygiene, meals and health; use of equipment and weapons; lack of safety measures, and human rights violations committed by immigration and public officers.

It has been consistently pointed out that such elongated custodial measures toward unregistered immigrants and operation of custody facilities do not satisfy the standards set in the U.N. Standard Minimum Rules for the Treatment of Prisoners (1955). Thus, policies should be reexamined in order to establish the internal zones of the facilities for minimal control as suitable for the purpose and nature of such facilities, while minimizing the restrictions placed on liberty within.

1.1.6 Issue of the Immigration Status of Marriage Immigrant Women

1.1.6.1 *Current Status of Marriage Immigrant Women*

As of March 2012, marriage immigrants numbered 145,604, having increased 1.8% from the year before; and by nationality, Chinese numbered 63,720 (43.8%), Vietnamese 38,101 (26.2%), Japanese 11,276 (7,7%), and Filipino 8,724 (6.0%). With such an increase of marriage immigrant women settling in as a new social phenomenon, new social issues with respect to their human rights also began to surface in relation to domestic violence, matchmaking system which comes close to human trafficking, and unstable immigration status.

1.1.6.2 *Uniqueness of Korea Regarding Marriage Immigrant Women*

Marriage immigrants to Korea are closely related to the issues of a decreasing Korean population in relation to low birth rates, the aging of society and the migration of farming and fishing villages. The fact that policies related to marriage immigration from nations of low economic status was promoted by the government in order to resolve such issues is what sets Korea apart from marriage immigration in nations such as the U.S. and Europe where individuals have opted to do so. In other words, marriage immigrants to Korea are the result of policies adopted to overcome the failure of population control such as the inability of males in economic peripheries like farming and fishing villages to get married and the resulting migration from the regional areas and the continued low birth rate that is one of the lowest in the world and the resulting crisis of labor reproduction. For these reasons, the number of women entering Korea, together with Japan, constitutes a high percentage compared to other Asian nations. In this context, these women have very much become a tool for the Korean government. From the early stages of the policy, these women were consistently expected to fulfill their "duties" of normalizing the farming population and economy through childbirth, but their human rights were not considered important. This also explains why the multicultural policies of the Korean government are focused on their children and family support rather than their human rights.

This "tool" of marriage migration, encouraged and pursued by the national government as part of its population control policy, not only evades the original framework of love or contract between two individuals but also eliminates arrival procedures that should be based on "justice." Numerous small matchmakers can conduct their businesses merely by reporting to the tax office when they receive up to 10 million won from the prospective husband or local governments for each successful case. Thus, their only objective is to succeed in the matchmaking. In order to achieve this goal, the process will involve false, exaggerated or too little information regarding the involved persons, explicit commercialization of the women's body and sexuality, coercive atmosphere, etc. In addition, gender inequality arising from the patriarchal traditions of the Confucian culture in East Asia and the economic superiority that Korea has over its surrounding Asian states caused the farming communities to impose upon these women from "poor" Asian nations the role of a "submissive" woman and daughter-in-law which had already been long criticized and undone in Korean society. Within this context, the violence of Korean husbands and cruel treatment of the in-laws towards them were frequent, but the Korean government did not intervene. Many studies have emphasized the human rights of immigrant women and the Korean government also raised issues concerning the assimilation forced upon these women; but as we can observe in the terminology of "marriage" immigrant women rather than just "immigrant" women used by Korean society, they are expected to play the role of traditional wife, daughter-in-law and mother acceptable to the patriarchal marriage system of Korean society. Furthermore, the legal provision allowing them to acquire citizenship only when they give birth within two years of their marriage clearly shows the extremely patriarchal nature of Korea's Nationality Act.

The 1948 Nationality Act, enacted based on the paternal *jus sanguinis* at the point of legislation, was the foundation for Korea's patriarchal Nationality Act. Although amended in 1997 to *jus sanguinis* following either parent, amendment of the law alone did not aggressively transform the gender-biased practical affairs concerning nationality. The image of female immigrants as the "bride of the farming village bachelor" is still deeply rooted in the paternal *jus sanguinis*. Most representative efforts of the government for resolution of the 2-year residence requirement of the Nationality Act for Simple Naturalization was to allow confirmation of fault by authorized women-related organizations in 2006. However, the issue of dependency of marriage immigrant women to their Korean husbands due to their residence requirement is continuously being raised. The exclusive immigration policies of the Korean government such as the current Support for Multicultural Families Act limiting its scope of application to "foreigners or naturalized persons having married and formed families with Korean nationals of lawful resident status" so that permanent residence is only permitted to marriage immigrants ultimately exclude a majority of foreign immigrants.

These issues can also be observed in the recommendations of international human rights organizations. The Committee on Economic, Social and Cultural Rights (CESCR), in its final comments upon evaluation of the third government report in 2009, expressed concern for the dependency of foreign spouses married to Korean citizens with regard to their resident status, and recommended additional support on the part of the Korean government to help these women married to Korean husbands to be able to acquire residence permits without depending upon their husbands or grant them the right to naturalize and thus overcome the discrimination they face. If they must depend upon their husbands for a basic right such as resident permits, the marriage immigrants cannot negotiate, compromise or resolve disputes at an equal level as that of their husbands. Thus, this provision reflects the male-centered marriage philosophy of Korea, which becomes the reason why marriage immigrant women "endure" the violence or unfair treatment they experience within marriage.

1.1.6.3 *Direction for Discussion*

The issue of human rights violation of marriage migrant women from whom childbirth was expected as part of Korea's population policy was perhaps foreseeable from the beginning. Their marriage process can be divided into premarital matchmaking and post-marital resident status acquisition. First, an issue in the process of marriage matchmaking is that commercial international matchmaking bears the characteristics of human trafficking, which has been confirmed numerous times through fact-finding reports. These international marriage systems were pointed out as being equivalent to human trafficking in the Protocol to prevent suppress and punish trafficking in persons, especially women and children, supplementing the United Nations Convention against transnational organized crimes adopted by the U.N. General Assembly in 2000.

In order to resolve this issue, the Korean government enacted in 2007 the Act concerning the Regulation of Marriage Matchmaking Business (Law no. 8688, Dec. 14, 2007) effective from May 2008; but its effectiveness has been questioned as it follows the market principle of freedom of contract rather than protecting the human rights of the parties entering into marriage.

In the recent fourth amendment of the National Assembly (amended Dec. 15, 2011), some of the existing issues in the matchmaking process were addressed such as prohibiting mass meetings and mass boarding, increasing the amount of information being provided to marriage immigrant women, a newly included a requirement of capital for matchmaking businesses in order to regulate the entry of small businesses, and reinforcing relevant punishments. However, in such an international matchmaking process, unlike typical domestic matchmaking, there is an extreme unbalance of power between the parties involved as the husband or his family pays an enormous amount of commission beyond his economic ability to the broker in order to "purchase" his bride. The brokers abuse this power imbalance to maintain the practice of forcing women into participating in "beauty contest-like" selection process or demanding sexual intercourse with men they have only met for a couple of days or hours. From this perspective, broker intervention under the market principle of freedom of contract, which is based upon equal rights of both parties, cannot be the solution for the fundamental problems of international marriage. Not only the control of the Korean central and local governments is necessary but also a system which notifies the brokers of the strict regulations applicable and continuous evaluation and management of them based on these standards. Also, not only the realization of marriage but also post-marital process should help these women adapt to Korean society while there also should be educational planning to help them meet the spouse and his family as equals within the family. It should not only be the women adjusting to Korean society but also her new Korean family surrounding her; and furthermore, Korean society should help prepare for changes that will result from their existence. To this end, government management of the brokers intervening with the arrival of the marriage immigrant women, as well as educational opportunities to help these women and their Korean families to mutually respect culture and practices are what the central and local governments need to implement. If policies concerning marriage immigrant women were created as part of Korea's population policy, the government naturally must provide educational opportunities to the newly incorporated members of the population and their families.

1.1.7 Significance of the Refugee Act and Its Limitations

1.1.7.1 *Current Status*

Refugee refers to any person who, "owing to well-founded fear of being persecuted for reasons of race, religion, nationality, membership of a particular social group or political opinion, is outside the country of his nationality and is unable or, owing to such fear, is unwilling to avail himself of the protection of that country; or who, not having a nationality and being outside the country of his former habitual residence as a result of such events, is unable or, owing to such fear, is unwilling to return to it." Korea became a party to the Convention and Protocol Relating to the Status of Refugees in December 1992. Following the signing of the convention, it added the provision on recognition of refugees in the Immigration Control Act in December 1993; and beginning in 1994, petitions for the recognition of refugee status were received.

Following the signing of the Refugee Convention, however, Korea did not recognize any refugees until 2000 when it became member of the executive board of the UNHCR. With the recognition of one Ethiopian in 2001, the total number of foreigners having applied for refugee status numbers 4,011 as of January 2012, of whom 268 have been granted refugee status and 146 the humanitarian residence permit, while 1,923 have been denied and 659 withdrawn. The remaining 1,015 are waiting the results of their evaluation. This has brought about criticism that the refugee recognition standards were too strict.

In order to resolve this issue, the Refugee Act was submitted by floor leader Hwang Woo-Yeo and passed by the National Assembly in December 30, 2011.

According to the purpose of the Refugee Act, it states that "After having signed the Convention and Protocol Relating to the Status of Refugees in December 1992, the Republic of Korea has been controlling the refugee recognition process by the Immigration Control Act. For the past 15 years, however, the petitioners have remained at about 2,000 persons, while those having been recognized as refugees numbered less than 100; so that compared to other developed countries, it has not received sufficient number of refugees and thus fulfilling its responsibilities within the international community." Further, while refugee applicants waiting the first level determination numbers 1,000, the process of which has been criticized internally and abroad for its lack of efficiency, transparency and fairness; and issues have also been raised because methods of sustaining livelihood for the applicants are blocked, while even those having been recognized as refugees have not been able to enjoy the rights guaranteed by the Refugee Convention. Thus, by enacting the Act concerning the status and treatment of refugees, Korea seeks to harmonize its domestic law with international law such as the Convention Relating to the Status of Refugees, while seeking to advance as a developed human rights nation by specifically providing for the recognition procedures and treatment of refugees.

In the Immigration Control Act, legislated from an immigration control perspective, rather than the Refugee Act from a refugee protection perspective, provisions concerning refugees are not a suitable legal regime for guaranteeing the human rights of refugees. Though the process of recognition and their treatment cannot be separated from the other, the problem with the Immigration Control Act is that it precisely does that in providing only for recognition procedures and not their treatment. The UNHCR recommended to the Korean government in August 2006 that the legislation of independent refugee protection law which would guarantee procedural rights in the refugee evaluation process limit the methods and duration of confinement, and determine not only the recognition procedures for refugee status but also the rights and duties of the refugees and asylum petitioners. The enacted Refugee Act is significant in that it reflected such discussions to establish the minimum standard of refugee protection towards meeting the international standards of a refugee regime and the guarantee of refugee rights.

1.1.7.2 *Specific Provisions of the Refugee Act*

The recently passed Refugee Act provisions include General Provisions, Refugee Status Application and Determination, the Refugee Committee, and Treatment of Recognized Refugees and Others. The significance of the regulation can be summarized as follows.

First of all, the Refugee Act defines refugees as "an alien who is unable or unwilling to avail him/herself of the protection of his/her country of nationality owing to well-founded fear of being persecuted for reasons of race, religion, nationality, membership of a particular social group or political opinion; or who, not having a nationality, is unable or, owing to such fear, unwilling to return to the country of his/her former residence (hereinafter 'the country of habitual residence')." This definition is clearer and more specific than the definition provided in the Immigration Control Act and also satisfies the objective of refugee recognition in international law. The Refugee Act also specifically provides for the prohibition of refoulement, a core principle of the Refugee Convention. In particular, the Act is significant in that it includes not only persons recognized as refugees but also humanitarian status holders and refugee status applicants in the scope of the application of the prohibition.

Due process was also reinforced in the refugee recognition procedure. The Refugee Act grants applicants the right to receive the assistance of an attorney, interpretation in filling out interview reports, and the presence of trusted individuals during the interview. The applicant may request access to or a copy of the interview record or relevant materials such as documentary evidence submitted by him/herself. This would be important court evidence if the applicant were to be denied refugee status, after which he/she appeal through an administrative appeal. The applicant can also prohibit the disclosure of personal information in order to protect privacy and safety.

Provisions for the treatment of recognized refugees, humanitarian status holders and refugee status applicants are also significant. An alien who is recognized as a refugee and stays in the country is provided social security at the same level as that of Korean nationals, and if his/her child is a minor as defined by the Civil Act, he/she can receive primary and secondary education as that provided to Korean nationals. Treatment of humanitarian status holders and refugee status applicants is also provided for. The Minister of Justice may permit a humanitarian status holder to engage in wage earning employment, and the Minister of Justice may provide living and other expenses to refugee status applicants until the Minister can permit the applicant to engage in wage-earning employment six months after the date on which the refugee application was received. The refugee status applicant can receive medical services support, as well as primary and secondary education at the same level as that of Korean nationals for family members who are minor aliens.

What the Ministry of Justice is most concerned with following the legislation of the Refugee Act is the practical difficulties in immigration control due to the abuse of the refugee system. If illegal aliens refuse to return to their own countries and apply for refugee status, the realistic issue will be how far that status can be recognized. With respect to this, the Refugee Act provides that the Minister of Justice may omit part of the determination procedure if "the refugee status applicant concealed facts in the application through means that include, but are not limited to, the submission of false documents or false statements," "the refugee status applicant re-applied for refugee status without material change in circumstances after a previous application was denied or previous refugee status recognition was cancelled," or "the refugee status applicant is an alien who has stayed in the Republic of Korea for one year or longer and who applied for refugee status when the expiration of the sojourn period was imminent, or is an alien subject to forcible removal who applied for refugee status for the purpose of delaying the enforcement of the removal order."

1.1.7.3 *Issues with the Simplified Procedures*

In spite of the positive significance of the passage of the Refugee Act, there is great potential for the original objectives to be abused pursuant to the simplified procedures. Because the simplified procedures do not specify what part of the process may be eliminated, if the core procedures such as "interview" or "fact-finding" were to be omitted, it would be difficult to judge whether the refugee application was one of an abuse of the system.

According to the current Refugee Act provisions, omission is permitted where the refugee status applicant concealed facts in the application through means that include, but are not limited to, the submission of false documents or false statements. In general, however, refugees having fled their countries due to persecution may not be able to clearly testify the facts during the first investigation. Thus, testimony before and after may contradict each other, or that objective facts may not be uniform. There may be cases where they inevitably change their statements in order to protect persons that have helped them. Under these circumstances, omitting part of the process upon determining that the applicant had concealed certain facts may be problematic.

Paragraph 199 of the Handbook on Procedures and Criteria for Determining Refugee Status under the 1951 Convention and the 1967 Protocol relating to the Status of Refugees states, "Untrue statements by themselves are not a reason for refusal of refugee status and it is the examiner's responsibility to evaluate such statements in the light of all the circumstances of the case." This shows that interview and fact-finding is minimal to such an evaluation. This should similarly be applied to cases where a statement differs from the facts that are given in reapplications without a significant change of circumstances. In order to find out whether there has been a significant change of circumstances, there needs to be fact-finding regarding the state of affairs in the nationality state after at least an interview with the applicant.

From the applicant's perspective in particular, applications for refugee status is often the last resort. Yet if they were to uniformly apply for refugee status after "over one year of stay" without consideration for their actual circumstances, they uniformly become subject to the simplified procedures which conflicts with the objective of the law. Further, the problem is serious where, though the scope of those subject to forced removal is comprehensive and ambiguous, if subject to these provisions, they are deemed to have abused the refugee law and thus subject to simplified procedures.

2 Border between North Korea and China

2.1 *Implications of the Border Regime between North Korea and China*

There is currently no information regarding the maritime boundary delimitation between North Korea and China. The single delimitation known to the world is based on the Sino-Korean Border Treaty and it subsequent protocol, which delimited the territorial seas in the West Sea (Yellow Sea). They were signed in 1962 and 1964 respectively.

Given the potential for the discovery and exploitation of oil deposits in the West Chosun Bay (Seo Han Man), it is timely to consider the possibility of a dualistic regime emerging from this situation. One regime can emerge from maritime boundary delimitation on the continental shelf and another from the cooperative system for joint development of resources that may emerge between the states. In the case of the latter, any possible agreement reached between North Korea and China for joint development of the area would have much larger and long term implications in a unified Korea's relationship with China.

It is just as possible to treat the succession of maritime boundary delimitations in the same way as we treat territorial borders and otherwise. Should we treat them differently, a cooperative system for joint development of maritime resources may launch a whole new set of legal issues with respect to succession—whether it can be treated like border regimes or other territorial regimes. Of course, in the current situation, where no publicly concluded maritime delimitations exist, predicting the existence of such a cooperative system is only speculative. However, if we consider the fact that China has already established a joint development zone with Vietnam when delimiting maritime boundaries in the waters around the Gulf of Tonkin and also established such zones with Japan, it is highly probable that China would do the same with

North Korea. As such, a consideration of the issue would be timely and necessary since the likelihood of such a pact now resides in the realm of probability rather than mere possibility.

The West Sea is not only important to North Korea and China for its major rich fishing grounds. The potentiality of oil and natural gas discovery makes it even more important. Thus, even in the absence of a boundary delimitation agreement the two states can forge an agreement for joint development if oil deposits were found along the hypothetical boundary. Such an agreement would be far more practical than the development zone between Korea and Japan and merits serious consideration and analysis.

This section discusses the issue of succession of joint development zones established around maritime boundaries, or temporary zones installed prior to the confirmation of maritime boundaries by treaty. It seeks to predict and discuss the border regimes settled in relation to borders rather than maritime boundaries since no treaty between North Korea and China has been publicized. Through an analysis of the cooperative systems around borders, we consider the hypothetical cooperative system for the joint development zone in the seas between North Korea and China and the issue of their succession.

2.1.1 Characteristics of the Border Regime between North Korea and China

Article 11 of the 1978 Vienna Convention on the Succession of States in respect of Treaties (hereinafter "1978 Vienna Convention") provides for an automatic succession for border regimes, while Article 12 regulates automatic succession of other territorial regimes. The 1974 Draft Articles on Succession of States in Respect of Treaties with commentaries defines "other territorial regimes" as including military bases, water rights and navigation on rivers, and neutralization or demilitarization of particular territories. The agreements between North Korea and China discussed below may fall under Article 11—Border Regimes; or Article 12—Other Territorial Regimes.

2.1.1.1 *Boundary Delimitation Agreement of the Waters between and among China, North Korea and Russia from the Tumen River*

This agreement was concluded on 3 November 1998 in Pyeongyang and entered into force on 19 June 1999. Comprising 6 articles, the Agreement states in its Preamble:

> Based on the existing border treaties, the three States agree to the following for the purpose of delimiting the Joint Boundary Waters between the People's Republic of China and the Democratic People's Republic

> of Korea, and the Boundary Waters between the Democratic People's Republic of Korea and the Russian Federation (hereinafter the 'Tri-junction of the Boundary Waters').

Article 1(1) further provides:

> The Tri-junction of the Boundary Waters from the Tumen River begins at the Sino-Russian Border Signpost No. 423 and runs in a straight line between the banks, perpendicular to the Tumen mainstream. This line is where the North Korean/Chinese Joint Border Zone ends in the Tumen River.

This puts the reader on notice of the existing borders between North Korea and China. Unlike the known Sino-Korean Border Treaty, however, this provision makes it possible to assume that in the case of the Tumen River, the river itself constitutes the joint border rather than a boundary line. In other words, when Article 1(1) is read in conjunction with the Preamble, there exists between North Korea and China a joint *border zone* rather than a *boundary* in the waters. One can also see from Article 1(1) that the Tumen River boundary between North Korea and Russia is the centre-point of the Tumen mainstream.

One question that arises from the foregoing is the possibility of utilizing the Amnok (Yalu) River itself as a border between North Korea and China. In other words, whether a bilateral treaty can realistically specify the Amnok River as Joint Boundary Waters. If this were true, one can presume the treaty will take the form of a bilateral agreement determining the entire river as the border and joint waters, while maintaining a border regime of joint usage. If this were possible, then the border delimitation in the Sino-Korean Border Treaty and its subsequent Protocol would consist, not of a line above the Amnok and Tumen Rivers. Instead, the rivers themselves would form the boundaries and jurisdiction of the riverbeds would be dealt with separately.

Furthermore, it is also possible that the stone marker above the Amnok River that appears to indicate a boundary between North Korea and China actually determines the jurisdiction of the territory below it. Article 2 of the Agreement states, "Unless the Party States otherwise agree, no matter what natural alterations may occur on the Tumen River, the Tri-junction of the Boundary Waters will not change." This means that even with natural (geographical) changes, the boundaries between the three states cannot change without the consent of all other parties. Considered as a whole, it is more appropriate to take the Amnok and Tumen Rivers in their entirety as forming the borders between

North Korea and China rather than as a boundary line. In addition, Article 2 allows us to infer that a provision requiring consent of both North Korea and China is likely to be found if the borders were to be altered.

2.1.1.2 *Agreement for the Cooperation of North Korea and China on the Floodgate Project of Amnok and Tumen Rivers*

The Agreement for the Cooperation of North Korea and China on the Floodgate Project of Amnok and Tumen Rivers was concluded in Pyeongyang on 24 May 1990 and became effective the same day. Comprising of 14 provisions, this treaty abolished an earlier agreement that bears the same name concluded in Beijing on 30 June 1978.

Unlike the 1978 agreement which comprised of 12 provisions, the 1990 agreement was based on the Agreement for the Cooperation on the Floodgate Project between the People's Republic of China Irrigation Department and the Democratic People's Republic of Korea Meteorological Observatory concluded on 31 December 1957. This means that the 1978 and 1990 agreements did not take the form of an inter-state treaty, but were instead agreements between state institutions. The germane question here is this: Are these agreements amenable to succession?

The 1990 Agreement deals mainly with cooperation regarding the hydrologic observatory installed in the Amnok and Tumen River mainstream and basins by North Korea and China. Among other things, it deals with issues such as the mutual exchange of hydrologic data, information and forecast; and the joint study of abnormal hydrologic phenomena. Even if the Treaty were to be determined as not having being automatically succeeded, mutual exchange of information in relation to non-navigational use of international rivers is an obligation that has obtained customary international law status and therefore binds the unified Korea regardless of its successive character.

2.1.1.3 *Agreement for the Cooperation of Joint Use and Management of the International Rivers between North Korea and China*

This Agreement for the Cooperation of Joint Use and Management of the International Rivers between North Korea and China was concluded and became effective on 5 May 1964 in Pyeongyang, and comprises 8 articles. Under the 1978 Vienna Convention, this particular agreement may either be categorized under Article 11 or Article 12. This is because it concerns the use of international rivers, the focus of which would make it an object of regulation under Article 12. However, since both the Amnok and Tumen Rivers in their entirety are the boundaries between North Korea and China, they can also be categorized as typical Article 11 border regimes. Some argue that where boundaries exist in international rivers, the phrase "other territorial regimes" under Article 12 is meant to deal with the authority to use the waters. This Agreement should therefore should be categorized under Article 11 (Border Regimes). Again, considering that the two rivers form the boundaries, their joint use would appear to ultimately form a border regime.

Regardless of their categorization, the International Court of Justice held in the *Gabcikovo-Nagymaros Project Case* (1997) that Article 12 also reflects customary international law. Therefore, even if a unified Korea was not a party to the 1978 Vienna Convention, the "other territorial regimes," like "border regimes," would be subject to automatic succession and such categorization would have no practical legal benefit. Ultimately, it does not matter whether this Agreement falls under Article 11 or Article 12 under the 1978 Vienna Convention since it is automatically succeeded. Should North Korea be absorbed by Korea in the course of unification, then the Korean government would shoulder the duties under the Agreement. Thus, an analysis of the content of cooperation is crucial.

Pursuant to the agreement, North Korea and China each appointed a five-member delegation (including one leader each) to form a 10-person Joint Commission for the Use of International Rivers, as well as individual and multiple expert bodies. The Joint Commission discusses and resolves issues such as: 1) issues unresolved by individual expert bodies; 2) issues related to the projects of individual and multiple expert bodies; and 3) other issues that do not fall under the scope of the individual expert bodies. For communication and quick resolution of issues, China stationed its contact personnel in Dandong and North Korea in Sinuiju.

The Joint Commission is one of the representative institutions that ought to be retained after unification. The contents of the agreement are generally about the establishment and operation of this Joint Commission; and in preparation for unification, the gathering of information and analysis of their activities and projects are urgently needed because their activities will directly be succeeded by the unified Korea. Only the specifics of their activities and projects may be renegotiated with China as long as the framework remains undisturbed.

2.1.1.4 *Agreement for the Cooperation of Navigation in the International Rivers between North Korea and China*

Signed and effective as of 23 May 1960, the Agreement for the Cooperation of Navigation in the International Rivers between North Korea and China contains 11 provisions, and two annexes: (a) Regulations for the Construction and Management of Canals and Signs along the International Rivers of Amnok and Tumen between North Korea and China; and (b) Rules for the Navigation of Ships in the International Rivers between North Korea and China.' While this Agreement is also susceptible to the problem of categorization under Articles 11 and 12 of the 1978 Vienna Convention, the categorization itself holds no significance or real benefits since their legal effects are the same.

Pursuant to the Agreement, ships under North Korean or Chinese jurisdiction can dock at designated ports and points whenever necessary, and the crew aboard these ships are free to disembark and pass through the port cities. Maintenance and repair of the international canals of Amnok and Tumen River, installation and management of the signs, amendment of navigational rules and other related administrative duties are under charge of the Cooperation Committee for the Navigation of Amnok and Tumen Rivers between North Korea and China which consists of 3 representatives nominated by the respective governments.

Article 4 of the annexed Rules of Navigation of Ships provides for accidents and rescue. In accidents where ships of different states collide, joint investigation is required. The implementation of the Joint Commission for the Use of International Rivers and the Cooperation Committee for the Navigation of Amnok and Tumen Rivers is significant in that the Commission's activities and cooperation constitute important "border regimes" or "other territorial regimes" that would be automatically succeeded after unification. The specific information regarding the practices of both groups is very important for the stability and effective management of the post-unification border regime. The practices of European joint commissions regarding international rivers are easily accessible and their study may prove instructive. However, information regarding European joint commissions only serve as reference points when considering the particular relationship between North Korea and China.

2.1.1.5 *Protocol for the Joint Protection/Proliferation and Use of Fishery Resources in Lake Supung between North Korea and China*

The Protocol for the Joint Protection/Proliferation and Use of Fishery Resources in Lake Supung between North Korea and China was concluded on 19 December 1972 to regulate the joint use of fishery resources Lake Supung, an artificial lake created by blocking the downstream area of Amnok River. It is comprised of 8 articles.

As may be observed from its title, this Protocol not only focuses usage but also protection and proliferation, i.e., maintenance, management and preservation. For example, it regulates the installation of artificial spawning grounds for carp and crucian, sets fishing zones and protective zones prohibiting fishing, as well as regulates pollution for the protection of fishery resources. It is interesting to note that while bilateral treaties regarding joint use of fishery resources are generally put into effect by establishing joint commissions, this Protocol does not stipulate this. Instead the Protocol regulates the use of the fishery resources and the number of fishing boats that may engage in fishing activities in order to ensure systematic proliferation. Because this Protocol deals with joint use of fishery resources, it has great implications for the issue of succession of joint development treaties regarding marine resources.

2.1.1.6 *Protocol Regarding Fish Farming in Lake Supung*

This protocol was concluded on June 28, 1959, effective immediately. Comprised of 12 articles, this protocol was concluded not between representatives of the central government as the above "Protocol for the Joint Protection/Proliferation and Use of Fishery Resources in Lake Supung" but rather between the Chinese representatives of Liaoning People's Committee and the North Korean representatives of Pyeonganbukdo People's Committee. In other words, it was concluded between regional representatives.

This protocol likewise gives attention to maintenance, management and preservation rather than limiting its focus solely to the development of fishery resources. Because it is related to fish farming, it does not regulate natural species except for its measures to decrease the number of mandarin fish that has been deemed harmful to the proliferation of economically viable species. Due to the emphasis of the effective development of fish farming, research institutions have been established, with requirements for mutual exchange of materials. North Korea and China have also sought protection and proliferation of fishery resources in Lake Supung through institutional mechanisms, namely the legislation for rational fishing jointly enacted in late 1960. Their efforts to achieve legislative harmony seem to have a rather contemporary approach. Further, the recognition of the importance of a basic biological study of Lake Supung and the subsequent requirements of Article 10—publication in 1959 of joint Sino-Korean research done in 1958 suggested to the international maritime institution of the Western Pacific Fisheries Commission Secretariat—can also be judged as being advanced.

In conclusion, both protocols of 1959 and 1972 are effective regimes that could be applied to the joint use and management of the fishery resources in the West Sea where North Korean and Chinese boundaries meet. These likewise can fall under Articles 11 and 12 of the 1978 Vienna Convention and bind the unified Korea to their duties.

2.1.1.7 *Agreement Regarding the Supung Hydroelectric Power Plant on the Amnok River between North Korea and China*

Concluded in Beijing on 17 April 1955 and becoming effective on 1 July that same year, the Agreement Regarding the Supung Hydroelectric Power Plant on the Amnok River between North Korea and China comprises 11 articles. Although hydroelectricity is a type of energy and can therefore be differentiated from resources, hydroelectricity can still fall under "border regimes" or "other territorial regimes" on the basis that it utilizes river water.

Article 1 of this Agreement provides that all the property of the Supung Hydroelectric Power Plant belongs jointly to North Korea and China. While the significance of joint possession in a socialist state is unclear, it certainly does not disturb the fact that the entire Amnok River forms the border between North Korea and China. The two governments established the Public Supung Waterworks for the joint operation of the power plant; and joint possession is implemented through joint management and operation of the plant entirely through the funds of the Public Supung Waterworks. The fact that the entire Amnok River forms the border itself is alluded to by Article 2 of the Agreement which states:

> All the buildings and facilities of Amnok River and Supung Hydroelectric Power Plant situated in the territories of both states do not interfere with their territorial sovereignty nor alter the borders of either state.

At the same time, North Korea and China concluded the Protocol Regarding the Supung Hydroelectric Power Company on the Amnok River on 7 May 1955. Several annexes were attached to this Agrement: (a) Articles of Incorporation for the Supung Hydroelectric Power Company on the Amnok River; (b) Agreement Regarding Inspection/Evaluation of the Property of Supung Hydroelectric Power Company on the Amnok River and Other Financial Issues; and (c) Agreement regarding Several Issues in Restoration of Supung Hydroelectric Power Company.

2.1.2 Implications of the Sino-Korean Treaties Regarding Border Regimes or Other Territorial Regimes

All the agreements and protocols discussed in this chapter are closely related to the border also established through the Amnok and Tumen Rivers and are representative of border and other territorial regimes. Of these, those having greater significance in relation to maritime delimitation are: (a) 1955 Agreement Regarding the Supung Hydroelectric Power Plant on the Amnok River Dealing with Joint Use of Energy and Natural Resources (e.g. fishery resources and hydroelectricity); (b) 1955 Protocol Regarding the Supung Hydroelectric Power Company on the Amnok River; (c) 1959 Protocol Regarding Fish Farming in Lake Supung; and (d) 1972 Protocol for the Joint Protection/Proliferation and Use of Fishery Resources in Lake Supung. According to the 1978 Vienna Convention, all these agreements and protocols have the potential of being automatically succeeded to by a unified Korea, while two of the protocols may also be subject to renegotiation of specific provisions. Even if a unified Korea is not bound by the 1978 Vienna Convention, Articles 11 and 12, being reflective of customary law, would still be binding.

Because these treaties and protocols can apply to marine natural resources including fishery resources, oil and energy, the existence of treaties regulating the cooperative systems between North Korea and China—or its future conclusion—is highly probable. However, whether such treaties fall under the scope of Articles 11 and 12 of 1978 Vienna Convention is subject to debate and is therefore difficult to presume an automatic succession.

It is even more difficult to find state practice regarding this. Even scholars asserting the automatic succession of treaties of a dispositive nature do not claim that every single provision of such treaties must be succeeded. In other words, each of the provisions is severable; and only dispositive or material provisions are to be succeeded. It would thus be wrong to assume that all four agreements and protocols discussed above would be succeeded simply because they regard border regimes or other territorial regimes. Therefore, from an administrative/practical point of view, an analysis of the provisions among the agreements and protocols mentioned above would be necessary. Further, with regard to agreements regulating the cooperative system for the joint development of marine resources, there remains the fundamental question of whether they even fall within the scope of Articles 11 or 12 of the 1978 Vienna Convention. Without a clear resolution of this issue, it would be impossible to discuss the possibility of succession.

3 Gando

3.1 *Analysis of Korea's Claim of Sovereignty over Gando (Jiandao) Area in China under International Law*

Today, there are scholars and civic groups in Korea that misconstrue the object of Korea's claim of sovereignty over Gando/Jiandao (hereinafter "Gando") due to distorted historical foundations. The recent considerations of the Northeast Project aggressively promoted by China gave rise to the fixation of the Gando issue as one of sovereignty, thus leading to concentrated efforts of developing relevant theories. In the midst of the aftershocks of the Northeast Project which had amplified the awareness of a crisis over the history of the northern territories of Korea, actions taken by China regarding Mount Baekdu have had nationwide repercussions. The desire for the restoration of ancient territory, together with the current fast changing state of affairs in Northeast Asia, has resulted in a re-examination of Korea's genuine, good-neighbourly approach towards China's actions in the northern territories.

Included in the Mount Baekdu Project are comprehensive plans including: Application for the designation of UNESCO World National Heritage and Global Geopark, Launching of Changbai Mountain Protection and Development Zone of Jilin Province, Establishment of the Changbaishan China International Tourism Festival, Commercial Industry, e.g., mineral water and ginseng, Completion of Changbaishan Airport, Construction of related roads and railroads, and implementation of various academic conferences and culture projects. There are differing views regarding the true intentions of these projects with one considering it as being part of the Northeast Project series and another as China's efforts to secure tourist industry resources for economic and cultural reasons.

Just as Dokdo symbolizes great historical significance in the relations between Korea and Japan, the Gando territory including Mount Baekdu is special to the Korean people. Just as solidifying sovereignty over Dokdo is emerging as one of the foundations for Korean-Japan relations, especially for having overcome colonial rule and having persevered through the pains of division, Gando is an indivisible part of the future of unified Korea. Adjacent to China and the northern territory, North Korea concluded the Sino-Korean Border Treaty (朝中邊界條約) in 1962, thereby delimiting their mutual boundary across the Cheonji, or the crater lake atop Mount Baekdu. There are differing academic theories regarding the legal status of North Korea as the principal agent of the agreement, as well as the validity of the agreement itself. However, apart from the legal debate, when assessing the opportunity cost for a unified Korea, there ought to be a sincere concern for the assertions to be made regarding the territories lying north of the border between North Korea and China.

The problem is that Korea's claim of sovereignty over the current Gando area has many legal challenges to overcome; furthermore, in relation to China's projects or their methods of strengthening sovereignty over the northern territory, the likelihood of Korea's success in its search for strategic solutions while excluding North Korea is remote.

Not only is Gando yet to be recognized as a disputed area by the international community, there is no official position taken by Korea regarding the issue. Thus, the current claims of sovereignty currently unfolding in the Korean academy, when approached in light of "the General Principles of International Law regarding Territorial Acquisition and Loss" (General Principles regarding Territorial Acquisition), is an issue that has yet to overcome numerous obstacles.

If the claim of sovereignty by the Korean academy ultimately signifies a territorial dispute between Korea and China, the approach toward Gando must take on a different orbit. In other words, it must be clarified that the Gando issue is, at its core, a "territorial dispute" and that such disputes entail a comprehensive understanding of history, politics and geography. However, considering that the actual existence of sovereignty is ultimately determined by the "awareness of international law" and perceptions thereof, the current approach of the Korean academy must be more systemized. What must be kept in mind is that in proving sovereignty over disputed territory, the evaluation of the legal significance or probative value of an international judicial or arbitral body is made according to the general principles of territorial acquisition, and thus, requires an approach from the perspective of such institutions.

Following the *Island of Palmas case* before the Permanent Court of Arbitration in 1928, decisions by the International Court of Justice and other international judicial organs regarding territorial disputes have given birth to the general principles of territorial acquisition, under which a state must satisfy the following factors in order to prove its exercise of sovereignty. First, its exercise of authority over a particular disputed territory must have been effective, continuous, peaceful and displayed over a certain length of time; second, territorial sovereignty takes on different forms depending upon the specific features of the territory in dispute; third, territorial sovereignty is established pursuant to the process of determining the marginally relative merits by evaluating the evidence provided by the states in dispute regarding the functional exercise of authority of the state and/or government; and fourth, the probative value must be related to the state actions that are directly relevant to the occupation of the territory in dispute.

However, recently international judicial organs have shown a set of legal principles different from that of the traditional one. One that is representative in this matter would be that in resolving sovereignty issues, the decisions of the colonial powers exercising authority over the disputed territories during the colonial era, as well as the interpretation and application of the treaties reflecting those decisions, were recognized to have an absolute evidentiary capacity. This approach continually denies the probative value of numerous, yet debatable, historical evidence.

When analyzing the issue of sovereignty over Gando pursuant to the principles generated from these recent functionalist decisions, at a glance, it appears that classifying the Gando issue as a territorial dispute leads to the conclusion that Korea is at a disadvantage in raising the issue and solidifying its claim. This is because international jurisprudence runs counter to the position taken by Korean scholars, namely, that the Gando Agreement is invalid in light of the Korea-Japan Protectorate Treaty. The grounds for invalidity are: 1) coercion invalidating the Treaty and subsequently the Agreement, and 2) exceeding the scope of protection; however, these do not coincide with the decisions mentioned above. Further, the position regarding the invalidity of the Sino-Korean Border Treaty of 1962, namely the lack of international legal rules requiring the succession of the Border Treaty upon unification, does not coincide with recent case law nor the understanding of international law.

In the end, in order for Korea to effectively and successfully claim sovereignty over Gando, it must overcome the international jurisprudence that only relies on evidence that has absolute probative value such as the decisions of colonial states, and analyze the substantive understanding of contemporary international law. It is only through these explorations that Korea's claim of sovereignty can maintain legitimacy under the international legal approach towards territorial disputes. This study provides a comprehensive, hypothetical opinion of how Korea should overcome the contemporary international jurisprudence in claiming sovereignty over Gando. By re-examining the traditional approach from the perspective of contemporary international law, this section aims to provide a direction for future studies towards a more effective claim.

The common issues related to the claim of sovereignty as put forth by Korean scholars are as follows: first, the nature of the Border Conferences of 1885 and 1888 and the legal force of the Baekdusan National Boundary Monument, including the interpretation of Tomun River as written on the Monument (西爲鴨綠 東爲土門: "Boundaries of Aprok on the west and Tomun on the east"); second, the confirmation of the Korean-Chinese borders pursuant to the 1909 Gando Agreement between China and Japan; and third, the legal force of the 1962 Sino-Korean Border Treaty and the issue of succession after unification. Because these three issues, in relation to the sovereignty claim over Gando, have long been introduced through numerous studies in Korea, this section will only briefly explain them below.

3.1.1 Legal Force of the Baekdusan National Boundary Monument

Korean scholars are divided on the issue of validity of the Baekdusan National Boundary Monument [hereinafter "Monument"], which was set up by Mok Geuk Deung pursuant to the orders of Kang Xi in the 38th year of King Sukjong (1712). The scholars that argue in favor of the valid legal status of the Monument as a border treaty emphasize that the mere stipulation of two states, the first of its kind, is significant in spite of its many problems, i.e., procedural defect in the construction of the Monument, the failure to mention specific demarcation of the Baekdusan area, and the lack of formal consent on the part of Chosun regarding the accurate name of the river or water sources forming the national boundaries.

The argument that denies the legal force of the Monument can be seen as being an extension of the claim of sovereignty over Shimyo (瀋遼) and Seogando (西間島) in the areas north of the Aprok River. Their grounds for denial are as follows: first, historically speaking, not only has Chosun peacefully exercised authority over the area north of the Aprok River and east of the Tomun River, but it has also continued control over the same after the establishment of the Monument; second, there are historical maps indicating the Gando area, as well as maps drawn under the orders of Gang Hee Jae; and third, although precise boundaries cannot be determined, proper boundaries must have been decided by the installation of the unoccupied zone (閑曠地) pursuant to the Kangdo Meeting (江都會盟) of 1627 between Chosun and the Qing Dynasty.

3.1.2 Legal Force of the 1909 China-Japan Gando Agreement

The traditional understanding of the 1909 China-Japan Gando Agreement in the Korean academy, as being invalid, runs parallel to the assertions of the Minister of Foreign Affairs and Trade. In evaluating the issue of validity together with sovereignty over Gando, the Korean academy has determined that the agreement should be considered null and void along with the conclusion of the Korea-Japan Protectorate Treaty of November 1905. They also argue any sense of validity should be examined within the context of "the effect of a treaty on third states."

In other words, the Korean scholars that assert Gando sovereignty also argue that "while it is impossible, in principle, for a third state not directly in dispute to intervene in the resolution with the same rights as that of a disputing party, Japan's intervention in the issue of jurisdiction over Gando between Chosun and China has been on the grounds of the Korea-Japan Protectorate Treaty." Therefore, if the Treaty is invalid, Japan's intervention would consequently be illegal, which leads to the invalidation of the Gando Agreement between China and Japan as being concluded by a third state without legitimate authority.

3.1.3 Validity of the 1962 Sino-Korean Border Treaty

Korean scholars asserting sovereignty over Gando also claim that the borders demarcated pursuant to the 1962 Sino-Korean Border Treaty, having been concluded in secret, is only valid between the parties involved. Further, assuming that the issue of succession following unification may differ depending upon the form of unification, these scholars also contend that it would be possible to deny the legal force of the Treaty should Korea absorb the North. The basis for this assertion is in designating North Korea as an anti-state group rather than a state under international law, thereby refuting any international legal significance to the Treaty.

However, should such unification occur, there have been opinions acknowledging the validity of the Treaty pursuant to settled international customary law giving rise to the duty of accommodation of border treaties. They emphasize that when a border treaty concluded by a divided state and subsequent boundaries are accommodated by a successor state by unification, it is international customary law that it is automatically succeeded.

3.1.4 Analysis of International Jurisprudential Challenges that Must be Overcome in order to Validate Korea's Claim over Gando

With regard to these sovereignty claims as put forth by the Korean academy, the author has already raised the following 9 issues in his previous work as challenges in contemporary international law that must be overcome in order to legitimize Korea's claim.

The issues were as follows: 1) threshold issues of international legal principles regarding territorial acquisition and Korea's claim of sovereignty over Gando; 2) overcoming the ICJ's recent trend of functionalist decisions and understanding colonialism; 3) analysis of China's state practice through its cases of territorial disputes; 4) the 1962 Sino-Korean Border Treaty and the application of *uti possidetis* after unification; 5) interpretation of the lack of Korea's public claim of sovereignty over Gando as the abandonment of title or acquiescence; 6) compatibility of Korea's claim related to the invalidity of the Gando Agreement and the current practices of international law; 7) possibility of claiming territory (Gando) without a precise indication of the geographical area or demarcation; 8) application of the principle of self-determination to the ethnic Koreans (*Joseon-jok*) currently residing in the Yanbian Korean Autonomous Prefecture (YBKAP) located in the Gando area; 9) the effect of Korea's claim over Gando on its current occupation of Dokdo.

Five issues have been selected for further analysis in this section by leaving out those issues that were repetitive or not directly relevant to the claim of sovereignty. They are: 1) the threshold issues; 2) the recent trend of ICJ decisions and colonialism; 3) China's territorial disputes; 4) the Sino-Korean Border Treaty; and 5) self-determination of YBKAP. The effect of Korea's claim over Gando on Dokdo will be briefly mentioned in the conclusion.

The points of dispute according to the understanding of the author regarding the five issues above can be summarized as follows:

3.1.4.1 *Threshold Issues for Korea's Claim over Gando*

As for the threshold issues that must be settled for Korea's claim over Gando, the following three points can be raised: first, whether it is possible to claim territory (Gando) without a precise indication of the geographical scope or demarcation; second, whether the lack of Korea's public claim of sovereignty over the Gando can be interpreted as the abandonment of title or acquiescence; and third, whether Korea's claim related to the invalidity of the Gando Agreement is compatible with current practices of international law.

3.1.4.2 *Whether the Claim of Sovereignty is Possible without Determining Its Precise Geographical Scope and Boundaries*

The precise geographical scope of Gando has long been an issue under debate in the Korean academy, and the general understanding of this issue has been introduced in various papers. They have also posed the impossibility of ascertaining the scope of Gando or Korea's claim of sovereignty. A number of cases have been hypothesized to determine the geographical scope of any potential claim. Should the Baekdusan National Boundary Monument not be recognized as a border demarcation treaty, it would be possible to claim sovereignty up to Seogando north of the Aprok River; but if the Monument is recognized as a treaty, the greatest extent that could be claimed would include the Monument—Totwe (土堆)—Seoktwe (石堆)—Tomun River (土門江)—Songhwa River (松花江)—and the Heukryong River (黑龍江), while the smallest claimed area (strictest interpretation of the Monument) would simply include the Monument—Totwe—Seoktwe—Tomun River. Besides these, there are a few more hypothetical cases.

Some have claimed that the territorial scope of Gando includes the areas of Seogando, Donggando, Bukgando, the Shimyo area, as well as Yeonhaeju and the Manchu area (北方故土), leading to concerns of territorial expansionism and irredentism. Unfortunately, even they have failed to settle the precise geographical scope of Gando. The problem is not that individual researchers cannot agree on a single understanding, but rather that they have failed to accurately understand the facts and have repeated their errors by studying secondary materials rather than the originals.

Regardless of whether determining the geographical scope of Gando is historically, theoretically and realistically impossible, it is an entirely different issue altogether from that of preparing for such a dispute without designation of the object for which Korea claims sovereignty. In other words, in claiming sovereignty over Gando, the very fact that the territory is not a specifically determined area is a basic issue that needs to be resolved even if the hypothetical cases above were to be considered. In territorial disputes generally where the states differ on the territory at issue, it would be hypothetically possible for the judicial body to settle the issue within the legal proceedings; but even in such cases, it would be unreasonable to produce several hypothetical scenarios for the scope of territory to simply to refute their parameters.

Also, without having confirmed the object of the claim, it would be unreasonable to approach the claim with the argument that the disputed territory can be settled through future discussions with the other party. Ultimately, one of the most urgent issues with Korea's sovereignty claim is this very issue of settling the precise geographical scope of Gando. If sovereignty could be claimed solely based on historical arguments, then nearly all borders as existing today would have to be changed. Considering this perspective of the international legal academy, the importance of settling the territorial scope of Gando only increases.

Along the same lines, those claiming sovereignty over Gando must also be warned against excessive nationalism in determining territorial scope. Maximum expansion or irredentism should not disregard the international legal principles relating to territorial acquisition but rather ought to be resolved within its framework. As the recent trend of dispute resolution shows, peaceful resolution is the aim of contemporary international law, and Korea's claim of sovereignty over Gando ought to be in compliance with this pursuit.

3.1.4.3 *Whether the Lack of Korea's Public Claim of Sovereignty over the Gando Area Results in the Abandonment of Its Title or Subsequent Acquiescence*

As mentioned above, at the core the Gando issue lies a territorial dispute, which thereby requires an approach from the perspective of an international judicial body. When seen in light of international principles of territorial acquisition, the most pressing matter is the formal manifestation of the position of the Korean government. As reported in the Korean press recently, should such a passive attitude continue, it may be interpreted as an abandonment of rights or acquiescence to China's claim of sovereignty, leading to perhaps a meaningless claim under international law. The *de facto* exercise of authority over Gando by the Chinese government, when seen in the light of the international principles of territorial acquisition, in one sense, does not face any problems with international recognition of its sovereignty.

Not having been recognized as a disputed territory by international society, and with the lack of a formal statements by the Korean government, the current sovereignty claim over Gando as put forth by the Korean academy and civic groups will ultimately have to overcome the challenge presented in the following answer given by then former Minister of Foreign Affairs and Trade, Ban, Ki-Moon. He stated before the Foreign Affairs, Trade and Unification Committee of the National Assembly in 2004: "It is possible to consider the Gando Agreement as being legally invalid.... However, simply because the Agreement is invalid does not solve all our problems.... It is the government's position that the problem of the Gando Agreement and the issue of Gando sovereignty ought to be approached separately...."

The official position of the Korean government is that the claim and proof of the invalidity of the Gando Agreement does not signify Korea's overt claims of sovereignty. It only helps to increase the probability of the current situation—silence on any claims of sovereignty—being interpreted as that of abandonment or acquiescence.

3.1.4.4 *Whether Korea's Claim of Invalidity of the Gando Agreement is Compatible with the Current Practices of International Law*

The traditional understanding of the Korean academy regarding the China-Japan Gando Agreement of 1909 can be judged as siding with the recent statement made by Minister Ban regarding its invalidity. The academy approaches the core issue, or the evaluation of the validity of this Agreement, together with the conclusion of the Protectorate Treaty of November 1905, as a continuation of failure or invalidity of the same. The argument regarding the status of the Gando Agreement is seen as directly connected with the issue of the effect of a treaty on third states under international law.

However, when analyzing the Gando sovereignty issue based on the jurisprudence generated from recent international decisions, one can only reach the conclusion that Korea is at a disadvantage in having to raise the issue of Gando as a territorial dispute and publicize its claim of sovereignty. In other words, the recent international jurisprudence regarding territorial dispute runs counter to the position taken by the Korean academy, namely that the Gando Agreement is invalid in relation to the Protectorate Treaty due to coercion and exceeding the scope of protection.

In reality, contemporary international law is loyal to the concept of legal stability, as can be observed in the strengthening of the legal effect of intertemporal law and the increase in the universal application of the functionalist/opportunist principle of *uti possidetis*. It holds fast to the international law of the colonial era, and the propriety of the claim of invalidity of the Gando Agreement ought to be re-evaluated. In this regard, it is worth noting that there is another approach which criticizes the general trend of the Korean academy that considers the Agreement as a simple border treaty, and emphasizes that the Agreement is at the same time a regulation of the lives of ethnic Koreans residing there, thereby asserting the need for re-evaluation of the Agreement as a legally valid treaty. Therefore, this approach provides an alternative to the limitation of the issue to that only of land and sovereignty. This approach also suggests other implications including that of the legal status of the *Joseon-jok* residing in the Gando area, which will be discussed later in this section.

3.1.5 The Validity of the 1962 Sino-Korean Border Treaty and the Problem of Demarcation after Re-Unification

Should Korea become unified with North Korea through succession, based on settled international customary law of the duty of accommodation of border treaties, it would be more compatible with international law to recognize the validity of the 1962 treaty. In other words, it is settled under international customary law that borders resulting from treaties concluded by one of the two divided states are automatically succeeded when the states succeed through unification.

With regard to the validity of the 1962 treaty, those who make sovereignty claims to Gando generally argue that: 1) regarding the border issue with Poland during the unification of Germany, the unified Germany and Poland newly concluded a border treaty in order to maintain the previous Oder-Neisse Line, and 2) the Vienna Convention on the Succession of States in Respect of Treaties, does not provide for situations in which divided nations become one. However, in the case of Oder-Neisse Line, unlike East Germany's ambiguous position regarding border delimitation between Poland and Germany prior to unification, the political dynamics surrounding the issue of unification ultimately resulted in the formal confirmation of this line as the border. This fact has great implications considering the current status of Gando.

The Vienna Convention on the Succession of States in Respect of Treaties, pursuant to article 49(1), entered into force on November 6, 1996. Article 11 provides that "[a] succession of States does not as such affect: (a) a boundary established by a treaty[,]" which also has implications for a unified Korea.

Overall, the 1962 treaty appears valid under international law, and it would be proper to acknowledge its interpretation as giving rise to the duty of a unified Korea to succeed to the same. The validity of the 1962 treaty will likely be debated when the issue of unification enters a full-fledged discussion in the process of securing the border with China, the point at which there must be a meticulous consideration of the international legal and political significance and benefit of denying its validity. Again, as mentioned above, the prospects of relations and benefits of Korea's claim of sovereignty over Gando, versus maintenance of peace on the Korean peninsula and peaceful diplomatic relations with neighbouring states, and the achievement/establishment of a unified Korea is a task that must urgently be debated.

Interestingly, when looking at the methods of resolution of the Gando sovereignty issue, the proponents of sovereignty propose a scheme of placing Gando under Chinese jurisdiction and securing some greater benefit from it, which seems to reflect the realistic problems and difficulties in the task of securing sovereignty against China.

3.1.6 The Applicability of Self-Determination to the Chinese-Koreans (Joseon-jok) Residing in the Yanbian Korean Autonomous Prefecture Currently Residing in the Gando Area

3.1.6.1 *Status of Self-Determination in International Law*

In territorial dispute resolution, history has unfortunately shown cases of determination not upon the concerns of residents of the respective areas but on other factors. After the founding of the U.N. in 1945, international law has made epochal developments that demand attention such as in the area of human rights. However, with the possible exception of peoples under colonialism, contemporary international law does not require a sovereignty determination of disputed areas to be made through plebiscites or in some other credible manner. Thus, in many disputed and inhabited areas of great economic concern, i.e., underground resources, the dispute is often settled entirely by the states involved without regard for the residents or their concerns.

The principle of self-determination has been developed over the years through numerous international treaties and resolutions including the U.N. Charter, International Covenant on Civil and Political Rights (ICCPR), International Covenant on Economic, Social and Cultural Rights (ICESCR), the Declaration on the Granting of Independence to Colonial Countries and Peoples, the Declaration on Permanent Sovereignty over Natural Resources, and the Declaration on Principles of International Law concerning Friendly Relations and Cooperation among States in accordance with the Charter of the United Nations.

The ICJ has also furthered this concept in its Advisory Opinion of 21 June 1971 on the *Legal Consequences for States of the Continued Presence of South Africa in Namibia (South West Africa) notwithstanding Security Council*

Resolution 276 (1970), where it stated that "the subsequent development of international law in regard to non-self-governing territories, as enshrined in the Charter of the United Nations, made the principle of self-determination applicable to all [nations])."

With regard to the process of decolonization, the Advisory Opinion on the *Status of Western Sahara* was a landmark decision in the theoretical development and structuring of the concept. In the opinion, the ICJ made determinations, with regard to the disposition of colonialism, of the rights of the peoples of newly independent states, namely their rights to their territory and other rights to be enjoyed under international law. With regard to this issue, the U.N. General Assembly requested an advisory on two questions: "1) Was Western Sahara (Rio de Oro and Sakiet El Hamra) at the time of colonization by Spain a territory belonging to no one (*terra nullius*)?; 2) If the answer to the first question was in the negative, what were the legal ties between this territory and the Kingdom of Morocco and the Mauritanian entity?"

The ICJ found "that at the time of colonization, Western Sahara was inhabited by peoples which, if nomadic, were socially and politically organized in tribes and under chiefs competent to represent them" and that the fact that Spain entered into agreements with local chiefs showed that Spain did not consider the land as *terra nullius*. The Court recognized that "in the case of claims to sovereignty over areas in thinly populated or unsettled countries, 'very little in the way of actual exercise of sovereign rights'... might be sufficient in the absence of a competing claim." The Court thereby concluded that Western Sahara was not *terra nullius*, and that at the time of Spain's colonization of Western Sahara, neither Morocco nor Mauritania exercised territorial sovereignty or co-sovereignty over the same. As a result, the ICJ concluded that regardless of the claim of sovereignty by Morocco or Mauritania, the people residing in Western Sahara had the right to determine their future.

The late Professor Thomas Franck of NYU Law School, in mentioning the superiority of self-determination over claims made on a historical basis, stated that "[g]enerally, neighboring states have not been allowed to help themselves to adjacent territories on the basis of historical claims; boundary readjustments must come as an expression of the democratically expressed will of those subject to the readjustment." If not, it "would lead to endless conflicts, as modern states [find] themselves under pressure to join a general reversionary march backward to a status quo ante...."

Although Professor Franck's proposal was made in the context of post-colonialism, the residents' surrender of sovereignty over their territory actually takes on a similar form. There is not much room for theory in the application of self-determination to the colonial era, but there is much debate about its application in a non-colonial context, to which there is no theoretical consensus.

Further, in the non-colonial context, the position that a plebiscite must be held for the residents of disputed territories is not strongly advocated for in the international legal arena. Thus, with regard to the cession of such territories and the exercise of self-determination by its residents, Jennings and Watts have stated, "The hardship involved for the inhabitants of the territory who remain and lose their old citizenship and are handed over to a new sovereign whether they like it or not, created a movement in favour of the claim that no cession should be valid until the inhabitants had by a plebiscite given their consent to the cession... But it cannot be said that international law makes it a condition of every cession that it should be ratified by a plebiscite."

In such circumstances, it is urgent that relevant norms of international law be examined and new norms subsequently developed that will highlight the miserable conditions of the residents of disputed areas. When certain residential areas come under territorial dispute or become the object of disposal by sovereign states, international law should obligate the execution of plebiscites in the respective areas. Whether the results can be a determinative factor in the resolution of such disputes will be influenced by factors like implanted settlers. Plebiscites in such cases are entirely different from other cases of debate, e.g., whether self-determination grants an independent national character to all races and religions in a non-colonial context. The issue of whether self-determination causes the repositioning on maps of states after colonization to conform to the racial arrangements that existed prior is also an issue to be debated. Regardless, the residents of disputed areas should at least be guaranteed the right to select a single or dual nationality.

Considering all of the situations mentioned above, it is indisputable that determining territorial sovereignty over areas according to principles without sufficiently recognizing the intentions and concerns of the residents can result in arbitrary suffering for the residents.

The issue of sovereignty over disputed territories have long been treated and resolved in a very abstract manner. Although stated in a post-colonial context, Judge Dillard's statement in his separate opinion for the *Western Sahara* case has implications for contemporary self-determination as well as the current Gando dispute: "It is for the people to determine the destiny of [a] territory and not [a] territory the destiny of the people."

3.1.6.2 *Sovereignty over Gando, Ethnic-Koreans (Joseon-jok), and Self-Determination*

Having analyzed the contemporary international jurisprudence that must be overcome in Korea's claim over Gando, one comes to the core issue of whether self-determination is applicable to the ethnic Koreans (*Joseon-jok*) residing in the YBKAP located in the Gando area. Even the Gando sovereignty proponents emphasize that should the resolution of the Gando issue not be in sight, there is a need to actively support the *Joseon-jok* in the long run so that they can take a sufficiently competent role, which would be a desirable approach considering the status of self-determination in contemporary international law.

Professor Son Choon Il of Yanbian University pointed out that the following areas must be studied more carefully with regard to the *Joseon-jok* issue. He largely categorized them into historical concerns and social concerns. Regarding historical concerns, he proposed the following: (1) methods of Japanese rule over Koreans residing in Manchuria; (2) social aspects of Koreans in the Manchu state; and (3) the comparative study of Japanese colonial rule over Manchuria, Korea and Taiwan. Regarding social concerns, he proposed: (1) developmental direction for the *Joseon-jok* society in China; (2) study of international marriages between the *Joseon-jok* women and Korean men; (3) causes for conflict between *Joseon-jok* and Koreans and methods of resolution; (4) dual culture of *Joseon-jok* and its utilization; (5) methods for Korea's support for the development of *Joseon-jok* economy and culture in China; (6) study of the identity of *Joseon-jok* and that of Koreans; and (7) the social role of *Joseon-jok* in the unification of Korea.

The issue of whether self-determination can be applied to the *Joseon-jok* and what long-term support strategy is necessary, though generating numerous debates, will require further examination and study, provided that, considering the internal limitations of self-determination discussed above, the issue of *Joseon-jok* should never be approached from a typical Korean perspective. Along the same lines, it should be noted that the problem with emotional nationalist movements, such as those recently proposed by support groups for the "Brothers in China," e.g., "Korean citizenship for the *Joseon-jok* in China" or "Koguryu Reconquista," is that they have taken actions and approaches that do not take into consideration the substance of the debates.

Even when most liberally interpreting the scope of self-determination, from the international legal perspective emphasizing the status quo of territorial stability and integration, it is questionable as to whether the current *Joseon-jok* policy of the Chinese government is antidemocratic and oppressive so as to legitimize their demand for certain territorial status. Even if this were to be taken in a positive light, the substantive direction that the Gando sovereignty issue ought to take will ultimately depend upon the autonomous and democratic intentions as reflected in the decisions of the *Joseon-jok* themselves. Simply put, their exercise of self-determination will have a dispositive effect. Their future should be determined on their own, and the very issue of Gando sovereignty should also be determined by their intentions.

Index

www.ingramcontent.com/pod-product-compliance
Lightning Source LLC
Chambersburg PA
CBHW031320230926
51848CB00001B/27

* 9 7 8 9 0 0 4 3 1 5 7 8 5 *